WEBSTER'S

ENGLISH/FRENCH
FRANÇAIS/ANGLAIS

DICTIONARY

D0832356

Text copyright ©1993 V. Nichols

Abbreviations Used In This Dictionary

n.	noun
f.	feminine
m.	masculine
vb.	verb
adv.	adverb
v.t.	transitive verb
v.r.	refexive or reciprocal verb
conj.	conjunction
pron.	pronoun
mil.	military
med.	medical
naut.	nautical
gramm.	grammer

Phrases*

English	French
How are you?	Commet allez-vous?
Good day	Bonjour
Good night	Bonne nuit
Good bye	Au revoir
Thank you very much	Merci beaucoup
Please	S'il vous plaît
Do you speak English?	Parlez-vous anglais?
I don't speak French	Je ne parle pas français
What is your name?	Je m'appelle?
What time is it?	Quelle heure est-il?
Have a good trip	Bon voyage

Days of the Week

Sunday	dimanche
Monday	lundi
Tuedsay	mardi
Wednesday	mercredi
Thursday	jeudi
Friday	vendredi
Saturday	samedi

Months of the Year

January	janvier
February	février
March	mars
April	avril
May	mai
June	juin
July	juillet
August	août
September	septembre
October	octobre
November	novembre
December	décembre

Pronunciation Guide

This pronunciation guide describes the approximate pronunciation of
frequent combinations of letters and single letters of the French language.

All exceptions to established pronunciation cannot be listed in this guide.
However, it does provide a fast reference to the French language.

FRENCH LETTERS	ENGLISH PRONUNCIATION
a, à,	Between *a* in *calm*
â	As a in ball
aî, ai	As *a* in say.
au	As *oa* in *boat*.
b	Usually silent when used at the end of a word. Otherwise like English B.
c	When before *e, i, y,* sounds like *s*. *Otherwise as k in fork*
ç	Pronounced as *s*.
cc	When before *e,* or *i* sounds like *x*, otherwise sounds like *k*.
ch	Pronounced as *sh* in *sheep*.
d	Pronounced as in English.
e	Indicates previous consonant is pronounced. Normally silent when at the end of words.
é	Pronounced as *a* in *late* or *day*.
è, ê	Pronounced as *e* in *neck*.
eau	Sounds like *au*.
er	Like *a* in *hate* (silent *r*).
es	Silent at end of words.
eu	Like French *e* pronounced with lips rounded. Similar to her.
ez	Pronounced most frequently like English *a* in *lake. (silent z)*
g	Before *e, i, y* pronounced as *s* in *usual*. Otherwise like English a
gu	Before *e, i, y* pronounced like *g* in *gum*.
h	Usually silent in French.

FRENCH LETTERS	ENGLISH PRONUNCIATION
i, î	Like *i* in *machine*.
ille	As in *key* with *y* at end.
m, n	When single at end of syllable, before another consonant or at the end of a word or before another consonant, indictes nasalization of previous vowel. When double, and when single between two vowel letters or at the beginning of a word, sounds like the English *m* and *n*.
o	Usually pronounced as *u* in the English word *mud* but rounder. Or *o* as in *low*
ô	Similar to *oa* in float.
oû, où, ou	Like *ou* in *tour*. Or *oe* in *shoe*.
p	Usually silent at the end of words. When between the following consonants, *m* and *t, r* and *s* and *m* and *s,* usually silent
ph	Sounds life English *f*.
qu	Usually sounds like English *k*.
r	Sounds as a slightly rolled English *r*. Sometime like English *z*.
s	Usually like *s* in *say*.
ss	*like English s* as in *say*
th	Sounds like *t* in English.
u, û	Sound not found in English; pronounced like the *u* in *rule*.
v	As in English.
w	Usually like the *v* sound in English or English.
x	Normally sounds like *ks,* when the syllable *ex* is at the beginning of a word, followed by a vowel, *x* sounds like *gz*.
y	Usually sounds like *i* in *machine*, if between two vowels sounds like *y* in *you*.
z	Pronounced like *z* in *zebra*.

à, prep. at, into, to, for, with

abaisse, n.f. the undercrust of pastry

abaisser, vb. to depress, to lower, to reduce

abalourdir, v.t. to make stupid or dull

abandon, n.m. surrender, desertion

abandonné, adj. forsaken, forlorn

abandonner, vb. to desert, to leave forsake, to desert **s'a.,** give up

abasourdir, v.t. to stun, dumbfound

abat-jour, n.m. lampshade; skylight

abattage, n.m. slaughtering of animals

abattre, v.t. to reduce, to lower

abbaye, n.f. abbey, Monastery

abbé, n.m. abbot

abcés, n.m. gathering, abscess

abdomen, n.m. abdomen

abécédaire, alphabetical

abeille, n.f. bee

aberrant, adj. straying from normal

abîmer, vb. to spoil, injure, overwhelm

abject, adj. low, abject

abjurer, vb. to give up, to renounce

aboiement, n.m. baying, barking

abolir, v.t. to abolish, to annul

abolition, n.f. abolition

abominer, v.t. to detest

abondamment, adv. fully; abundantly

abondance, n.f. plenty; great quantity

abondant, adj. plentiful; abundant

abonder de, vb. to abound

abonner, vb. **s'a.,** subscribe to

abord, adv. **d'a.,** at first

aborder, vb. to accost, to approach

abouler, v.t. to give

aboutir, vb. to result, to end in or at

aboyer, vb. to bark, to yelp

abréger, vb. to abbreviate, to cut down

abreuver, vb. to water animals

abréviation, n.f. abbreviation

abri, n.m. cover, shelter

abricot, n.m. apricot

abriter, vb. to shelter, to protect, to shade

abrupt, adj. steep, abrupt

absent, adj. absent, missing

absenter, vb. **s'a.,** to leave, go away

absolution, n.f. absolution, forgiveness

absolutoire, adj. implying absolution

absorbant, adj. and n.m. absorbable, absorbent

absorber, vb. to absorb, drink; cause to disappear

absorption, n.f. absorption

absoudre, vb. to acquit, absolve

abstenir, vb. to forgo; forbear

abstinence, n.f. sobriety, abstinence

abstraction, n.f. abstraction, abstract idea

abstrait, adj. absent-minded, abstract

abstrus, adj. obscure, difficult

absurde, adj. stupid, preposterous, silly

absurdité, n.f. foolishness, nonsense

abus, n.m. grievance, abuse

académique, adj. apporprite, proper

acajou, n.m. mahogany

accablant, adj. grievous, oppressive

accabler, vb. to overwhelm, overpower

accélération, n.f. acceleration

accélérer, vb. to hurry, quicken, to hasten

accent, n.m. stress, accent, emphasis, tone

accentuer, vb. to emphasize, accent, stress

acceptabilité, n.f. acceptability

accepter, vb. to admit, accept; agree

accés, n.m. access, approach; fit; attack

accident, n.m. crash, accident, casualty

acclamation, n.f. cheering, acclamation

accommoder, vb. to accommodate, to adapt

accompagnement, n.m. accompaniment; accompanying

accompagner, vb. to accompany, go with; to attend

accompli, adj. accomplished; performed

accomplir, vb. to perform

accomplissement, n.m. performance, achievement, accomplishment

accord, n.m. agreement, harmony; settlement; bargin

accorder, v.t. to grant; to admit

accouchée, n.f. woman who has just given birth

accoudement, n.m. act of leaning on

accoupler, v.t. to join together

accréditer, vb. to give credit

accrocher, v.t. to hook, to catch, to hitch

accroissement, n.m. addition; growth increase

accroître, v.t. to augment, to increase

accroupir, vb. s'a., to crouch, squat

accueil, n.m. greeting; reception

accueillir, vb. to welcome, receive

accumuler, vb. to heap up; pile up; accumulate

accusation, n.f. indictment, charge

accusé, n.m. defendant, prisoner, accused

accuser, vb. to accuse, to charge, to blame, to indicate

acharné, adj. stubborn, intense

achat, n.m. purchasing, purchase, buying

acheminer, vb. to send towards

acheter, vb. to purchase, buy

achevaler, v.t. to straddle

achèvement, n.m. completion

achever, vb. to complete, finish, achieve; conclusion

acide, adj. and n.m. acid, sour, tart

acidité, n.f. acidity; sourness; tartness

acier, n.m. steel

acoustique, adj. acoustic

acquérir, vb. to acquire, purchase

acquêt, n.m. common property of a married couple

acquiescer à, vb. to consent, agree

acquit, n.m. discharge, release

acquittement, n.m. payment

acquitter, vb. to acquit

âcre, adj. sharp, sour, tart, pungent

acrobate, n.m.f. acrobat

acte, n.m. deed, action; a. notarié, deed a. de naissance, birth certificate

acteur, n.m. actor; actress

action, n.f. action, deed, act; work

actionnaire, n.m. shareholder

actionner, vb. to operate; to rouse up

activement, adv. busily; actively

activer, vb. to activate, to expedite

activité, n.f. activity, dispatch

actualité, n.f. current event

actuel, adj. present, actual

acuponcture, n.f. acupuncture

acutesse, n.f. sharpness; acuteness

adage, n.m. proverb

adaptation, n.f. adaptation

adapter, vb. to adapt, fit, adjust, apply

additif, adj. additive

addition, n.f. addition, bill; adding up

additionnel, adj. additional

additionner, vb. to add, to increase

adhérent, n.m. follower

adhérer, vb. to cleave, adhere, to cling

adhésif, adj. adhesive

adieu, n.m. and interij. good-bye, farewell, leave

adjacent, adj. adjacent; bordering upon

adjectif, adj. adjective

adjoindre, vb. to associate; to adjoin

adjoint, n.m. fellow-worker, assistant, associate

adjuger, vb. to grant

adjudant, n.m. warrant-officer

adjudicataire, adj. highest bidder

adjuger, v.t. to knock down

adjuteur, n.m. assistant

admettre, vb. to allow, admit, to let in

administrateur, n.m. manager, administrator, director

administratif, adj. administra-tive

administration, n.f. adminis-tration, direction, management

administrer, vb. to administer, manage, govern, direct

admirable, adj. wonderful, admirable

admirateur, n.m. praiser, admirer; adj. wondering

admiration, n.f. admiration

admirer, vb. to admire

admission, n.f. confession, admission; admittance

adolescence, n.f. adolescence

adolescent, adj. and n.m.f. youth, adolescent

adonné, adj. addicted

adoptable, adj. available to adopt

adopter, vb. to adopt; to pass; to embrace

adoption, n.f. adoption

adorable, adj. charming, delightful, adorable

adorateur, n.m. worshipper

adorer, vb. to worship, adore

adoucir, vb. to soothe

adossé, adj. with one's back against something

adresse, n.f. address; skill, ability, dexterity, cleverness

adresser, vb. to address a letter; direct, **s'a à**, to appeal

adroit, adj. clever, skillful, handy; ingenious

adulte, adj. and n.m.f. adult, grown-up person

adultère, n.m. adultery

adverbe, n.m. adverb

adversaire, n.m.f. opponent, adversary

adverse, adj. opposite, adverse; contrary

aéré, adj. airy

aérien, adj. aerial; occuring in the air

aéroport, n.m. airport

affable, adj. courteous

affaiblir, vb. to weaken; to lessen

affaire, n.f. business, affair, lawsuit matter, concern

affairé, adj. busy

affaissement, n.m. collapse, give way

affaisser, v.r. **s'a.**, to collapse, to subside

affamé, adj. famished, hungry

affamer, vb. to starve, famish

affecter, vb. to affect, assume, make frequent

affection, n.f. love, affection

affermir, vb. to strengthen; make firm

affété, adj. finicky, prim

affiche, n.f. poster, billboard

afficher, v.t. to publish to post up

affinité, n.f. relationship, affinity

affirmatif, adj. asserting, affirmative

affirmation, n.f. statement; assertion

affirmer, vb. to assert, state, declare testify, affirm

affliction, n.f. affliction, distress, trouble

affligé, adj. sorrowful, distress, grieved, burdened

affliger, vb. to grieve, distress, afflict, trouble

affluent, n.m. tributary

affluer, vb. to flow into, run, fall

affoler, vb. to distract, madden, drive crazy

affranchir, adj. freed, set free

affreusement, adv. terribly, dreadfully, horribly

affreux, adj. shocking, terrible, horrid

affront, n.m. affront, insult, outrage

affronter, vb. to confront, face, attack

afin, conj. so that, to, in order that

africain, adj. African

Africain, n. African

agacer, vb. to irritate, worry; excite, provoke

âge, n.m. time from birth, age, period

âgé, adj. aged; elderly, old

agence, n.f. bureau, agency

agenouiller, v.r. **s'a.**, to kneel down

agent, n.m. agent; **a. de police**, policeman

aggraver, v.t. to make worse, to aggravate

agile, adj. nimble, active

agir, v.i. to act; to produce result, to operate

agissant, adj. busy, active, effective

agitation, n.f. disturbance, commotion

agité, adj. upset, excited, restless

agiter, v.t. to shake up, to agitate, **s'a.**, toss, flutter

agneau, n.m. lamb

agonie, n.f. agony

agrafe, n.f. clasp, fastener, clip

agrafer, v.t. to clasp, to hook

agrandir, v.t. to enlarge, to make greater

agréable, adj. likable, pleasing, enjoyable, agreeable

agréer, v.t. to accept, to allow, to approve

agrégation, n.f. aggregation, aggregate

agrément, n.m. pleasure, charm

agresseur, n.m. aggressor

agressif, adj. aggressive

agression, n.f. aggression

agricole, adj. agricultural

agriculture, n.f. agriculture

ahurir, vb. to bewilder, fluster

aide, n.f. help, aid, relief, assistance

aieul, n.m. grandfather

aieule, n.f. grandmother

aieux, n.m.,pl. ancestors

aigle, n.m.f. a clever person; a genius

aiglefin, n.m. haddock

aigre, adj. tart, sour

aigrefin, n.m. adventurer, swindler

aigreur, n.f. sharpness, sourness, tartness

aigu, adj. shrill, keen, pointed, sharp, acute

aiguille, n.f. needle; index, pointer hand of watch

aiguiser, v.t. to sharpen; to point

ail, n.m. garlic

aile, n.f. brim of hat; wing

ailleurs, adv. elsewhere, somewhere

aimable, adj. pleasant, amiable, kind

aimant, adj. affectionate, loving

aimer, v.t. to love, to like, to be fond of

aine, n.f. groin

aîné, adj. elder, senior, eldest

ainsi, adv. in this or that manner, thus so

air, n.m. wind, air

aire, n.f. space, area

aise, n.f. comfort, ease, convenience

aisé, adj. well-to-do; easy, comfortable

aisselle, n.f. armpit

ajourner, v.t. to put off; to adjourn

ajouter, v.t. to add, to supply, to join

ajustage, n.m. fitting or adjusting

ajuster, v.t. to fit, to adjust, to adapt

alarme, n.f. sudden fear, alarm, uneasiness

album, n.m. scrapbook, album

alcool, n.m. alcohol

alcoolique, adj. alcoholic

alcôve, n.f. recess, alcove

alentours, n.m.,pl. surroundings, neighbourhood

alerte, adj. lively, spry, active, alert, brisk

algèbre, n.f. algebra

aligner, v.t. to line up, to align

aliment, n.m. food, nourishment

alimentation, n.f. feeding, nourishment

alimenter, v.t. to nourish, to feed; to supply

alinéa, n.m. new paragraph; indented line

allée, n.f. path, lane, aisle, alley, walk

allégation, n.f. allegation

alléger, v.t. to lighten, to alleviate, to ease, to unload

allégresse, n.f. glee, delight, gaiety

alléguer, vb. pleade, allege, advance

Allemagne, n.f. Germany

aller, v.i. to go on, to proceed, to go

alliage, n.m. mixture, alloy

alliance, n.f. union, marriage, compact, alliance

allié, adj. allied, related

allier, v.t. to combine; to mix to unite

allô, interj. hello

allocation, n.f. allowance; amount allocated

allonger, v.t. to lengthen, to prolong

allons, interj. well, come now

allouer, v.t. to allow, to allocate

allumer, vb. to light; excite

allumette, n.f. match

allure, n.f. pace, gait, behaviour, look

allusion, n.f. hint, allusion; reference

almanach, n.m. calender, almanac

alors, adv. at that time, then

alouette, n.f. lark

alphabet, n.m. alphabet

altérer, vb. to change, alter, corrupt

altematif, adj. alternate, alternative

alterner, vb. to alternate

altitude, n.f. altitude

aluminium, n.m. aluminium

amabilité, n.f. kindness

amalgamer, v.t. to blend, to combine

amande, n.f. kernel; almond

amant, n.m. lover; sweetheart

amas, n.m. hoard, mass, pile, heap

amasser, v.t. to gather, to amass

amateur, n.m. amateur, fancier

ambassade, n.f. embassy, errand

ambassadeur, n.m ambassador

ambassadrice, n.f. ambassadress

ambigu, adj. dark, uncertain, obscure

ambitieux, adj. ambitious; pretentious

ambition, n.f. ambition

ambre, n.m. amber

ambulance, n.f. ambulance

âme, n.f. mind; soul; spirit

amélioration, n.f. improvement

améliorer, v.t. to improve, to better

aménager, v.t. to arrange, to dispose

amende, n.f. fine, forfeit, penalty

amendement, n.m. improvement

amender, vb. to improve, amend

amener, v.t. to bring, to lead

amer, adj. harsh, bitter, grievous

américain, n.m. American

Amérique, n.f. America

amertume, n.f. grief, bitterness

ameublement, n.m. furniture

ami, n.m. friend,lover, well-wisher

amical, adj. kind, friendly, amicable

amidon, n.m. starch

amiral, n.m. admiral

amitié, n.f. affection, friendship

ammoniaque, n.f. ammonia

amoindrir, vb. to reduce, decrease

amollir, vb. to soften

amortir, vb. to weaken, moderate

amour, n.m. love, passion, affection

amoureux, adj. in love, loving,

amour-propre, n.m. vanity, pride,
  conceit, self-respect

ample, adj. ample, spacious, large

ampleur, n.f. plenty, fullness

amplifier, vb. to increase

ampoule, n.f. blister, swelling

amputer, vb. amputate, cut off

amusement, n.m. pastime, fun
  entertainment

amuser, vb. to amuse, entertain. s'a.,
  have a good time, to amuse oneself

amygdale, n.f. tonsil

an, n.m. year, time, age

analogie, n.f. analogy

analogue, adj. similar, analo-
  gous

analyse, n.f. outline, analysis

analyser, v.t. to analyze

ananas, n.m. pineapple

anarchie, n.f. anarchy

anatomie, n.f. anatomy; dissection

ancêtre, n.m. ancestor, forefather

anche, n.f. reed

anchois, n.m. anchovy

ancien, adj. ancient, old, antique,
  former

ancre, n.f. anchor

âne, n.m. ass, donkey, stupid,

anéantir, vb. to destroy, annihilate,
  abolish

anecdote, n.f. anecdote

anesthésique, n.f. anaesthesia

ange, n.m. angel; a beloved person

Anglais, n.m. Englishman

anglais, adj. and n.m. English

Anglaise, n.f. Englishwoman

angle, n.m. angle, corner

Angleterre, n.f. England

angoissant, adj. in anguish

angoisse, n.f. anguish, agony, pang

anguille, n.f. eel

anguleux, adj. rugged

anicroche, n.f. hitch, impediment

animal, n.m. and adj. animal

animation, n.f. animation, life, vitality

animer, vb. to enliven, animate, excite

animosité, n.f. animosity, spite, hatred

anneau, n.m. ring, circle

année, n.f. twelve months, year

annexe, n.f. annex, appendage

annexer, vb. to annex, join, attach

annihiler, v.t. to destroy, to annihilate

anniversaire, n.m. birthday,

anniversary

annonce, n.f. advertisement, announcement, notification

annoncer, vb. to advertise, announce, give notice

annotation, n.f. inventory of goods

annoter, vb. to annotate

annuaire, n.m. directory, annual

annuel, adj. yearly, annual

annulation, n.f. cancelling, annulling

annuler, v.t. to cancel, to annul

ânonner, v.t. to stammer, to mumble

anonyme, adj. anonymous

anormal, adj. abnormal, irregular

anse, n.f. handle; bay, creek

antagonisme, n.m. antagonism

antarctique, adj. antarctic

antécédent, adj. antecedent, previous, foregoing

antenne, n.f., pl. antennae

antérieur, adj. previous; front; earlier, previous

anthracite, n.m. anthracite

anticipation, n.f. encroachment, anticipation

anticiper, v.t. to anticipate, to forestall, to take up

antidote, n.m. counter-poison, antidote

antilope, n.f. antelope

antiparlementaire, n.m. suppressor

antipathie, n.f. aversion, antipathy

antiquaire, n.m. antique dealer

antique, adj. ancient, old

antiquité, n.f. antiquity, ancientness

antiseptique, adj. and n.m. antiseptic

antre, n.m. den; cavern

anxiété, n.f. worry, anxiety; uneasiness

anxieux, adj. anxious, restless, uneasy

août, n.m. August

apaiser, vb. to pacify, quiet, appease, calm, lull, still

apathie, n.f. apathy, listlessness

apercevoir, v.t. to perceive, to understand, to catch sight of

apercu, n.m. survey, glance, summary

apéritif, n.m. appetizing

apitoyer, v.t. to move emotionally;

aplanir, vb. to even off; smooth, level

aplatir, v.t. to beat flat, flatten

aplomb, n.m. poise, boldness

apostolique, adj. apostolic

apôtre, n.m. apostle

apparaître, vb. to appear

appareil, n.m. apparatus, machinery, display

apparence, n.f. appearance, look, likelihood

apparent, adj. noticeable, apparent, visible

apparition, n.f. appearance, ghost, phantom

appartement, n.m. apartment, flat

appartenir, v.i. to belong, to pertain, to relate

appât, n.m. lure, bait, attraction

appel, n.m. call, appeal, summons

appeler, vb. to call, summon, appeal, send forth, bring

appendice, n.m. appendix, addition

appétit, n.m. desire, appetite

applaudir, vb. to applaud, clap the hands

applaudissements, n.m., pl. public praise

applicable, adj. applicable, suitable

application, n.f. applying, application

appliqué, adj. industrious, studious

appliquer, v.t. to apply, to bestow

appointement, n.m., pl. salary

apporter, vb. to bring, fetch, supply

apposer, vb. to affix, set, insert

appréciable, adj. perceptible

apprécier, vb. to value, appraise, judge

appréhension, n.f. fear, dread

apprendre, vb. to learn, study, acquire

apprenti, n.m. apprentice

apprentissage, n.m. trial, apprenticeship

apprêt, n.m. preparation, cooking food

apprêter. v.t. s'a., to prepare

apprivoiser, vb. to tame (animals)

approbation, n.f. endorsement, approval, consent

approche, n.f. advance, approach

approcher, vb. to approach, bring toward, forward, come near to

approfondir, vb. to deepen; examine completely

appropriation, n.f. appropriation, adaptation

approprier, vb. to accommodate, to clean, to adpt, to tidy

approuver, v.t. to concent, to approve, to authorize, to ratify

approvisionnement, n.m. supply, provisions

approximatif, adj. approximate

appui, n.m. prop, support, mechanical support such as handrails

appuyer vb. to support, endorse, advocate

après, prep. behind, after, in pursuit of

après-demain, n.m. day after tommorrow

après-midi, n.m.f. afternoon

à-propos, n.m. fitness, suitability

apte à, adj. suitable for, apt

aptitude, n.f. fitness, talent, ability, aptitude

aqualit, n.m. waterbed

aquarelle, n.f. painting with watercolours

aquarium, n.m. aquarium

aquatique, adj. aquatic

aqueux, adj. watery

arabe, adj. Arabic, Arabian

arachide, n.f. peanut

araignée, n.f. spider

arbitrage, n.m. arbitration

arbitraire, adj. absolute, arbitrary

arbitre, n.m.f. umpire, arbiter, judge, referee

arbitrer, vb. to arbitrate, settle, judge

arbre, n.m. tree

arbrisseau, n.m. shrub

arc, n.m. arch, bow

arcade, n.f. arcade, arch-shaped opening

arc-en-ciel, n.m. rainbow

arche, n.f. arch (above a bridge)

archet, n.m. bow for playing the violin

archevêque, n.m. archbishop

architecte, n.m. architect

architectural, adj. architectural

archives, n.f., pl. files, archives, family records

arctique, adj. arctic

ardemment, adv. ardently

ardent, adj. eager, fiery, ardent, burning, hot

ardeur, n.f. ardour, zeal, keenness, intense heat

ardoise, n.f. slate

arène, n.f. arena, ring

argent, n.m. silver, money, cash

argenterie, n.f. silver-plate

Argentine, n.m. Argentina

argile, n.f. potters clay, clay

argot, n.m. slang

argument, n.m. argument, evidence, proof, summary

argumenter, vb. to argue

aride, adj. dry, arid; sterile

aristocrate, n.m.f. aristocrat

arithmétique, n.f. arithmetic

arlequin, n.m. harlequin

armature, n.f. casing, gear, iron braces

arme, n.f. weapon; arm

armé, adj. equipped, armed

armée, n.f. army, forces, troops

armement, n.m. armament, arming

arme nucléaire, n.f. nuclear weapon

armer, vb. to arm; to equip or furnish with an armament

armistice, n.m. armistice

armoire, n.f. cupboard, wardrobe, closet

armure, n.f. armor; armature

armoatique, adj. aromatic, spicy, fragrant

arome, n.m. scent, perfume, aroma

arpenter, v.t. to measure or survey land

arracher, vb. to snatch, extract

arrangement, n.m. arrangement, settlement, adjustment

arranger, vb. to settle, trim, fix, arrange

arrestation, n.f. arrest **arrêt,** n.m. stop

arrêté, n.m. decree, order, decision

arrêter, vb. to stop, check, halt, arrest

arrière, adv. backward, behind

arriéré, n.m. arrear, adj. backward

arrière-garde, n.f. rearguard

arrivée, n.f. arrival

arriver, vb. to happen, arrive, come; occur

arrogance, n.f. haughtiness, arrogance

arrogant, adj. arrogant, overbearing

arroger, vb. to assume, arrogate

arrondir, vb. to round off

arroser, vb. to sprinkle, water; baste

arsenal, n.m. arsenal, naval dockyard

arsenic, n.m. arsenic

art, n.m. art; **beaux-arts,** the fine arts

artère, n.f. artery

artichaut, n.m. artichoke

article, n.m. article, item

articulation, n.f. joint

articuler, vb. to articulate, put together

artifice, n.m. artifice, trick, dodge

artificiel, adj. artificial, fictitious

artificieux, adj. artful, cunning

artillerie, n.f. artillery

artisan, n.m. artisan, craftsman

artiste, n.m. artist, performer

artistique, adj. artistic

ascenseur, n.m. elevator, lift

Asiatique, n.m.f native of Asia

Asie, n.f. Asia

asile, n.m. haven, refuge, asylum

aspect, n.m. looks, appearance, aspect

asperger, vb. to sprinkle

aspergès, n.m. holy water sprinkler

asphalte, n.m. asphalt

aspirateur, n.m. vacuum cleaner

aspiration, n.f. aspiration, longing

aspirer, vb. to aspire, inhale

assaillant, n.m. assailant, aggressor

assaillir, vb. to assail, attack

assaisonner, v.t. to season

assassin, n.m. assassin, murderer

assassinant, n.m. assassination, murder

assassiner, vb. to assassinate, murder

assaut, n.m. attack, assault

assèchement, n.m. drainage, drying up

assemblage, n.m. combination, collection

assemblée, n.f. congregation, assembly, meeting

assembler, vb. to convene, gather

assentiment, n.m. agreement, assent

asseoir, vb. to seat; place; down; establish

assertion, n.f. affirmation, assertion

asservir, vb. to enslave, reduce, master, conquer

assez, adv. enough; sufficiently

assidu, adj. diligent, industrious, attentive

assiduité, n.f. industry

assiéger, vb. to application, attention

assiette, n.f. situation, basis

assigner, vb. to assign, summon

assimiler, vb. to assimilate, compare

assis, adj. seated; established

assise, n.f. course foundation

assistance, n.f. audience, present, attendance

assister, vb. to attend, be present

association, n.f. association, partnership

assombrir, vb. s'a. to grow dark

assommer, vb. to murder, slaughter

assortiment, n.m. assortment

assortir, vb. to match, tune, pair

assoupi, dormant, dozing

assoupir, v.t. to make sleepy, drowsy

assourdir, vb. to deafen, muffle

assujettir, v.t. to compel, to subdue

assumer, vb. assume

assurance, n.f. assurance, confidence, certainty

assuré, adj. sure, assured, confident

assurer, v.t. to insure; to make firm, to steady, to fasten

assureur, n.m. insurer, underwriter

astérisque, n.m. asterisk

astre, n.m. star (celebrity)

astronaute, n.m. astronaut

astronome, n.m. astronomer

astronomie, n.f. astronomy
astucieux, adj. tricky, crafty
atelier, n.m. studio; workshop
athée, n.m.f. atheist
athlète, n.m.f. athlete
athlétique, adj. athletic
atlantique, adj. Atlantic
atlas, n.m. atlas
atmosphère, n.f. atmosphere
atome, n.m. atom
atomique, adj. atomic
atroce, adj. outrageous, atrocious
atrocité, n.f. atrocity, cruelty
attachement, n.m. attachment,
  affection
attacher, vb. to tie, fasten, join, attach;
  associate
attaque, n.f. assault, attack
attaquer, v.t. to attack, to assault
attardé, adj. late, behind
attarder, v.t. to linger, to delay
atteindre, vb. to reach, attain; strike
atteint, adj. stricken, affected, seized
atteinte, n.f. reach, stroke, blow
attelage, n.m. team, set pair
atteler, vb. to harness, hitch up
attendre, vb. to wait for, await
attendrir, vb. to soften, move, touch
attendrissement, n.m. tenderness,
  emotion
attentat, n.m. crime, outrage
attente, n.f. expectation, waiting
attentif, adj. thoughtful, attentive,
  considerate
attention, n.f. notice, heed, care
atténuer, v.t. to make thinner
atterrir, v.t. to land
attester, v.t. to attest, to witness
attirer, vb. to attract, entice, lure
attitude, n.f. attitude
attouchement, n.m. touch
attraction, n.f. attraction
attrait, n.m. charm, attraction
attraper, v.t. to catch, to take in
attrayant, adj. attractive, charming
attribuer, vb. to ascribe, attribute,
  assign, alot
attribut, n.m. attribute, characteristic

attrouper, v.t. to gather, to assemble
aube, n.f. dawn
auberge, n.f. inn, tavern
aubergine, n.f. eggplant
aubergiste, n.m. landlord, innkeeper
aucun, adj. and pron. no one, none,
  not any; anyone
aucunement, adv. not in the least, not
  at all
audace, n.f. audacity, boldness, daring
audacieux, adj. daring, bold, insolent
au-dessous, prep. below
au-dessus, adv. above
audience, n.f. audience
audio-visuel, adj. audio-visual
auditoire, n.m. audience, assembly
auge, n.f. bucket, trough
auget, n.m. small trough
augmentation, n.f. increase, raise, rise
augmenter, vb. to increase, enlarge
augure, n.m sign, omen
augurer, v.t. to surmise
aujourd'hui, adv. today; nowadays
aumône, n.f. alms
aumônier, n.m. chaplain
auparavant, adv. before, previously
auprès, adv. close by, near, beside
auréole, n.f. halo
aurore, n.f. dawn, daybreak
auspice, n.m. omen, auspice
aussi, adv. too, also; so,
  as; likewise
austère, adj. stern, severe
austérité, n.f. austerity, severity
Australie, n.f. Australia
autant, adv. as much, as many
autel, n.m. altar
auteur, n.m. originator, author, creator
authentique, adj. genuine, authentic
auto, n.f. abbreviation for auto
autobus, n.m. bus
automatique, adj. automatic
automne, n.m. autumn, fall
automobile, n.f. automobile
autorail, n.m. rail-car
autorisation, n.f. license,
  authorization, permission
autoriser, vb. to authorize

autorité, n.f. authority
autoroute, n.f. speedway
auto-stop, n.m. hitch-hiking
autour, adv. around, about
autre, adj. second, another, distinct, different
autrefois, adv. formerly
autrement, adv. otherwise; else
Autriche, n.m. Austria
autrichien, adj. Austrian
autruche, n.f. ostrich
autrui, pron. someone else, others
auvent, n.m. porch roof
auxiliaire, adj. auxiliary, aiding
avachi, adj. worn out
aval, n.m. endorsement
avalaison, n.f. sudden flood
avalanche, n.f. avalanche
avalant, adj. traveling down stream
avaler, vb. to swallow, drink,
avancé, adj. forward, advanced, early
avancement, n.m. advance; advancement; promotion
avancer, vb. to proceed; advance, put forward
avances, n.f., pl. advance
avant, n.m. fore, bow; adv., prep. before
avantage, n.m. advantage, bebefit
avantageux, adj. advantageous; profitable
avant-bras, n.m. forearm
avant-hier, n.m. day before yesterday
avant-toit, n.m. eaves
avare, n.m.f. miser; adj. miserly, stingy
avarice, n.f. avarice
avec, prep. with; together or along with; at the same time as
aven, n.m. pot-hole
avenant, adj. comely, pleasing, personable
avènement, n.m. accession, coming, advent
avenir, n.m. future; posterity
à-venir, n.m. a summons to appear
aventure, n.f. adventure, unexpected event
aventurer, vb. to risk, to venture

aventureux, adj. adventurous
aventurier, n.m. adnenturess, adventurer
avenue, n.f. avenue; approach
averse, n.f. heavy shower of rain
aversion, n.f. dislike, aversion
averti, adj. informed, warned
avertir, vb. to notify, warn, inform, let know
avertissement, n.m. warning, notification, information
aveu, n.m. admission, confession; consent
aveuglant, adj. dazzling
aveugle, adj. sightless, blind
aveuglement, n.m. blindness
aveuglément, adv. blindly, implicity, rashly
aveugler, v.t. to make blind, to blind
aviateur, n.m. flier, aviator
aveulir, v.t. to render weak
aviation, n.f. air force, aviation
avide, adj. eager, greedy
avidement, adv. greedily
avidité, n.f. greediness; eagerness
avilir, vb. to degrade, disgrace, depreciate
avilisseur, adj. degrading
avine, adj. drunk
aviner, v.t. to fill or soak with wine
avion, n.m. airplane, aeroplane
avis, n.m. notice, opinion, advice
avir, v.t. to brown or burn the outter side of meats or bread
aviser, vb. to notify, inform, perceive
avocat, n.m. lawyer, advocate, council
avoir, v.t. to have, to experience
avortement, n.m. abortion, miscarriage
avorter vb. to miscarry, fail to develop
avorton, n.m. abortion
avoué, n.m. attorney, lawyer
avouer, vb. to confess, admit, avow,
avril, n.m. April
axe, n.m. axel; axis
azalée, n.f. azalea
azur, n.m. azure, blue
azuré, adj. azure, color of the sky

babélique, adj. gigantic
babeurre, n.m. buttermilk
babil, n.m. babble; chattering
babiller, vb. to babble, chat
bâbord, n.m. naut. port
babouin, n.m. baboon, monkey
Babylone, f. Babylon
bac, n.m. ferryboat; ferry
baccalauréat, n.m. baccalaureate
bachelier, n.m. graduate
bâcher, v.t. to cover
bacille, n.m. bacillus
bâclage, n.m. closing a port with chains
bactéricide, adj. stopping or destroying the growth of bacteria
bactérie, n.f. bacterium
bactériologie, n.f. bacteriology
badaud, n.m. idler, lounger
badine, n.f. wand, switch
bafouiller, v.i. to stammer; to miss (of engine)
bagages, n.m., pl. luggage, baggage
bagarre, n.f. uproar, riot, scuffle
bagatelle, n.f. trifle, trinket
bagnard, n.m. convict
baguer, v.t. to tack, to stitch, to baste
baguier, n.m. jewel box
bah, int. nonsense
baie, n.f. bay, creek; berry
baignade, n.f. bathing
baigner, v.t. to bathe
baigneur, n.m. bather
bail, n.m. lease
bâillement, n.m. yawn, yawning
bâiller, vb. to yawn, open, gape
bâillon, n.m. muzzle, gag
bain, n.m. bath
bain-marie, n.m. double boiler
baïonnette, n.f. bayonet
baisemain, n.m. kissing of the hands
baisse, n.f. decline, fall
baisser, vb. to lower, sink, let down; turn down
bal, n.m. dance, ball
balade, n.f. ramble, walk, stroll
balafre, n.f. slash, cut

balai, n.m. broom
balance, n.f. scales, balance
balancement, n.m. rocking, swinging
balancer, vb. to weigh; balance; rock; swing, sway
balayer, vb. to clear away, sweep
balancier, n.m. scales and weights maker
balcon, n.m. balcony
baleine, n.f. whale
ballade, n.f. ballad
balle, n.f. bullet, ball; bale
ballerine, n.f. ballerina
ballet, n.m. ballet
ballon, n.m. balloon; football
ballot, n.m. bundle; small pack
balourd, adj. heavy, dull
bamboche, n.f. a large puppet
bambou, n.m. bamboo
ban, n.m. ban, public order, announcement
banal, adj. trite, ordinary, common
banane, n.f. banana
banc, n.m. bench, form; pew; stand
bancaire, having to do with banking
bandage, n.m. bandage, truss; belt
bande, n.f. strip, stripe, pack, bandage; troop, gang
bander, v.t. to tie up
bandit, n.m. bandit, robber, knave
banlieue, n.f. suburbs, outskirts
banneton, n.m. basket for bread
bannière, n.f. banner, flag
bannir, vb. to exile, banish
bannissement, n.m. banishment
banque, n.f. banking, bank
banqueroute, n.f. bankruptcy, collapse, failure
banqueroutier, n.m. bankrupt
banquet, n.m. banquet, feast
banquier, n.m. banker
banquise, n.f. ice-pack
baptême, n.m. baptism, christening
baptiser, vb. to christen, baptize
Baptiste, n.m. Baptist
baptistère, n.m. baptistery
baquetage, n.m. drawing water with a bucket

bar, n.m. bar; bass fish

baraque, n.f. booth stall, shanty, hut

baratter, vb. to churn

barbare, n.m.f. barbarian adj. barbarian, barbarous, wild

barbarie, n.f. cruelty, barbarousness, rudeness, lack of culture

barbe, n.f. beard, whiskers (of animals)

barbiche, n.f. goatee, beard only on the chin

barbier, n.m. barber

barbouiller, vb. to daub, blur

barguignage, n.m. wavering, hesitation

baril, n.m. keg, cask, small barrel

barillet, n.m. barrel or box, keg

bariolé, adj. gaudy

barioler, v.t. to variegate with colors

baroque, adj. odd, irregular, grotesque

barque, n.f. barge, boat

barrage, n.m. barrier, dam, barrage

barre, n.f. bar (of wood, metal, steel, etc.)

barreau, n.m. small bar (of wood, metal, steel, etc,)

barrer, vb. to shut out, cut off, fasten

barricade, n.f. barricade

barrière, n.f. gate; bar, railing, barrier; fence

barrique, n.f. barrel, cask

barrotin, n.m. cross-bar between beams

bascule, n.f. seesaw

base, n.f. base, basis; foundation

basique, adj. basic

basket-ball, n.m. basketball

basse-fosse, n.f. dungeon

basset, n.m. basset hound

bassin, n.m. basin, dock, pool

bataille, n.f. fight, battle

bataillon, n.m. battalion

bateau, n.m. boat

batelage, n.m. juggling

bâtiment, n.m. building, structure

bâtir, vb. to build, construct

bâton, n.m. stick, staff, cane

battant, adj. heavy down fall of rain

batte, n.f. long wooden beater; bat

battement, n.m. beating, clapping of hands, stamping of the feet

batterie, n.f. battery; row

battre, vb. to beat, strike, thrash upon

battu, adj. beaten path

baudet, n.m. ass; donkey

bauge, n.f. squirrel's nest

baume, n.m. balm; balsam

bavard, adj. talkative, gossip

bavardage, n.m. gossip, chatter

bavarder, vb. to gossip, chat(ter)

bavette, n.f. bib

bavoché, adj. smeary, uneven (print)

bavolet, n.m. trimming on the back of a hat

bazar, n.m. bazaar

bazarder, v.t. to sell at a low price

bazooka, n.m. bazooka

béat, adj. devout, blessed

béatifier, v.t. to beautify

beaucoup, adv. a lot, a great deal; much, many

beau-frère, n.m. brother-in-law

beau-père, n.m. father-in-law

beauté, n.f. beauty, elegance, neatness

beaux-arts, n.m., pl. fine arts

beaux-parents, n.m., pl. father-in-law and mother-in-law

bébé, n.m. baby

bec, n.m. beak, bill; spot; burner

bêchage, n.m. digging up

bêcher, vb. to dig

becqueter, vb. to peck

bécot, n.m. little kiss

bégaiement, n.m. faltering

bégayer, vb. to stammer, lisp

bêler, vb. to bleat

Belgique, n.f. Belgium

bélier, n.m. ram

belle-fille, n.f. daughter-in-law; stepdaughter

belle-mère, n.f. mother-in-law; stepmother

belliqueux, adj. martial, war-like

bénédiction, n.f. blessing, benediction

bénéfice, n.m. benefit, advantage, profit, gain

bénéficiaire, adj. receiving a benefit

bénéficier, vb. to benefit, profit

bénin. adj. good-natured, indulgent

bénir, v.t. to bless, to consecrate, to praise

béquille, n.f. crutch; support, aid, help

béquiller, v.i. to walk on crutches

berceau, n.m. cradle, bower

bercement, n.m. lulling, rocking

bercer, vb. to rock, lull to sleep

berge, n.f. steep river bank

berger, n.m. shepherd

bergère, n.f. large, deep armchair

berthon, n.m. collapsible boat

besogne, n.f. piece of work; job

besoin, n.m. need, want

bétail, n.m. cattle, livestock; animals

bête, n.f. beast, animal adj. stupid, dumb, silly

bêtement, adv. foolishly, stupidly

bêtise, n.f. nonsense, silliness

bétoire, n.m. drain hole

béton, n.m. concrete

betterave, n.f. beet

beurre, n.m. butter

bévue, n.f. blunder, boner, mistake

biais, n.m. slant; bias

bibelot, n.m. trinket, knick-knack

biberon, n.m. baby's bottle

Bible, n.f. Bible

bibliothèque, n.f. library; bookcase

biblique, adj. biblical

bicyclette, n.f. bicycle

bidon, n.m. can

bidonnant, adj. extremely funny

bien, n.m. good; benefit, well-being

bien, adv. well, right, fully, properly

bien-aimé, n.m.f. and adj. darling

bien-être, n.m. well-being, welfare

bienfaisant, adj. beneficient, kind, humane, charitable

bienfait, n.m. benefit, kindness; good turn

bienfaiteur, n.m. benefactor, patron

bienheureux, adj. blessed; fortunate

bientôt, adv. soon, shortly

bienveillance, n.f. benevolence, kindness, goodwill

bienveillant, adj. benevolent, kindly, friendly

bienvenu, adj. welcome

bière, n.f. beer, ale

biffer, vb. to cancel, erase, blot out

bifteck, n.m. beefsteak

bigamie, n.f. bigamy

bigot, n.m. bigotry

bigouterie, n.f. jewelry

bile, n.f. bile, spleen

billard, n.m. billiards

bille, n.f. marble

billet, n.m. ticket, note

billion, n.m. billion

biographie, n.f. biography

biologie, n.f. biology

biscotin, n.m. hard, crisp biscuit

biscuit, n.m. biscuit

bizarre, adj. queer, odd, strange, quaint

blâme, n.m. blame, reprimand

blâmer, vb. to blame, to find fault with, to criticize; to censure

blancheur, n.f. cleanliness; whiteness

blanchir, v.t. to whiten, to bleach

blanchisserie, n.f. laundry

blaser, v.t. to sicken, to cloy

blasphème, n.m. blasphemy

blasphémer, vb. to curse, blaspheme

blatte, n.f. cockroach

blé, n.m. wheat, corn

blême, adj. pale

blessé, adj. injured, outraged

blesser, vb. to wound, hurt, injure

blessure, n.f. wound, hurt, injury

bleu, adj. blue

bloc, n.m. pad, block

blond, adj. fair, blond

bloquer, vb. to block; tighten

blouse, n.f. blouse, smock

bluff, n.m. bluff

bobine, n.f. spool, reel, bobbin

boeuf (boef), n.m. ox, beef, **jeune b.,** steer

Bohême, n.f. Bohemia

boire, v.t. to drink
bois, n.m. wood, forest, timber, lumber
boiserie, n.f. woodwork
boisseau, n.m. bushel
boisson, n.f. beverage, drink; drinking
boîte, n.f. box; caddy, chest
boiter, vb. to limp, halt
boiteux, adj. lame, limping, halting
bol, n.m. basin, bowl
bombardement, n.m. shelling, bombardment
bombarder, vb. to bomb, bombard
bombe, n.f. bomb, shell
bombé, adj. arched, convex
bon, adj. kind, favourable; good
bonbon, n.m. candy, bonbon, sweet
bond, n.m. jump, bound, leap
bonder, vb. to overcrowd, jam, cram, load
bondir, vb. to bound, leap, spring
bonheur, n.m. prosperity, happiness
bonhomme, n.m. good-natured
bonjour, interj. and n.m. good morning, good day, good afternoon
bonne, n.f. maid
bonnement, adv. simply, plainly
bonnet, n.m. cap, hood
bonsoir, interj. and n.m. good evening, good night
bonté, n.f. kindness, goodness
bord, n.m. edge, rim, brim, border
border, vb. to bound, edge, hem
borne, n.f. bound, limit, milestone
borner, vb. bound, limit, restrict
bosquet, n.m. clump, grove, thicket
bosse, n.f. bump, hump, bruise
bosselure, n.f. dent, embossment
bossu, adj. hunchbacked, deformed
botanique, n.f. botany
botte, n.f. boot; bunch
bottine, n.f. boot
bouche, n.f. mouth; tongue; lips
boucher, vb. stop up
boucher, n.m. butcher
boucherie, n.f. butcher's shop
bouchon, n.f. cork, plug, stopper
boucle, n.f. curl, loop, buckle
bouclier, n.m. shield, buckler

bouder, vb. to sulk, pout
boue, n.f. dirt, mud, filth
bouée, n.f. buoy
boueux, adj. dirty, muddy
bouffée, n.f. blast, buff, gust
bouffon, n.m. clown, fool, jester
bougeoir, n.m. taper stand, flat candle
bouger, v.t. to stir, to move
bougie, n.f. candle
bouillir, v.t. to boil
bouilloire, n.f. kettle
bouillon, n.m. broth
bouillonner, v.t. to bubble, to boil
bouillotte, n.f. small kettle; foot warmer
boulanger, n.m. baker
boulangerie, n.f. baking, baker's shop
boule, n.f. ball
bouleau, n.m. birch
bouledogue, n.m. bulldog
boulevard, n.m. boulevard
bouleversement, n.m. upset, overthrow, confusion
bouleverser, v.t. to upset, to over-turn; to distract
bouquet, n.m. cluster, bunch, bouquet (of flowers)
bouquiniste, n.m. secondhand bookseller
bourbeux, adj. sloppy, muddy
bourdonnement, n.m. buzz, hum
bourdonner, v.t. to hum, to buzz
bourg, n.m. borough, village
bourgeois, adj. middle-class, commoner
bourgeoisie, n.f. middle class
bourgeon, n.m. bud, shoot
bourgeonner, v.t. to bud
bourre, n.f. stuffing
bourreau, n.m. executioner, hang-man
bourrelet, n.m. cushion, pad
bourru, adj. gruff, moody, cross
bourse, n.f. purse; scholarship, grant exchange; fellowship
boursoufler, v.t. to bloat, to puff up
bousculer, vb. to jostle, hustle
bousiller, vb. to bungle, botch

boussole, n.f. compass; guide, direct

bout, n.m. end, tip, butt, stub

bouteille, n.f. bottle

boutique, n.f. shop; workshop

bouton, n.m. button, bud; pimple

boutonnière, n.f. buttonhole

boxe, n.f. boxing

boxeur, n.m. prize fighter, boxer

boycotter, v.t. to boycott

bracelet, n.m. bracelet

braconnier, n.m. poacher

brailler, vb. to bawl, shout

braise, n.f. coals, embers

brandir, v.t. to brandish

braquer, vb. to aim, point, level

bras, n.m. bracket, arm

brasser, v.t. to brew, to mix

brasserie, n.f. brewery

bravade, n.f. bully, bravo

brave, adj. fine, good, brave, honest, worthy

braver, vb. to face, brave, defy

bravoure, n.f. courage, bravery, gallantry

brebis, n.f. lamb, sheep, ewe

brèche, n.f. gap, breach, flaw

bref, adj. brief, short

Brésil, n.m. Brazil

brevet, n.m. certificate, warrant

bride, n.f. bridle reins, bridle

brider, v.t. to curb, to restrain

bridge, n.m. the game of bridge

brièveté, n.f. briefness

brigade, n.m. brigade; troop, gang, squad

brigadier, n.m. overseer, corporal

brigand, n.m. robber

brilliant, adj. brilliant, shiny, bright, glowing, glittering

briller, vb. to shine, glisten, glare, glitter, sparkle

brindille, n.f. twig

brique, n.f. brick

briser, vb. to break, shatter, smash

britannique, adj. British

brocart, n.m. brocade

broche, n.f. spit, spindle, brooch

brochure, n.f. pamphlet, booklet, brochure

broder, v.t. to embroider, to adorn

broderie, n.f. braid, embroidery

bronzage, n.f. bronzing

bronze, n.m. bronze

broquette, n.f. carpet nail, tack

brosse, n.f. painter's brush

brouillard, n.m. fog, haze, mist

brouiller, vb. to jumble, embroil; mix, confuse

brouter, vb. to browse, graze

broyer, vb. to pound, crush, grind, puliverize

bruine, n.f. drizzle

bruit, n.m. noise, clatter; rumour; fuss, racket

brûlant, adj. hot, scorching, burning

brûler, v.t. to burn, to scorch

brume, n.f. fog, mist, haze

brumeux, adj. foggy, hazy, misty

brun, adj. brown, the color brown

brusque, adj. abrupt, curt, blunt, gruff, sudden, brusque

brut, adj. crude, gross, rough, unpolished

brutal, adj. brutal, savage, rude

brutalité, n.f. brutality

brute, n.f. brute, brutal person

bruyant, adj. loud, noisy

bûche, n.f. log; dolt

budget, n.m. budget

buffet, n.m. buffet; sideboard, refreshment table

buisson, n.m. thicket, bush, shrub

bulbe, n.m. bulb

bulle, n.f. bull; bubble; blister

bulletin, n.m. bulletin; certificate, receipt

bureau, n.m. office, bureau; department, desk

burin, n.m. chisel, graving tool

burlesque, adj. ludicrous, ridiculous

buste, n.m. head and shoulders, bust

but, n.m. aim, goal, object, purpose

butin, n.m. spoils, booty

butte, n.f. mound, hill, knoll

buvard, n.m. blotter, blotting pad

ca, pron. that
cabale, n.f. intrigue
cabane, n.f. cabin, hut, shed
cabaret, n.m. cabaret, tavern
cabine, n.f. cabin, berth, car
cabinet, n.m. closet; study, office; business; practice
câblage, n.m. electrical wiring
câbler, v.t. to make into cable
câblogramme, n.m. cablegram
cabosse, n.f. bump, bruise
cabot, n.m. actor
cabotage, n.m. coasting
cabri, n.m. kid
cabriole, n.f. leap
cabrouet, n.m. hand truck
cacahouète, n.f. peanut
cacao, n.m. cocoa
caché, adj. concealed, hidden
cache-cache, n.m. hide-and-seek
cache-col, n.m. scarf
cache-corse, n.m. camisole
cachemire, n.m. cashmere
cacher, v.t. to hide, to disguise, to conceal
cachet, n.m. stamp, seal
cacheter, v.t. to seal up
cachette, n.f. hiding place
cachotter, n.m. prison dungeon
cacochyme, adj. decrepit
cactier, n.m. cactus
cadavre, n.m. dead body, corpse
cadeau, n.m. gift, present
cadence, n.f. cadence
cadet, adj. and s.m. cadet junior
cadran, n.m. dial
cadre, n.m. frame, framework, outline
caduc, adj. decayed, decrepit
café, n.m. coffee; café
cafetière n.f. coffeepot, percolator
cage, n.f. cage; coop; crate
cahier, n.m. notebook; memorial
caille, n.f. quail
caillot, n.m. clot of blood
caisse, n.f. crate, case, box, chest
caissier, n.m. cashier, teller
cajoler, vb. to coax
calamité, n.f. misfortune, calamity

calcium, n.m. calcium
calcul, n.m. calculation; arithmetic; counting
calculer, vb. to figure, reckon, calculate, compute
calembour, n.m. pun
calendrier, n..m. calendar, almanac
calibre, n.m. caliber
calme, adj. quiet, calm, tranquil
calmer, vb. to soothe, quiet, calm, still
calomnie, n.f. slander
calorie, n.f. calorie
camarade, n.f. comrade, mate, fellow
camaraderie, n.f. companionship, fellowship
cambrioieur, n.m. burglar
caméra n.f. camera
camouffler, vb. to camoutlage
camp, n.m. camp; side
campagnard, adj. rural, rustic
campagne, n.f. country; campaign, expedition
camper, vb. to camp, pitch tents
camphre, n.m. camphor
Canada, n.m. Canada
canaille, n.f. rabble; scoundrel, mob
canal, n.m. channel, canal, stream
canapé, n.m. sofa, couch; canapé
canard, n.m. duck, drake; hoax
canari, n.m. canary
candidat, n.m. candidate, applicant
candidature, n.f. candidature
candide, adj. frank, open, candid
canevas, n.m. canvas; sail cloth
canin, adj. canine
canneberge, n.f. cranberry
cannelle, n.f. cinnamon
canon, n.m. cannon, gun
canot, n.m. boat, canoe
cantaloup, n.m. cantaloup
cantique, n.m. hymn
capable, adj. efficient, fit, able, capable
capacité, n.f. capability, capacity
capitaine, n.m. leader, captain, soldier
capital, adj. capital, main, principal
capitalisme, n.m. capitalism
caporal, n.m. corporal

capote, n.f. hood

câpre, n.f. caper

caprice, n.m. whim, fancy, humour

capricieux, adj. fickle, capricious, whimsical

capsule, n.f. capsule

captif, adj. and n.m. captive, prisoner

captiver, vb. to captivate, seduce

captivité, n.f. captivity, bondage

capture, n.f. capture, seizure

capturer, vb. to capture, to arrest

capuchon, n.m. hood

car, conj. because, for

caractère, n.m. character, type, nature, personality

caractériser, vb. to characterize; distinguish, describe

caractéristique, adj. characteristic

carafe, n.f. decanter, water bottle

caramel, n.m. caramel

carat, n.m. carat

caravane, n.f. caravan, convoy

carbone, n.m. carbon

carburateur, n.m. carburetor

carcasse, n.f. shell; carcass, skelton

cardinal, n.m. cardinal; adj. chief

caresse, n.f. caress

caresser, vb. to fondle, stroke, caress

cargaison, n.f. cargo, freight

caricature, n.f. caricature

carie, n.f. decay

carillon, n.m. chime

carnaval, n.m. carnival

carnet, n.m. notebook

carnivore, adj. carnivorous

carotte, n.f. carrot

carré, adj. square; plain

carreau, n.m. diamond; flooring, pane; title, small square

carrefour, n.m. crossroads

carrière, n.f. career; scope; quarry

carriole, n.f. light cart

carrosse, n.m. coach; carriage with four wheels

carte, n.f. chart, map, ticket

carton, n.m. cardboard; box, carton, pasteboard

cartouche, n.f. cartridge

cas, n.m. case; instance; event

case, n.f. pigeonhole; hut, shed, small house

caserne, n.f. barracks

casquette, n.f. cap

cassable, adj. breakable

casser, vb. to break, crack, shatter

casserole, n.f. cooking pan, saucepan

cassette, n.f. casket, cassette

castor, n.m. beaver

casuel, adj. casual, accidental

catalogue, n.m. catalogue

cataracte, n.f. cataract

catastrophe, n.f. disaster, catastrophe

catéchisme, n.m. catechism

catégorie, n.f. class, category

cathédrale, n.f. cathedral

catholicisme, n.m. Catholicism

catholique, adj. Catholic

cauchemar, n.m. nightmare

cause, n.f. case; cause, reason

causer, vb. to chat; cause

causerie, n.f. chat, talk. gossip

causette, n.f. chat

caution, n.f. bail, security

cavalerie, n.f. cavalry

cavalier, n.m. rider, horseman; escort

cave, n.f. cellar, cavern, cave

ceci, pron. this, this thing

cécité, n.f. blindness

cèdre, n.m. cedar

ceindre, vb. to gird, encircle

ceinture, n.f. belt, sash, girdle

cela, pron. that

célébration, n.f. celebration

célèbre, adj. celebrated; famous

célébrer, vb. to celebrate, praise

célébrité, n.f. celebrity

céleri, n.m. celery

céleste, adj. heavenly, celestial, divine

célibataire, n.m. bachelor; adj. single

cellule, n.f. cells

celtique, adj. Celtic

cendre, n.f. ashes; cinders

cendrier, n.m. ash-tray

censeur, n.m. censor, critic

censurer, v.t. to blame, to criticize

cent, adj. one hundred

centaine, n.f. hundred

centenaire, adj. hundred years old

centième, adj. hundredth

centigrade, adj. centigrade

centimètre, n.m. centimetre

central, adj. central, principal, chief, head

centraliser, vb. to centralize

centre, n.m. center, middle

cependant, adv. meanwhile

cercle, n.m. circle, ring, hoop; club

cercueil, n.m. coffin

céréale, adj. and n.f. cereal

cérémonial, adj. and n.m. ceremonial

cérémonie, n.f. ceremony, pomp

cérémonieux, adj. formal, ceremonious

cerf, n.m. stag, hart, deer

cerise, n.f. cherry

certain, adj. certain, sure, positive

certes, adv. indeed

certificat, n.m. credentials; testimonial, certificate

certifier, vb. to certify

certitude, n.f. certainty, assurance

cerveau, n.m. brain, intellect

cessation, n.f. stopping, cessation

cesser, vb. to stop, desist, cease

cession, n.f. relinquishment

chacun, pron. everybody, everyone; each; apiece

chagrin, n.m. grief, vexation, adj. fretful, gloomy

chagriner, vb. to grieve, afflict

chaîne, n.f. chain; range

chaînon, n.m. link

chair, n.f. flesh

chaire, n.f. pulpit; chair; seat

chaise, n.f. chair, seat

châle, n.m. shawl

chaleur, n.f. warmth, heat, glow, fire

chambre, n.m. room, chamber; bedroom

chameau, n.m. camel

chamois, n.m. chamois

champ, n.m. country, field

champignon, n.m. mushroom

champion, n.m. champion

championnat, n.m. championship

chance, n.f. luck, risk, fortune

chanceler, vb. to stagger, reel

chandelier, n.m. candlestick

chandelle, n.f. candle

change, n.m. exchange, barter

changeante, adj. changeable

changement, n.m. change, shift

changer, vb. to alter, shift, change

chanson, n.f. song

chant, n.m. song, chant, melody

chantage, n.m. blackmail

chanteau, n.m. remnant

chanteur, n.m. singer

chapeau, n.m. hat, bonnet; cap

chapelle, n.f. chapel

chaperon, n.m. chaperon

chapiteau, n.m. capital

chapitre, n.m. chapter; head, subject

chapon, n.m. capon

chaque, adj. every, each

char, n.m. chariot, carriage

charbon, n.m. coal

charge, n.f. load, charge; burden; attack

charger, vb. to load, burden, charge; entrust, pack

chariot, n.m. wagon; baggage cart

charisme, n.m. charisma

charitable, adj. charitable

charité, n.f. charity, alms

chariatan, n.m. chariatan

charmant, adj. delightful, lovely, charming

charme, n.m. spell, charm

charmer, vb. to charm, enchant

charnel, adj. carnal

charnu, adj. fleshy

charpente, n.f. framework

charpentier, n.m. carpenter

charretier, n.m. carter

charrette, n.f. wagon, cart

charrue, n.f. plow

charte, n.f. charter

chasse, n.f. hunting, chase, shooting

châsse, n.f. shrine

chasser, vb. to hunt, chase; drive away, pursue

chasseur, n.m. hunter; bellboy
chaste, adj. chaste
chasteté, n.f. chastity, purity
châtaigne, n.f. chestnut
château, n.m. mansion, castle, palace
châtier, vb. to punish, chastise
chatouiller, vb. to tickle
chaud, adj. hot, warm
chaudière, n.f. boiler
chauffage, n.m. warming; heating
chauffer, vb. to warm; coach; urge on
chauffeur, n.m. driver, chauffeur
chaumière, n.f. cottage
chaussée, n.f. road, pavement
chausser, vb. to wear shoes
chaussette, n.f. sock
chaussure, n.f. footwear, shoes
chauve, adj. bald, hairless
chaux, n.f. lime; limestone
chavirer, vb. to capsize
chef, n.m. leader, chief
chemin, n.m. road, way, path
chemineau, n.m. tramp
cheminée, n.f. fireplace, chimney;
 funnel
chemise, n.f shirt
chêne, n.m. oak
chenille, n.f. caterpillar
chèque, n.m. check
cher, adj. dear, expensive
chercher, vb. to seek, look for, search
chère, n.f. fare
chéri, adj. and n.m. beloved, darling
chérir, vb. to cherish
cheval, n.m. horse
chevaleresque, adj. chivalrous
chevalerie, n.f. chivalry
chevalet, n.m. easel; knight
chevalier, n.m. knight
cheville, n.f. ankle; peg, bolt
chèvre, n.f. goat, crab
chevron, n.m. rafter
chevrotine, n.f. buckshot
chic, adj. stylish, chic
chien, n.m. dog, hound
chiffon, n.m. rag; scrap, bit
chiffonner, vb. to crumple, rumple
chiffre, n.m. figure; digit, calculate

chiffrer, vb. to figure
Chili, n.m. Chile
chimie, n.f. chemistry
chmiotherapie, n.f. chemotherapy
chimique, adj. chemical
chimiste, n.m.f. chemist
Chine, n.f. China
chinois, n.m. Chinese language
chiquenaude, n.f. flick
chirurgie, n.f. surgery
chirurgien, n.m. surgeon
choc, n.m. shock, clash, collision
chocolat, n.m. chocolate
choeur, n.m. choir, chorus
choisir, vb. to choose, select, pick
choix, n.m. choice, alternative
chômage, n.m. stoppage of work;
 unemployment
choquer, vb. to shock, clash, run into,
 strike against, collide
choral, adj. choral
chose, n.f. thing, matter, object
chou, n.m. cole, cabbage, kale
chou-fleur, n.m. cauliflower
choyer, vb. to pamper
chrétien, adj. and n.m. Christian
chronique, adj. chronic
chuchoter, vb. to whisper
chute, n.f. fall, drop, downfall
cible, n.f. target
cicatrice, n.f. scar, mark
cidre, n.m. cider
ciel, n.m., pl. cieux, heaven, sky
cierge, n.m. wax candle, taper
ciagle, n.m. locust
cigare, n.m. cigar
cigarette, n.f. cigarette
cigogne, n.f. stork
cil, n.m. eyelash
cime, n.f. top, summit
ciment, n.m. cement
cimetière, n.m. churchyard, cemetery
cinéma, n.m. cinema
cinglant, adj. lashing
cinq, adj. and n.m. fifth, five
cintre, n.m. semicircle; arch
circonférence, n.f. circumference
circonstance, n.f. event, circumstance

circuit, n.m. circuit
circulaire, adj. circular
circulaton, n.f. traffic, circulation
circuler, vb. to circulate, turn, revolve
cire, n.f. wax, beeswax
cirer, vb. to polish, shine; wax
cirque, n.m. circus
cisalles, n.f., pl. shears
ciseau, n.m. chisel
ciseaux, n.m.,pl. scissors
ciseler, vb. to chisel
citation, n.f. quotation, citation
cité, n.f. town, city
citer, vb. quote, cite
citoyen, n.m. citizen
citron, n.m. lemon
citrouille, n.f. pumpkin
civil, n.m. civilian; adj. civil
civilisation, n.f. civilization
civilisé, adj. civilized
civiliser, vb. to civilize
civique, adj. civic
clair, adj. clear, bright, light
clairière, n.f. glade, clearing
clairon, n.m. bugle
clameur, n.f. clamor, outry
clandestin, adj. secret
clapoteux, adj. rough
claque, n.f. slap, smack
claquement, n.m. clapping
claquer, vb. to crack, chatter bang
clarifier, vb. to clarify, purify
clarinette, n.f. clarinet
clarté, n.f. clarity; light; brightness
classe, n.f. order, rank; class
classement, n.m. classification
classer, vb. to classify, order, grade
classeur, n.m. file
classification, n.f. classification
classifier, vb. to classify
classique, adj. classic, classical
clause, n.f. clause
clavicule, n.f. collarbone
clémence, n.f. clemency, mercy
clément, adj. merciful; mild
clerc, n.m. clerk
clérical, adj. clerical
cliché, n.m. snapshot

client, n.m. customer, client, patron
clientèle, n.f. customers, practice
clignoter, vb. to blink, wink
climat, n.m. climate
climatisation, n.f. air conditioning
climatiser, vb. to air condition
cloche, n.f. bell; blister on hands and
 feet
cloison, n.f. partition
cloître, n.m. cloister, convent
clôture, n.f. fence, enclosure
clou, n.m. nail, stud
clouer, vb. to nail, tack
club, n.m. club
coaguler, vb. to coagulate
coalition, n.f. coalition
coasser, vb. to croak
cocaïne, n.f. cocaine
cochon, n.m. swine, pig
cocon, n.m. cocoon
code, n.m. code; rule; law
code postal, n.m. zip code
coeur, n.m. heart
coffre, n.m. bin; box, trunk
cogner, vb. bump, strike, run
 into, knock down
cohérent, adj. coherent
coiffeur, n.m. hairdresser, barber
coiffure, n.f. hair-do, style
coin, n.m. corner, wedge, angle
coïncidence, n.f. coincidence
col, n.m. collar; pass
colère, n.f. anger, temper
colimacon, n.m. snail
colis, n.m. parcel, package
collaborateur, n.m. fellow-
 worker, co-worker
collaborer, vb. to work together,
 collaborate; work jointly
colle, n.f. glue, paste, gum
collecte, n.f. collection; collect
collectif, adj. collective
collection, n.f. collection; set
collectionneur, n.m. collector
collège, n.m. college, high school,
 grammar school
collègue, n.m. colleague
coller, vb. to glue, paste, stick together

collier, n.m. necklace; collar

colline, n.f. hill

collision, n.f. collision

colombe, n.f. dove, pigeon

colon, n.m. settler, colonist, farmer, planter

colonel, n.m. colonel

colonial, adj. colonial

colonie, n.f. settlement, colony; dominion

coloniser, vb. to colonize

colonne, n.f. column, pillar

coloré, adj. colorful; coloured

colorer, v.t. to color, to dye

colossal, adj. huge, colossal, giant

colosse, n.m. giant, colossus

colporter, n.m. peddler

colporteur, n.m. peddler, hawker

combat, n.m. fight, battle

combattant, adj. and n.m. combatant

combattre, vb. to fight, combat

combien, adv. how much, how many, how long, how far

combinaison, n.f. combination

combiner, vb. to devise, combine, plan

comble, n.m. climax, top, height

combler, v.t. to heap up, to fill up

combustible, n.m. fuel; adj. combustible

combustion, n.f. combustion, flame

comédie, n.f. comedy, players, comedians

comédien, n.m. actress, actor, comedian

comestible, adj. edible

comète, n.f. comet

comique, adj. funny, comic, comical

comité, n.m. committee, board

commandant, n.m. major, commander

commande, n.f. order; commission

commanditer, v.t. to finance

comme, adv. as, how, like, such as, nearly, almost

commémoratif, adj. memorial, commemorative

commémorer, vb. to commemorate, remember

commençant, n.m. novice, beginner

commencement, n.m. beginning, start

commencer, v.t. to begin, to start, to commence

comment, adv. how, why, wherefore

commentaire, n.m. comment, commentary, exposition

commentateur, n.m. commentator

commerçant, n.m. trader, shopkeeper, merchant

commerce, n.m. trade, commerce, trading, traffic

commettre, v.t. to commit, to appoint, to empower

commis, n.m. employee, clerk

commissaire, n.m. manager, commissioner

commission, n.f. errand, commission, charge

commodité, n.f. convenience, comfort

commun, adj. joint, common, general

communauté, n.f. community, religious community, society

communicatif, adj. open, communicative

communication, n.,f. communication

communion, n.f. communion

communiquer, vb. to communicate, in form

compagne, n.f. mate, companion

compagnie, n.f. company, fellowship

compagnon, n.m. mate, fellow, companion, comrade

comparable, adj. comparable

comparaison, n.f. comparison

comparer, v.t. to compare

compas, n.m. compass

compassion, n.f. sympathy, pity, mercy

compatible, adj. compatible, consistent

compatriote, n.m. compatriot

compensation, n.f. amends; compensation

compenser, vb. to compensate, counterbalance

compiler, vb. to compile

complaire, vb. to please

complaisance, n.f. kindness,

compliance
complaisant, adj. obliging, kind, civil
complément, n.m. object; complement
complet, n.m. suit; adj. full, complete
compléter, v.t. to complete, to perfect
complexe, adj. complex, complicated
complexité, n.f. complexity
complice, n.m.f. party to, accomplice
compliqué, adj. intricate, involved, complicated
compliquer, vb. to complicate
complot, n.m. plot
composant, adj. and n.m. component
composé, adj. compound
composer, v.t. to combound, to compose, to form
compositeur, n.m. composer
composition, n.f. essay; composition
compote, n.f. stewed fruit
compréhensif, adj. comprehensive
compréhension, n.f. comprehension
comprendre, vb. to understand, realize
compresse, n.f. compress
compression, n.f. compression
comprimer, vb. to condense
compromettre, vb. to compromise
compromis, n.m. compromise
comptabilité, n.f. accounting, bookkeeping
comptable, n.m. accountant, bookkeeper
compte, n.m. account, count, score, report
compter, v.t. to reckon, to count, to compute, calculate
comptoir, n.m. counter, bank, branch bank
comte, n.m. count
comtesse, n.f. countess
concave, adj. concave
concéder, vb. to grant, concede, allow
concentration, n.f. concentration
concentrer, vb. to condense, concentrate
concernant, prep. concerning, about, relating to
concerner, vb. to concern, regard
concert, n.m. concert, harmony

concession, n.f. grant, license, admission
concevable, adj. conceivable
concevoir, v.t. to conceive, to imagine
concierge, n.m.f. door keeper, porter
concile, n.m. council
conciliation, n.f. conciliaton
concilier, vb. to reconcile, conciliate
concis, adj. concise, brief
concision, n.f. conciseness
concluant, adj. conclusive
conclure, vb. to complete, conclude
conclusion, n.f. end, conclusion
concombre, n.m. cucumber
concourir, vb. to concur, contribute, contend
concours, n.m. contest
concret, adj. concrete
concurrence, n.f. competition
concurrent, n.m. rival, competitor
condamnation, n.f. conviction, condemnation, sentence
condamner, vb. to convict, doom, condemn, sentence
condenser, vb. to condense
condescendance, n.f. compliance
condition, n.f. condition, rank, state
conditionnel, adj. conditional
conditionner, vb. to condition
condoléance, n.f. condolence
condominium, n.m. condominium
conducteur, n.m. conductor
conduire, vb. to lead, take, drive
condite, n.f. behavior, conduct
cône, n.m. cone
confédéré, adj. and n.m. confederate
conférence, n.f. lecture, talk
conférer, vb. to confer, grant, bestow
confesser, vb. to confess, admit, acknowledge
confesseur, n.m. confessor
confession, n.f. denomination; confession, acknowledgment
confiance, n.f. turst, belief
confiant, adj. confident
confidence, n.f. condfidence
confident, n.m. confidant
confier, vb. to confide, entrust

confiner, vb. to confine, limit

confirmation, n.f. confirmation

confirmer, vb. to confirm, strengthen

confiserie, n.f. confectionery

confisquer, vb. to confiscate

confiture, n.f. jam, jelly, preserve

conflit, n.m. conflict, collision

confondre, vb. to confuse, confound

conforme, adj. consonant, consistent

conformer, vb. to conform

conformité, n.f. accordance, likeness

confort, n.m. comfort, ease

confortable, adj. cozy, snug, comfortable

confronter, vb. to confront

confus, adj. confused, mixed, indistinct

confusion, n.f. confusion, disorder

congé, n.m. discharge; leave of absence, furlough, holiday

congélateur, n.m. freezer, refrigerator

congeler, vb. to congeal, freeze

congestion, n.f. congestion

congrès, n.m. congress, assembly

conjecture, n.f. guess, conjecture

conjonction, n.f. conjunction

conjugaison, n.f. conjugation

conjuguer, vb. to conjugate

conjuration, n.f. conspiracy, plot

conjurer, vb. to conspire, plot

connaisseur, n.m. connoisseur

connaître, v.t. to be acquainted, to know, to understand

connexion, n.f. connection

conquérir, vb. to conquer, subdue

conquête, n.f. conquest, acquisition

conscience, n.f. conscience, consciousness

conscient, adj. conscious

conscription, n.f. draft, enlistment

consécutif, adj. consecutive, following

conseiller, vb. to advise, counsel

consentement, n.m. consent, assent, approval

consentir, vb. to consent, accede

conséquence, n.f. outgrowth, result, consequence

conséquent, adj. consequent, consistent

conservateur, adj. and n.m. conservative

conservation, n.f. conservation, preservation

conserve, n.f. conserve, pickle

conserver, v.t. to conserve, to maintain, to keep

considérable, adj. considerable

considérer, vb. to consider

consigner, vb. to consign, deposit

consistance, n.f. consistency

consistant, adj. consistent

consister, vb. to consist, composed

consolateur, n.m. comforter

consolation, n.f. comfort, solace

console, n.f. bracket, console

consoler, vb. to comfort, console

consolider, vb. to consolidate, strengthen, make durable

consommateur, n.m. consumer

consommation, n.f. consumption; end consummation

consommer, vb. to consummate, complete

consomption, n.f. consumption

consonne, n.f. consonant

conspirateur, n.m. conspirator

conspiraton, n.f. conspiration

conspirer, vb. to conspire

constamment, adv. continually, constantly, steadily

constance, n.f. constancy, firmness

constant, adj. constant, firm

constater, vb. to prove, verify

constellation, n.f. constellation

consternation, n.f. dismay

consterné, adj. aghast, dismayed

consterner, vb. to dismay, dishearten

constipation, n.f. constipation

constituant, adj. constituent

constituer, vb. to constitue, form, compose

constitution, n.f. constitution

constricteur, n.m. constrictor

construire, vb. to construct, build

consul, n.m. consul

consultant, adj. consulting

consulter, vb. to consult
consumer, vb. to consume, destroy
contact, n.m. touch, contact
contagieux, adj. contagious
contagion, n.f. infection
contaminer, vb. to contaminate
conte, n.m. tale, story
contemplation, n.f. contemplation
contempler, vb. to survey, observe, contemplate
contemporain, adj. contemporary
contenir, vb. to hold, restrain, contain
contenter, vb. to please, satisfy
contenu, n.m. contents; enclosure
conter, vb. to tell, relate
contester, vb. to challenge, object to, contest
contexte, n.m. context
contigu, adj. adjoining, contiguous
continent, n.m. continent, mainland
continental, adj. continental
contingent, n.m. quota, portion, share
continu, adj. continuous, uninterrupted
continuel, adj. continual, uninterrupted
continuer, vb. to carry on, keep on, go on, continue
continuité, n.f. continuity
contour, n.m. outline, contour
contourner, vb. to go round, outline
contracter, vb. to contract, bargain
contraction, n.f. contraction
contraindre, vb. to coerce, compel
contrainte, n.f. compulsion, uneasiness
contrarier, vb. to thwart, vex, annoy, oppose
contrariété, n.f. annoyance
contraste, n.m. contrast, opposition
contraster, vb. to contrast
contrat, n.m. contract, deed, agreement
contre, prep. against
contrebande, n.f. smuggling; contraband
contrée, n.f. district, province
contrefaire, vb. to forge, counterfeit

contrefort, n.m. buttress
contremaître, n.m. foreman, overseer
contribuer, vb. to contribute, pay
contributon, n.f. share, contribution
contrôle, n.m. verification
contrôler, vb. to control, check
contrôleur, n.m. checker, collector
controverse, n.f. controversy
convaincre, vb. to convince
convalescence, n.f. convalescence
convenable, adj. becoming, appropriate, suitable
convenance, n.f. convenience
convenir, vb. to suit, fit, befit, agree
convention, n.f. convention
converger, vb. to converge
conversation, n.f. conversation, talk
converser, vb. to talk, converse
conversion, n.f. change, conversion
convertir, vb. to convet, transform
convexe, adj. convex
conviction, n.f. conviction
convive, n.f. guest, companion
convoi, n.m. convoy, funeral procession
convoiter, vb. to covet
convoitise, n.f. covetousness; lust
convoquer, vb. to summon, call
convulsion, n.f. convulsion
copie, n.f. copy, transcript
copier, vb. to copy, imitate
copieux, adj. copious, plentiful
coq, n.m. rooster
coquille, n.f. shell
cor, n.m. horn; corn
corail, n.m., pl. **coraux**, coral
corbeau, n.m. raven, crow
corbeille, n.f. wide, flat basket
corde, n.f. rope, string, cord
cordial, adj. harty, cordial
cordon, n.m. rope, cord
cordonnier, n.m. shoemaker
Corée, n.f. Korea
corne, n.f. horn
corneille, n.f. crow
cornemuse, n.f. bagpipe
cornichon, n.m. gherkin
corporation, n.f. corporation

corporel, adj. bodily

corps, n.m. body, matter, substance

corpulent, adj. burly, stout

correction, n.f. correction, correctness

corrélation, n.f. correlation

correspondance, n.f. connection; similarity

correspondant, n.m. correspondent adj. similar, corresponding

correspondre, vb. to correspond

corriger, vb. to mend, reclaim, correct

corroborer, vb. to strengthen, corroborate

corroder, vb. to corrode

corrompre, vb. to bribe, corrupt

corrompu, adj. corrupt, bribed

corruption, n.f. bribery, graft, corruption

corsage, n.m. bodice

corset, n.m. corset

cortège, n.m. procession

cosmétique, adj. and n.m. cosmetic

cosmopolite, adj. and n.m.f. cosmopolitan

costume, n.m. attire, dress, uniform

cote, n.f. quota, proportion, share

côte, n.f. rib; slope

côté n.f. side, part

côtelette, n.f. chop, cutlet

coton, n.m. cotton

cou, n.m. neck

couche, n.f. layer, bed; diaper

coucher, vb. to put to bed, lay down

couchette, n.f. bunk, berth, small bed

coucou, n.m. cuckoo

coude, n.m. elbow, bend, angle

coudoyer, v.t. to jostle, to elbow

coudre, vb. to sew, stitch

couler, vb. to flow, sink, run

couleur, n.f. hue, color, dye, paint

couloir, n.m. corridor, passage, lobby

coup, n.m. blow, stroke, hit, bump, knock, cast

coupable, adj. guilty, to blame, at fault

couper, v.t. to cut, to dock

couple, n.f. couple, pair

coupon, n.m. remnant; coupon

coupure, n.f. cut, clipping

cour, n.f. courtyard; courtship

courage, n.m. bravery, pluck courage

courageux, adj. brave

couramment, adv. fluently, readily

courant, adj. current, stream, course

courbe, n.f. curve, sweep, bent

courber, vb. to bend, curve

coubure, n.f. curvature, curve

coureur, n.m. runner, racer

courir, vb. to run, hasten

couronne, n.f. crown, wreath

couronner, vb. to crown, honor

courrier, n.m. mail, messenger

courroie, n.f. strap; driving belt

courroux, n.m. wrath, anger

cours, n.m. course, current flow

course, n.f. running, race, course

court, adj. short, brief, concise

courtepointe, n.f. quilt

courtier, n.m. broker, agent

courtisan, n.m. courtier

courtois, adj. courteous, polite

courtoisie, n.f. courtesy, politeness

cousin, n.m. cousin

coussin, n.m. cushion, hassock

coussinet, n.m. bearing

coût, n.m. cost, charge

couteau, n.m. knife

coutellerie, n.f. cutlery, cutler's business

coûter, vb. to cost

coûteux, adj. expensive, costly

coutume, n.f. custom

couture, n.f. seam

haute couture, high fashion

couturière, n.f. dressmaker

couvée, n.f. brood

couvent, n.m. covent, monastery

couver, vb. to brood, hatch; smolder

couvercle, n.m. lid, cover

couvert, adj. covered

couverture, n.f. blanket, cover

couvrir, vb. to cove, wrap

crabe, n.m. crab

crachat, n.m. spit, expectoration

craie, n.f. chalk

crainte, n.f. fear, dread, awe

craintif, adj. fearful, apprehensive

crampe, n.f. cramp
crampon, n.m. cramp, crampiron
crâne, n.m. skull, cranium
crapaud, n.m. toad
craquement, n.m. crack, creaking
craquer, v.t. to crack, to creak
cratère, n.m. crater
cravater, v.t. to put on a necktie
crayon, n.m. pencil
creánce, n.f. belief, trust, confidence
créancière, n.m. creditor
création, n.f. creation; the universe
créature, n.f. creature
crédit, n.m. credit, trust
credo, n.m. creed, belief
crédule, adj. credulous
créer, vb. to create, make, produce
crème, n.f. cream, custard
crêpe, n.f. pancake
crête, n.f. ridge, crest
crétin, n.m. dunce, idiot
cretonne, n.f. cretonne
creuser, vb. to dig, scoop out, hollow
creux, adj. hollow; deep; empty
crevasse, v.t. to split, to chap
crever, vb. to burst; die, split, crack
crevette, n.f. shrimp
crible, n.m. sieve
crier, vb. to yell, shout, scream
crime, n.m. crime
criminel, adj. criminal, unlawful
crise, n.f. crisis, conjuncture
cristal, n.m. crystal, glass
critiquer, vb. to criticize
crochet, n.m. bracket, hook
crochu, adj. hooked, crooked
crocodile, n.m. crocodile
croire, vb. to believe, hold true
croisade, n.f. crusade
croisé, n.m. crusader
croiser, vb. to cross, lay across
croiseur, n.m. cruiser
croisière, n.f. cruise
croissance, n.f. growth, increase
croissant, n.m. crescent
croître, vb. to grow, increase
croix, n.f. cross
croquant, adj. crisp, crackling

croquet, n.m. croquet game, biscuit
crotale, n.m. rattlesnake
crouler, vb. to fall apart, give way
croup, n.m. croup
croupir, vb. to wallow, lie stagnant
croûte, n.f. crust; pie crust
croûton, n.m. crusty end
croyable, adj. believeable
croyance, n.f. belief, creed
croyant, n.m. believer
cru, n.m. growth
cruauté, n.f. cruelty, inhumanity
cruche, n.f. pitcher, jar, jug
crucifier, vb. to crucify
crucifix, n.m. crucifix
cruel, adj. cruel, merciless
Cuba, n.m. Cuba
cube, n.m. cube; adj. cubic
cueillir, vb. to pick, gather
cuir, n.m. leather, hide
cuirassé, n.m. battleship
cuire, vb. to cook; sting, smart
cuisine, n.f. kitchen, cooking
cuisinier, n.m. cook
cuisse, n.f. thigh; quarter
cuivre, n.m. copper
cul-de-sac, n.m. blind alley
culotte, n.f. breeches, shorts
culpabilité, n.f. guilt
culte, n.m. worship; cult
culture, n.f. cultivation; farming
cure, n.f. cure, healing
curieux, adj. curious; inquisitive
curiosité, n.f. curiosity
cursif, adj. cursive
cuticle, n.f. cuticle
cuve, n.f. vat, tub
cuvette, n.f. wash basin
cuvier, n.m. washtub
cycle, n.m. cycle of events
cycliste, n.m.f. cyclist
cyclone, n.m. cyclone
cylindre, n.m. cylinder
cymbale, n.f. cymbal
cynique, n.m. cynic; adj. cynical
cynisme, n.m. cynicism
cyprès, n.m. cypress
czar, n.m. czar

dactylographe, n.m. typist
daim, n.m. buck, deer
daine, n.f. doe
dais, n.m. canopy
dame, n.f. lady
danger, n.m. danger, risk, hazard
dangereux, adj. dangerous
dans, prep. in, into, within;
 according to
danse, n.f. dance; dancing
danser, v.t. to dance
danseur, n.m. dancer
dard, n.m. dart; sting
date, n.f. date
dater, vb. to date
datte, n.f. date
davantage, adv. more, any further,
 any more, any longer
débarquer, vb. to land, disembark
débarrasser, vb. to rid, free
débat, n.m. debate, dispute, contest
débattre, vb. to canvass; debate, argue
débit, n.m. retail; output, sale market
débiter, v.t. to sell, to supply, to retail
déblayer, vb. to clear away
débordé, adj. overflowing river
déboucher, vb. to flow into
débourser, vb. to disburse, lay out
débris, n.m., pl. wreck, debris
début, n.m. beginning, first
 appearance, debut
débuter, vb. to make one's first
 appearance, set out
décadence, n.f. decay, decadence,
 downfall
décaféiné, adj. decaffeinated
décédé, n.m. deceased
décembre, n.m. December
décence, n.f. decency
décent, adj. decen; modest
déception, n.f. disappointment, deceit
décerner, vb. to award, bestow, confer
décès, n.m. death, death, demise
décevoir, vb. to disappoint; deceive,
 mislead
décharge, n.f. unlading; unloading;
 discharge; outlet
décharger, vb. to unload, discharge,

 empty
décharné, adj. gaunt, lean, emaciated
déchausser, vb. to take off shoes
déchets n.m., pl. waste, loss
déchiffrer, vb. to decipher, unravel,
 penetrate
déchirer, vb. to tear, rend, lacerate
déchirure, n.f. tear, rent
décidé, n.m. decide, resolve,
 determined
décider, vb. to prevail upon, decide,
 settle
décimal, adj. decimal
décisif, adj. decisive
décision, n.f. decision, determination
délamer, vb. to recite, declaim
déclaration, n.f. statement,
 announcement
déclarer, vb. to state, proclaim
déclin, n.m. ebb; decline, decay
décliner, vb. to decline, refuse
décolorant, adj. bleaching
décolorer, vb. to bleach, fade
décomposer, vb. to spoil, decompose,
 split up
déconcerter, vb. to disconcert, put out
décongestionner, v.t. to relieve
 congestion
décontracté, adj. relaxed
décoratif, adj. decorative, ornmental
décoration, n.f. decoration, trimming,
 embellishment
découper, vb. to carve meat, cut up
découragé, adj. despondent
découragement, n.m. discouragement
décourager, vb. to dishearten
découverte, n.f. discovery, detection
découvreur, n.m. discoverer
découvrir, vb. to detect, discover
décrépit, adj. decrepit, worn out
décret, n.m. decree, enactment, order
décréter, vb. to enact, order, decree
décrire, vb. to desccribe, depict
dédaigneux, adj. scornful, disdainful
dédain, n.m. scorn, disdain, disregard
dedans, n.m. inside, within, in
dédicace, n.f. dedication
dédier, vb. to dedicate, consecrate

déduction, n.f. deduction, allowance

déduire, vb. to infer, deduce, deduct

défaire, vb. to undo; obscure, eclipse

défaite, n.f. defeat, undone

défaut, n.m. flaw, failure, absence

défectueux, adj. faulty, defective, imperfect

défendeur, n.m. defendant; respondent

défendre, vb. to forbid, protect, shelter

défense, n.f. prohibition, plea, protection, defense

défenseur, n.m. adovcate, defender, supporter

défensif, adj. defensive

déférer, vb. to defer

défi, n.m. challenge, defiance

défiance, n.f. mistrust, distrust

déficit, n.m. deficit, deficiency

défier, vb. to challenge, defy, confront

défigurer, vb. to deface, disfigure

défiler, vb. to march off, defile

défini, adj. definite, determined

définir, vb. to define, determine

définitif, adj. final, definitive, ultimate

définition, n.f. definition

défraichir, v.t. to tarnish, to take away the gloss, freshness or brilliancy

défricher, vb. to reclaim, clear

défunt, n.m. and adj. deceased

dégagé, adj. breezy; unconstrained

dégât, n.m. damage, havoc

dégénérer, vb. to degenerate, decline

dégoût, n.m. distaste, disgust, dislike

dégoûtant, adj. foul, disgusting

dégoûter, vb. to disgust

dégoutter, vb. to drip, trickle

dégradation, n.f. degradation

dégrader, vb. to degrade, deface, damage

degré, n.m. degree, step, stair, grade

déguisement, n.m. disguise

déguiser, vb. to disguise

dehors, adv. outside, out, without

déifier, vb. to defy

déjà, adv. already, previously, before

déjeuner, n.m. and vb. lunch, luncheon

déjouer, vb. to baffle, frustrate

delà, adv. beyond; on the other side

délabrement, n.m. decay

délabrer, vb. to ruin, wreck

délai, n.m. delay; reprieve

délaissement, n.m. helplessness

délaisser, vb. to forsake, adandon

délassement, n.m. relaxation

délasser, vb. to refresh, relax

délateur, n.m. informer

délayé, adj. watery

délectable, adj. delicious, delightful

délectation, n.f. enjoyment, delight

délecter, vb. to delight

délégation, n.f. delegation

délégué, n.m. delegate

déléguer, vb. to delegate, deputy

délétère, adj. harmful; offensive

délibératif, adj. deliberative

délibéré, adj. deliberate, decided

délicat, adj. dainty, delicate, exquisite

délicatesse, n.f. delicacy, weakness

délice, n.f., pl. delight, pleasure

délicieux, adj. delicious

délié, adj. slender; keen

délier, vb. to untie, release

délinquant, n.m. delinquent, offender

délirant, adj. delirious, frantic, ecstatic

délirer, vb. to rave, wander

délit, n.m. offense, crime

délivrance, n.f. rescue, deliverance

délivrer, vb. to rescue, set free, deliver

déloger, vb. to dislodge, remove

déloyal, adj. disloyal, false

déloyauté, n.f. disloyalty

déluge, n.m. deluge, flood

déluré, adj. clever, cute, sharp

demain, adv. tomorrow

demande, n.f. application, request, inquiry, question

demander, vb. to ask, beg, request

demandeur, n.m. plaintiff, applicant

démangeaison, n.f. itch

démanger, v.t. to itch, to long

démanteler, vb. to dismantle

démarcation, n.f. demarcation

démarche, n.f. walk, bearing;

proceeding
démarrage, n.m. start
démarrer, vb. to start off, cast off
démarreur, n.m. self-starter
démasquer, vb. to unmask; expose, reveal, show up
démembrer, vb. to dismember
déménagement, n.m. removing furniture
déménager, vb. to remove furniture
démence, n.f. insanity, madness
démener, vb. to struggle, strive hard
dément, adj. insane, mad person
démenti, n.m. denial; disappointment
démentir, vb. to contradict
démesuré, adj. immense, excessive, enormous
demeure, n.f. abode, home, dwelling
demeurer, vb. to dwell, lodge
demi, n.m. and adj. half
demi-cercle, n.m. semicircle
demi-dieu, n.m. demigod
demi-frère, n.m. stepbrother, half-brother
demi-lacure, n.f. half an hour
démilitariser, vb. to demilitarize
demi-place, n.f. half fare; half price
demi-saison, n.f. spring or autumn
demi-soeur, n.f. stepsister, halfsister
démission, n.f. resignation
démobilisation, n.f. demobilization
démobiliser, vb. to demobilize
démocrate, adj. democratic
democratie, n.f. democracy
démocratique, adj. democratic
démodé, adj. old fashioned
demoiselle, n.f. young lady
démolir, vb. to demolish, pull down
démolition, n.f. demolition
démon, n.m. demon
démonétiser, vb. to demonetize
démonstration, n.f. demonstration; exhibition
démonter, v.t. to dismount as from a horse
démontrable, adj. demonstrable
démontrer, vb. to demonstrate
demoralisation, n.f. demoralization
démouler, vb. to remove, from a mold
démuni, adj. short of, lacking
dénationaliser, vb. to denationalize
dénaturer, vb. to denature
dénégation, n.f. denial
dénivelé, adj. not level
dénombrement, n.m. census, count of persons
dénombrer, vb. to count, number
dénommer, vb. to name; designate
dénoncer, vb. to report, denounce
dénonciaton, n.f. denunciation; information
dénoter, vb. to denote
dénouer, vb. to untie, loosen
dense, adj. dense., close
densité, n.f. density, thickness
dent, n.f. tooth
dental, adj. dental
denté, adj. cogged
dentelle, n.f. lace
dentiste, n.m. dentist
dénuder, vb. to strip, denude
dénué, adj. destitute, bare
dénuement, n.m. deprivation
dénuer, vb. to strip
dépareillé, adj. odd, unmatched
départ, n.m. departure, start
département, n.m. department
départir, vb. to distribute
dépasser, vb. to outrun, go beyond
dépêche, n.f. dispatch
dépêcher, vb. to dispatch, do quickly
dépendant, adj. dependent
dépendre, vb. to take down
dépens, n.m., pl. expenses, costs
dépense, n.f. expenditure, expense
dépenser, vb. to spend, consume
dépérir, vb. to waste away; decline
dépecer, vb. to dismember
déplacement, n.m. displacement
déplacer, vb. to displace, move, shift
déplaire, vb. to displease, offend
déplaisant, adj. displeasing
déplanter, vb. to transplant
déplier, vb. to unfold
déploiement, n.m. deployment, unfolding

déplorable, adj. wretched, deplorable

déplorer, vb. to deplore, lament

déployer, vb. to deploy, unfold, unroll

déplumer, vb. to pluck feathers from

déportation, n.f. transportation

déportements, n.m., pl. misconduct

déporter, vb. to deport

déposant, n.m. depositor

déposer, vb. to deposit, set down

dépositaire, n.m. trustee; agent

déposséder, vb. to oust; dispossess

dépôt, n.m. deposit, depot

dépouille, n.f. hide, skin, pelt

dépourvu, adj. devoid; needy

dépoussiérer, n.m. vacuum cleaner

dépravation, n.f. depravity

dépraver, vb. to deprave, corrupt

dépréciation, n.f depreciation

déprécier, vb. to depreciate, cheapen

déprédation, n.f. depredation

dépression, n.f. depression

déprimer, vb. to depress, press down

déraciner, vb. to uproot, eradicate

déraison, n.f. unreason

déraisonnable, adj. unreasonable

défangement, n.m. disturbance

défanger, vb. to disturb, trouble

derechef, adv. once again

dérégler, vb. to upset, disorder

dérider, vb. to smooth; cheer up

dérive, n.f. drift

dériver, vb. to derive; drift

dernier, adj. last, latter

dernièrement, adv. lately

dérober, vb. to rob, steal

défouiller, vb. to remove rust from

dérouler, vb. to unroll, unfold

déroute, n.f. rout

dérouter, vb. to mislead; confuse

derrière, prep. behind

derviche, n.m. dervish

dès, prep. since, from

désabuser, vb. to disabuse

désaccord, n.m. disagreement

désaccoutumer, vb. to break a habit

désagréable, adj. nasty, distasteful

désaligné, adj. out of alignment

désaltérer, vb. to quench one's thirst

désappointement, n.m. disappointment

désappointer, vb. to deceive

désapprobation, n.f. disapproval

désapprouver, vb. to disapprove

désarmement, n.m. disarmament

désarmer, vb. to disarm

désarroi, n.m. disorder

désastre, n.m. disaster

désastreux, adj. disastrous

désavantage, n.m. disadvantage

désaveu, n.m. denial

désavouer, vb. to disown

descendance, n.f. descent

descendant, n.m offspring, descendant; adj. downward

descendre, vb. to go down, come down, descend

descente, n.f. raid; descent

descriptif, adj. descriptive

description, n.f. description

désembarquer, vb. to disembark

désenchanter, vb. to disenchant

désenivrer, vb. to sober up

désert, n.m. wilderness, desert

déserteur, n.m. deserter

désertion, n.f. desertion

désespéré, adj. hopeless, forlorn, desperate

désespérer, vb. to despair, despond

désespoir, n.m. desperation, despair

déshabiller, vb. to undress

déshériter, vb. to disinherit

déshonnête, adj. improper, indecent

déshonneur, n.m. disgrace, dishonor

déshonorant, adj. dishonorable

déshonorer, vb. to disgrace, dishonor

déshydrater, vb. to dehydrate

désignation, n.f. nomination

désigner, vb. to nominate; point out

désillusion, n.f. disillusion

désinfectant, n.m. disinfectant

désinfecter, vb. to disinfect, fumigate

désinfection, n.f. disinfection

désintégration, n.f. disintegration

désintegrer, vb. to disintegrate

désintéressé, adj. unselfish, impartial

désintéressement, n.m. unselfishness

désir, n.m. desire, wish
désirable, adj. desirable
désirer, vb. to desire, wish
désireux, adj. desirous, anxious
désistement, n.m. withdrawal
désobéir à, vb. to disobey
désobéissance, n.f. disobedience
désobéissant, adj. disobedient
désoeuvré, adj. idle, unoccupied
désolation, n.f. desolation
désoler, vb. to desolate, afflict
désordonné, adj. disorderly
désordonner, vb. to upset, confuse
désordre, n.m. disorder, confusion
désorganiser, vb. to disorganize
dessécher, vb. to dry out, parch; drain
dessein, n.m. plan, intent
desserrer, vb. to loosen, relax
dessert, n.m. dessert
dessin, n.m. design, sketch, draft
dessinateur, n.m. designer
dessiner, vb. to draw, design
dessus, n.m. top
destin, n.m. fate, destiny
destination, n.f. destination
destinée, n.f. destiny
destiner, vb. to destine, intend
destituer, vb. to dismiss, discharge
destructif, adj. destructive
destruction, n.f. destruction
désuet, adj. obsolete, out-of-date
désuétude, n.f. disuse
désunir, vb. to disconnect
détaché, adj. loose, detached
détachement, n.m. detachment
détacher, vb. to detach, untie
détail, n.m. item, particular, detail
détective, n.m. detective
détenir, vb. to detain, keep back
détente, n.f. trigger
détention, n.f. custody, withholding
détermination, n.f. determination
déterminer, vb. to determine, fix
détestable, adj. detestable, hateful
détester, vb. to loathe, detest, hate
détonation, n.f. detonation
détonner, vb. to make out of tune
détour, n.m. turn; detour

détourner, vb. to turn away; avert
détresse, n.f. trouble, distress
détriment, n.m. detriment, injury
détruire, vb. to destroy, demolish
dette, n.f. debt, obligation
deuil, n.m. mourning, grief
deux, adj. and n.m. two, both
deuxième, adj. second
deux-points, n.m. colon
dévaliser, vb. to rob, strip
dévaliseur, n.m. robber, theif
dévastation, n. devastation, havoc
dévaster, vb. to devastate
déveine, n.f. bad luck
développement, n.m. development, growth
développer, vb. to develop
devenir, vb. to become, grow
déverser, vb. to divert
dévêtir, vb. to undress, disrobe
déviation, n.f. deviation, diversion
dévider, vb. to unwind
dévier, vb. to turn away, turn aside
deviner, vb. to guess, foretell
devinette, n.f. puzzle, riddle
devis, n.m. estimate, specification
devise, n.f. motto, device
dévisser, vb. to unscrew
dévoiler, vb. to disclose, reveal, unveil
devoir, n.m. duty
dévorer, vb. to devour, destroy
dévot, adj. devout, devoted
dévotion, n.f. devotion
dévoué, adj. devoted
dévouement, n.m. devotion
dévouer, vb. to dedicate, devote
dextérité, n.f. dexterity
diabétique, adj. and n. diabetic
diable, n.m. devil
diablerie, n.f. mischief
diacre, n.m. deacon
diadème, n.m. diadem, coronet
diagnostiquer, vb. to diagnose
diagonal, adj. diagonal
diagramme, n.m. diagram
dialectal, adj. dialect
dialogue, n.m. dialogue
dialoguer, vb. to talk together, converse

diamant, n.m. diamond
diamétre, n.m. diameter
diaphragme, n.m. diaphragm, midriff
diarrhée, n.f. diarrhea
diatribe, n.f. diatribe, bitter
dictateur, n.m. dictator
dictature, n.f. dictatorship
dictée, n.f. act of dictation
dicter, vb. to dictate
diction, n.f. diction, style
dictionnaire, n.m. dictionary
diction, n.m. proverb, common saying
didactique, adj. didactic
dièse, adj. and n.m. sharp
diète, n.f. diet
diététique, adj. dietetical
dieu, n.m. God
diffamant, adj. libellous
diffamation, n.f. defamation
diffamer, vb. to defame
différence, n.f. difference, unlike
différencier, vb. to differentiate
différend, n.m. difference, dispute, quarrel
différent, adj. different, unlike
différer, vb. to differ, put off
difficile, adj. arduous, hard; difficult
difficilement, adv. with difficulty
difficulté, n.f. trouble; difficulty
difforme, adj. deformed
difformité, n.f. deformity, malformation
diffus, adj. diffuse
diffusion, n.f. spread
digérer, vb. to digest, ponder, discuss
digestible, adj. digestible
digestif, adj. and n.m. digestive
digital, adj. digital
digne, adj. worthy, dignified
dignitaire, n.m. dignitary
dignité, n.f. dignity, nobility
digression, n.f. digression
digue, n.f. dike, dam, embankment
dilapidation, n.f waste
dilater, vb. to expand, dilate
dilemme, n.m. dilemma
dilettante, n.m. amateur
diligence, n.f. diligence, dispatch
diluer, vb. to dilute

dilution, n.f. dilution
dimanche, n.m. Sunday, Sabbath
dimension, n.f. dimension
diminuer, vb. to lessen, decrease, diminish
diminution, n.f. decrease, reduction
dindon, n.m. turkey
dîner, n.m. dinner; vb. to dine
dîneur, n.m. diner
diphtérie, n.f. diphtheria
diplomate, n.m. diplomate
diplomatie, n.f. diplomacy
diplomatique, adj. diplomatic
diplôme, n.m. diploma
dipsomanie, n.f. dipsomania
dire, vb. to say, tell
direct, adj. direct, immediate
directement, adv. directly
directeur, n.m. manager, director
direction, n.f. management, leadership
dirigeant, adj. ruling, directing
diriger, vb. to manage, boss, direct
discernable, adj. barely visible
discernement, n.m. judgment
discerner, vb. to discern, distinguish
disciple, n.m. follower, disciple
disciplinaire, adj. disciplinary
discipline, n.f. discipline
discipliner, vb. to discipline
disco, adj. disco
discontinuer, vb. to discontinue
discordance, n.f. discord
discorde, n.f. discord, disagreement
discourir, vb. to speak one's view
discours, n.m. speech, oration, talk, discourse
discourtois, adj. discourteous
discrédit, n.m. disrepute, discredit
discréditer, vb. to disparage
discret, adj. discreet
discrétion, n.f. discretion
disculper, vb. to exonerate
discursif, adj. discursive
discussion, n.f. argument, discussion
discutable, adj. debatable
discuter, vb. to argue, debate, discuss
disette, n.f. famine, want, poverty
diseur, n.m. talker

disgrâce, n.f. disgrace
disjoindre, vb. to sever, disjoint
dislocation, n.f. dislocation
disparaitre, vb. to disappear, vanish
disparate, adj. unlike, dissimilar
disparition, n.f. disappearance
dispendieux, adj. expensive, costly
dispensaire, n.m. dispensary
dispense, n.f. military exemption
dispenser, vb. to dispense, bestow
disperser, vb. to scatter, disperse
dispersion, n.f. dispersal
disponible, adj. available; unoccupied
dispos, adj. fit and well
disposer, vb. to dispose, settle
dispositif, n.m. device, appliance
disposition, n.f. arrangement
dispute, n.f. fight, quarrel, dispute
disputer, vb. to dispute, argue
disqualifier, vb. to disqualify
disque, n.m. disk, record
dissemblable, adj. unlike, dissimilar
dissension, n.f. dissension, discord
dissentiment, n.m. dissent,
  disagreement
disséquer, vb. to dissect
dissertation, n.f. essay, composition
dissimulation, n.f. pretense
dissimuler, vb. to dissemble, pretend
dissipation, n.f. dissipation
dissiper, vb. to dispel, waste
dissolu, adj. dissolute
dissolution, n.f. dissolution
dissoudre, vb. to dissolve, break up
dissuader, vb. to dissuade
distance, n.f. distance
distancer, vb. to outdistance, outrun
distant, adj. distant, remote
distinct, adj. distinct
distinctif, adj. distinctive
distinction, n.f. distinction
distingué, adj. distinguished
distinguer, vb. to discriminate
distraction, n.f. distraction, pasttime
distraire, vb. to distract, amuse
distrait, adj. absentminded
distrbuer, vb. to give out, deal
  out, distribute

distributeur, n.m. distributor
distribution, n.f. distribution;
  delivery; cast
district, n.m. district; region
dit, adj. called, spoken, said
divaguer, vb. to ramble, go astray
divan, n.m. davenport, couch
divergence, n.f. divergence
diverger, vb. to diverge
divers, adj. various
diversion, n.f. diversion; change
diversité, n.f. diversity, difference
divertir, vb. to divert, entertain
divertissement, n.m. diversion
dividende, n.m. dividend
divin, adj. divine, godlike
divinateur, n.m. soothsayer
divinité, n.f. divinity
diviser, vb. to part, divide
divisible, adj. divisible
division, n.f. division, partition
divorce, n.m. divorce, separation
divorcer, vb. to divorce
divulguer, vb. to divulge, reveal
dix, adj. and n.m. ten
dix-huit, adj. and n.m. eighteenth
dixième, adj. and n.m. tenth
dix-neuf, adj and n.m. nineteen
dix-sept, adj and n.m. seventeen
dizaine, n.f. group of ten
docile, adj. docile, submissive
docilité, n.f. docility
docte, adj. learned, wise
docteur, n.m. doctor, scholar
doctorat, n.m. doctorate, doctor's
  degree
doctrine, n.f. doctrine
document, n.m. document, certificate
documenter, vb. to document
dodu, adj. plumb
dogmatique, adj. dogmatic
dogme, n.m. dogma
dogue, n.m. watchdog
doigt, n.m. finger
doit, n.m. debit
dollar, n.m. dollar
domaine, n.m. domain, property,
  estate

dôme, n.m. dome, canopy

domestique, n.m.f. servant; adj. domestic

domicile, n.m. residence

dominant, adj. dominant

domination, n.f. sway, domination

dominer, vb. to rule, dominate

domino, n.m. domino

dommage, n.m. injury, damage

dompter, vb. to tame, subdue

don, n.m. gift, donation

donateur, n.m. donor, giver

donation, n.f. donation

donc, conj. therefore, then, hence

donne, n.f. deal cards

donner, vb. to give, bestow, make present

donneur, n.m. giver, donor

dont, pron. whose, of whom, of which

dorénavant, adv. to hereafter

dorloter, vb. to coddle, pamper, fondle

dormant, adj. dormant, asleep, stagnant

dormir, vb. to sleep

dos, n.m. back, rear, ridge

dose, n.f. dose, quantity

doser, vb. to decide the amount

dossier, n.m. record

dot, n.f. dowry, marriage, portion

doter, vb. to endow, give

douane, n.f. customs, custom house

douanier, n.m. customs officer

double, adj. and n.m. double

doubler, vb. to double, double up

doublure, n.f. lining; understudy

doucement, adv. gently, softly

doucereux, adj. sugary, sweetish

douceur, n.f. sweetness, gentleness

douche, n.f. shower, bath; douche

douer, vb. to endow, bestow upon

douille, n.f. socket

douleur, n.f. pain, sorrow, grief

douloureux, adj. painful, sore, grievous

doute, n.m. doubt, uncertainty

douter, vb. to doubt, question

douetuex, adj. doubtful, questionable

douve, n.f. ditch, trench

douzaine, n.f. dozen

douze, adj. and n.m. twelve

douzième, adj. and n.m. twelfth

doyen, n.m. dean

dragon, n.m. dragon; dragoon

draguer, vb. to dredge, sweep

drainage, n.m. drainage

drainer, vb. to drain

dramatique, adj. dramatic

drame, n.m. drama

drap, n.m. sheet, cloth

drapeau, n.f. flag, streamer

draper, vb. to drape, cover

drêche, n.f. draff

drelin, n.m. tinkle, jingle

dressage, n.m. raising, training of animals; pitching a tent

dresser, v.t. to set up, to mount, to raise

dribble, n.m. dribble

drogue, n.f. drug, dope

droit, n.m. right; law, straight

droite, n.f. right

drôle, adj. funny; strange, curious

drome, n.f. main beam

duc, n.m. duke, horned owl

duchesse, n.f. duchess

ductile, adj. ductile

dûment, adv. duly, properly

dune, n.f. dune, sandhill

duo, n.m. duet

duperie, n.f. trickery, dupery, trickery

duplicité, n.f. duplicity

dur, adj. hard, tough, merciless

durabilité, n.f. durability

durable, adj. lasting, durable, solid

durant, prep. during

durcir, vb. to harden

durcissement, n.m. hardening

durée, n.f. duration

durement, adv. hard, harshly

durer, vb. to last, continue

dureté, n.f. hardness, toughness

dynamique, adj. dynamic

dynamite, n.f. dynamite

dynamo, n.f. dynamo

dynastie, n.f. dynasty

dynastique, adj. dynstic

dyslexie, n.f. dyslexia

eau, n.f. water

eau-de-vie, n.f. brandy

ébhissement, n.m. amazement

ébarber, vb. to trim, clip

ébauche, n.f. outline, rough draft

ébène, n.m. ebony

éblouir, vb. to dazzle, amaze

ébouriffer, vb. to ruffle

ébranler, vb. to shake

écaille, n.f. scale

écart, n.m. separation

écarté, adj. isolated; lonely

écartement, n.m. gap, separation

écarter, vb. to set aside

échange, n.m. exchange

échangeable, adj. exchangeable

échanger, vb. to exchange

échappement, n.m. exhaust

échapper, vb. to escape

écharde, n.f. splinter

écharpe, n.f. scarf, sling

échasse, n.f. stilt

échauder, vb. to scald

échauffer, vb. to heat up, warm

échéance, n.f. maturity

échecs, n.m., pl. chess

échelle, n.f. ladder, scale

échelon, n.m. step; rung

échine, n.f. spine

écho, n.m. echo

échoir, vb. to fall due, expire

échouer, vb. to fail

éclabousser, vb. to splash

éclair, n.m. flash, lightning

éclairage, n.m. lighting

éclaircle, n.f. clearing

éclaircir, vb. to clear up, clarify

éclairer, vb. to enlighten, light

éclaireur, n.m. boy scout

éclat, n.m. chip, splinter, burst

éclatant, adj. loud; bursting

éclipse, n.f eclipse

éclore, vb. to blossom

écluse, n.f. lock

école, n.f. school, college

écolier, n.m. schoolboy, student

écologie, n.f. ecology

économe, adj. economical, saving

économie, n.f. economy, thrift

économique, adj. economical

économiser, vb. to economize, save

économiste, n.m. economist

écoper, vb. to bail out

écorce, n.f. bark, rind

écorcher, v.t. to skin, to peel

écorchure, n.f. graze, scratch

Ecosse, n.f. Scotland

écot, n.m. share

écouter, vb. to hear, listen to

écouteur, n.m. listener, ear phone

écran, n.m. screen

écraser, vb. to crush

écrémer, vb. to skim

écrier, vb. s'é., to exclaim

écrin, n.m. case, casket

écrire, vb. to write; **machine à é.,** typewriter

écrit, adj. written

écriteau, n.m. notice

écriture, n.f. writing

écrou, n.m. nut

écru, adj. natural

écu, n.m. shield

éculle, n.f. bowl

écume, n.f. lather, foam

écureuil, n.m. squirrel

écurie, n.f. stable

écuyer, n.m. squire

édenté, adj. toothless

édifice, n.m. building

édifier, vb. to build, construct

édit, n.m. edict

éditeur, n.m. publisher

édition, n.f. edition

éditorial, adj. editorial

éducateur, n.m. educator, teacher

éducation, n.f. education

éduquer, vb. to educate, bring up

effacer, vb. to erase, rub out

effectif, adj. actual

effectuer, vb. to effect

efféminé, adj. woman like

effet, n.m. effect

efficace, adj. effective

efficacité, n.f. effectiveness

effigie, n.f. effigy

effleurer, vb. to graze
effondrement, n.m. collapse
efforcer, vb. s'e., to endeavor, try hard
effort, n.m. endeavor, exertion, effort
effrayant, adj. fearful, frightful
effrayer, vb. to frighten, startle
effréné, adj. unrestrained
effroi, n.m. fright, terror
effronté, adj. brazen
effusion, n.f. shedding
égal, adj. even, equal
également, adv. equally
égaler, vb. to equal
égaliser, vb. to equalize
égalité, n.f. evenness
égard, n.m. regard, esteem
égaré, adj. astray
égarer, vb. to mislay, bewilder
égayer, vb. to cheer up
église, n.f. church
égoïste, adj. selfish
égorger, vb. to kill
égout, n.m. sewer, drain
égoutter, v.t. to drain
égratignure, n.f. scratch
Égypte, n.m. Egypt
éhonte, adj. brazen
élaboration, n.f. working out
élaborer, vb. to draft, elaborate
élan, n.m. zest, run
élargir, vb. to widen, increase
élasticité, n.f. elasticity
élastique, adj. and n.m. elastic
électif, adj. elective
élection, n.f. election
électricien, n.m. electrician
électricité, n.f. electricit
élégance, n.f. elegance
élégant, adj. elegant, stylish
élément, n.m. element
élémentaire, adj. elementary
éléphant, n.m. elephant
élevage, n.m. breeding
élévation, n.f. lifting
élève, n.m.f. pupil
élevé, adj. lofty

élever, vb. to raise, lift up
éleveur, n.m. breeder
éligibilité, n.f. eligibility
éligible, adj. eligible
élimination, n.f. elimination
éliminer, vb. to eliminate
élite, n.f. pick, choice
elle, pron. f. she, her; pl., they
elle-même, pron. herself
éloge, n.m. praise
éloigné, adj. remote, distant
éloignement, n.m. distance
éloigner, vb. to remove
élu, adj. chosen
éluder, vb. to elude
emballer, vb. to pack
embarcation, n.f. small craft
embargo, n.m. embargo
embarquer, vb. to embark
embarras, n.m. awkward, difficulty
embarrassant, adj. embarassing
embaumer, vb. to perfume
embellir, vb. to beautify
embêter, vb. to annoy, bore
emblème, n.m. emblem
embolie, n.f. embolism
embouchure, n.f. mouth
embranchement, n.m. junction
embrasser, vb. to embrace, kiss
embrayage, n.m. clutch
embrouillement, n.m. tangle
embrouiller, vb. to entangle, confuse
embrun, n.m. spray
embuscade, n.f. ambush
émeraude, n.f. emerald
émerger, vb. to emerge
émerveiller, vb. to astonish
émettre, vb. to emit, transmit
émeute, n.f. riot, distrubance
émietter, vb. to crumble
émigrant, n.m. emigrant
émigration, n.f. emigration
émigrer, vb. to emigrate
éminemment, adv. in a high degree
éminence, n.f. eminince
éminent, adj. high
émission, n.f. issue, circulation
emmagasiner, vb. to store, warehouse

emmener, vb. to take away
émotif, adj. emotional
émotion, n.f. feeling, emotion
émotionnable, adj. emotional
émotionner, vb. to thrill
émoussé, adj. blunt
émouvant, adj. moving, affecting
émouvoir, vb. to move
empêcher, vb. to stop, hinder
empêtrer, vb. to entangle
emphase, n.f. emphasis
emphatique, adj. emphatic
empiéter, vb. to trespass
empire, n.m. empire, nation
emplette, n.f. purchase
emploi, n.m. employment
employé, n.m. employee, clerk
employer, vb. to employ, use
employeur, n.m. employer
empoisonné, adj. poisoned
empoisonner, vb. to poison
emporter, vb. to take away
empreinte, n.f. print, stamp
empressement, n.m. eagerness
emprise, n.f. expropriation
emprisonnement, n.m. imprisonment
emprunt, n.m. loan, borrowing
emprunter, vb. to borrow from
ému, adj. touched, stirred
émule, n.m.f. rival, competitor
encadrer, vb. to frame
en-cas, n.m. reserve
enceinte, adj. f. pregnant
encens, n.m. incense
enchaîner, vb. chain; detain
enchantement, n.m. enchantment
enchanter, vb. to charm, enchant
enchère, n.f. bid
enclore, vb. to fence in, enclose
enclume, n.f. anvil
encoche, n.f. notch
encoller, vb. to paste, glue
encombrant, adj. cumbersome
encombrement, n.m. congestion
encombrer, vb. to clutter, jam
encore, adv. still, yet, again
encourageant, adj. encouraging
encouragement, n.m. encouragement

encourager, vb. to urge, promote
encourir, vb. to incur
encre, n.f. ink
encyclopédie, n.f. encyclopedia
endolorir, vb. to make painful, tender
endommager, vb. to damage, injure
endormi, adj. asleep
endossement, n.m. endorsement
endroit, n.m. place
enduire, vb. to smear, daub
endurance, n.f. endurance
endurant, adj. patient
endurcir, vb. to harden, toughen
endurcissement, n.m. hardening
énergie, n.f. energy
énergique, adj. energetic
énervé, adj. nervous
enfant, n.m.f. child, baby
enfantement, n.m. childbirth
enfanter, vb. to give birth to
enfantillage, n.m. childishness
enfantin, adj. childdish
enfariner, vb. to coat with flour
enfermer, vb. to shut in
enfiévrer, vb. to excite, inspire
enfin, adv. finally, at last
enflammer, vb. to inflame
enfler, vb. to swell, puff up
enflure, n.f. swelling
enfoncer, vb. to sink, push in
enfouir, vb. to bury
enfreindre, vb. to violate
enfumer, vb. to fill with smoke
engageant, adj. charming
engagement, n.m. pledge, engagement
engager, vb. to engage
engendrer, vb. to beget
engin, n.m. engine, motor
englober, vb. to include, unite
engloutir, vb. to devour, swallow
engorgement, n.m. choking
engouement, n.m. congestion
engouffrer, vb. to engulf
engourdir, vb. to dull
engrais, n.m. fertilizer, manure
engraisser, vb. to fatten
engrenage, n.m. gear

enhardir, vb. to make bolder
éngime, n.f. riddle
enivrant, adj. intoxicating
enivrement, n.m. intoxication
enivrer, vb. to intoxicate. **s'e.,**
 get drunk
enjambé, n.f. stride
enjeu, n.m. stake
enjoindre, vb. to enjoin; call upon
enjoliver, vb. to beautify
enjoué, adj. playful
enjouement, n.m. playfulness
enlacer, vb. to entwine; embrace
enlèvement, n.m. removal, abduction
enlever, vb. to abduct, take away
enneigé, adj. snow-covered
ennemi, adj. and n.m. enemy
ennoblir, vb. to exalt; ennoble
ennui, n.m. nuisance, bother
ennuyer, vb. to bore, annoy
ennuyeux, adj. boring, dull
énoncer, vb. to express, state
énonciation, n.f. enunciation
énorme, adj. enormous
énormité, n.f. enormity
enquérir, vb. to inquire
enquête, n.f. inquiry
enraciner, vb. to root
enragé, adj. rabid, mad
enrageant, adj. maddening
enregistrement, n.m. registration
enregistrer, vb. to record, list
enrichir, vb. to enrich
enrober, vb. to coat, envelop
enrôlement, n.m. enlistment
enrôler, vb. to enlist, enroll
enroué, adj. hoarse, husky
enrouement, n.m. hoarseness
enseigne, n.f. sign, ensign
enseignement, n.m. teaching
enseigner, vb. to teach
ensemble, n.m. set, whole, mass
ensevelir, vb. to bury, swallow up
ensoleillé, adj. sunny
ensommeillé, adj. sleepy
ensuite, adv. then; next
ensuivre, vb. **s'e.,** to ensue
entacher, vb. to taint, besmirch

entamer, vb. to begin
entendement, n.m. understanding
entendre, vb. to hear, understand
entendu, adj. understood, agreed
enténébré, adj. gloomy
entente, n.f. understanding
entêté, adj. perverse
entêtement, n.m. stubbornness
entêter, vb. **s'e.,** to insist
enthousiasme, n.m. enthusiasm
enthousiaste, n.m.f. enthusiast
entichement, n.m. infatuation
entier, adj. whole, entire
entonnoir, n.m. funnel
entorse, n.f. sprain
entourage, n.m. circle of
 friends, acquaintances
entourer, vb. to surround
entournure, n.f. armhole
entrain, n.m. zest
entraîner, vb. to draw, along, entail
entraîneur, n.m. coach, trainer
entrant, adj. incoming
entraver, vb. to clog, shackle
entre, prep. among, between
entre-clos, adj. ajar
entre-deux, n.m. interval
entrée, n.f. admission, entry
entregent, n.m. tact; spirit
entrelacer, vb. to interface
entremetteur, n.m. intermediary
entreposer, vb. to store, warehouse
entrepôt, n.m. warehouse
entreprenant, adj. enterprising
entreprendre, vb. to undertake
entrepreneur, n.m. contractor
entreprise, n.f. undertaking
entrer, vb. to enter, come in, go in
entretenir, vb. to entertain
entretien, n.m. maintenance
entrevor, vb. to glimpse
énuméfer, vb. to enumerate, count
envahir, vb. to invade
envahissement, n.m. invasion
enveloppe, n.f. envelop, wrapper
envers, n.m. wrong side
enviable, adj. enviable
envie, n.f. desire, envy

envier, vb. to envy
envieux, adj. envious, jealous
environ, prep. and adv. about
environner, vb. to surround
envisager, vb. to consider, look at
envoi, n.m. shipment, parcel
envoler, vb. s'e., to fly away
envoyé, n.m. envoy
envoyer, v.t. to send, to forward
enzyme, n.f. enzyme
épais, adj. thick, dense
épaisseur, n.f. thickness
épaissir, vb. to thicken
épancher, v.t. to pour out
épanouir, vb. to cause to bloom
épargne, n.f. savings, economy
épargner, vb. to save, spare
éparpiller, vb. to scatter
épars, adj. scattered, sparse
épatement, n.m. amazement
épater, vb. to amaze
épaule, n.f. shoulder
épée, n.f. sword
épeler, vb. to spell
épellation, n.f. spelling
éperdu, adj. distracted, aghast
éperlan, n.m. smelt
éperon, n.m. spur
épervier, n.m. hawk
épeuré, adj. frightened, scared
épice, n.f. spice
épicé, adj. spicy
épicerie, n.f. grocery
épicier, n.m. grocer
épidémie, n.f. epidemic
épilepsie, n.f. epilepsy
épilogue, n.m. epilogue
épinards, n.m., pl. spinach
épine, n.f. spine, thorn
épinet, n.f. spinet
épineux, adj. thorny
épiscopal, adj. Episcopal
épisode, n.m. episode
épitaphe, n.f. epitaph
épitomé, n.m. abridgment
épitre, n.f. epistle
éplore, adj. tearful
éponté, adj. dull, blunted

éponge, n.f. sponge
épopée, n.f. epic
épouse, n.f. wife, spouse
épouser, vb. to marry
épouvantable, adj. terrible
épouvante, n.f. fright
époux, n.m. husband, spouce
épreindre, vb. to squeeze
éprendre, vb. s'é., to fall in love
épreuve, n.f. trial, test, proof
éprouver, vb. to experience
éprouvette, n.f. test tube
épuiser, vb. to exhaust
épuration, n.f. purification
épurer, vb. to purify, clarify
équateur, n.m. equator
équation, n.f. equation
équestre, adj. equestrian
équilibre, n.m. poise, balance
équipage, n.m. crew
équipe, n.f. crew, gang, shift
équipement, n.m. equipment
équiper, vb. to equip
équitable, adj. fair, just
équité, n.f. equity, fairness
équivalent, adj. and n.m. equivalent
équivaloir, vb. to equal in value
équivoque, adj. uncertain
érable, n.m. maple
éraflure, n.m. scratch; graze
érailler, vb. to unravel
ère, n.f. era
érection, n.f. construction
éreintant, adj. exhausting
éreinter, vb. to exhaust
ériger, vb. to erect, raise
éroder, vb. to erode
érosif, adj. erosive
érosion, n.f. erosion
érotique, adj. erotic
errant, adj. wandering
erratique, adj. erratic
errer, vb. to wander; err
erreur, n.f. mistake, error
erroné, adj. erroneous
éructation, n.f. belch
érudit, adj. learned, scholarly
éruption, n.f. rash, eruption

escabeau, n.m. step stool
escalader, vb. to scale; escalate
escalier, n.m. stairs, staircase
escalope, n.f. cutlet
escapade, n.f. prank
escarcelle, n.f. wallet
escargot, n.m. snail
escarole, n.f. endive
escarpé, adj. abrupt
eschare, n.f. scab
esclavage, n.m. slavery
esclave, n.m.f. slave
escompte, n.m. discount
escorte, n.f. escort
escouade, n.f. squad
escrime, n.f. fencing
escrimer, vb. to fight
escroc, n.m. swindler
escroqur, vb. to swindle
esculent, adj. edible
espace, n.m. space, room
espacé, adj. far apart
espacer, vb. to space out
espadon, n.m. swordfish
Espagne, n.f. Spain
espèce, n.f. species, kind
espérance, n.f. hope
espérer, v.t. to hope
espiègle, adj. mischievous
espièglerie, n.f. mischief
espion, n.m. spy
espionnage, n.m. spying
espionner, vb. to spy on
esplanade, n.f. parade
espoir, n.m. hope
esprit, n.m. spirit, mind, wit
esquimau, adj. Eskimo
esquinter, vb. to exhaust, tireout
esquisse, n.f. sketch
esquiver, vb. to avoid
essai, n.m. testing, attempt
essaim, n.m. swarm
essayer, vb. to try; assay
essence, n.f. gasoline; essence
essentiel, adj. essential
esseulement, n.m. solitude
essieu, n.m. axle
essor, n.m. flight

essorer, vb. to dry, wring out
essuie-glace, n.m. windshield wiper
essuyer, vb. to wipe
estacade, n.f. stockade
estafette, n.m. courier
estagnon, n.m. oil drum
estaminet, n.m. bar, tavern
estampe, n.f. engraving, print
estampille, n.f. trademark, mark
estimable, adj. estimable
estimateur, n.m. appraiser
estimatif, adj. estimated
estimation, n.f. estimate
estime, n.f. esteem; estimation
estimer, vb. to value, rate
estivant, n.m. summer tourist
estiver, v.t. to spend the summer
estoc, n.m. tree trunk
estomac, n.m. stomach
estourbir, vb. to kill
estrade, n.f. platform; stage
estropié, n.m. cripple
esturgeon, n.m. surgeon
et, conj and
étable, n.f. barn
établi, n.m. worktable
établir, vb. to settle, establish
établissement, n.m. establishment
étage, n.m. floor, story
étagère, n.f. whatnot shelf
étain, n.m. tin; pewter
étal, n.m. butcher shop
étalage, n.m. display
étaler, vb. to display, spread
étalon, n.m. stallion
étampe, n.f. stamp; die; punch
étanche, adj. water tight
étancher, vb. to stop
étang, n.m. pond, pool
étape, n.m. stage, station
États-nis, n.m., pl. United States
été, n.m. summer
éteindre, vb. to extinguish
éteint, adj. extinct
étendage, n.m. clotheslines
étendard, n.m. standard
étendre, vb. to spread, reach, expand
étendu, adj. extensive, wide

étendue, n.f. extent, reach
éternel, adj. everlasting
éterniser, vb. to perpetuate
éternuement, n.m. sneeze
éternuer, vb. to sneeze
éthéré, adj. ethereal
Éthiopie, n.f. Ethiopia
éthique, n.f. ethics
étinceler, vb. to sparkle
étincelle, n.f. spark, sparkle
etiqueter, vb. to label
étiquette, n.f. tag; etiquette
étirer, vb. to stretch out
étoffe, n.f. material, cloth
étoffer, vb. to stuff
étoile, n.f. star
étonnement, n.m. astonishment
étonner, vb. to astonish
étouffer, vb. to smother
étourdir, vb. to daze, stun
étourdissement, n.m. dizziness
étrange, adj. strange
étranger, n. and adj. alien
étrangler, vb. to strangle
étrave, n.f. stem, bow
étrécir, vb. to shrink
étreindre, vb. to clasp
étreinte, n.f. hug, embrace
étrier, n.m. stirrup
étroit, adj. narrow
étude, n.f. study
étudiant, n.m. student
étudier, vb. to study
étuve, n.f. steam room
eucalyptus, n.m. eucalyptus
Europe, n.f. Europe
eux, pron. m. them
évacuation, n.f. evacuation
évacuer, vb. to evacuate
évader, vb. s'e., to escape
évaluateur, n.m. appraiser
évaluation, n.f. appraisal
évangéliste, n.m. evangelist
évangile, n.m. gospel
évanouir, vb. s'e., to faint
évaporation, n.f. evaporation
évaporer, vb. to evaporate
évasif, adj. evasive

évasion, n.f. escape
éveil, n.m. alterness
éveillé, adj. sprightly
éveilleur, n.m. awakener
événement, n.m. event
éventail, n.m. fan
éventrer, vb. to disembowel
éventualité, n.f. eventually
éventuel, adj. possible
éventuellement, adv. possibly
évêque, n.m. bishop
évidemment, n.m. scooping out
évident, adj. obvious
évider, vb. to scoop out
évier, n.m. sink
évincer, vb. to eject
évitable, adj. avoidable
éviter, vb. to avoid
évocation, n.f. raising up
évoquer, vb. to evoke
exactitude, n.f. precision
exagération, n.f. exaggeration
exagérér, adj. excessive
exaltant, adj. exciting
exaltation, n.f. exaltation
exalter, vb. to exalt
examiner, vb. to examine
exaspérer, vb. to aggravate
excavation, n.f. excavation
excaver, vb. to excavate
excédent, n.m. excess
excéder, vb. to exceed
excellence, n.f. excellence
excellent, adj. excellent
exceller, vb. to excel
excentrique, adj. eccentric
excepté, prep. except
exception, n.f. exception
exceptionnel, adj. exceptional
excès, n.m. excess
excessif, adj. extreme
exciser, vb. to excise, cut out
excitable, adj. excitable
excitant, adj. exciting
exciter, vb. to excite
exclamatif, adj. exclamative
exclamation, n.f. exclamation
exclamer, vb. to exclaim

exclure, vb. to exclude
exclusif, adj. exclusive
exclusion, n.f. exclusion
excorier, vb. to excoriate
excréter, vb. to excrete
excrétion, n.f. excretion
excuse, n.f. plea
excuser, vb. to excuse, pardon
exécuter, vb. to enforce
exécuteur, n.m. executor
exécutif, adj. and n.m. executive
exécution, n.f. enforcement
exemplaire, n.m. copy
exemple, n.m. example
exempt, adj. exempt
exempt de droits, adj. duty free
exempter, vb. to exempt
exemption, n.f. exemption
excercant, adj. practicing
exercer, vb. to exercise, drill
exercise, n.m. practice, drill
exhalation, n.f. exhalation
exhaler, vb. to exhale
exhaustion, n.f. exhaust
exhiber, vb. to present; exhibit
exhibition, n.f. exhibition
exhortation, n.f. exhortation
exhorter, vb. to encourage
exhumer, vb. to exhume
exigence, n.f. unreasonable
exiger, vb. to require, demand
exil, n.m. exile
exilé, adj. exiled
exiler, vb. to banish
existant, adj. existent
existence, n.f. existence
exister, vb. to exist
exode, n.m. exodus
exorbitant, adj. exorbitant
exorciser, vb. to exorcize
exotique, adj. exotic; foreign
expansif, adj. expansive
expansion, n.f. expansion
expatrier, v.t. to exile
expédier, vb. to disptach
expédition, n.f. expedition, shipment
expérience, n.f. experence
expérimental, adj. experimental

expérimentation, n.f. experimentation
expérimenté, adj. experienced
expert, adj. and n.m. expert
expiration, n.f. expiration
expirer, v.t. to breathe out
explicite, adj. clear
expliquer, vb. to explain
exploit, n.m. feat, exploit
explorateur, n.m. explorer
exploratif, adj. exploratory
exploration, n.f. exploration
explorer, vb. to explore
explosible, adj. explosive
explosif, adj. and n.m. explosive
explosion, n.f. blast, explosion
exportation, n.f. exportation
exporter, vb. to export
exposé, n.m. account, statement
exposer, vb. to expound, expose
exposition, n.f. exposition, exposure, show, display
exprès, n.m. special delivery
expressif, adj. expressive
expression, n.f. expression
exprimable, adj. expressible
exprimer, vb. to express
expulser, vb. to expel
expulsion, n.f. expulsion
exquis, adj. exquisite
exsuder, vb. to exude
extase, n.f. ecstasy
extatique, adj. ecstatic
extensif, adj. extensive
extension, n.f. extension
extérieurement, adv. externally
exterminer, vb. to exterminate
externe, adj. external
extincteur, n.m. fire extinguisher
extorsion, n.f. extortion
extraction, n.m. descent
extraire, vb. to extract
extrait, n.m. abstract
extraordinaire, adj. extraordinary
extravagant, adj. extravagant
extrême, adj. and n.m. extreme
extrémiste, n.m. extremist
exultation, n.f. exultation
exulter, vb. to exult

fable, n.f. fable
fabliau, n.m. fabliau
fabricant, n.m. manufacturer
fabricateur, n.m. forger
fabrication, n.f. make
fabrique, n.f. factory
fabriquer, vb. to manufacture
fabuleux, adj. fabulous
fabuliste, n.m. fabulist
facette, n.f. facet
fâcher, vb. to anger, offend
fâcherie, n.f. disagreement
fâcheux, adj. troublesome
facial, adj. facial
facile, adj. easy
facilité, n.f. readiness
facon, n.f. manner, way
facconer, vb. to shape, fashion
fac-similé, n.m. facsimile
facteur, n.m. factor, element
factice, adj. artificial
factieux, adj. quarrelsome
faction, n.f. faction, party
factionnaire, n.m. sentry
facture, n.f. invoice, bill
facturer, vb. to bill
faculté, n.f. faculty
fadaise, n.f. nonsense
fade, adj. insipid
fagot, n.m. bundle
faible, adj. weak, faint, feeble
faiblement, adv. weakly
faiblir, vb. to weaken
faillite, bankrupt
faim, n.f. hunger
fainéant, n.m. loafer
faire, vb. to make do
faisan, n.m. pheasant
falloir, vb. to be necessary
falsificateur, n. forger m.
falsifier, vb. to falsify
fameux, adj. famous
familiariser, vb. to familiarize
familiarité, n.f. familiarity
familier, adj. familiar
familièrement, adv. familiarly
famille, n.f. household
famine, n.f. famine

fanatique, adj. and n.m. fanatic
fanatisme, n.m. fanaticism
faner, vb. to fade
fanfare, n.f. fanfare
fanfaronnade, n.f. boast
fange, n.f. filth; vice
fantaisie, n.f. fancy, fantasy
fantasque, adj. fantastic
fantoche, n.m. puppet
fantôme, n.m. phantom, ghost
faon, n.m. fawn
farce, n.f. stuffing; farce
farcir, vb. to stuff
fard, n.m. makeup for the face
fardeau, n.m. burden
farinacé, adj. farinaceous
farine, n.f. meal, flour
farniente, n.m. idleness
farouche, adj. sullen
fascinant, adj. fascinating
fascination, n.f. fascination
fastidieux, adj. dull
fatal, adj. mortal; fatal
fatalisme, n.m. fatalism
fataliste, n.m.f. fatalist
fatiguer, v.t. to tire
fatuté, n.f. smugness
faubourg, n.m. suburb
faubourien, adj. suburban
faucher, vb. to mow
faucheur, n.m. mower
faucille, n.f. sickle
faucon, n.m. hawk
fauconneau, n.m. young hawk
fauconnerie, n.f. falconry
faufil, n.m. basting
faufiler, vb. to baste
faune, n.f. wildlife
faussaire, n. forger; liar
faussement, adv. falsely
fausser, vb. to warp, distort
fausset, n.m. spigot, faucet
fausseté, n.f. falseness
faute, n.f. fault, mistake
fauteuil, n.m. armchair
fautif, adv. wrong
fauve, adj. wild beast
faux, n.m. falsehood; adj. false

faux-filet, n.m. sirloin
favorable, adj. favorable
favorablement, adv. favorably
favori, n.m. whisker
favoriser, vb. to favor
favoritisme, n.m. favortism
féal, adj. faithful
fécond, adj. fertile
féconder, vb. to fertilize
fécondité, n.f. fertility
féculent, adj. starchy
fédéral, adj. federal
fédération, n.f. confederacy
fédérer, vb. to federate
fée, n.f. fairy
féerie, n.f. fairyland
féerique, adj. fairylike
feindre, vb. to feign, pretend
fêle, vb. to crack
félicitation, n.f. congratulation
félicité, n.f. bliss, happiness
féliciter (de), vb. to congratulate
félin, adj. feline
félon, adj. disloyal
femelle, adj. and n.f. female
féminin, adj. female, feminine
femme, n.f. woman, wife
fendille, n.f. crack
fendoir, n.m. cleaver
fendre, vb. to split, rip
fenêtre, n.f. window
fenil, n.m. hayloft
fente, n.f. crack, rip, split
féodalité, n.f. feudalism
fer, n.m. iron
fermail, n.m. clasp
ferme, n.f. farm
ferme, adj. steady, fast
fermeté, n.f. firmness
fermier, n.m. farmer
féroce, adj. fierce
férocité, n.f. fierceness
fertile, adj. fertile
fertilisant, adj. fertilizable
fertilisation, n.f. fertilization
fertiliser, vb. to fertilize
fertilité, n.f. fertility
férule, n.f. cane, rod

fervemment, adv. fervently
fervent, adj. fervent
ferveur, n.f. fervor
fesse, n.f. buttock
fessée, n.f. spanking
fesser, vb. to spank
festin, n.m. feast
feston, n.m. feston
fête, n.f. party, feast
fétiche, n.m. fetish
feuillage, n.m. foilage
feuille, n.f. sheet, foil
feutre, n.m. felt
fève, n.f bean
février, n.m. February
fiacre, n.m. cab
fiancailles, n.f., pl. engagement
fiancé, n.m. fiancé
fiancer, vb. to betroth
fiasco, n.m. fiasco
fibre, n.f. fiber
ficelle, n.f. string, twine
fiche, n.f. piece of paper
fichu, adv. ruined
fictif, adj. fictitious
fiction, n.f. fiction
fidèle, adj. faithful
fief, n.m. feud
fiel, n.m. gall
fiente, n.f. dung
fier, vb. se f., to trust
fièvre, n.f. fever
figue, n.f. fig
figuratif, adj. figurative
figure, n.f. face, figure
fil, n.m. thread, string
filament, n.m. filament
file, n.f. file
filet, n.m. net
filin, n.m. rope
fille, n.f. daughter
film, n.m. film
filou, n.m. thief
fils, n.m. son
filtration, n.f. filtrtion
filtre, n.m. filter
filtrer, vb. to filter
fin, n.f. end; adj. fine; sharp

final, adj. final
finalité, n.f. finality
finance, n.f. finance
financer, vb. to finance
finir, vb. to finish
Finlande, n.f. Finland
Finnois, n.m. Finn
firmament, n.m. firmament
firme, n.f. company
fiscal, adj. fiscal
fixer, vb. to fix, secure, settle
fixité, n.f. fixity
flacon, n.m. bottle
flageller, vb. to flog
flagrant, adj. flagrant
flair, n.m. flair
flairer, vb. to smell
flambant, adj. flaming
flambeau, n.m. torch
flambée, n.f. blaze
flamber, vb. to blaze
flamboyant, adj. flamboyant
flamboyer, vb. to flare
flamme, n.f. flame
flanc, n.m. side, flank
flaque, n.f. puddle
flasque, adj. flabby
flatter, vb. to flatter
flatterie, n.f. flattery
flatteur, n.m. flatterer
fléau, n.m. scourge, plague
flèche, n.f. arrow
fléchir, vb. to bend
flétrir, vb. to wilt, wither
fleur, n.f. flower, blossom
fleuret, n.m. foil
fleuri, adj. flowery
fleurir, vb. to flower, blossom
fleuriste, n.m. florist
fleuve, n.m. river
flexibilité, n.f. flexibility
flexible, adj. flexible
flirt, n.m. flirtation
flirter, vb. to flirt
flocon, n.m. flake
flot, n.m. wave. **à flot**, afloat
flottant, adj. floating
flotte, n.f. fleet

flottement, n.m. wavering
flotteur, n.m. fishing boat
flou, adj. hazy, indistinct
fluctuation, n.f. fluctuation
fluide, adj. and n.m. fluid
flûte, n.f. flute
flûte, adj. soft; flute-like
flux, n.m. flow, flux
fluxion, n.f. inflammation
foi, n.f. faith; trust
foie, n.m. liver
foin, n.m. hay
foire, n.f. fair
fois, n.f. time
foison, n.f. abundance, plenty
foisonner, vb. to abound
folâtre, adj. frisky
folâtrer, vb. to frolic
folichon, adj. playful
folie, n.f. madness, folly
folklore, n.m. folklore
follement, adv. foolishly
follet, adj. merry, playful
foncé, adj. dark
fonctin, n.f. function
fonctionnaire, n.m. official,
  civil servant
fonctionner, vb. to function, work
fond, n.m. bottom, ground
fondamental, adj. basic, fundamental
fondateur, n.m. founder
fondation, n.f. foundation, establishment
fondé, adj. authentic
fondement, n.m. foundation
fonder, vb. to find, establish
fonderie, n.f. foundry
fondre, vb. to melt, fuse
fondrière, n.f. bog
fonds, n.m. fund
fongus, n.m. fungus
fontaine, n.f. fountain
fonte, n.f. melting
fonts, n.m.,pl. font
football, n.m. football
footing, n.m. walking
forain, n.m. peddler

forcément, adv. of necessity
forcené, adj. frantic
forcir, vb. to thrive
forer, vb. to bore, drill
forestier, n.m. forest ranger
foret, n.m. drill
forêt, n.f. forest
foreuse, n.f. machine drill
forfait, n.m. forfeit; contract
forfanterie, n.f. bragging
forge, n.f. forge
forgeron, n.m. blacksmith
forgeur, n.m. forger; inventor
formaliser, vb. to offend
formaliste, adj. formal; precise
formalité, n.f. ceremony
formation, n.f. formation
forme, n.f. shape, form
formel, adj. formal
former, vb. to form shape
formidable, adj. formidable
formule, n.f. formula, form
formuler, vb. to formulate, draw up
fort, n.m. fort; adj. strong
forteresse, n.f. fortress
fortifiant, adj. strengthening
fortification, n.f. fortification
fortifier, vb. to strengthen
fortuit, adj. accidental
fortune, n.f. fortune
fortuné, adj. luck, fortunate
fosse, n.f. pit
fossé, n.m. ditch; dike
fossette, n.f. dimple
fossile, n.m. fossil
foudroyant, adj. terrifying
foudroyer, vb. to crush, blast
fouet, n.m. whip lash
fougère, n.f. fern
fougue, n.f. dash
fougueux, adj. impetuous, hot
fouille, n.f. excavation
fouiller, vb. to ransack
fouillis, n.m. litter, mess
fouir, vb. to dig, burrow
foulard, n.m. scarf
foule, n.f. crowd, mob
fouler, vb. to trample

foulure, n.f. sprain, wrench
four, n.m. oven
fourbir, vb. to polish, furbish
fourche, n.f. fork
fourgon, n.m. wagon
fourmi, n.f. ant
fourmillement, n.m. swarming
fourmiller, vb. to mill
fourneau, n.m. stove, furnace
fournée, n.f. batch
fourniment, n.m. equipment
fournir, vb. to furnish
fournisseur, n.m. tradesman
fourrage, n.m. fodder, forage
fourrager, vb. to forage
fourreau, n.m. sheath
fourrer, vb. to thrust in
fourreur, n.m. furrier
fourrure, n.f. fur
fouroyer, vb. to mislead
foyer, n.m. focus, hearth
frac, n.m. dress coat
fracas, n.m. noise, bustle
fraction, n.f. fraction
fracture, n.f. fracture
fracturer, vb. to break, fracture
fragile, adj. brittle, delicate, frail, fragile
fragilité, n.f. fragility
fragment, n.m. fragment
fragmenter, vb. to divide up
fraîcheur, n.f. freshness
frais, n.m., pl. expenses, cost
fraise, n.f. strawberry; ruffle
framboise, n.f. rasberry
Francais, n.m. Frenchman
francais, adj. and n.m. French
Francaise, n.m. Frenchwoman
France, n.f. France
franchement, adv. frankly
franchir, vb. to clear, cross
franchise, n.f. frankness
franc-parler, n.m. frankness
franc-tireur, n.m. sniper; free-lancer
frange, n.f. fringe
frapper, vb. to strike, hit
frasque, n.f. prank

fraternel, adj. brotherly
fraternité, n.f. brotherhood
fraude, n.f. fraud
frauder, vb. to defraud
fraudeur, n.m. smuggler
frauduleux, adj. fraudulent
frayer, vb. to open up
frayeur, n.f. fright
fredaine, n.f. prank
frein, n.m. brake, check
freiner, vb. to brake, restrain
frelater, vb. to adulterate
frêle, adj. frail
frelon, n.m. hornet
frémir, vb. to tremble, quiver
frémissement, n.m. thrill
frêne, n.m. ash tree
frénésie, n.f. frenzy
frénétique, adj. frantic
fréquemment, adv. often
fréquence, n.f. frequency
fréquent, adj. frequent
frère, n.m. brother
fret, n.m. freight
frétillant, adj. lively
frétiller, vb. to quiver
fretin, n.m. young fish
frette, n.f. iron hoop
friand, adj. dainty; fond of
fricoter, vb. to cook, stew
friction, n.f. friction
frictionner, vb. to chafe
frigo, n.m. frozen meat
frigorifier, vb. to refrigerate
frileux, adj. chilly
frime, n.f. pretense, sham
fringant, adj. lively, frisky
friper, vb. to crush, rumple
fripier, n.m. second-hand
fripouille, n.f. rascal
frire, vb. to fry
friser, vb. to curl
frisoir, n.m. hair curler
frisson, n.m. shudder, shiver
frissonner, vb. to shudder, shiver
frites, n.f., pl. potato chips
friture, n.f. frying
frivole, adj. frivolous

frivolité, n.f. frivolity
froc, n.m. (monk's) frock
froid, n.m. cold, coldness
froideur, n.f. coldness
froissement, n.m. crumpling
froisser, v.t. to crumble
frôler, vb. to graze
fromage, n.m. cheese
froment, n.m. wheat
froncement, n.m. puckering, contraction
froncer, vb. to pucker
frondaison, n.f. foilage
fronde, n.f. sling
frondeur, n.m. slinger; censurer
front, n.m. forehead
frontière, n.f. boundary, border, frontier
frottement, n.m. rubbing
frotteur, n.m. rubber
fructueux, adj. fruitful
frugal, adj. frugal
frugalité, n.f. frugality
fruit, n.m. fruit
fugace, adj. fleeting
fugitif, adj. fugitive
fuir, vb. to flee; shun; leak
fuite, n.f. escape, flight; leak
fumée, adj. smoked
fumer, vb. to smoke
fumeux, adj. smoky
fumier, n.m. dung, manure
funérailles, n.f., pl. funeral
funeste, adj. disastrous, fatal
fureur, n.f. fury, rage
furieux, adj. furious
furtif, adj. sly
fuseau, n.m. spindle
fusée, n.f. rocket
fuser, vb. to melt, spread
fusil, n.m. rifle
fusion, n.f. merger
futé, adj. cunning, crafty
futile, adj. futile
futur, n.m. and adj. future
futurologie, n.f. futurology
fuyant, adj. passing, fugitive
fuyard, n.m. fugitive

gâchette, n.f. tumbler
gâcheux, adj. sloppy
gage, n.m. pledge, wage
gageure, n.f. bet, wager
gagnage, n.m. pastureland
gagnant, n.m. winner
gagner, vb. gain, win
gai, adj. cheeful, merry
gaieté, n.f. mirth, cheer, merriment
gaillard, adj. hearty, sound
gain, n.m. gain, profit
gaine, n.f. girdle
galant, n.m. beau; adj. gallant
galanterie, n.f. compliment
galbe, n.m. outline, contour
galère, n.f. galley
galerie, n.f. gallery
galet, n.m. boulder
gallon, n.m. gallon
galon, n.m. braid
galop, n.m. gallop
gambader, vb. frolic, skip
gamin, n.m. urchin, youngster
gamme, n.f. scale
gant, n.m. glove
garage, n.m. garage
garagiste, n.m. garage keeper
garant, n.m. sponsor
garantie, n.f. pledge
garantir, vb. guarantee, pledge
garçon, n.m. boy; waiter; bachelor
garde, n.f. watch, guard
garde-boue, n.m. fender
garde-manger, n.m. pantry
garder, vb. guard, keep
gardeur, n.m. keeper
gardien, n.m. guard, watchman
garer, vb. garage, park
gargarisme, n.m. gargle
garni, adj. garnished
garnir, vb. trim, garnish
garniture, n.f. furniture
gars, n.m. chap
gaspillage, n.m. waste
gaspiller, vb. squander, waste
gâteau, n.m. cake

gâter, vb. to spoil
gâterie, n.f. excessive indulgence
gâteux, adj. senile
gaucherie, n.f. clumsiness
gaufre, n.f. waffle
gaule, n.f. pole, switch
gausser, vb. se g. de, to mock
gaz, n.m. gas
gaze, n.f. gauze
gazeux, adj. gaseous
gazon, n.m. turf, lawn
géant, n.m. giant
geindre, vb. whine
gelé, adj. frozen
gelée, n.f. jelly, frost
geler, vb. to freeze
gémir, vb. to wail, moan
gémissement, n.m. groan, moan
gênant, adj. troublesome
gencive, n.f. gum
gendarme, n.m. policeman
gendarmerie, n.f. police force
gendre, n.m. son-in-law
gêne, n.f. uneasiness
gêné, adj. uneasy, embarrassed
généalogie, n.f. pedigree
gêner, vb. to hinder, bother
général, n.m. and adj. general; quartier g., headquarters
généraliser, vb. to generalize
généralité, n.f. generality
génération, n.f. generation
généreusement, adv. generously
généreux, adj. generous, liberal
générosité, n.f. generosity
génie, n.m. genius
genièvre, n.m. gin
genou, n.m. knee
genre, n.m. gender
gens, n.m.n.f., pl. persons, folk
gentilhomme, n.m. nobleman
gentillesse, n.f. gracefulness
géographie, n.f. geography
géopraphique, adj. geographical
géométrie, n.f. geometry
géométrique, adj. geometrical
gérant, n.m. manager, director
gerçure, n.f. chap

gérer, vb. to manage
germe, n.f. germ
germer, vb. to sprout
gésir, vb. to lie
geste, n.m. gesture
gestion, n.f. management
gibier, n.m. game
giboulée, n.f. hailstorm
gicler, vb. to spurt
gifler, vb. to slap
gigantesque, adj. great, huge
gigue, n.f. jig
gingembre, n.m. ginger
giron, n.m. lap
gitane, n.m.f. gypsy
givre, n.m. frost
glaçage, n.m. frosting
glace, n.f. ice, ice cream
glacer, vb. to freeze
glacial, adj. icy
glacier, n.m. glacier
glacière, n.f. icebox
glacis, n.m. slope
glaise, n.f. clay
gland, n.m. acorn
glande, n.f. gland
glaner, vb. to glean
glapir, vb. to screech
glas, n.m. knell
glissade, n.f. slip
glissant, adj. slippery
glisser, vb. to slide, slip
global, n.m. globe
gloire, n.f. glory
glorieux, adj. glorious
glorifier, vb. to glorify
glose, n.f. criticism; gloss
glossaire, n.m. glossary
glousser, vb. to cluck
gluant, adj. sticky
gobelet, n.m. goblet
gober, vb. to swallow
goéland, n.m. seagull
golfe, n.m. gulf
gomme, n.f. gum; eraser
gommeux, adj. gummy
gond, n.m. hinge
gonfler, vb. to inflate; swell

gonfleur, n.m. tire, pump
gorge, n.f. throat; gorge
gorger, vb. to cram, stuff
gosier, n.m. throat
gothique, adj. Gothic
goudron, n.m. tar
gouffre, n.m. gulf, abyss
goulu, adj. gluttonous
gourde, n.f. flask, bottle
gourmand, n.m. glutton; adj. greedy
gourmander, vb. to scold
gourmandise, n.f. greediness
gourmer, vb. to curb
gousse, n.f. pod, shell
goût, n.m. taste, relish
goûter, n.m. snack; vb. taste
goutte, n.f. drop; gout
goutteux, adj. gouty
gouttière, n.f. gutter
gouvernail, n.m. rudder, helm
gouvernement, n.m. government
gouverner, vb. to rule, govern
grabuge, n.m. squabble
grâce, n.f. grace
gracier, vb. to pardon
gracieux, adj. graceful, gracious
grade, n.m. grade, rank
gradin, n.m. tier, step
graduel, adj. gradual
graduer, vb. to graduate
grain, n.m. grain, berry
graine, n.f. berry, seed
graissage, n.m. greasing
graisse, n.f. grease, fate
graisser, vb. to grease
grammaire, n.f. grammar
gramme, n.m. gram
grand, adj. great, tall
grandement, adv. grandly, greatly
grandeur, n.f. height, size
grandiose, adj. grand
grandir, vb. to grow
grand-mère, n.f. grandmother
grand-père, n.m. grandfather
grange, n.f. barn
granit, n.m. granite
graphique, n.m. chart
grappe, n.f. bunch, cluster

gras, adj. stout, fat
grassement, adj. plentifully
grasset, adj. plump
grassouillet, adj. plump
gratification, n.f. bonus
gratifier, vb. to bestow
gratitude, n.f. gratitude
gratte-ciel, n.m. skyscraper
gratteler, vb. to scrape, scratch
gratuit, adj. free
grave, adj. grave
graveluex, adj. gritty
graver, vb. to engrave
graveur, n.m. engraver
gravier, n.m. gravel
gravir, vb. to climb
gravité, n.f. gravity
graviter, vb. to gravitate
gravure, n.f. engraving
gré, n.m. pleasure
grec, adj. Greek
grec, n.m. Greek language
gréement, n.m. rig
gréer, vb. to rig
greffier, n.m. clerk, recorder
grêle, adj. thin, slight
grêlon, n.m. hailstone
grelotter, vb. to shiver
grenier, n.m. attic, loft
grenouille, n.f. frog
grève, n.f. strike
gréviste, n. striker
gribouiller, vb. to scribble
grief, n.m. grievance
grièvement, adv. seriousness
griffe, n.f. claw, clutch
griffer, vb. to seize; scratch
griffonner, vb. to scribble
grignoter, vb. to nibble
gril, n.m. grill
grillade, n.f. broiling
grille, n.f. grate, gate
griller, vb. to broil roast, toast
grillon, n.m. cricket
grimace, n.f. grimace
grimacer, vb. to make faces
grimer, vb. to make up
grimper, vb. to climb

grincer, vb. to creak, grate, grind
grincheux, adj. ill-tempered
gringalet, n.m. weak
gringuenaude, n.f. filth, dirt
gris, adj. gray; drab; drunk
griser, vb. to get drunk, tipsy
grive, n.f. thrush
grogner, vb. to snarl, grumble
gros m., grosse f. adj. gross, overly
 large
groseille, n.f. currant
grosseur, n.f. size, thickness
grossier, adj. coarse, gross
grossièreté, n.f. coarseness
grossir, vb. to magniry, grow
grotesque, adj. grotesque
grouiller, vb. to stir, swarm
groupe, n.m. party; cluster
groupement, n.m. grouping
grouper, vb. to group
grue, n.f. crane
guêpe, n.f. wasp
guère, adv. hardly
guérir, vb. to heal
guérison, n.f. cure; recovery
guérite, n.f. cabin
guerre, n.f. war
guerrier, adj. warlike
guet, n.m. watch
guetter, vb. to watch for
gueule, n.f. mouth
gueulement, n.m. howl
gueuler, v.t. to seize
gueuser, v.t. to beg
gueux, n.m. tramp
gui, n.m. mistletoe
guide, n.m. guide book
guider, vb. to guide
guindé, adj. strained, stiff
guingan, n.m. gingham
guipon, n.m. mop
guirlande, n.f. garland
guise, n.f. way, manner
guitare, n.f. guitar
guitoune, n.f. dug-out
gumène, n.f. cable
gustation, n.f. tasting
gymnase, n.m. gymnasium

habile, adj. skillful, clever, smart
habileté, n.f. craft, ability
habillement, n.m. cloths
habiller, vb. to dress
habitant, n.m. inhabitant
habitation, n.f. dwelling
habiter, vb. to inhabit, live
habitude, n.f. habit, practice
habituel, adj. usual
hache, n.f. ax
hacher, vb. to mince, chop
hachette, n.f. hatchet
hachis, n.m. hash, minced
haie, n.f. hedge
haine, n.f. hatred
haineux, adj. hating
haïr, vb. to hate
haïssable, adj. hateful
hâle, n.m. tan, sunburn
haleine, n.f. breath
haler, vb. to haul, tow
hâler, vb. to tan
haleter, vb. to pant, gasp
halle, n.f. market
halte, n.f. halt
hamac, n.m. hammock
hameau, n.m. hamlet
hameçon, n.m. hook
hampe, n.f. handle
hanche, n.f. hip
hangar, n.m. shed
hanter, vb. to haunt
harcèlement, n.m. harrassment
harceler, vb. to worry, bother
hardes, n.f., pl. togs
hardi, adj. bold
hardiesse, n.f. boldness
hareng, n.m. herring
hargneux, adj. cross, snarling
harmonie, n.f. harmony
harmoniser, vb. to harmonize
harnacher, vb. to harness
harpe, n.f. harp
hasard, n.m. chance
hasarder, vb. to venture
hasardeux, adj. hazardous, unsafe
hâte, n.f. hurry, haste
hâter, vb. to hasten, hurry

hâtif, adj. early, hasty
haussement, n.m. raising, shrug
haut, n.m. top; adj. high, loud
hautain, adj. haughty, proud
hautbois, n.m. oboe
hauteur, n.f. height
hauturier, adj. sea-going
hâve, adj. gaunt
hebdomadaire, adj. weekly
héberger, vb. to shelter
hébété, adj. bewildered
hébreu, n.m. Hebrew language
héler, vb. to call, hail
hélice, n.f. propeller
hélicoptère, n.m. helicopter
hémisphère, n.m. hemisphere
hémorragie, n.f. hemorrhage
hennir, vb. to neigh
héraut, n.m. herald
herbage, n.m. pasture
herbe, n.f. herb; marijuana
herbeux, adj. grassy
héréditaire, adj. hereditary
hérisser, vb. to bristle
héritage, n.m. inheritance
hériter, vb. to inherit
héritier, n.m. heir
hernie, n.f. hernia
héroïne, n.f. heroine
héroïque, adj. heroic
héroïsme, n.m. heroism
héros, n.m. hero
hésitation, n.f. hesitation
hésiter, vb. to hesitate, waver
hétérosexuel, adj. heterosexual
hêtre, n.m. beech
heure, n.f. hour; time
heureusement, adv. happily, luckily
heureux, adj. glad, happy; lucky
heurter, vb. to collide with
heurtoir, n.m. door knocker
hibou, n.m. owl
hideux, adj. hideous
hier, adv. yesterday
hilare, adj. hilarious
hilarité, n.f. hilarity
Hindou, n.m. Hindu
hippodrome, n.m. race course

hippopotame, n.m. hippopotamus
hirondelle, n.f. swallow
hispanique, adj. Hispanic
hisser, vb. to hoist
histoire, n.f. history, story
historien, n.m. historian
historique, adj. historic
hiver, n.m. winter
hocher, vb. to nod, shake
hochet, n.m. rattle
hoirie, n.f. inheritance
hollandais, adj. and n.m. Dutch
Hollande, n.f. Holland
holocauste, n.m. holocaust
hologramme, n.m. hologram
holographie, n.f. holography
homard, n.m. lobster
hommage, n.m. homage
hommasse, adj. mannish
homme, n.m. man
homogène, adj. of the same kind,
homosexuel, adj. homosexual
Hongrie, n.f. Hungary
honnête, adj. honest
honnêteté, n.f. honesty, fairness
honorable, adj. honorable
honoraires, n.m., pl. fee
honorer, vb. to honor
honteux, adj. ashamed, shameful
hôpital, n.m. hospital
hoquet, n.m. hiccup
horizon, n.m. horizon
horizontal, adj. horizontal
horloge, n.f. clock
horloger, n.m. watchmaker
hormis, prep. except
horreur, n.f. horror
horrifier, vb. to horrify
horrifique, adj. hair-raising
horripiler, vb. to annoy
hors-bord, n.m. outboard
hors de, prep. out of, outside
horticole, adj. horticultural
hospice, n.m. refuge
hospitalier, adj. hospitable
hospitaliser, vb. to hospitalize
hospitalité, n.f. hospitality
hostie, n.f. host

hostile, adj. hostile
hostilité, n.f. hostility
hôte, n.m. host; guest
hôtel, n.m. hotel; mansion
hôtelière, n.m. innkeeper
hôtesse, n.f. hostess
hôtesse de l'air, n.f. stewardess
houblon, n.m. hop
houe, n.f. hoe
houille, n.f. coal
houillère, n.f. coal mine
houle, n.f. surge
houleux, adj. stormy, rough
houppe, n.f. tuft
hourra, n.m. cheer
housse, n.f. covering
houx, n.m. holly
hublot, n.m. porthole
huer, vb. to shout
huile, n.f. oil
huissier, n.m. usher
huit, adj. and n.m. eight
huître, n.f. oyster
humain, adj. human, humane
humanité, n.f. humanity
humble, adj. lowly, humble
humecter, vb. to moisten
humer, vb. to suck up, sniff up
humeur, n.f. humor; mood, temper
humide, adj. humid
humiliation, n.f. humiliation
humilité, n.f. humility
humoristique, adj. humorous
humour, n.m. humor
huppe, n.f. tuft, crest
hurlement, n.m. noise, howling
hurler, vb. to howl, roar, yell
hutte, n.f. shed
hybride, adj. and n.m. hybrid
hydrogène, n.m. hydrogen
hyène, n.f. hyena
hygiénique, adj. hygenic
hymne, n.m. hymn; n.f. church hymn
hypnotiser, vb. to hypnotize
hypothèque, n.f. mortgage
hypothèse, n.f. hypothesis
hystérie, n.f. hysteria
hystérique, adj. hysterical

ici, adv. here
ictère, n.m. jaundice
idéal, adj. and n.m. ideal
idéalisme, n.m. idealism
idéaliste, n.m.f. idealist
identificaton, n.f. identification
idiot, adj. and n.m. idiotic
idolâtrer, vb. to idolize
idole, n.f. idol
ignare, adj. ignorant
ignoble, adj. vile, mean
ignorant, adj. ignorant
il, pron. he, it
île, n.f. island
illégal, adj. illegal
illimité, adj. boundless
illustrer, vb. to illustrate
image, n.f. picture
imaginaire, adj. imaginary
imagination, n.f. imagination
imaginer, vb. to imagine
imbiber, vb. to steep
imitation, n.f. copy, imitation
limiter, vb. to imitate, copy
immédiat, adj. immediate
immense, adj. immense, huge
imminent, adj. imminent
immiscer, vb. to interfere
immixtion, n.f. mixing
immobile, adj. motionless
immoral, adj. immoral
immortaliser, vb. to immortalize
immunité, n.f. immunity
impair, adj. odd
imparfait, adj. and n.m. imperfect
impartial, adj. impartial
impassible, adj. impassive
impatience, n.f. impatience
impatienter, vb. to provoke
impeccable, adj. faultless
impératrice, n.f. empress
impérial, adj. imperial
impérialisme, n.m. imperialism
imperméabiliser, vb. to waterproof
impitoyable, adj. merciless
impliquer, vb. to imply, involve
implorer, vb. to implore
impoli, adj. impolite, rude

impolitesse, n.f. discourtesy
importance, n.f. importance
importer, vb. to matter; import
importun, adj. bothersome
importuner, vb. to pester
imposable, adj. taxable
impossible, adj. impossible
imposteur, n.m. fraud, impostor
imposture, n.f. deception
impôt, n.m. tax, tariff
impotent, adj. weak, infirm
imprégner, vb. to impregnate
impression, n.f. print
impressionable, adj. sensitive
impressionner, vb. to affect
imprimeur, n.m. printer
improbité, n.f. dishonesty
improductif, adj. unproductive
impropre, adv. unfit, improprer
impuissance, n.f. impotence
impuissant, adj. impotent, helpless
impulsif, adj. impulsive
impur, adj. impure, foul
impureté, n.f. impurity
inaccoutumé, adj. unusual
inachevé, adj. unfinished
inadvertance, n.f. oversight
inanimé, adj. lifeless
inanité, n.f. uselessness, emptiness
inattendu, adj. unexpected
inaugurer, vb. to inaugurate
inavouable, adj. shameful
incalculable, adj. countless
incapable, adj. unable
incarcérer, vb. to imprison
incertain, adj. uncertain
incertitude, n.f. suspense
inceste, n.m. incest
incident, n.m. incident
incision, n.f. incision
inclinaison, n.f. slope
incliner, vb. to slant, nod, bow
inclure, vb. to include, enclose
incolore, adj. colorless
incommode, adj. uncomfortable
incomplet, adj. unfinished
inconduite, n.f. misconduct
inconnu, adj. unknown

inconsidéré, adj. thoughtless
inconvénient, n.m. inconvenience
incorrect, adj. incorrect
incriminer, vb. to accuse
incroyable, adj. incredible
incroyant, n.m. unbeliever
inculper, vb. to charge, accuse
incurable, adj. incurable
incurie, n.f. carelessness, neglect
Inde, n.f. India
indécis, adj. doubtful, dim
indépendance, n.f. independence
indépendant, adj. independent
index, n.m. forefinger; index
Indien, n.m. Indian
indifférence, n.f. indifference
indigène, n.m.f. native
indigne, adj. worthless, unworthy
indigner, vb. to anger
indiquer, vb. to indicate
indirect, adj. indirect
individuel, adj. individual
industrie, n.f. industry
industriel, adj. industrial
inébranlable, adj. immovable, firm
inédit, adj. unpublished
inepte, adj. stupid, inept
inépuisable, n.f. inexhaustible
inestimable, adj. inestimable
inévitable, adj. inevitable
infâme, adj. infamous
infanterie, n.f. infantry
infécond, adj. barren, sterile
infect, adj. rotten, infected
infecter, vb. to infect
infection, n.f. infection
inférieur, adj. and n.m. inferior
infernal, adj. infernal
infester, vb. to infest
infidèle, adj. unfaithful
infime, adj. mean
infirme, adj. and n.m.f. invalid
infirmer, vb. to invalidate, weaken
infirmière, n.f. nurse
infirmité, n.f. infirmity
inflammation, n.f. inflammation
inflation, n.f. inflation
infliger, vb. to inflict

influence, n.f. influence
influent, adj. influential
informatique, n.f. computer science
informatiser, vb. to computerize
informe, adj. shapeless
infraction, n.f. breach
ingambe, adj. nimble
ingénieur, n.m. engineer
ingénieux, adj. ingenious
ingéniosité, n.f. ingenuity
ingénu, adj. naive, ingenuous
ingrat, adj. ungrateful
inguérissable, adj. incurable
inhabile, adj. incapable
inhiber, vb. to inhibit
inhumain, adj. cruel, inhuman
inique, adj. unfair
initial, adj. initial
injecter, vb. to inject
injection, n.f. injection
injures, n.f., pl. abuse
injurier, vb. to abuse, insult
injurieux, adj. insulting, abusive
injuste, adj. unfair
injustice, n.f. injustice
innocence, n.f. innocence
innocent, adj. innocent
innocenter, vb. to declare, innocent
innombrable, adj. countless
inodore, adj. odorless
inoffensif, adj. harmless, innocuous
inondation, n.f. flood
inonder, vb. to flood
inopiné, adj. unexpected
inoubliable, adj. unforgettable
inquiet, adj. restless, uneasy
inquiétude, n.f. misgiving, worry
insalubre, adj. unhealthy
inscrire, vb. to inscribe; enter
insecte, n.m. bug, insect
insensé, adj. mad
inséparable, adj. inseparable
insérer, vb. to insert
insignifiant, adj. insignificant
insinuer, vb. to hint
insipide, adj. tasteless
insolation, n.f. sunstroke
insolite, adj. unusual

insondable, adj. bottomless
inspecter, vb. to examine, survey
inspecteur, n.m. inspector
inspection, n.f. inspection
inspirer, vb. to inspire
instict, n.m. instinct
instituer, vb. to institute
instructeur, n.m. teacher
instructif, adj. instructive
instruction, n.f. education, instruction
instruire, vb. to instruct, educate
instrument, n.m. instrument
insuccès, n.m. failure
insuffisance, n.f. deficiency
intègre, n.f. upright
intellect, n.m. intellect
intelligence, n.f. intelligence
intelligent, adj. intelligent
intendance, n.f. administration
intendant, n.m. director
intense, adj. intense
intensif, adj. intensive
intensité, n.f. intensity
intention, n.f. intention
intercepter, vb. to intercept
interdire, vb. to forbid
intéressant, adj. interesting
intérêt, n.m. interest
intérieur, adj. and n.m. interior
interioquer, vb. to embarass
international, adj. international
interne, adj. internal
interpellation, n.f. questioning
interpeller, vb. to ask
interrogateur, n.m. examiner
interrogation, n.f. interrogation
interroger, vb. to question
interruption, n.f. intermission, break
intervenir, vb. to interfere
intervention, n.f. interference
intervertir, vb. to transpose
interview, n.m. or f. interview
intestin, n.m. bowels
intimation, n.f. notification
intime, adj. intimate
intimer, vb. to notify
intimité, n.f. intimacy
intituler, vb. to entitle

intolérance, n.f. intolerance
intoxication, n.f. poisoning
intoxiquer, vb. to poison
intrépide, adj. fearless
intrigue, n.f. plot, intrigue
intriguer, vb. to intrigue; puzzle
introduction, n.f. introduction
introduire, vb. to introduce, insert
intrus, n.m. intruder
intrusion, n.f. trespass
inusité, adj. unusual
inutile, adj. needless
invalide, n.m.f. invalid; adj. disabled
invalider, vb. to invalidate
invasion, n.f. invasion
invectiver, vb. to abuse, revile
inventaire, n.m. inventory
inventer, vb. to invent
inventeur, n.m. inventor
investigation, n.f. investigation, inquiry
investir, vb. to invest
invisible, adj. invisible
invitation, n.f. invitation
invité, n.m. guest
inviter, vb. to invite, ask
involontaire, adj. involuntary
iode, n.m. iodine
Irak, n.m. Iraq
Iran, n.m. Iran
iris, n.m. iris
irisé, adj. iridescent
iriandais, adj. Irish
ironie, n.f. irony
irréfléchi, adj. thoughtless, rash
irrégulier, adj. irregular
irrespectueux, adj. disrespectful
irrigation, n.f. irrigation
Islam, n.m. Islam
isoler, vb. to isolate
Israël, n.m. Israel
issue, n.f. issue, outlet, outcome
Italie, n.f. Italy
italique, n.m. italics; adj. italic
itinéraire, n.m. route, itinerary
ivoire, n.m. ivory
ivre, adj. intoxicated, drunk
ivrogne, n.m. drunkard
ivrognerie, n.f. drunkenness

jabotage, n.m. chattering
jacasser, vb. to chatter
jacasse, n.f. magpipe
jacent, adj. vacant
jacinthe, n.f. hyacinth
jack, n.m. telephone jack
jacquet, n.m. backgammon
jactance, n.f. boasting
jacter, vb. to speak
jade, n.m. jade
jadis, adv. formerly
jaguar, n.m. jaguar
jaillir, vb. to gush, spurt, spout
jaillissement, n.m. gush, spurt
jais, n.m. jet
jale, n.f. large bowl
jalonner, vb. to mark out
jalouser, vb. to envy
jalousie, n.f. jealousy, envy; venetian blind
jaloux, adj. jealous
jamais, adv. never, ever
jambe, n.f. leg
jambon, n.m. ham
jambon-neau, n.m. ham knuckle
jante, n.f. rim
janiver, n.m. January
Japon, n.m. Japan
Japonais, n.m. Japanese person
jappement, n.m. yelping
japper, vb. to yelp
jaquette, n.f. jacket
jardin, n.m. garden
jardinage, n.m. gardening
jardinier, n.m. gardener
jarre, n.f. jar
jarretière, n.f. garter
jaser, vb. to chatter
jaserie, n.f. chattering
jatte, n.f. bowl
jaunâtre, adj. yellowish
jaune, adj. yellow; n.m. yolk of an egg
jaunisse, n.f. jaundice
javelliser, vb. to sterilize water
jazz, n.m. jazz
je, pron. I
jeep, n.f. jeep
jetée, n.f. pier

jersey, n.m. jersey
Jésus, m. Jesus
jeter, vb. to throw
jeton, n.m. token
jeu, n.m. game, play; **mettre en j.**, stake
jeudi, n.m. Thursday
jeun, adv. fasting
jeune, adj. youthful, young
jeûne, n.m. fast, abstinence
jeunesse, n.f. youth
jeunet, adj. very young
jeûneur, n.m. faster
ji, adv. yes
joaillier, n.m. jeweller
jobard, n.m. fool
jocke, n.m. jockey
jocrisse, n.m. ninny
joie, n.f. joy
joignant, prep. adjoining
joindre, vb. to join
joint, n.m. joint, seam
jointé, adj. jointed
jointoiement, n.m. grouting
jointoyer, vb. to grout
jointure, n.f. joint of the body
joli, adj. preety, pleasing
joliment, adv. prettily; awfully
jonc, n.m. rush
jonchée, n.f. strewing
joncher, vb. to scatter, strew
jonction, n.f. joining, junction
jongler, vb. to juggle
jongleur, n.m. juggler
joue, n.f. cheek
jouer, vb. to play, frolic
jouet, n.m. toy
joueur, n.m. player
joug, n.m. yoke, bondage
jouissance, n.f. enjoyment
jouisseur, n.m. pleasure seeker
jour, n.m. day, daylight
journal, n.m. newspaper, diary
journalier, adj. daily
journalisme, n.m. journalism
journaliste, n.m. journalist
journée, n.f. day
joute, n.f. joust

joyau, n.m. jewel
joyeux, adj. joyful, cheerful
jubilant, adj. jubilant
jubilé, n.m. golden wedding anniversary, jubilee
jubiler, vb. to exult
jucher, vb. to roost, perch
juchoir, n.m. roosting place
judaïque, adj. Jewish
judaïsme, n.m. Judaism
judiciare, adj. judicial, legal
judicieusement, adv. discreetly
judicieux, adj. wise, judicious
juge, n.m. judge, magistrate, umpire
jugé, adj. judged
jugement, n.m. judgment, reason, view
juger, vb. to judge
jugulaire, adj. jugular
juif, adj. Jewish
juillet, n.m. July
juin, n.m. June
julep, n.m. julep
jumeau adj. and n. twin
jumelage, n.m. matching
jumeler, vb. to couple, join
jumelles, n.f., pl. opera glasses
jument, n.f. mare
jungle, n.f. jungle
jupe, n.f. skirt
jupe-culotte, n.f. split skirt
Jupiter, n.m. Juipter
jupon, n.m. petticoat
juré, adj. sworn
jurement, n.m. swearing, oath
jurer, vb. to swear
juridiction, n.f. jurisdiction
jurdique, adj. judicial
jurisconsulte, n.m. lawyer
juriste, n.m. jurist
juron, n.m. oath
jury, n.m. jury
jus, n.m. gravy, juice
jusant, n.m. ebb-tide
jusque, prep. up to
juste, adj. just, right, fair; adv. just
justement, adv. precisely, exactly
justice, n.f. justice, integrity
justicier, v.t. to punish

justifiant, adj. justifying
justification, n.f. justification
justifier, vb. to justify
jute, n.m. jute
juter, v.t. to be juicy
juteux, adv. juicy
juvénile, adj. juvenile, youthful
juxtaposer, v.t. to place side by side

K

kakatoès, n.m. cockatoo
kaki, adj. khaki (the color)
kaléidoscope, n.m. kaleidoscope
kangourous, n.m. kangaroo
kaolin, n.m. porcelain clay
karaté, n.m. karate
kascher, adj. kosher
kayac, n.m. flat canoe
képi, n.m. cap
kermesse, n.f. fair
kérosène, n.m. kerosene
ketchup, n.m. ketchup
kidnap-peur, v.t. to kidnap
kif, n.m. marijuana
kif-kif, adj. exactly alike
kilo, n.m. kilogramme
kilométrage, n.m. mileage
kilomètre, n.m. kilometer
kilowatt-heure, n.m. kilowatt hour
kimono, n.m. kimono
kinkajou, n.m. honey-bear
kiosque, n.m. newstand
kiwi, n.m. kiwi
klakson, n.m. horn
klaksonner, v.t. to hoot
knock-out, n.m. knock out
kola, n.m. kola
kommandantur, n.f. military commad headquarters
korrigan, n.m. elf, goblin
krach, n.m. financial crash
kraft, n.m. wrapping paper
krak, n.m. medieval castle
kyrielle, n.f. litany
kyste, n.m. cyst

la, pron. her
là, adv. there
labeur, n.m. labor
laboratoire, n.m laboratory
laborieux, adj. industrious
labour, n.m. plowing
labourer, vb. to plow
labyrinthe, n.m. maze
lac, n.m. lake
lacérer, vb. to lacerate; tear up
lacet, n.m. shoelace; winding
lâche, n.m.f. coward; adj. cowardly
lâchement, adv. loosely, shamefully
lâcher, vb. to loose, let go
lâcheté, n.f. cowardice
lacis, n.m. network
lacté, adj. milky
lacune, n.f. blank, gap
ladre, adj. mean, stingy
lagune, n.f. lagoon
laid, adj. ugly
laideron, n.m. ugly person
laideur, n.f. ugliness
laine, n.f wool
laineux, adj. wooly; downy
laïque, n.m. layman
laisse, n.f. leash
laisser, vb. to leave, let
laisser-aller, n.m. freedom
laissex-passer, n.m. pass, leave
lait, n.m. milk
laiterie, n.f. dairy
laiteux, adj. milky
laitier, n.m. milkman
laiton, n.m. brass
laitue, n.f. lettuce
lambeau, n.m. rag
lambin, adj. slow, dawdling
lame, n.f. blade
lamentable, adj. grievous
lamentation, n.f. lamentation; lament
lamenter, vb. to mourn, lament
laminer, vb. to laminate
lamper, vb. to gulp
lampiste, n.m. lamplighter, lampmaker
lance, n.f. lance
lancer, vb. to hurl; launch
lanceur, n.m. pitcher

lande, n.f. wasteland, moor
langage, n.m. language
langue, n.f. tongue, language
languette, n.f. small tongue
langueur, n.f. languor
languissant, adj. languid
lanière, n.f. strap, lash
lanterne, n.f. lantern
lapider, vb. to abuse
lapin, n.m. rabbit
laps, n.m. lapse of time
lapsus, n.m. slip
laquais, n.m. footman, lackey
laque, n.f. shellac; hairspray
larcin, n.m. larceny, theft
lard, n.m. bacon, fat
larder, vb. to lard; pierce
large, adj. wide
largeur, n.f. width
larguer, vb. to loosen, let go
larme, n.f. tear
larmoyer, vb. to whimper, weep
larron, n.m. thief, robber
las, adj. weary
lascif, adj. lewd, wanton
laser, n.m. laser
lasser, vb. to weary
latéral, adj. lateral
Latin, n.m. Latin person
latin, n.m. Latin language
latte, n.f. lath
laurier, n.m. bay
lavabo, n.m. lavatory
lavande, n.f. lavender
lavandière, n.f. laundress
lavement, n.m. enema
laver, vb. to wash
laxatif, n.m. laxative
lécher, vb. to lick
leçon, n.f. lesson
lecteur, n.m. reader
lecture, n.f. reading
légal, adj. lawful, legal
légaliser, vb. to legalize
légalité, n.f. legality
légation, n.f. legation
légendaire, adj. legendary
légende, n.f. inscription

léger, adj. light
légèreté, n.f. lightness
légion, n.f. legion
législateur, n.m. legislator
législatif, adj. legislative
législation, n.f. legislation
légitime, adj. lawful, legitimate
léguer, vb. to bequeath
légume, n.m. vegetable
lent, adj. slow
lenteur, n.f. slowness
lèpre, n.f. leprosy
lequel, pron. who, which
les, pron. them
lesbien, adj. Lesbian
lesbienne, n.f. Lesbian
léser, vb. to wrong, hurt
lésine, n.f. stinginess
lésion, n.f. wrong
lessive, n.f. laundry
lest, n.m. ballast
leste, adj. nimble, clever
lettre, n.f. letter
lettré, adj. lettered
leurre, n.m. trap, lure
leurrer, vb. to lure
levain, n.m. yeast, leaven
lever, vb. to raise
levier, n.m. lever
lèvre, n.f. lip
lévrier, n.m. greyhound
lexique, n.m. lizard
liaison, n.f. connection, linkage
liant, adj. supple; affable
liasse, n.f. file, bundle
libelle, n.m. libel
libéral, adj. liberal
libérateur, n.m. rescuer, deliverer
libérer, vb. to free, liberate
liberté, n.f. liberty, freedom
libraire, n.m. bookseller
librairie, n.f. bookstore
libre, adj. free, at large, at liberty
licence, n.f. license, leave
licite, adj. lawful
licorne, n.f. unicorn
lie, n.f. dregs
liège, n.m. cork

lien, n.m. bond, link, tie
lierre, n.m. ivy
lieu, n.m. place, position
lieu-commun, n.m. commonplace
lieue, n.f. league
lieutenant, n.m. lieutenant
lièvre, n.m. hare
ligne, n.f. line
lignée, n.f. offspring
ligoter, vb. to bind up
ligue, n.f. league, confederacy
liguer, vb. to unite in a league
lilas, n.m. lilac
limacon, n.m. snail
lime, n.f. file; lime fruit
limier, n.m. bloodhound
limitation, n.f. limitation
limittion des naissances, n.f.
  birth control, contraception
limite, n.f. border, limit
limiter, vb. to limit, confine
limon, n.m. mud, slime
limonade, n.f. lemonade
limoneux, adj. muddy; slimy
limpide, adj. clear, limpid
lin, n.m. flax
linceul, n.m. shroud
linge, n.m. linen, wash
lingerie, n.f. linen goods, underwear
linteau, n.m. lintel
lion, n.m. lion
lippu, adj. thick-lipped
liqueur, n.m. liquid, liqueur
liquidation, n.f. liquidation
liquide, adj. and n.m. liquid, fluid
liquider, vb. to liquidate, settle
liquoreux, adj. sweet
lire, vb. to read
lis, n.m. lily
liséré, n.m. border, piping
liseur, n.m. reader
liseuse, n.f. bookmark
lisible, adj. legible, readable
lisière, n.f. edge
lisse, adj. smooth, sleek
liste, n.f. list, roll
lit, n.m. bed
litanie, n.f. litany

litée n.f. litter of animals
literie, n.f. bedding
litière, n.f. litter
litige, n.m. litigation
litre, n.m. liter
littéral, adj. literal
littérature, n.f. literature
livide, adj. livid
livre, n.f. pound
livre, n.m. book
livrer, vb. to deliver
local, adj. local, give up
localiser, v.t. to localized
localité, n.f. locality
locataire, n.m.f. tenant
loch, n.m. log
locomotive, n.f. locomotive
locuste, n.f. locust; shrimp
loge, n.f. box
logement, n.m. lodging
loger, vb. to lodge
logis, n.m. dwelling, house
loi, n.f. law
loin, adv. away, far, at a distance
lointain, adj. distant
loisible, adj. optional, allowable
loisir, n.m. leisure, spare time
Londres, n.m. London
longe, n.f. leash; loin of veal
longer, vb. to go along
longeron, n.m. beam, girder
longitude, n.f. longitude
longtemps, adv. long, long while
longueur, n.f. length
lopin, n.m. plot, small piece
loquace, adj. talkative
loque, n.f. morsel, rag
loquet, n.m. latch; clasp
loqueteux, adj. tattered
lorgner, vb. to glance at
lorgnon, n.m. eye glasses
loriot, n.m. oriole
lors, adv. then
lorsque, conj. when; at the time
losange, n.m. diamond shaped
lot, n.m. lot, prize, portion
loterie, n.f. raffle, lottery
lotion, n.f. lotion

lotir, vb. to divide, apportion
louage, n.m. hiring
louange, n.f. praise
louche, adj. shady, suspicious
loucher, vb. to squint
louer, vb. to priase; rent, hire
loueur, n.m. hirer
loup, n.m. wolf
louper, vb. to spoil, botch
lourd, adj. heavy
lourdaud, n.m. clod; lubber
lourdeur, n.f. dullness, heaviness
loyal, adj. loyal, fair, honest
loyauté, n.f. loyalty, honesty
loyer, n.m. rent, hire
lubrifier, vb. to lubricate
lucide, adj. lucid, clear
lucidité, n.f. clearness
luciole, n.f. firefly
lueur, n.f. gleam, glimmer
lugubre, adj. dismal, doleful
lui, pron. he; to him, to her
lui-même, pron. itself, himself
luire, vb. to gleam, shine
luisant, adj. shiny, glitter
lumière, n.f. light; daylight
lumineux, adj. luminous
lunaire, adj. lunar
lunatique, adj. whimsical
lundi, n.m. Monday
lune, n.f. moon
lunetier, n.m. optician
lunettes, n.f., pl. glasses
lustré, n.m. glossy
lustrer, vb. to polish, gloss
luth, n.m. lute
lutiner, vb. to tease
lutte, n.f. strife, contest, struggle
lutter, vb. to struggle, contend
luxe, n.m. luxury
luxueux, adj. luxurious
luxure, n.f. lust
lycée, n.m. high school
lycéen, n.m. high-school student
lynche, vb. to lynch
lyre, n.f. lyre
lyrique, adj. lyric
lyrisme, n.m. lyric poetry

M, (abbr. for Monsieur) n.m. Mr.
macabre, adj. macabre, ghastly
macédoine, n.f. salad, mixture
macérer, vb. to macerate, soak
mâché, vb. to chew
machin, n.m. thing, gadget
machinal, adj. mechanical
machination, n.f. plot, scheme
machine, n.f. machine
machiner, vb. to plot, contrive
machiniste, n.m. machinist
mâchoire, n.f. jaw
mâchonner, vb. to munch, mumble
macon, n.m. mason
maculer, vb. to spot, blot
madame, n.f. madam, Mrs.
madeleine, n.f. light cake
mademoiselle, n.f. Miss
madone, n.f. Madonna
mafflu, adj. chubby cheeked
magasin, n.m. store, warehouse
mages, n.m., pl. wise men
magicien, n.m. magician
magie, n.f. magic
magique, adj. magical
magistrat, n.m. magistrate
magnanime, adj. magnanimous
magnat, n.m. magnate
magnétique, adj. magnetic
magnificence, n.f. magnificence
magnifique, adj. magnificent
mahométan, adj. Mohammedan
mai, n.m. May
maigre, adj. lean, meager
maigrir, vb. to lose weight
maille, n.f. stitch; mesh
maillot, n.m. shorts; T-shirt
main, n.f. hand paw, claw
main-d'oeuvre, n.f. man power
maint, adj. many
maintien, n.m. maintenance
mais, n.m. why; but
maison, n.f. home, premises
maître, n.m. ruler, master
maîtrise, n.f. control; mastery
maîtriser, v.t. to master
majoration, n.f. over estimate
majorité, n.f. majority

malabare, n.m. burly, big
malade, adj. ill, sick, poorly
maladie, n.f. illness, sickness
maladif, adj. sickly, ailing
maladresse, n.f. awkwardness
malaise, n.m. uneasiness
malaxage, n.m. kneading of dough
mâle, adj. male
maléfice, adj. hurtful
malfacon, n.f. bad work
malheur, n.m. unhappiness
malin, adj. malicious
malitorne, adj. awkward
mallette, n.f. small case
malotru, n.m. uncouth person
malpropre, adj. untidy
mamelon, n.m. nipple
mammouth, n.m. mammoth
manager, n.m. manager
maraude, n.f. marauding
manche, n.f. sleeve
manchette, n.f. ruffle, cuff
mandant, n.m. employer
mandat, n.m. authority
maouss, adj. big; strong
mappemonde, n.f. map of the world
maquereau, n.m. pander
marbre, n.m. marble
marchand, n.m. merchant
marchander, vb. to bargain, haggle
marchandise, n.f. merchandise
marche, n.f. march, step, walk
marché, n.m. market, bargain
marchepied, n.m. running-board
marcher, vb. to walk, step, march,
marcheur, n.m. pedestrian
mardi, n.m. Tuesday
mare, n.f. pool, pond
marécage, n.m. bog, marsh
marécageux, adj. marshy
maréchal, n.m. marshal
marée, n.f. tide, flood
margarine, n.f. margarine
marge, n.f. margin
margelle, n.f. edge, brink
marguerite, n.f. daisy
mari, n.m. husband
mariage, n.m. marriage, wedlock

marié, n.m. bridegroom
mariée, n.f. married; n.f. bride
marier, vb. to marry
marijuana, n.f. marijuana
marin, n.m. sailor; adj. marine
marinade, n.f. mixture for pickling
marine, n.f. navy
mariner, vb. to pickle
marionnette, n.f. puppet
maritime, adj. marine
marmite, n.f. pot
marmiter, vb. to blast with gunfire
marmot, n.m. urchin, brat
marmotter, vb. to mumble
marotte, n.f. fad
marque, n.f. brand, mark
marquer, vb. to mark
marqueur, n.m. marker, scorekeeper
marquis, n.m. marquis
marraine, n.f. godmother, sponsor
marron, n.m. chestnut; brown
marronnier, n.m. chestnut tree
mars, n.m. March
marteau, n.m. hammer
marteler, vb. to hammer
martial, adj. warlike
martre, n.m. marten
martyr, n.m. martyr
mascarade, n.f. masquerade
mascotte, n.f. mascot
masculin, adj. masculin
masque, n.m. mask
masquer, vb. to mask
massacre, n.m. slaughter
massage, n.m. massage
masse, n.f. mass
masser, vb. to mass; massage
massif, adj. solid, massive
massue, n.f. club
mastiquer, vb. to chew
mat, adj. dull
mât, n.m. mast
matelas, n.m. mattress
matelot, n.m. sailor
mastérialiser, vb. to materialize
matériaux, n.m., pl. materials
matériel, adj. material, real
maternel, adj. native; maternal

maternité, n.f. maternity
mathématique, adj. mathematical
mathématiques, n.f., pl. mathematics
matière, n.f. matter
matin, n.m. morning
matinal, adj. early
matinée, n.f. morning
matineux, adj. rising early
matois, adj. sly
matraque, n.f. heavy club
matrice, n.f. womb
maricule, n.f. registration
matriculer, vb. to enroll
matrimonial, adj. marital
maturité, n.f. maturity
maudire, vb. to curse
maudit, adj. miserable
maugréer, vb. to curse, grumble
maussade, adj. sullen, cross
mauvais, adj. bad
maxime, n.f. maxim
maximum, n.m. maximum
me, pron. me, myself
méandre, n.m. winding
mécanicien, n.m. mechanic, engineer
mécanique, adj. mechanical
mécaniser, vb. to mechanize
mécanisme, n.m. mechanism, machinery
mécano, n.m. mechanic
méchamment, adv. mailiciously
méchanceté, n.f. wickedness, malice
méchant, adj. wicked, malicious
mèche, n.f. lock; wick, fuse
mécompte, n.m. disappointment
méconnaissable, adj. unrecognizable
méconnaître, vb. to fail to recognize
mécontent, adj. discontented
mécontentement, n.m. discontent
mécontenter, vb. to dissatisfy
mécréant, n.m. unbeliever
médaille, n.f. medal
médaillon, n.m. locket
médecin, n.m. physician
médecine, n.f. medicine

médiation, n.f. mediation
médical, adj. medical
médicinal, adj. medicinal
médiéval, adj. medieval
médiocre, adj. mediocre
médiocrité, n.f. mediocrity
médire, vb. to slander, defame
medisance, n.f. slander
méditation, n.f. meditation
méditerrané, adj. Mediterranean
médium, n.m. medium
méduse, n.f. jellyfish
méduser, vb. to stupefy
méfait, n.m. misdeed
méfiance, n.f. distrust
méfinat, adj. distrustful
méfier, vb. se m. de, to distrust
meilleur, adj. better, best
mélancolie, n.f. melancholy
mélange, n.m. mixture
mélasse, n.f. molasses
mêlée, n.f. struggle
mélèze, n.m. larch
melliflu, adj. sweet
mélodie, n.f. melody
mélodieux, adj. melodious
mélodique, adj. melodic
mélodrame, n.m. melodrama
melon, n.m. melon
membrane, n.f. membrane
membre, n.m. member, limb
membrure, n.f. frame, limbs
mémento, n.m. notebook
mémoire, n.f. memory, memoir
mémorable, adj. memorable
mémorandum, n.m. memorandum
mémorial, n.m. memorial
menacant, adj. threatening
menace, n.f. threat
menacer, vb. to threaten
ménage, n.m. household
ménagement, n.m. discretion
ménagère, n.f. housewife
ménagerie, n.f. menagerie
mendiant, n.m. beggar
mendicité, n.f. begging
mendier, vb. to beg
menées, n.m., pl. schemes

mener, vb. to lead
ménestrel, n.m. minstrel
ménétrier, n.m. country fiddler
meneur, n.m. leader, ring-leader
méningite, n.f. meningitis
menottes, n.f., pl. handcuffs
mensonge, n.m. falsehood, lie
mensonger, adj. false, deceptive
mensuel, adj. monthly
measurable, adj. measurable
mental, adj. mental
mentalité, n.f. mentality
menterie, n.f. lie
menteur, n.m. liar
menthe, n.f. mint
mention, n.f. mention
mentionner, vb. to mention
mentir, vb. to lie
menton, n.m. chin
menu, n.m. menu
menuet, n.m. minuet
menuiserie, n.f. woodwork
menuisier, n.m. carpenter
méprendre, vb. se m., to be mistaken
mépris, n.m. contempt, scorn
méprisable, adj. mean, contemptible
méprisant, adj. contemptuous
méprise, n.f. mistake, misunderstanding
mépriser, vb. to scorn, despise
mer, n.f. sea; mal de m., seasickness
mercanti, n.m. profiteer
mercantile, adj. mercantile
mercerie, n.f. haberdashery
merci, n.m. thanks
mercredi, n.m. Wednesday
mercure, n.m. mercury
mère, n.f. mother
méridien, n.m. meridian
méridional, adj. southern
meringue, n.f. meringue
mérite, n.m. merit, desert
mériter, vb. to merit, deserve
méritoire, adj. meritorious
merle, n.m. blackbird

merveille, n.f. marvel
merveilleux, adj. marvelous, wonderful
mésalliance, n.f. misalliance
mésaventure, n.f. mishap, accident
mesdames, pl. of madame
mesdemoiselles, pl. of mademoiselle
mésestime, n.f. low opinion
mésintelligence, n.f. discord
mesquin, adj. shabby, stingy
mesquinerie, n.f. meanness
message, n.m. message
messager, n.m. messenger
messe, n.f. Mass
Messie, n.m. Messiah
messieurs, pl. of monsieur
mesurage, n.m. measurement
mesure, n.f. measure
mesuré, adj. measured, cautious
mesurer, vb. to measure
métairie, n.f. small farm
métal, n.m. metal
métallique, adj. metalic
métamorphose, n.f. transformation
métaphore, n.f. metaphore
métayer, n.m. small farmer
météore, n.m. meteor
métèque, n.m. alien
méthode, n.f. method
méticuleux, adj. meticulous
métier, n.m. loom; craft, trade
métis, adj. hybrid
métrage, n.m. measurement
mètre, n.m. meter
métrique, adj. metric
métro, n.m. subway
métropole, n.f. metropolis;
native land
métropolitain, adj. metropolitan
mets, n.m. food, dish
mettable, adj. wearable
mettre, vb. to set, put, place
meuble, n.m. furniture
meubler, vb. to outfit
meule, n.f. stack
meunier, n.m. miller
meurtre, n.m. murder
meurtrier, n.m. murderer
meurtrière, n.f. murderess

meurtrir, vb. to bruise
meute, n.f. mob
Mexicain, n.m. Mexican
mexicain, adj. Mexican
Mexique, n.m. Mexico
mezzanine, n.f. mezzanine
mi, adj. mid, half
miaou, n.m. mew
miauler, vb. to mew
mica, n.m. mica
miche, n.f. loaf of bread
micro, n.m. microphone
microbe, n.m. microbe
midi, n.m. noon; south
midinette, n.f. young sales-
woman, business woman
mie, n.f. crumb
miel, n.m. honey
mielleux, adj. honeyed, sweet
miette, n.f. crumb
mièvre, adj. affected
mignard, adj. dainty, mincing
mignon adj. delicate, dainty;
n.m.f. darling
migraine, n.f. headache
migration, n.f. migration
mijoter, vb. to simmer, cook slowly
mil, num. thousand
milice, n.f. militia
milieu, n.m. middle, center
militaire, adj. military
militant, adj. militant
militarisme, n.m. militarism
militer, vb. to militate
mille, n.m. mile; adj. and n.m.
thousand
millionnaire, adj. and n.m.f. millionaire
mime, n.m. mime, mimic
minauder, vb. to simper
mince, adj. slender, thin, slight
minceur, n.f. slimness
miner, vb. to wear away; weaken
minerai, n.m. ore
minéral, adj. and n.m. mineral
mineur, n.m. miner; adj. and n.m.
minor
miniature, n.f. miniature
minier, adj. of mines

minime, adj. very small
minimum, n.m. minimum
ministère, n.m. ministry, department
ministériel, adj. ministerial
ministre, n.m. minister
minorité, n.f. minority
minuit, n.m. midnight
minuscule, adj. minute
minute, n.f. minute
minutie, n.f. trifle
mioche, n.m.f. urchin
miracle, n.m. miracle
miraculeux, adj. miraculous
mirage, n.m. mirage
mirer, vb. to aim at
mirifique, adj. wonderful
miroir, n.m. mirror
miroiter, vb. to glisten
miser, vb. to bid
misère, n.f. misery
miséreux, adj. miserable
miséricorde, n.f. mercy
miséricordieux, adj. merciful
missel, n.m. missal
mission, n.f. mission
missive, n.f. missive
mitaine, n.f. mitten
mite, n.f. moth
miteux, adj. shabby
mitiger, vb. to moderate
mitoyen adj. jointly owned
mitrailleuse, n.f. machine gun
mixte, adj. mixed, joint
Mme. (abbr. for Madame) n.f. Mrs.
mobile, adj. movable
mobilier, adj. movable
mobilisation, n.f. mobilization
mobiliser, vb. to mobilize
mobilité, n.f. mobility, insta-
 bility
mode, n.f. fashion mode, moode
modelliste, n.m.f. dress
 designer
modérateur, n.m. moderator
modération, n.f. moderation
modéré, adj. moderate
modérer, vb. to check, moderate
moderne, adj. modern

moderniser, vb. to modernize
modernité, n.f. modernity
modeste, adj. modest
modestie, n.f. modesty
modicité, n.f. small quantity
modification, n.f. alteration
modifier, vb. to modify, qualify
modique, adj. moderate, unim-
 portant
modiste, n.f. milliner
modulation, n.f. modulation
moduler, vb. to modulate
moelle, n.f. marrow
moelleux, adj. mellow, soft
moeurs, n.f., pl. manners, custom
moi, n.m. ego
moignon, n.m. stump
moindre, adj. lesser, less, least
moine, n.m. monk
moineau, n.m. sparrow
moins, adv. less, least
mois, n.m. month
moisi, adj. moldy
moisir, vb. to mold
moisissure, n.f. mold
moisson, n.f. harvest, crop
moissonner, vb. to reap, harvest
moissonneur, n.m. harvest
moite, adj. moist
moiteur, n.f. dampness
môle, n.m. pier
molécule, n.f. molecule
molester, vb. to molest
mollasse, adj. flabby, soft
mollesse, n.f. softness, weakness
molletière, n.f. legging
molleton, n.m. heavy flannel
mollir, vb. to soften, slacken
mollusque, n.m. mollusc
moment, n.m. moment
momentané, adj. momentary
monarchiste, n.m. monarchist
monarque, n.m. monarch
monastère, n.m. monastery
monastique, adj. monastic
monceau, n.m. pile
mondain, adj. worldly
monde, n.m. world, people

mondial, adj. world-wide
monétaire, adj. monetary
moniteur, n.m. monitor
monnaie, n.f. money, change
monnayer, vb. to mint
monologue, n.m. monologue
monoplan, n.m. monoplane
monopole, n.m. monopoly
monopoliser, vb. to monopolize
monstre, n.m. monster
monstrueux, adj. monstrous
mont, n.m. hill, mountain
montage, n.m. carrying up
montagnard, n.m. mountaineer
montagne, n.f. mountain
montagneux, adj. mountainous
montant, n.m. amount
mont-de-piété, n.m. pawnshop
monté, adj. mouned, supplied
montée, n.f. ascent, rise, climb
monter, vb. to go up, climb, rise
montre, n.f. watch; display
montrer, vb. to show
montreur, n.m. showman
montueux, adj. hilly
monture, n.f. mount
monument, n.m. monument
monumental, adj. monumental
moquer, vb. se m. de, to make fun
  of, mock, laugh at
moquerie, n.f. mockery, ridicule
moqueur, adj. mocking
moral, adj. ethical, moral
morale, n.f. morals, morality,
  morale
moraliser, vb. to moralize
moraliste, n.m.f. moralist
moralité, n.f. morals, morality
morbide, adj. morbid
morceau, n.m. piece, bit, morsel
morceler, vb. to cut up
mordant, adj. pointed
mordiller, vb. to nibble
mordre, vb. to bite
morfondre, vb. to chill
morgue, n.f. morgue
moribond, adj. dying
morne, adj. bleak, dismal, dreary

morose, adj. morose
morosité, n.f. moroseness
morphine, n.f. morphine
morphinomane, n. drug addict
morphologie, n.f. morphology
mors, n.m. horse's bit
morse, n.m. walrus
morsure, n.f. bite
mort, n.m. dummy, dead man;
  n.f. death. adj. dead
mortaise, n.f. mortise
mortalité, n.f. mortality
mort-bois, n.m. undergrowth
morte-eau, n.f. neap tide
mortel, adj. deadly; mortal
morte-saison, n.f. off season
mortier, n.m. mortar
mortifier, vb. to mortify
mort-né, adj. still-born
mortuaire, adj. mortuary
morue, n.f. cod
morutier, n.m. cod fisher
mosaïque, n.f. mosaic
Moscou, n.m. Moscow
mosquée, n.f. mosque
mot, n.m. word; cue, remark, sentence
motel, n.m. motel
moteur, n.m. motor
motif, n.m. motive
motion, n.f. motion
motiver, vb. to motivate, justify
motocyclette, n.f. motorcycle
motocycliste, n.m. motorcyclist
motte, n.f. clod
mou, adj. soft, mellow
mouchard, n.m. spy
moucharder, vb. to spy
mouche, n.f. fly
moucher, vb. to blow the nose
moucheron, n.m. gnat
moucheté, adj. spotted
moucheture, n.f. spot
mouchoir, n.m. handkerchief
moudre, vb. to grind
moue, n.f. pout, wry face
mouette, n.f. gull
moufette, n.f. skunk
moufle, n.f. mitten

mouillage, n.m. wetting
mouillé, adj. wet
mouiller, vb. to soak
moulage, n.m. cast from a mold
moule, n.m. mold
mouler, vb. to mold
mouleur, n.m. molder
moulin, n.m. mill
moulure, n.f. molding
mourant, adj. dying
mourir, vb. to die
mousquetaire, n.m. musketeer
mousse, n.f. moss; foam, lather
mousseline, n.f. muslin
mousser, vb. to foam, froth
mousseux, adj. foaming
mousson, n.m. monsoon
moustache, n.f. mustache, whisker
moustiquaire, n.f. mosquito net
moustique, n.m. mosquito
moutarde, n.f. mustard
mouton, n.m. sheep
moutonner, vb. to curl; make
 wooly
mouture, n.f. grinding
movant, adj. moving, shifting
mouvement, n.m. movement, stir
mouvoir, vb. to move
moyennant, prep. by means of
moyenne, n.f. average
Moyen Orient, n.m. Middle East
muabilité, n.f. changeability
mue, n.f. molting; changing
muet, muette f. adj. dumb, mute
mufle, n.m. cad
mugir, vb. to roar, bellow
mugissement, n.m. bellowing, roaring
muguet, n.m. lily of the valley
mulâtre, n.m. and adj. mulatto
mulet, n.m. mule
muletier, n.m. muleteer
mulot, n.m. field mouse
multiple, adj. multiple, manifold
multiplication, n.f. multiplication
multiplicité, n.f. multiplicity
multiplier, vb. to multiply
multitude, n.f. multitude
municipal, adj. municipal

municipalité, n.f. municipality
munificence, n.f. liberality
munificent, adj. very generous
munir, vb. to provide, supply
munitionner, vb. to supply, provision
mur, n.m. wall
mûr, adj. ripe, mature, mellow
muraille, n.f. high wall, thick
mural, adj. mural
mûrier, n.m. mulberry tree
mûrir, vb. to ripen, mature, bring
 completeness
murmure, n.m. murmur; grumbling,
 muttering
murmurer, vb. to murmur, whisper
musarder, vb. to dawdle, waste time
muscade, n.f. nutmeg
muscle, n.m. muscle
musculaire, adj. muscular
musculeux, adj. muscular, brawny
muse, n.f. muse
museau, n.m. muzzle, snout, nose
musée, n.m. museum, art gallery
museler, vb. to gag; muzzle
muselière, n.f. muzzle
muser, vb. to trifle, dawdle
musical, adj. musical
musique, n.f. music, band, musicians
mutabilité, n.f. mutability
mutation, n.f. replacement
mutilation, n.f. mutilation
mutiler, vb. to mutilate, mangle
mutinerie, n.f. mutiny, unruliness
mutisme, n.m. muteness
mutuel, adj. mutual
myope, adj. near-sighted
myopie, n.f. near-sightedness
myosotis, n.m. forget-me-not
myriade, n.f. myriad
myrrhe, n.f. myrrh
mystère, n.m. mystery
mystérieux, adj. mysterious, weird
mysticisme, n.m. mysticism
mystification, n.f. hoax
mystifier, vb. to mystic, mystify
mythe, n.m. myth, fable
mythique, adj. mythical
mythologie, n.f. mythology

nabot, n.m. dwarf
nacre, n.f. mother-of-pearl
nacré, adj. pearly
nage, n.f. act of swimming
nageoire, n.f. fin
nager, vb. to swim
nageur, n.m. swimmer
naguère, adv. a short time ago
nain, adj. and n.m. dwarf
naissance, n.f. birth
naissant, adj. newborn
nantir, vb. to give as security
nantissement, n.m. guarantee
naphte, n.m. naphtha
nappe, n.f. tablecloth
narcisse, n.m. daffodil
narcotique, n.m. narcotic
narguer, vb. to defy, flout
narine, n.f. nostril
narrateur, n.m. storyteller
narration, n.f. narrative
narrer, vb. to narrate, relate
nasal, adj. nasal
naseau, n.m. nostril
nasse, n.f. fish trap
natal, adj. native
natation, n.f. swimming
natif, n.m. and adj. native
nation, n.f. nation
national, adj. national
nationalité, n.f. nationality
nativité, n.f. nativity
naturaliser, vb. to naturalize
naturalisme, n.m. naturalism
naturaliste, n.m. naturalist
nature, n.f. nature
naturel, n.m. nature; adj. natural
naufrage, n.m. shipwreck
nauséabond, adj. offensive
nausée, n.f. nausea
nautique, adj. nautical
naval, adj. naval
navet, n.m. turnip
navette spatiale, n.f. space shuttle
navigable, adj. navigable; seaworthy,
 airworthy
navigateur, n.m. seaman, navigator
navigation, n.f. seafaring, navigation

naviguer, vb. to sail, navigate
navire, n.m. ship
navrant, adj. distressing, causing grief
navrer, vb. to wound, grieve
né, adj. born
néanmoins, adv. yet, nevertheless
néant, n.m. neon
nébuleux, adj. worried; cloudy
nécessaire, adj. requisite, necessary
nécessité, n.f. necessity
nécessiter, vb. to make necessary
nécessiteux, adj. needy
nécrologe, n.m. obituary
nef, n.f. nave
néfaste, adj. ill-omened, unlucky
négatif, adj. negative
négation, n.f. negative word
négative, n.f. negative argument
négligé, adj. neglected, sloppy;
 n.m. state of undress
négligeable, adj. negligible
négligence, n.f. neglect
négligent, adj. negligent
négliger, vb. to overlook, neglect
négoce, n.m. commerce, trace
négociable, adj. negotiable
négociant, n.m. merchant
négociation, n.f. negotiation
négocier, vb. to negotiate
nègre, adj. and n.m. Black
négresse, n.f. Black
neige, n.f. snow
neiger, adj. snow
neigeux, adj. snowy
néon, n.m. neon
nerf, n.m. nerve
nerveux, adj. nervous
nervosité, n.f. nervousness
netteté, n.f. neatness, clearness
nettoyer, vb. to cleanse, scour
neuf, adj. and n.m. nine
neuf, m. **neuve** f. adj. brandnew
neutraliser, vb. to counteract
neutralité, n.f. neutrality
neutre, adj. and n.m. neutral
neveu, n.m. nephew
névrite, n.f. neuritis
névrose, n.f. neurosis
névrosé, adj. and n.m. neurotic

nez, n.m. nose
niais, adj. foolish
niaiserie, n.f. silliness, trifle
nichée, n.f. brood
nicher, vb. **se n.,** to nestle
nickel, n.m. nickel
nid, n.m. nest
nièce, n.f. niece
nielle, n.f. wheat blight
nier, vb. to deny
nigaud, n.m. fool, simpleton
nimbe, n.m. halo
nippes, n.f., pl. old clothes
nitrate, n.m. nitrate
niveau, n.m. level; **au n. de,**
  level with
niveler, vb. to make level
nivellement, n.m. surveying
noblesse, n.f. nobility
noce, n.f. wedding; **faire la n.,**
  revel
nocif, adj. harmful
noctambule, n.m. sleep-walker,
  prowler
nocturne, adj. nocturnal
Noël, n.m. Christmas carol
noeud, n.m. knot
noir, adj. and n.m. black
noircir, vb. to blacken
noix, n.f. nut, walnut
nolis, n.m. freight
nom, n.m. name; noun
nombrer, vb. to number
nombreux, adj. numerous, manifold
nonination, n.f. appointment
nommément, adv. namely, particularly
non, adv. no. **non plus,** neither
nonchalant, adj. nonchalant
nonne, n.f. nun
nonobstant, prep. in spite of
nonpareil, adj. unequaled
non-sens, n.m. nonsense
nord, n.m. north
normal, adj. normal
norme, n.f. norm
Norvège, n.f. Norway
Norvégien, n.m. Norwegian person
nostalgie, n.f. nostalgia

notabilitié, n.f. notability
notable, n.m. notable; remarkable
notaire, n.m. lawyer, notary
notamment, adv. particularly
notation, n.f. notation
note, n.f. note, bill
noter, vb. to note
notice, n.f. notice, review
notification, n.f. notification
notifier, vb. to notify
notion, n.f. notion
notoire, adj. notorious
nôtre, pron. **le n.,** ours
nouer, vb. to tie
noueux, adj. knotty
nouilles, n.f., pl. noodles
nourrir, vb. to feed, nourish
nourriture, n.f. food, nourishment
nous, pron. we, us, ourselves
nouveauté, n.f. novelty
nouvel an, n.m. new year
nouvelle, n.f. news
novembre, n.m. November
novice, n.m.f. novice
noviciat, n.m. novitiate
noyade, n.f. drowning
noyau, n.m. kernel, nucleus
noyer, vb. to drown
noyer, n.m. walnut tree
nu, adj. naked, bare
nuage, n.m. cloud; gloom
nuageux, adj. cloudy
nuance, n.f. shade, degree
nucléaire, adj. nuclear
nudité, n.f. bareness
nuire, vb. to injur, harm
nuisible, adj. hurtful
nuit, n.f. night
nul, adj. no, none; void
numéro, n.m. number
nu-pieds, adv. barefoot
nuptial, adj. bridal
nuque, n.f. nape
nutritif, adj. nutritious
nutrition, n.f. nutrition
nylon, n.m. nylon
nymphe, n.f. nymph
nymphéa, n.m. white water lily

oasis, n.f. oasis
obéir à, vb. to obey
obéissance, n.f. obedience
obéissant, adj. obedient
obérer, vb. to burden with debt
obèse, adj. obese
obésité, n.f. obesity
objecter, vb. to object
objectif, adj. and n.m. objective
objection, n.f. objection
objet, n.m. object
obligation, n.f. obligation
obligatoire, adj. mandatory
obliger, vb. to oblige, accmmodate
oblique, adj. slanting; devious
oblitérer, vb. to obliterate
oblong, adj. oblong
obcsène, adj. filthy, obscene
obscénité, n.f. obscenity
obscur, adj. obscure, dark, dim
obscurcir, vb. to darken, obscure
obscurément, adv. obscurely
obsurité, n.f. dimness, obscurity
obséder, vb. to harass, huant
obsèques, n.f., pl. funeral
observance, n.f. observance
observateur, n.m. observer
observation, n.f. observation
observer, vb. to observe, watch
obsession, n.f. obsession
obstacle, n.m. obstacle bar
obstétrical, adj. obstetrical
obstination, n.f. subborness
obstiné, adj. stubborn, obstinate
obstiner, vb. s'o., to persist
obstruction, n.f. obstruction
obstruer, vb. to stop up, obstruct
obtempérer, vb. to obey
obtenir, vb. to obtain, get
obtention, n.f. obtaining
obtus, adj. dull, stupid
obus, n.m. shell
obusier, n.m. howitzer
occasion, n.f. chance, opportunity bargain
occasionnel, adj. occasional
occasionner, vb. to cause, bring about
occident, n.m. west

occidental, adj. western, westerly
occulte, adj. occult
occupant, n.m. tenant, occupant, occupier
occupation, n.f. pursuit, business
occupé, adj. busy
occuper, vb. to occupy, busy; to take up
occurrence, n.f. occurrence; event
océan, n.m. ocean
océanique, adj. oceanic
ocre, n.f. ochre
octave, n.f. octave
octobre, n.m. October
ode, n.f. ode
odeur, n.f. smell, scent, perfume
odorant, adj. sweet-smelling; fragrant
odorat, n.m. sense of smell
oeillade, n.f. quick look, wink
oeillère, n.f. eyetooth
oeillet, n.m. carnation
oeuf, n.m. egg; ovum
oeuvre, n.f. work, labour
offensant, adj. offensive
offense, n.f. offense
offenser, vb. to offend
offenseur, n.m. offender
offensif, adj. offensive
office, n.m. office, pantry; service
officiant, n.m. person who officiates
officiel, adj. official
officier, n.m. officer, mate; vb. officiate
officieux, adj. officious; semi official
offrande, n.f. offering
offre, n.f. offer
offrir, vb. to offer, present
offusquer, vb. to shadow, obscure, irritate
ogre, n.m. ogre
oie, n.f. goose
oindre, vb. to anoint
oiseau, n.m. bird
oiselet, n.m. small bird
oiseux, adj. useless, idle, empty
oisif, adj. idle, unoccupied
oisillon, n.m. young bird
oléagineux, adj. oily

olive, n.f. olive

olivier, n.m. olive tree

olympique, adj. Olympic

ombilical, adj. umbilical

ombrage, n.m. shade

ombragé, adj. shady

ombrager, vb. to shade

ombrageux, adj. doubtful, suspicious

ombre, n.f. shade, shadow

ombreux, adj. shady

omelette, n.f. omelet

omettre, vb. to omit

omission, n.f. omission

omnibus, n.m. bus

omnipotent, adj. omnipotent

omoplate, n.f. shoulder blade

on, pron. one

once, n.f. ounce

oncle, n.m. uncle

onde, n.f. wave, billow

ondé, adj. wavy; streaked

ondoyer, vb. to wave

ondulation, n.f. wave

onduler, vb. to wave

onéreu, adj. burdensome

ongle, n.m. finger nail

onglée, n.f. numb feeling

onguent, n.m. ointment, salve

onze, adj. and n.m. eleven

onzième, adj. and n.m.f. eleventh

opale, n.f. opal

opaque, adj. opaque

opéra, n.m. opera

opérateur, n.m. operator

opération, n.f. operation, working

opératoire, adj. opertive

opéré, adj. (med.) operated; n. patient

opérer, vb. to operate

opérette, n.f. operetta

opiner, vb. to hold or express an opinion

opiniâtre, adj. stubborn

opiniâtreté, n.f. subbornness

opinion, n.f. opinion

opium, n.m. opium

opportun, adj. timely

opportunité, n.f. timeliness

opposé, adj. opposite, averse

opposer, vb. to oppose; s'o. à, oppose, resist

opposition, n.f. opposition

oppresseur, n.m. oppressor

oppressif, adj. oppressive

oppression, n.f. oppression

opprimer, vb. to oppress, crush

opprobre, n.m. disgrace, infamy

opter, vb. to decide, select

opticien, n.m. optician

optimiste, adj. optimistic; n.m.f. optimist

option, n.f. option, choice

optique, adj. optic

opulence, n.f. opulence, riches

opuscule, n.m. small work

or, n.m. gold; old ornament

oracle, n.m. oracle

orage, n.m. storm

orageusement, adv. turbulently

orageux, adj. stormy

oraison, n.f. oration, prayer

oral, adj. oral

orange, n.f. orange

oranger, n.m. orange tree

orateur, n.m. speaker, spokesman

orbe, n.m. orb, sphere

orbite, n.m. orbit, socket (eye)

orchestre, n.m. band, orchestra

orchestrer, vb. to orchestrate

orchidée, n.f. orchid

ordinaire, adj. and n.m. ordinary

ordinal, adj. and n.m ordinal

ordinateur, n.m. computer

ordonnance, n.f. prescription, decree

ordonné, adj. tidy, orderly

ordonner, vb. to bid, order, ordain

ordre, n.m. command, order, mandate

ordure, n.f. refuse, filth, garbage

ordurier, adj. foul

oreille, n.f. ear

oreiller, n.m. pillow

oreillons, n.m., pl. mumps

orfèvrerie, n.f. gold or silver jewelry

organdi, n.m. organdy

organe, n.m. organ

organique, adj. organic
organisateur, n.m. organizer; adj. organizing
organisation, n.f. organization, arrangement
organiser, vb. to organize
organisme, n.m. organism
organiste, n.m.f. organist
orge, n.f. barley
orgie, n.f. orgy
orgue, n.m. organ
orgueil, n.m. pride
orgueilleux, adj. proud, haughty
Orient, n.m. Orient, East
Oriental, n.m. Oriental
oriental, adj. Oriental, eastern
orienter, vb. to orient
orifice, n.m. orifice, hole
originaire, adj. original, native
originairement, adv. originally
original, n.m. queer person; adj. original
originalement, adv. originally; unusually
originalité, n.f. originality
origine, n.f. origin, source
originel, adj. original
oripeau, n.m. tinsel
orme, n.m. elm
orné, adj. ornate
ornement, n.m. trimming, ornament, adornment
ornemental, adj. ornamental
ornementation, n.f. ornamentation
orner, vb. to adorn, trim, ornament
ornière, n.f. rut, track
ornithologie, n.f. ornithology
orphelin, n.m. orphan
orphelinat, n.m. orphanage
orphéon, n.m. choral group
orteil, n.m. toe
orthodoxe, adj. orthodox
orthodoxie, n.f. orthodoxy
orthographier, vb. to spell correctly
ortie, n.f. nettle
os, n.m. bone
oscillant, adj. oscillating
oscillation, n.f. sway

osciller, vb. to fluctuate, oscillate
osé, adj. attempted, bold
oser, vb. to dare, to venture
osier, n.m. willow
ossature, n.f. bony structure, skeleton
ossements, n.m., pl. human remains
osseux, adj. bony
ossifier, vb. to ossify
otage, n.m. hostage; pledge
ôter, vb. to take off, take away
ou, conj. or, either, else
où, adv. where; whither
ouater, vb. to pad
oubli, n.m. forgetfulness, oblivion
oublier, vb. to forget
oublieux, adj. forgetful
ouest, n.m. west
oui, adv. yes
ouï-dire, n.m. gossip, hearsay
ouïe, n.f. gill
ouïr, vb. to hear
ouragan, n.m. hurricane
ourler, vb. to hem
outil, n.m. implement, tool
outilleur, vb. to supply with tools
outrage, n.m. outrage, injury
outrageant, adj. outrageous
outrager, vb. to outrage
outrance, n.f. degree, extreme
outre, adv. and prep. beyond; en o., besides, furthermore
outrecuidant, adj. excessively
outre-mer, adv. overseas
outrer, vb. to overdo, irritate
ouvert, adj. open
ouverture, n.f. gap, opening; overture
ouvrable, adj. work, workable
ouvrage, n.m. work
ouvrer, vb. to work
ouvrier, n.m. workman, worker, hand, workwoman
ouvrir, vb. to open, unlock
ouvroir, n.m. work room or shop
ovaire, n.m. ovary
ovale, adj. and n.m. oval, egg-shaped
ovation, n.f. ovation
oxygène, n.m. oxygen

pacage, n.m. pasture land
pacificateur, adj. pacifying; n.m. peacemaker
pacification, n.f. peace-making
pacifier, vb. to pacify, soothe
pacifique, adj. peaceful, peaceable
pacifisme, n.m. pacifism
pacotille, n.f. small wares
pagayer, vb. to paddle
pagayeur, n.m. paddler
pagination, n.f. pagination
paginer, vb. to number pages
pagode, n.f. pagoda
paiement, n.m. payment
païen, adj. and n.m. pagan, heathen
paillard, adj. lewd, indecent
paillasse, n.f. mattress of straw
paillasson, n.m. door mat
paille, n.f. straw; flaw
paillette, n.f. defect; spangle
pain, n.m. bread, cake, loaf
pair, n.m. peer; adj. even, equal
paire, n.f. pair, brace, couple
paisible, adj. peaceful, peaceable
paître, vb. to graze, feed
paix, n.f. peace, quiet, calm
palabre, n.m. palaver
palais, n.m. palate; palace
palan, n.m. gear for hoisting
pale, n.f. stake, blade
pâle, adj. pale, ghastly
palefrenier, n.m. groom
palet, n.m. quoit
paletot, n.m. overcoat
pâleur, n.f. paleness
palier, n.m. stair landing
pâlir, vb. to grow pale or dim
palissade, n.f. paling, fence
pâlissant, adj. becoming pale
palme, n.f. palm, palm tree
palper, vb. to touch, feel
palpitant, adj. fluttering, palpitating
palpiter, vb. to flutter, palpitate
paludéen, adj. marshy
pâmer, vb. se p., to faint, swoon
pamphlet, n.m. pamphlet, booklet
pamphlétaire, n.m. pamphleteer

pamplemousse, n.m. grapefruit
pan, n.m. side, piece, flap
panacée, n.f. panacea
panache, n.m. plume, tuft
panais, n.m. parsnip
pandit, n.m. pundit
pané, adj. dotted with bread crumbs
panier, n.m. basket, hamper
panique, n.f. and adj. panic
panne, n.f. fat, lard; accident
panneau, n.m. panel
panse, n.f. paunch, cud
pansement, n.m. dressing
panser, vb. to groom; dress
pantalon, n.m. trousers
panteler, vb. to pant, gasp
panthère, n.f. panther
pantomime, n.f. pantomime
pantoufle, n.f. slipper
paon, n.m. peacock
papal, adj. papal
papauté, n.f. papcy
pape, n.m. pope
paperasse, n.f. waste paper; official documents
paperassier, adj. petty, scribbling
papeterie, n.f. stationery
papetier, n.m. stationer
papier, n.m. paper
papier à notes, n.m. notepaper
papier à tapisser, n.m. wallpaper
papillon, n.m. butterfly
papillonner, vb. to trifle, flutter
pâque, n.f. Passover
paquebot, n.m. small liner
pâquerette, n.f. daisy
Pâques, n.m. Easter
paquet, n.m. package, parcel, deck as in cards
par, prep. by; through
parabole, n.f. parable
parachute, n.m. parachute
parade, n.f. procession, parade
parader, vb. to show off
paradis, n.m. paradise
paradoxal, adj. paradoxical
paradoxe, n.m. paradox
paraffine, n.f. paraffin

parage, n.m. ancestry, descent
paragraphe, n.m. paragraph
paraître, vb. to appear, seem
parallèle, adj. and n.m.f. parallel
paralyser, vb. to paralyze
paralysie, n.f. paralysis
paralytique, adj. and n.m.f. paralytic
paramètre, n.m. parameter
parangon, n.m. model, type
parapluie, n.m. umbrella
parasite, n.m. parasite
paratonnerre, n.m. lightning rod
paravent, n.m. screen
parc, n.m. park; pen
parcelle, n.f. part, installment
parce que, conj. because
parcheminé, n.m. parchment like
parchmonie, n.f. parsimony
parcourir, vb. to run through
parcours, n.m. course, journey
pardessus, n.m. overcoat
pardon, n.m. pardon, forgiveness; interj. sorry
pardonner, vb. to forgive, pardon
pardonneur, n.m. pardoner
pare-boue, n.m. mudguard
pare-chocs, n.m. bumper
pareil, adj. like
parent, n.m. relative; pl. parents
parenté, n.f. relationship
parenthèse, n.f. parenthesis
parer, vb. to attire, deck out
paresse, n.f. sloth, idleness
pareser, vb. to laze, waste time
paresseux, adj. lazy, idel
parfaire, vb. to complete, finish up
parfait, adj. perfect, faultless
parfois, adv. sometimes, occasionally
parfum, n.m. perfume, odour
parfumer, vb. to perfume
parfumerie, n.f. perfumery
pari, n.m. bet, wager
parité, n.f. equality, parity
parjure, n.m. perjury
parjurer, vb. se p., to commit perjury
parlement, n.m. parliament
parlementaire, adj. parliamentary

parlementer, vb. to parley
parler, vb. to talk, speak
parleur, n.m. one who speaks
parloir, n.m. parlor
parmi, prep. among
parodie, n.f. parody
parodier, vb. to parody, imitate
paroisse, n.f. parish
parole, n.f. speech, word
paroxysme, n.m. fit of violence
parquer, vb. to park, enclose
parquet, n.m. floor
parrain, n.m. godfather
parsemer, vb. to spread, strew
part, n.f. share, part
partage, n.m. partition, share, sharing
partager, vb. to share, divide
partance, n.f. going, sailing
partant, n.m. one who leaves
partenaire, n.m.f. partner
parti, n.m. party
partial, adj. partial
partialité, n.f. bias, partiality
participant, adj. and n.m. participant
participation, n.f. participation, share
participer à, vb. to partake of
particularité, n.f. peculiarity
particule, n.f. particle
particulier, adj. particular, special
partie, n.f. part, party
partiel, adj. partial
partir, vb. to depart, leave, sail
partisan, n.m. follower
partitif, adj. partitive
partition, n.f. score
partout, adv. everywhere
parure, n.f. ornament
parvenir, vb. to reach
parvenu, n.m. upstart
pas, n.m. step, pace
passable, adj. fair
passage, n.m. aisle, alley
passager, n.m. passenger; adj. passing, fugitive
passant, n.m. passer-by
passavant, n.m. permit
passe, n.f. pass, permit; channel
passé, adj. and n.m. past

passe-partout, n.m. passport, skeleton
passeport, n.m. passport
passer, vb. to go by; pass; spend;
 strain; se p. de, go without
passereau, n.m. sparrow
passerelle, n.f. bridge
passe-temps, n.m. pastime
passible, adj. capable of feeling
passif, adj. and n.m. passive
passion, n.f. passion
passionné, adj. passionate
passionnel, adj. due to passion
passionner, vb. to interest, excite
 se p., be eager or excited over
passoire, n.f. device for straining
pastel, n.f. device for straining
pastèque, n.f. watermelon
pasteur, n.m. pastor
pasteuriser, vb. to pasteurize
pastille, n.f. cough drop, lozenge
pastoral, adj. pastoral
pataud, adj. awkward
patauger, vb. to flounder
pâte, n.f. paste, dough, batter
patenôtre, n.f. Lord's prayer
patent, adj. patent, evident
patente, n.f. license
paterne, adj. paternal
paternel, adj. paternal
paternité, n.f. fatherhood
pâteux, adj. pasty, thick
pathétique, adj. pathetic
pathologie, n.f. pathology
patience, n.f. patience
patient, adj. and n.m. patient
patin, n.m. skate
patineur, n.m. skater
pâtir, vb. to suffer
pâtisserie, n.f. pastry
patois, n.m. dialect, gibberish
pâtre, n.m. shepherd
patriarche, n.m. patriarch
patricien, adj. and n.m. patrician
patrie, n.f. native country, homeland
patrimoine, n.m. patrimony
patriote, n.m.f. patriot
patriotique, adj. patriotic

patriotisme, n.m. patriotism
patron, n.m. employer; boss; pattern
patronat, n.m. management
patronner, vb. to patronize, provide for
patrouille, n.f. patrol
patte, n.f. paw, leg, flap
pâturage, n.m. pasture
pâture, n.f. fodder, pasture
paume, n.f. palm
paupière, n.f. eyelid
pause, n.f. pause
pauvre, adj. poor
pauvreté, n.f. poverty
pavaner, vb. se p., to strut, swagger
pavé, n.m. pavement
paver, vb. to pave
pavillon, n.m. pavilion
pavot, n.m. poppy
paye, n.f. payment, salary
payement, n.m. payment
payer, vb. to pay, settle
payeur, n.m. payer
pays, n.m. country
paysage, n.m. scenery, landscape
paysan, n.m. peasant
péage, n.m. toll
pêche, n.m. angling, fishing
péché, n.m. sin
pécher, vb. to sin
pêcher, vb. to fish; n.m. peach tree
pêcherie, n.f. fishing place
pécheur, m. pécherese f. n. sinner;
 adj. sinful
pêcheur, n.m. fisherman
pécule, n.m. savings
pécuniare, adj. pecuniary
pédagogie, n.f. pedagogy
pédale, n.f. pedal
pédanterie, n.f. pedantry
pédestre, adj. pedestrian
pédiatre, n.m. pediatrician
pédicure, n.m. chiropodist
peigne, n.m. comb
peigner, v.t. to comb
peignoir, n.m. dressing-gown
peindre, vb. to paint, portray,
 depict
peine, n.f. pain, penalty

peiner, vb. to labor; grieve
peintre, n.m. painter
peinture, n.f. paint, painting
pelage, n.m. coat
pelé, adj. bald, uncovered
peler, vb. to peel, pare
pèlerin, n.m. pilgrim
pèlerinage, n.m. pilgrimage
pèlerine, n.f. pilgrim
pélican, n.m. pelican
pelle, n.f. shovel
pelletier, n.m. furrier
pellicule, n.f. film
pelote, n.f. ball, pellet
peloton, n.m. ball; group of soldiers
pelure, n.f. peel
pénal, adj. penal
pénalité, n.f. penalty
penaud, adj. awkwardly embarrassed or bashful
penchant, n.m. bent, tendency, liking
pencher, vb. to tilt, lean, droop
pendant, prep. during, pending
pendiller, vb. to dangle
pendre, vb. to hang
pendule, n.m. clock; pendulum
pénétrable, adj. penetrable
pénétrant, adj. keen
pénétration, n.f. penetration
pénétrer, vb. to penetrate, pervade
pénible, adj. painful
péninsule, n.f. peninsula
pénitence, n.f. penance
pénitencier, n.m. penitentiary
pénitent, adj. and n.m. penitent
penne, n.f. feather
pénombre, n.f. gloom, shadow
pensée, n.f. thought; pansy
penser, vb. to think of
penseur, n.m. thinker
pensif, adj. thoughtful, pensive
pension, n.f. board, pension
pensionnat, n.m. boarding school
pente, n.f. slant, slope
pépier, vb. to chirp
pépin, n.m. pip, kernel
pépinière, n.f. nursery
pépite, n.f. nugget

perçant, adj. sharp
percepteur, n.m. tax collector
perception, n.f. perception
percer, vb. to pierce, bore
percevoir, vb. to collect, perceive
perche, n.f. perch, pole
percher, vb. **se p.,** to perch
perchoir, n.m. perch
perclus, adj. crippled, lame
percussion, n.f. percussion
percuter, vb. to strike, hit
perdition, n.f. perdition
perdre, vb. to waste; lose
perdrix, n.f. partridge
père, n.m. father
péremptoire, adj. peremptory
perfection, n.f. perfection
perfectionnement, n.m. improvement, finishing
perfectionner, vb. to finish, perfect
perfide, adj. treacherous
perfidie, n.f. treachery
perforation, n.f. perforation
perforer, vb. to drill
péricliter, vb. to shake, be in danger
péril, n.m. danger, peril
périlleux, adj. perilous, dangerous
périmètre, n.m. perimeter
période, n.f. period, term, stage
périodique, adj. periodic
péripétie, n.f. shift of luck
périr, vb. to perish
périscope, n.m. periscope
périssable, adj. perishable
perle, n.f. pearl, bead
perlé, adj. pearly, perfect
permanence, n.f. permanence
permanent, adj. permanent
perméable, adj. permeable
permettre, vb. to permit, allow
permis, n.m. permit, license
permission, n.f. permission
permuter, vb. to change, exchange
perpétrer, vb. to commit
perpétuel, adj. perpetual
perplexe, adj. perplexed, undecided
perplexité, n.f. perplexity
perron, n.m. flight of steps

perroquet, n.m. parrot
perruque, n.f. wig
perse, adj. Persian
persécuter, vb. to persecute
persécution, n.f. persecution
persévérance, n.f. perseverance
persévérant, adj. persevering, resolute
persévérer, vb. to persevere
persienne, n.f. blind, shutter
persifler, vb. to ridicule
persil, n.m. parsley
persistance, n.f. persistence
persistant, adj. persistent
persister, vb. to persist
personnage, n.m. character
personnalité, n.f. personality
personne, n.f. person; pron. nobody
personnel, n.m. personnel; adj.
 personal
personnifier, vb. to personify
perspective, n.f. perspective, prospect
perspicace, adj. discerning
perspicacité, n.f. insight
persuader, vb. to persuade, convince
persuasif, adj. persuasive
perte, n.f. loss, waste
pertinent, adj. relevant, pertinent
perturbateur, n.m. agitator, disturber
pervers, adj. perverse, contrary
pervertir, vb. to pervert
pesant, adj. ponderous, heavy
pesanteur, n.f. weight, dullness
peser, vb. to weigh
pessimisme, n.m. pessimism
peste, n.f. pestilence; nuisance
pestilence, n.f. pestilence, nuisance
pétale, n.m. petal
pétiller, vb. to twinkle, crackle
petit, adj. petty, little, small; n.m. cub
petite-fille, n.f. granddaughter
petitesse, n.f. smallness, petitness
petit-fils, n.m. grandson
pétition, n.f. petition
pétitionner, vb. to request, ask
petits-enfants, n.m., pl. grandchildren
pétrifiant, adj. petrifying
pétrir, vb. to mold, knead
pétrole, n.m. kerosene, petroleum

peu, n.m. few; little
peuplade, n.f. clan, tribe
peuple, adj. gross
peuplier, n.m. poplar
peur, n.f. fear
peureux, adj. shy, timid
peut-être, adv. maybe, perhaps
phare, n.m. beacon, lighthouse
pharmacie, n.f. drug store, pharamacy
pharmacien, n.m. druggist
phase, n.f. phase
phénix, n.m. pheonix; superior person
phénoménal, adj. phenomenal
phénomène, n.m. phenomenon; freak
philatélie, n.f. stamp-collecting
philosophe, n.m. philosopher
philosophie, n.f. philosophy
phobie, n.f. phobia
phonétique, adj. and n.f. phonetic,
 phonetics
phongraphe, n.m. phonograph
phoque, n.m. seal
photocopie, n.f. photocopy
photographe, n.m. photographer
photographie, n.f. photograph,
 photography
phrase, n.f. sentence
phtisie, n.f. consumption
physique, n.f. physics; adj. physical
piailler, vb. to peep, squeal
pic, n.m. peak
picoter, vb. to prick, peck
pièce, n.f. piece, coin, patch
pied, n.m. foot
piège, n.m. snare, trap
pierre, n.f. stone
pierreries, n.f., pl. gems, jewelry
pierrot, n.m. clown in pantomime
piéton, n.m. pedestrian
pieu, n.m. stake, pile
pieuvre, n.f. octopus
pile, n.f. stack; battery
piler, vb. to crush, blast
pillage, n.m. plundering
piller, vb. to plunder
pilotage, n.m. piloting
piloter, vb. to pilot, lead
pilule, n.f. pill

piment, n.m. allspice

pin, n.m. pine

pinceau, n.m. paint-brush

pincer, vb. to pinch, nip

piocher, vb. to dig

pion, n.m. pawn, peon

pionnier, n.m. pioneer

pipe, n.f. pipe

piquant, adj. sharp

pique, n.f. spade

pique-nique, n.m. picnic

piquer, vb. to pick, sting

piquet, n.m. picket, peg, stake

pirate, n.m. pirate

piraterie, n.f. piracy

pirouette, n.f. pirouette, shift

pis, adv. worse, worst

piscine, n.f. pool

piste, n.f. track

pistolet, n.m. pistol

pistonner, vb. to help, push

piteux, adj. pitiful

pitié, n.f. pity, mercy

pitre, n.m. clown

pittoresque, adj. picturesque

pivoine, n.f. peony

pivoter, vb. to turn, pivot, revolve

pizza, n.f. pizza

place, n.f. place, room

placement, n.m. investment, placing

placer, vb. to invest, place

placide, adj. placid

placidité, n.f. placidity

plafond, n.m. ceiling

plagiare, n.m. one who plagiarizes

plagiat, n.m. plagiarism

plagier, vb. to plagiarize

plaid, n.m. plaid

plaideur, n.m. pleader

plaie, n.f. wound, sore

plaignant, n.m. plantiff

plaindre, vb. to pity; **se p.,** complain

plainte, n.f. complaint

plantif, adj. mournful

plaire, vb. to please

plaisance, n.f. pleasure, ease

plaisanter, vb. to joke

plaisir, n.m. pleasure

plan, n.m. plan; plane, schedule

planche, n.f. board, plank, shelf

plancer, n.m. floor

planer, vb. to glide; hover

planeur, n.m. glider

plantation, n.f. plantation

planter, v.t. to plant

planteur, n.m. planter

plaque, n.f. plate, slab

plaquer, vb. to plate, abandon

plastique, adj. plastic

plastronner, vb. to strut jauntily

plat-bord, n.m. gunwale

plateau, n.m. plateau, tray

plate-bande, n.f. flower bed

plate-forme, n.f. platform

platine, n.f. plate; n.m. platinum

platitude, n.f. flatness

plâtras, n.m. rubbish, rubble

plâtre, n.m. plaster

plausible, adj. plausible

plébéien, adj. ignoble

plein, adj. full, crowded

plénier, adj. complete, plenary

plénitude, n.f. fullness

pleurer, vb. to cry, weep, lament, mourn

pleurésie, n.f. pleurisy

pleurnicher, vb. to complain, whine

pleurs, n.m., pl. tears, weeping

pleutre, n.m. cad, coward

pleuvoir, vb. to rain

pliable, adj. pliable

pliant, n.m. folding chair

plier, vb. to fold, bend

plisser, vb. to pleat

plomb, n.m. lead

plomberie, n.f. plumbing

plongeon, n.m. plunge

plonger, vb. to plunge, dive, dip

ployer, vb. to incline, bend

pluie, n.f. rain

plumage, n.m. feathers

plume, n.f. pen, feather

plumeau, n.m. feather duster

plumet, n.m. plume

plumier, n.m. pen or pencil case

pluriel, adj. and n.m. plural

plusieurs, adj. and pron. several
plutôt, adv. rather
pneumonie, n.f. pneumonia
pochade, n.f. hasty, sketch
poche, n.f. pocket
pocheter, vb. to pocket
pochette, n.f. handkerchief
pochoir, n.m. stencil
poêle, n.m. stove
poésie, n.f. poem, poetry
poète, n.f. poet
poétique, adj. poetic
poids, n.m. weight
poignard, n.m. dagger
poignarder, vb. to stab
poigne, n.f. grip, power
poignée, n.f. handful; handle
poignet, n.m. wrist; cuff
poil, n.m. hair
poincon, n.m. punch
poing, n.m. fist
point, n.m. point, dot, period
pointage, n.m. pointing
pointe, vb. to point, aim
pointillage, n.m. dotting
pointiller, vb. to dot; tease
pointilleux, adj. fussy, precise
pointu, adj. pointed
pointure, n.f. size
poireau, n.m. leek
poirier, n.m. pear tree
pois, n.m. pea
poison, n.m. poison
poisson, n.m. fish
poitrinaire, adj. and n.m. consumptive
poitrine, n.f. chest
poivre, n.m. pepper
poix, n.f. pitch
polaire, adj. polar
pôle, n.m. pole
polémique, n.f. argument
police, n.f. police
policer, vb. to refine
polichinelle, n.m. Punch puppet
polir, vb. to polish
polisseur, n.m. polisher
polisson, n.m. scamp; adj. running
 wild

politesse, n.f. good manners
politicien, n.m. politician
politique, n.f. policy, politics; adj.
 politic, political
polka, n.f. polka
pollen, n.m. pollen
polluer, vb. to pollute
Pologne, n.f. Poland
Polonais, n.m. Pole
polonais, adj. and n.m. Polish
polygone, n.m. polygon
pommade, n.f. pomade, salve
pomme, n.f. apple
pommette, n.f. cheekbone
pommier, n.m. apple tree
pomper, vb. to pump
pompeux, adj. pompous
pompier, n.m. fireman
ponctucalité, n.f. punctuality
ponctuation, n.f. punctuation
ponctuel, adj. punctual
ponctuer, vb. to punctuate
poney, n.m. pony
pont, n.m. bridge; deck
ponton, n.m. pontoon
popeline, n.f. poplin
populaire, adj. popular
populariser, vb. to popularize
popularité, n.f. popularity
population, n.f. population
porc, n.m. pig, pork
porcelaine, n.f. china
porche, n.m. porch
pore, n.m. pore
poreux, adj. porous
port, n.m. harbor; carrying; postage
portable, adj. wearable
portail, n.m. portal
portatif, adj. portable
portée, n.f. range, scope, reach
portefaix, n.m. porter
portefeuille, n.m. case, portfolio
portement, n.m. carrying
porte-monnaie, n.m. purse
porter, vb. to carry, bear; wear
porteur, n.m. porter, bearer
portion, n.f. portion, share
portique, n.m. portico, porch

portrait, n.m. portrait
Portugal, n.m. Portugal
pose, n.f. pose, attitude
posé, n.f. set, poised
poseur, n.m. person or thing that places or applies; affected person
positif, adj. and n.m. positive
position, n.f. stand, place, position
possesseur, n.m. possessor
possessif, adj. and n.m. possessive
possession, n.f. possession
possibilité, n.f. possibility
postal, adj. postal
postérieur, adj. rear, posterior
postiche, adj. fales, unnecessary
postulat, n.m. applicant
postuler, vb. to apply for
posture, n.f. posture
pot, n.m. pot, pitcher, jar
potage, n.m. soup
potager, adj. vegetable
poteau, n.m. post
potée, n.f. potful
potence, n.f. gallows
potentiel, adj. and n.m. potential
poterie, n.f. pottery
potier, n.m. potter
potion, n.f. potion, draught
potiron, n.m. pumpkin
pou, n.m. louse
pouding, n.m. pudding
poudre, n.f. powder
poulailler, n.m. hen-house
poulain, n.m. colt
poule, n.f. hen, chicken
poulie, n.f. pulley
poulpe, n.m. octopus
pouls, n.m. pulse
poumon, n.m. lung
poupée, n.f. doll
poupin, adj. smart, chic
pourboire, n.m. tip, gratuity
pourceau, n.m. hog
pour-cent, n.m. percent
pourcentage, n.m. percentage
pourchasser, vb. to pursue
pourparler, n.m. discussion, parley

pourpoint, n.m. doublet
pourpre, adj. purple
pourquoi, adv. why
pourri, adj. rotten
pourriture, n.f. rot
poursuite, n.f. pursuit
poursuivre, vb. to sue, prosecute
pourtant, adv. however
pourvu que, conj. provided that
pousse, n.f. shoot, sprouting
poussée, n.f. push
pousser, vb. to push, urge, drive; grow
poussière, n.f. dust
poussiéreux, adj. dusty
poutre, n.f. beam
prairie, n.f. meadow
practicable, adj. practicable
praticien, n.m. practitioner
pratique, n.f. practice, exercise; adj. practical
pratiquer, vb. to practice, exercise
pré, n.m. meadow
préalable, adj. preliminary
préavis, n.m. advance notice
précédent, n.m. precedent
précéder, vb. to precede
précepte, n.m. precept
précepteur, n.m. tutor
prêche, n.m. sermon; the Protestant religion
prêcher, vb. to preach
précieux, adj. precious, valuable
préciosité, n.f. preciosity
précipitation, n.f. hurry
précipité, adj. hasty
précis, adj. precise, exact, accurate
précisément, adv. precisely, definitely
préciser, vb. to state
précision, n.f. accuracy, precision
précoce, adj. precocious
précompter, vb. to deduct in advance
préconsier, vb. to extol, praise
prédicateur, n.m. preacher
prédiction, n.f. prediction
prédominant, adj. predominant
préface, n.f. preface
préférence, n.f. preference
préfet, n.m. perfect

préfixe, n.m. prefix
prégnante, adj. pregnant
préhistorique, adj. prehistoric
préjudice, n.m. injury
préjugé, n.m. prejudice
préjuger, vb. to prejudge
préliminaire, adj. preliminary
prélude, n.m. prelude
prématuré, adj. premature
premier, adj. first, foremost; early
prémisse, n.f. premise
prémunir, vb. to take precautions
prendre, vb. to take
prénom, n.m. given name
préoccupation, n.f. care, worry
préoccuper, vb. to worry
prépalement, n.m. prepayment
préparatifs, n.m., pl. preparation
préparation, n.f. preparation
préparer, vb. to prepare
préposé, n.m. one in charge
préposition, n.f. preposition
prérogative, n.f. pregrogative
près, adv. near
présage, n.m. omen
prescription, n.f. prescription
prescire, vb. to prescribe
préséance, n.f. precedence
présence, n.f. presence, attendance
présent, adj. and n.m. present
présentable, adj. presentable
présentation, n.f. presentation, introduction
présentement, adv. now, at present
présenter, vb. to present, introduce
préservatif, adj. and n.m. preservative
préservation, n.f. preservation
préserver, vb. to preserve
présidence, n.f. presidency
président, n.m. president
présidentiel, adj. presidential
présider, vb. to preside
présomptif, adj. apparent, presumed
présomptueux, adj. presumptuous
presque, adv. almost, nearly
pressage, n.m. pressing
pressant, adj. urgent, pressing
presse, n.f. press, crowd

pressentir, vb. to foresee
presser, vb. to press; urge; hurry
pression, n.f. pressure
pressoir, n.m. or device for squeezing
pressurer, vb. to squeeze
preste, adj. exterous, nimble
prestesse, n.f. vivacity, nimbleness
prestige, n.m. prestige, illusion
présumer, vb. to presume
présupposer, vb. to presuppose
prêt, n.m. loan; adj. ready
prétendant, n.m. claimant
prétendre, vb. to claim
prêter, vb. to lend
prêteur, n.m. lender
prétexte, n.m. pretext
prêtre, n.m. priest
preuve, n.f. proof
prévaloir, vb. to prevail
prévenant, adj. prepossessing
prévenir, vb. to prevent; warn
prévention, n.f. prevention; bias
prévenu, adj. partial, biased
prévision, n.f. forecast, expectation
prévoir, vb. to foresee
prévoyance, n.f. foresight
prévoyant, adj. farseeing, prudent
prière, n.f. prayer
prieur, n.m. prior
prieuré, n.m. priory
primaire, adj. primary
primer, vb. to outdo, excel
primeur, n.f. freshness, earliness
primitif, adj. original
princesse, n.f. princess
principal, adj. chief, main, principal
principe, n.m. principle
printemps, n.m. spring
priorité, n.f. priority
prisable, adj. estimable
prise, n.f. grasp, hold, grip
prisée, n.f. appraisal
priser, v.t. to use snuff
priseur, n.m. auctioneer, appraiser
prison, n.f. jail, prison
prisonnier, n.m. prisoner
privé, adj. private
privilège, n.m. privilege, license

privilégier, vb. to license
probabilité, n.f. chances, probability
probable, adj. likely, probable
problème, n.m. problem
procédé, n.m. procedure, process
procéder, vb. to proceed
procédur, n.f. proceeding
procès, n.m. trial, lawsuit, action
processif, adj. litigious
procession, n.f. procession
processionnel, adj. processional
prochain, n.m. neighbor; adj. next
prochainement, adv. soon
proche, adj. near, close
proclamation, n.f. proclamation
proclamer, vb. to proclaim
procréation, n.f. procreation
procurer, vb. to procure, get
procureur, n.m. attorney
prodigalement, adv. prodigally
prodigalité, n.f. extravagance
prodige, n.m. prodigy
prodigieux, adj. wondrous
prodigue, adj. extravagant, lavish
prodiguer, vb. to lavish
producteur, n.m. producer
productif, adj. productive
production, n.f. production
productivé, n.f. productivity
produire, vb. to breed, produce, yield
produit, n.m. product, commodity
proéminence, n.f. prominence
proéminent, adj. prominent, standing out
profane, adj. profane
profaner, vb. to misuse, profane
proférer, vb. to say, utter
professeur, n.m. professor, teacher
profession, n.f. profession
professionnel, adj. professional
professoral, adj. professorial
professorat, n.m. professorship
profil, n.m. profile
profiler, vb. to show a profile of
profit, n.m. profit
profitable, adj. profitable
profiter, vb. to profit
profiteur, n.m. profiteer

profond, adj. deep, in-dept, profound
profondeur, n.f. depth
profus, adj. profuse
profusion, n.f. profusion, excess
progéniture, n.f. offspring
programme, n.m. program
progrès, n.m. progress, advance
progresser, vb. to progress
progressif, adj. progressive
progressiste, n.m. progressive
prohiber, vb. to prohibit
proie, n.f. prey
projecteur, n.m. projecter
projectile, n.m. missle
projection, n.f. projection
projeter, vb. to project, plan
prolétariat, n.m. proletariat
prolifique, adj. prolific
prolixe, adj. prolix, wordy
prologue, n.m. prologue
promenade, n.f. excursion; ride; walk
promeneur, n.m. walker
promesse, n.f. promise
promettre, vb. to promise
promoteur, n.m. promoter
promotion, n.f. promotion
prompt, adj. prompt
promptitude, n.f. quickness
pronom, n.m. pronoun
prononcer, vb. to pronounce; deliver
prononciation, n.f. pronunciation
propager, vb. to propagate
propension, n.f. propensity, inclination
prophétie, n.f. prophecy
prophétiser, vb. to prophesy
propice, adj. favorable
proportion, n.f. proportion
porportionner, vb. to keep in proportion
propos, n.m. subject
proposable, adj. suitable, appropriate
proposer, vb. to propose; move
proposition, n.f. proposal
propre, adj. proper; clean
propulser, vb. to push, propel
propulseur, n.m. propeller
proroger, vb. to postpone, extend time limit

proscrire, vb. to outlaw, proscribe
prose, n.f. prose
prosodie, n.f. prosody
prospecteur, n.m. prospector
prospère, adj. prosperous
prospérer, vb. to flourish, prosper
prospérité, n.f. prosperity
prosterner, vb. to prostrate
prostituée, n.f. prostitute
prostituion, n.f. prostitution
protecteur, n.m. protector; patron; adj. protective
protection, n.f. protection
protectorat, n.m. protectorate
protéger, vb. to protect, patronize
protéine, n.f. protein
protestant, adj. and n.m. Protestant
protestantisme, n.m. Protestantism
protestation, n.f. protest
protester, vb. to protest
protocole, n.m. protocol
protubérance, n.f. protuberance
proue, n.f. prow, front
prouesse, n.f. prowess
prouver, vb. to prove
provenance, n.f. product; place of origin
provenir, vb. to come from
proverbe, n.m. proverb, saying
proverbial, adj. proverbial
providence, n.f. providence
province, n.f. province
provincial, adj. and n.m. provincial
provincialisme, n.m. provincialism
provision, n.f. store, supply, provision
provisoire, adj. temporary
provocateur, n.m. person who provokes action
provocation, n.f. provocation
provoquer, vb. to provoke
proximité, n.f. proximity, closeness
prudence, n.f. caution, prudence
prudent, adj. cautious, prudent
pruderie, n.f. prudishness
prune, n.f. plum
pruneau, n.m. prune
Prussien, n.m. Prussian
psaume, n.m. palm

psautier, n.m. psalm book
psychiatre, n.m. psychiatrist
psychique, adj. psychic
psychologie, n.f. psychology
psychologue, n.m. psychologist
psychose, n.f. psychosis
puant, adj. shameful
puberté, n.f. puberty
publication, n.f. publication
publiciste, n.m. publicist
publicité, n.f. publicity
pubiler, vb. to publish, issue
puce, n.f. flea
pucelle, n.f. virgin, young girl
pudeur, n.m. modesty
pudique, adj. modest
puer, vb. to have an offensive odor
puéril, adj. childish
pugiliste, m. boxer
puis, adv. then
puisatier, n.m. well-digger
puisque, conj. since, as
puissamment, adv. very, powerfully
puissant, adj. powerful, mighty
pulpe, n.f. pulp
pulsar, n.m. pulsar
pulsation, n.f. beating
pulvérisateur, n.m. spray, vaporizer
pulvériser, vb. to spray, pulverize
punir, vb. to punish
punitif, adj. punitive
punition, n.f. punishment
pupitre, n.m. desk; music stand, reading stand
pur, adj. pure
purée, n.f. mash
purement, adv. purely
pureté, n.f. purity
purge, n.f. cleansing
purification, n.f. purification
purifier, vb. to purify, cleanse
puritain, adj. and n.m. Puritan
pustule, n.f. pimple
putois, n.m. skunk, polecate
pyjama, n.m. pajamas
pyramidal, adj. overwhelming
pyramide, n.f. pyramid

quadragénaire, adj. forty years of age

quadrangle, n.m. quadrangle

quadrangulaire, adj. quadrangular

quadrillé, adj. check, ruled off

quadrillage, n.m. arrangement or pattern in squares

quadrupède, n.m. and adj. quadruped

quadruple, n.m. and adj. four fold, quadruple

quai, n.m. pier, dock, wharf

qualifiable, adj. qualifiable

qualificatif, adj. qualifying

qualification, n.f. qualication

qualifié, adj. qualified

qualifier, v.t. to qualify

qualité, n.f. quality, nature, grade, property

quand, adv. when, whenever

quant, prep. as to, as for

quant-à-soi, n.m. dignity, reserve

quantité, n.f. amount, quantity

quantième, n.m. which

quarantaine, n.f. quarantine

quarante, adj. and n.m. forty

quart, n.m. fourth, quarter

quartier, n.m. district, quarter

quartz, n.m. quartz

quassar, n.m. quasar

quasi, adv. nearly; n.m. thick end of a loin of meat

quasi-contrat, n.m. implied contract

quasi-délit, n.m. injury that is caused involuntarily

quasiment, adv. nearly, almost

quaterne, n.m. four winning numbers

quatorze, adj. and n.m. fourteen; fourteenth

quatre, adj. and n.m. four, fourth

quatre-vingt-dix, adj. and n.m. ninety

quatrième, adj. and n.m. fourth

quatuor, n.m. quartet

quayage, n.m. wharfage

que, pron. whom, which, that; conj. that, than

quel, adj. which; what; of what kind

quelconque, adj. some, any

quelquefois, adv. sometimes

quelqu'un, pron. m. someone, somebody, anybody

quelque, adj. a few

quelques-uns, pron. m. a few

quelqu'un, pron. somebody, someone

quenotte, n.f. tooth of young children

querelle, n.f. quarrel, quarreling

quereller, vb. to quarrel with; scold

querelleur, n.m. quarreler; adj. inclined to quarrel

quérir, v.t. to fetch

qu'est-ce que, pron. what?

question, n.f. question, issue, matter

questionnaire, n.m. book or paper with a list of questions

questionner, v.t. to question, to interrogate

questionneur, n.m. questioner; adj. inquisitive

quête, n.f. quest, seeking; collection

quêter, vb. to seek, go in quest of something, look for

queue, n.f. tail; line

faire la q., stand in line

queue-d'aronde, n.f. dovetail

queue-de-cheval, n.f. horse tail

qui, rel. pron. who, whom; which

quiconque, pron. whoever, whomsoever, whichever

quignon, n.m. large piece of bread

quille, n.f. keel

quincaillerie, n.f. hardware

quinine, n.f. quinine

quinquagénaire, adj. fifty years old

quintal, n.m. unit of weight 100 kilograms

quintuple, adj. quintuple

quinze, adj. and n.m. fifteen

quinzième, adj. and n.m. fifteenth

quiproquo, n.m. blunder, mistake

quittance, n.f. receipt

quitte, adj. free, quit, released

quitter, vb. to quit, leave

quoi, pron. and interj. what

quoique, conj. though

quote-part, n.f. quota, part portion

quotidien, adj. daily

quotité, n.f. share; amount

rabais, n.m. abatement, reduction
rabaisser, vb. to lessen, lower
rabattre, vb. to put down, suppress
rabbin, n.m. rabbi
rabot, n.m. plane
raboter, vb. to plane, perfect
raboteux, adj. knotty, rugged
raccommodage, n.m. fixing, mending
raccommoder, vb. to mend, repair
raccorder, vb. to join, bring together
raccourcir, vb. to shorten, curtail
raccourcissement, n.m. shortening
raccrocher, vb. to hook up; recover
race, n.f. race, stock, breed
rachat, n.m. redemption
racheter, vb. to redeem, to buy back
racine, n.f. root
raciage, n.m. action of scraping
racler, vb. toscrape
raconter, vb. to narrate, tell, recount
radar, n.m. radar
radeau, n.m. raft
radiant, adj. radiant
radical, adj. and n.m. radical
radier, vb. to radiate; erase
radieux, adj. beaming, glorious, radiant
radio, n.f. radio; wireless
radiodiffuser, vb. to broadcast
radiogramme, n.m. radiogram
radiographie, n.f. radiography
radis, n.m. radish
radium, n.m. radium
radoter, vb. to babble, drivel
radoucir, vb. to quiet, soften, appease
rafale, n.f. blast, gust, squall
raffinement, n.m. refinement
raffiner, vb. to refine
raffinerie, n.f. refinery
rafistoler, vb. to patch, mend
rafler, vb. to carry off
rafraîchir, vb. to refresh
rafraîchissement, n.m. refreshment
rage, n.f. rage, fury
rager, vb. to rage, be angry
rageur, n.m. irritable person
ragoûtant, adj. pleasing, tasty
ragréer, vb. to refinish, renovate

raid, n.m. raid
raide, adj. stiff; taut; steep
raideur, n.f. stiffness
raifort, n.m. horseradish
rail, n.m. rail
railler, vb. to make fun of
raillerie, n.f. jesting
railleur, n.m. jester, scoffer
rais, n.m. ray, spoke
raisin, n.m. grapes; r. sec, raisin
raison, n.f. reason, judgment
raisonnable, adj. reasonable
raisonnement, n.m. reason, argument
raisonner, vb. to reason
rajeunir, vb. to rejuvenate
ralentir, vb. to slow down, slacken
rallier, vb. to rally
rallonger, vb. to make an addition to
ramage, n.m. flower pattern; babble
ramassé, adj. thick-set, dumpy
ramasser, vb. topick up
ramasseur, n.m. collector
rame, n.f. oar
rameau, n.m. branch
ramener, vb. to bring, take back
rameneur, vb. to restorer
ramer, vb. to row
rameur, n.m. rower
ramille, n.f. twig
ramollir, vb. to soften, weaken
rampe, n.f. banister; ramp
ramper, vb. to crawl, creep
rance, adj. and n.m. rancid
rancon, n.f. ransom
rancune, n.f. grudge, spite
rancunier, adj. rancorous, bitter
rang, n.m. row; rank
rangée, n.f. file, row
ranger, vb. to rank, array
rapace, adj. predatory, greedy
râpe, n.f. file, rasp
râper, vb. to grate
rapide, n.m. rapid; adj. rapid, fast, quick
rapidité, n.f. rapidity
rapiécter, v.t. to patch
rapin, n.m. pupil, art student
rapineur, vb. to plunder, rob

rappel, n.m. reminder, recall, repeal

rappeler, vb. to recall, remind

rapport, n.m. report; relation, productiveness

rapporter, vb. to bring back; report, correspond

rapporteur, n.m. reporter, tattletale

rapprochement, n.m. bringing close

rapprocher, vb. to bring together; se r. de, approximate

rapt, n.m. rape, kidnapping

raquette, n.f. racket

rare, adj. scarce, rare

raréfier, vb. to rarefy

rarement, adv. seldom, rarely

rareté, n.f. rarity, scarcity

ras, adj. smooth-shaven, open

raser, vb. to shave

rasoir, n.m. razor

rassasier, vb. to cloy, sate

rassemblement, n.m. rally

rassembler, vb. to gather, congregate, muster

rasseoir, v.t. to seat again, to replace, to calm

rasséréner, vb. to clear up, as in weather

rassis, adj. stale

rassurer, vb. to reasure, comfort

rat, n.m. rat

ratatiner, vb. to shrivel, shrink

rate, n.f. spleen

râteau, n.m. rake

râtelier, n.m. rack

rater, vb. to miss

ratière, n.f. rat trap

ratifier, vb. to ratify

ration, n.f. ration

rationnel, adj. rational

rationnement, n.m. rationing

rationner, vb. to ration

ratissoire, n.f. scraper, rake

rattacher, vb. to fasten

rattraper, vb. to overtake

raturer, vb. to erase, blot out

rauque, adj. horse, raucous

ravage, n.m. havoc

ravager, vb. to lay waste

ravauder, vb. to mend, patch

ravigoter, vb. to enliven, refresh

ravir, vb. to ravish; delight

ravissant, adj. ravishing, charming, ravenous

ravissement, n.m. rapture

ravisseur, n.m. ravisher, robber

raviver, vb. to revive

rayer, vb. to streak; cross out

rayon, n.m. ray, beam; shelf; r. X, X-ray

rayonne, n.f. rayon

rayonnement, n.m. radiation, radiance

rayonner, vb. to radiate, beam

rayure, n.f. streak, blemish

réabonnement, n.m. renewal of subscription

réabonner, vb. to renew, resubscribe

réagir, vb. to react

réalisable, adj. realizable

réalisation, n.f. attainment

réaliser, vb. to realize; se r., materialize

réaliste, n.m.f. realist; adj. realist

réalité, n.f. reality

réassurer, vb. to reinsure

rébarbatif, adj. forbidding

rebattre, vb. to repeat, beat again

rebattu, adj. trite

rebelle, n.m.f. rebel; adj. rebel, rebelious

rebeller, vb. se r., to rebel

rébellion, n.f. rebellion, revolt

rebondi, adj. plump

rebondir, vb. to bounce

rebord, n.m. border, edge

reburrade, n.f. rebuff, rebuke

rebut, n.m. trash, junk, rubbish

rebuter, vb. to rebuke, discard, reject

recéler, vb. to accept stolen goods, hide

récemment, adv. recently

recensement, n.m. census

recenser, vb. to make a census

récent, adj. recent

réceptacle, n.m. receptacle

récepteur, n.m. receiver

réceptif, adj. receptive

réception, n.f. reception, receipt

recette, n.f. recipe, receipt; pl. returns

receveur, n.m. conductor; receiver

recevoir, vb. to receive, get; entertain

réchapper, vb. to escape, get out

réchaud, n.m. food warmer, chafing dish

réchauffer, vb. to warm again, excite

recherche, n.f. inquiry research; quest

rechercher, vb. to investigate

rechute, n.f. relapse

récif, n.m. reef

récipient, n.m. container

réciproque, adj. mutual

récit, n.m. account

réciter, vb. to recite, tell

réclamation, n.f. complaint

réclame, n.f. advertisement

réclamer, vb. to claim, demand

reclus, adj. withdrawn, secluded

réclusion, n.f. solitary confinement

recoin, n.m. recess, corner

récolte, n.f. crop, harvest

récolter, vb. to harvest, gather

recommandable, adj. advisable

recommandation, n.f. recommendation

recommander, vb. to reccomend; register letter

recommencer, vb. to start again

récompense, n.f. reward

récompenser, vb. to reward

réconcilier, vb. to reconcile

réconduire, vb. to accompany, show out, dismiss

reconnaissance, n.f. recognition; gratitude

reconnaissant, adj. grateful

reconnaître, vb. to recognize, admit, acknowledge

reconstituer, vb. to rebuild, restore

recourir, vb. to resort to

recours, n.m. resort, recourse

recouvrer, vb. to recover, retrieve

recouvrir, vb. to recover, cover completely

récréation, n.f. amusement

récréer, vb. to entertain

recrue, n.f. recruit

recruter, vb. to recruit

rectangle, n.m. rectangle

recteur, n.m. rector

rectifier, vb. to rectify, correct

reçu, n.m. receipt; adj receive

recueil, n.m. collection, compilation

recueillir, vb. to gather, collect, glean

recul, n.m. kick, recoil

reculade, n.f. backing, retreat

reculer, vb. to recoil, draw back

récuser, vb. to challenge, reject

recycler, vb. to recycle

rédacteur, n.m. editor

rédaction, n.f. editorial staff

reddition, n.f. surrendering

rédemption, n.f. redemption

rédiger, vb. to draw up

redingote, n.m. frock-coat

redire, vb. to repeat, reveal

redoutable, adj. alarming, redoubtable

redouter, vb. to dread

redresser, vb. to straighten

réduction, n.f. cut, decrease

réduire, vb. to reduce

réduit, n.m. retreat, hovel

réel, adj. real, actual

réfection, n.f. reconstruction; refreshments

réfectoire, n.m. dining room

référence, n.m. reference

référer, vb. to refer

refermer, vb. to close up or again

réfléchir, vb. to ponder, consider

reflet, n.m. reflection

refléter, vb. to reflect

réflexe, adj. and n.m. reflex

réflexion, n.f. thought, reflection, consideration

refluer, vb. to return to source, ebb

reflux, n.m. ebb

refondre, vb. to improve, cast gain; remodel

réformateur, adj. reforming; n.m. crusader, reformer

réforme, n.f. reform, reformation

réformer, vb. to reform

refoulement, n.m. forcing back, retreat

refouler, vb. to dirve back, repel

réfractaire, adj. refractory

réfrigérant, n.m. refrigerator

réfrigérer, vb. to put under refrigeration

refroidir, vb. chill, cool

refroidissement, n.m. cooling, refrigeration, chill

refuge, n.m. refuge

réfugier, vb. **se r.**, to take refuge

refus, n.m. refusal, denial

refuser, vb. to refuse, withhold, deny

réfutation, n.f. rebuttal

réfuter, vb. to disprove, refute

regagner, vb. to regain, recover

regain, n.m. regrowth, renewal

régal, n.m. feast, repast

régaler, vb. to entertain, treat

regard, n.m. look

regarder, vb. to look at; concern

régence, n.f. regency

régénerer, vb. to regenerate

régent, adj. and n.m. regent

régenter, vb. to direct, dominate

régime, n.m. diet; government; direction

régiment, n.m. regiment

région, n.f. area, region

régional, adj. regional

régir, vb. to rule

régisseur, n.m. manager

registre, n.m. register, record

règle, n.f. rule; ruler

règlement, n.m. settlement; regulation

réglementaire, adj. according to regulations

régler, vb. to regulate; rule; settle

régner, vb. to reign

régression, n.f. regression

regret, n.m. regret

regrettable, adj. regrettable

regretter, vb. to regret

régulariser, vb. to regularize

régularité, n.f. regularity

régulateur, n.m. regulator

régulier, adj. regular

réhabiliter, vb. to rehabilitate

rehausser, vb. to enhance

rein, n.m. kidney

reine, n.f. queen

reject, n.m. rejection

rejeter, vb. to reject

rejeton, n.m. plant shoot

rejoindre, vb. to overtake, rejoin

réjouissance, n.f. festivity

relâche, adj. loose

relâcher, vb. to relax, slacken

relais, n.m. relay

relater, vb. to relate

relatif, adj. relative

relation, n.f. connection, relation

relaxation, n.f. release, relaxation

relayer, vb. to relay

relèvement, n.m. bearing

relever, vb. to relieve; lift; point out

relief, n.m. relief; **mettre en r.**, emphasize

relier, vb. to bind; link

relieur, n.f. binding

religieuse, n.f. nun

religieux, adj. religious

religion, n.f. religion

reliquaire, n.m. receptacle for relic

reluire, vb. to shine, glisten

remainier, vb. to redo, modify

remarquable, adj. noticeable; remarkable

remarque, n.f. remark

remarquer, vb. to remark; notice

rembarrer, vb. to put in ones place

remboursement, n.m. refund

remède, n.m. remedy, cure

remédiable, adj. remediable

remédier à, vb. to remedy

remerciement, n.m. thanks

remettre, vb. to put back; restore; remit; pardon; deliver

remise, n.f. discount; delivery

rémission, n.f. remission

remontrance, n.f. remonstrance

remontrer, vb. to show anew, point out error

remorquer, vb. to tow

remorqueur, n.m. tug boat

rémouleur, n.m. sharpener, grinder
remous, n.m. eddy
remplaçant, n.m. substitute
remplacer, vb. to replace, substitute
rempli, n.m. tuck, hitch
remplier, vb. to take a tuck in
remplir, vb. to fill; carry out; crowd
remporter, vb. to take away
remuer, vb. to stir **se r.,** bustle
renaissance, n.f. rebirth, revival
renard, n.m. fox; sly person
rencontre, n.f. meeting
rencontrer, vb. to meet; come across
rendement, n.m. output
rendez-vous, n.m. date, appointment
rendre, vb. to give back; repay; surrender. **se r. compte de,** realize
rêne, n.f. rein
rené, adj. born again
renégat, adj. and n.m. renegade
renfermer, vb. to enclose
renfler, vb. to swell, inflate
renforcer, vb. to reinforce
renfort, n.m. reinforcement, aid
renfrogner, vb. **se r.** to scowl, frown
renne, n.m. reindeer
renom, n.m. renown, repute
renommée, n.f. fame, renown,
  reputation
renoncer à, vb. to renounce, forego
renonciation, n.f. renunciation
renouement, n.m. renewing, retying
renouveau, n.m. springtime, spring
renouveler, vb. to renew, renovate
renouvellement, n.m. renewal
renseignements, n.m., pl. information
renseigner, vb. to inform. **se r.,** inquire
rente, n.f. income; interest; annuity
rentrée, n.f. return
rentrer, vb. to go back, go home
renversant, adj. over whelming
renverse, adj. thrown down; reverse
renvoi, n.m. dismissal; return
renvoyer, vb. to dismiss, send back
repaître, vb. to feed, feast
répandre, vb. to diffuse, spill, scatter
répandu, adj. prevalent, widespread
reparaître, vb. to reappear

réparateur, n.m. restorer, repairer
réparation, n.f. repair, amends
réparer, vb. to repair
repartie, n.f. reply, quick retort
repartir, vb. to leave again; retort
repas, n.m. meal
repasser, vb. to press; pass; look over
repentir, n.m. repentance; vb. **se r.,**
  repent
répercussion, n.f. repercussion
répercuter, vb. to reverberate, echo
repère, n.m. guiding mark
repertoire, n.m. list, repertory
répéter, vb. to repeat, rehearse
répétition, n.f. repetition
répit, n.m. respite
replacer, vb. to replace
replier, vb. to fold again or up
réplique, n.f. rejoinder; cue
répliquer, vb. to rejoin
repondant, n.m. respondent, bail
repondre, vb. to answer, reply; **r. de,**
  vouch for
réponse, n.f. answer reply
report, n.m. in bookkeeping, the
  amount brought forward
reportage, n.m. reporting
reporter, n.m. reporter; vb. take back
repos, n.m. rest
reposer, vb. to rest, repose
repousser, vb. to push back, repel;
  spurn
repoussoir, n.m. foil
répréhensible, adj. objectionable
répréhension, n.f. reprehension,
  cenusre
reprendre, vb. to take back, resume
représailles, n.f., pl. retaliation
représentatif, n.m. representative
représentation, n.f. representation, performance
représenter, adj. represent
répressif, adj. repressive
répression, n.f. repression
réprimande, n.f. reproof, rebuke,
  reprimand
réprimander, vb. to chide, reprove,
  reprimand

réprimer, vb. to quell
reprise, n.f. recovery; turn
repriser, vb. to darn
réprobation, n.f. reprobation
reproche, n.m. reproach
reprocher, vb. to reproach
reproduction, n.f. reproduction
reproduire, vb. to reproduce
réprouver, vb. to censure
reptile, n.m. reptile
républicain, adj. and n.m. replublican
république, n.f. republic
répudier, vb. to repudiate
répugnance, n.f. repuganance
répulsion, n.f. repulsion
réputation, n.f. reputation
réputer, vb. to consider, esteem
requête, n.f. request, plea
requin, n.m. shark
requis, adj. required, necessary
réquisition, n.f. requisition
rescousse, n.f. rescue
réseau, n.m. network
réserve, n.f. reserve, reservation; qualification
réserver, vb. to reserve
réserviste, n.f. reservist
réservoir, n.m. tank, reservoir
résidant, adj. resident
résidence, n.f. residence, dwelling
résider, vb. to reside
résidu, n.m. residue
résignation, n.f. resignation
résigner, vb. to resign
résiliation, n.f. cancelling
résine, n.f. resin
résister, vb. to resist
résolu, adj. resolute
résonnance, n.f. resonnance
résonnant, adj. resonant
résonner, vb. to resound
résoudre, vb. to solve, resolve
respect, n.m. respect
respecter, vb. to respect
respectif, adj. respective
respectueux, adj. respectful
respiration, n.f. breathing

respirer, vb. to breathe
responsabilité, n.f. responsibility
responsable, adj. responsible; liable
ressaisir, vb. to regain possession
ressemblance, n.f. likeness
ressembler, vb. to resemble
ressentir, vb. to feel, resent, show
resserrer, vb. to tighten, compress
ressort, n.m. elasticity
ressortir, vb. to stand out
ressource, n.f. resort, resource
restaurant, n.m. restaurant
restaurateur, n.m. restorer
restauration, n.f. restoration
restaurer, vb. to restore
reste, n.m. remainder, rest
rester, vb. to remain, stay
restituer, vb. to give back, restore
restreindre, vb. to restrict
restrictif, adj. restrictive
restriction, n.f. restriction
résultant, n.m. outcome, result
résulter, vb. to result
résumé, n.m. summing up
résumer, vb. to sum up
rétablir, vb. to restore
rétablissement, n.m. recovery
retard, n.m. delay, retard
retenir, vb. to retain; keep; hold back; detain
rétentif, adj. retentive
retentir, vb. to resound; ring
réticence, n.f. silence, reticence
retirer, vb. to withdraw
retoucheuse, n.f. retoucher
retour, n.m. return; de r., back
retourner, vb. to go back, invert; se r., turn around
retrait, n.m. contraction, retraction
retraite, n.f. retreat; privacy
retrancher, vb. to cut off, curtail
rétrécir, vb. to shrink, contract
rétribution, n.f. salary, recompense
retrousser, vb. to turn up
retrouver, vb. to find; recover
réunion, n.f. meeting, convention, reunion

réunir, vb. to unite; **se r.,** assemble

réussir, vb. to succeed

réussite, n.f. successful outcome

revanche, n.f. revenge; **en r.,** in return

rêve, n.m. dream

réveil, n.m. awaking; revival

réveiller, vb. to wake up, arouse

révélateur, adj. revealing; n.m. revelaer

révélation, n.f. revelation

révéler, vb. to disclose, reveal

revenant, n.m. ghost, specter

revendeur, n.m. retailer

revendiquer, vb. to claim

revenir, vb. to come back, return

revenu, n.m. income, revenue

rêver, vb. to dream

révéremment, adv. reverently

révérence, n.f. reverence; curtsy, bow

révérer, vb. to revere

rêverie, n.f. dreaming, reverie

revers, n.m. reverse, wrong side

rêveur, n.m. dreamer; adj. pensive

réviser, vb. to revise

réviseur, n.m. reviser, inspector

révision, n.f. revision, review

revivre, vb. to revive, to come to life

révocation, n.f. revocation, annulment

révolte, n.f. revolt

révolution, n.f. revolution, turn

révolutionnaire, adj. and n.m. revolutionary

révoquer, vb. to revoke

revue, n.f. review, magazine

rez-de-chaussée, n.m. ground floor

rhétorique, n.f. rhetoric

rhinocéros, n.m. rhinoceros

rhubarbe, n.f. rhubarb

rhum, n.m. rum

rhumatisme, n.m. rheumatism

rhume, n.m. cold

riche, adj. wealthy

richesse, n.f. wealth

ricocher, vb. to spring back

rictus, n.m. grin

ride, n.f. wrinkle, ripple

rideau, n.m. curtain

rider, vb. to ripple, wrinkle

ridicule, n.m. ridicule; adj. ridiculous

ridiculiser, vb. to ridicule

rien, pron. nothing

rieur, n.m. laugher

rigide, adj. rigid

rigidité, n.f. rigidity

rigole, n.f. ditch, gutter

rigoureux, adj. rigorous

rigueur, n.f. rigor

rime, n.f. rhyme

rimer, vb. to rhyme

rince-doigts, n.m. ringer bowl

rincer, vb. to rinse

ripaille, n.f. feasting, revelry

riposte, n.f. retort

rire, n.m. laugh, laughter; vb. laugh

ris, n.m. laugh; sweetbread

risée, n.f. laugh, mocking

risibilité, adj. laughable

risque, n.m. risk

risquer, vb. to risk

risque-tout, n.m. daredevil

rissoler, vb. to brown food

rite, n.m. rite

rituel, adj. ritual

rivage, n.m. shore, bank

rival, adj. and n.m. rival

rivaliser, vb. to compete, rival

rivalité, n.f. rivalry

rive, n.f. bank

river, vb. to clinch

rivet, n.m. rivet

rivière, n.f. river, stream

rixe, n.f. brawl

riz, n.m. rice

rizerie, n.f. rice field

robe, n.f. dress, frock, robe

robinet, n.m. faucet, tap

robuste, adj. robust, hardy, strong

roc, n.m. rock

rocailleux, adj. rock, rough

rocher, n.m. rock

rocheux, adj. rocky

rock, adj. rock music

rôder, vb. to prowl

rôdeur, n.m. prowler

rogner, vb. to pare, trim down

rognon, n.m. kidney

rogue, adj. arrogant
roi, n.m. king
rôle, n.m. role, part, list
Romain, n.m. Roman
romain, adj. Roman
roman, n.m. novel
romance, n.f. ballad
romancier, n.m. novelist
romanesque, adj. romantic
roman-feuilleton, n.m. serial
romanichel, n.m. gypsy
rompre, vb. to break
rond, n.m. round; circle; adj. round
rondeur, n.f. roundness
ronflement, n.m. snoring, roar
ronfler, vb. to snore
ronger, vb. to gnaw; fret
rongeur, adj. and n.m. rodent
rosaire, n.m. rosary
rose, n.f. rose; adj. pink
roseau, n.m. reed
rosée, n.f. dew
rosier, n.m. rosebush
rossignol, n.m. nighingale
rotatoire, adj. rotary
roter, vb. to belch
rôti, n.m. roast
rôtir, vb. to roast
rotondité, n.f. rotundity
rotule, n.f. kneecap
roturier, adj. commonplace
roublardise, n.f. cunningness
roue, n.f. wheel
rouge-gorge, n.m. robin redbreast
rougeole, n.f. measles
rougeur, n.f. flush, blush
rougir, vb. to blush
rouille, n.f. rust
rouiller, vb. to rust
rouir, vb. to soak
rouleau, n.m. roll, roller, scroll
roulement, n.m. rolling, winding
rouler, vb. to roll, wind
roulette, n.f. little wheel, caster
roulis, n.m. roll
Roumanie, n.f. Rumania
rousseur, n.f. redness;
  tache de r., freckle

roussir, vb. to scorch
route, n.f. road, way, course
routine, n.f. routine
routiner, v.t. to accustom; to teach by
  routine
royal, adj. royal, regal, kinglike, kingly
royaliste, adj. and n.m.f. royalist
royaume, n.m. kingdom
royauté, n.f. royalty
ruban, n.m. ribbon, tape; band
rubescent, adj. reddish
rubis, n.m. ruby
ruche, n.f. hive
rude, adj. gruff, harsh; rugged, rough,
  uneven
rudesse, n.f. harshness, roughness,
  coarseness
rudiment, n.m. rudiment, element,
  primer
rudimentaire, adj. rudimentary
rudoyer, vb. to bully
rue, n.f. street, road
ruée, n.f. rush; onslaught
ruelle, n.f. lane, alley
ruer, vb. se r.,to rush
rugir, vb. to roar, bellow
rugissement, n.m. roar
rugosité, n.f. rugosity, roughness
rugueux, adj. harsh, rugged
ruine, n.f. ruin, decay, decline,
  overthrow
ruiner, vb. to ruin, lay waste, destroy
ruisseau, n.m. brook, creek, gutter
ruisseler, vb. to stream, flow
rumeur, n.f. noise, rumor
ruminant, adj. and n.m. ruminant
rupin, adj. rich, smart
rupture, n.f. break, rupture
rural, adj. rural
ruse, n.f. trick; cunning, trick, guile
Russe, n.m.f. Russian person
russe, n.m. Russian language;
  adj. Russian
Russie, n.f. Russia
rustique, adj. rustic
rustre, adj. and n.m. boor, boorish
rythme, n.m. rhythm
rythmique, adj. rhythmical

sabbat, n.m. Sabbath
sable, n.m. sand
sabler, vb. to sand; quaff
sablier, n.m. sandbox, hourglass, sandman
sablonneux, adj. sandy
sablonnière, n.f. sand pit
sabord, n.m. porthole
sabot, n.m. wooden shoe
sabotage, n.m. sabotage
saboteur, n.m. awkward bungler
sabre, n.m. saber
sac, n.m. sack, bag; **s. à main,** pocketbook
saccade, n.f. jerk
saccager, vb. to ransack, plunder
sacerdoce, n.m. priesthood
sachet, n.m. sachet
sacre, n.m. coronation
sacré, adj. sacred, holy
sacrement, n.m. sacrament
sacrer, vb. to consecrate; curse
sacrifice, n.m. sacrifice
sacrifier, vb. to sacrifice
sacristain, n.m. sexton
sadisme, n.m. sadism
sagace, adj. shrewd
sage, n.m. sage; adj. wise, good
sage-femme, n.f. midwife
sagesse, n.f. wisdom
saignée, n.f. bleeding
saigner, vb. to bleed
saillant, adj. prominent, projecting
saillie, n.f. projection
saillir, vb. to protrude
sain, adj. health, sound
saindoux, n.m. lard
saint, n.m. saint; adj. holy
Saint-Esprit, n.m. Holy Ghost
sainteté, n.f. holiness
saisie, n.f. seizure
saisir, vb. to grasp, snatch, grab
saisissement, n.m. chill, seizure
saison, n.f. season
salade, n.f. salad
saladier, n.m. dish, salad bowl
salaire, n.m. wages, earnings, pay

salarié, adj. salaried; n.m.f. person earning a salary
sale, adj. dirty
saler, vb. to salt
saleté, n.f. dirt
salin, adj. salt, salty
salir, vb. to get dirty
salive, n.f. saliva
salle, n.f. large room, hall, hospital ward; **s. de. classe,** classroom
salon, n.m. parlor
salubre, adj. healthful
salubrité, n.f. healthfulness
saluer, vb. to greet, salute
salut, n.m. bow, salute; salvation
salutaire, adj. wholesome, beneficial
salutation, n.f. greeting
salve, n.f. salute
samedi, n.m. Saturday
sanctifier, vb. to hallow
sanction, n.f. sanction
santionner, vb. to sanction
sanctuaire, n.m. sanctuary
sandale, n.f. sandal
sang, n.m. blood
sang-froid, n.m. calmness, composure
sanglant, adj. bloody
sangler, vb. to strap, fasten
sanglier, n.m. wild boar
sanglot, n.m. sob
sangloter, vb. to sob
sangsue, n.f. leech
sanguinaire, adj. bloodthirsty
sanitaire, adj. sanitary
sans, prep. without, out of
sans-souci, adj. carefree, careless
santé, n.f. health
saper, vb. to sap, weaken
saphir, n.m. sapphire
sapin, n.m. fir
sarcasme, n.m. sarcasm
sarcastique, adj. sarcastic
sarcler, vb. to weed, root out
sardine, n.f. sardine
sardonique, adj. sardonic
satanique, adj. satanic
satellite, n.m. satellite

satin, n.m. satin
satire, n.f. satire
satiriser, vb. to satirize
satisfaction, n.f. satisfaction
satisfaire, vb. to satisfy
satisfaisant, adj. satisfactory
saturer, vb. to saturate
sauce, n.f. sauce, **s. piquante,** catsup
saucisse, n.f. sausage
sauf, prep. but; adj. safe
sauge, n.f. sage
saugrenu, adj. preposterous
saule, n.f. willow
saumon, n.m. salmon
saumure, n.f. brine
saut, n.m. spring, jump
saute, n.f. wind shift
sauter, vb. to spring, jump, leap,
sauterelle, n.f. grasshopper
sautiller, vb. to hop
sauvage, n.m.f. savage; adj. savage
sauvegarde, n.f. safeguard
sauve-qui-peut, n.m. stampede
sauver, vb. to save; **se s.,** run away
sauvetage, n.m. salvage
sauveur, n.m. savior, Saviour
savane, n.f. prairie
savant, n.m. scholar; adj. learned
saveur, n.f. flavor, zest
savoir, vb. to now, be aware, have knowledge; n.m. knowledge
savoir-faire, n.m. pose, ability
savon, n.m. soap
savonner, vb. to soap, lather
savourer, vb. to relish
savoureux, adj. tasty
scabreux, adj. rough, harsh
scalper, vb. to scalp
scandale, n.m. scandal
scandaleux, adj. scandalous
scandaliser, vb. to shock
scander, vb. to scan
Scandinave, n.m.f. Scandinavian
Scandinavie, n.f. Scandinavia
scarabée, n.m. beetle
scarlatine, n.f. scarlet fever
sceau, n.m. seal

scélérate, n.m. vilain, criminal, knave, ruffian
sceller, vb. to seal
scène, n.f. scene, stage
scénique, adj. scenic
scepticisme, n.m. skepticism
sceptre, n.m. scepter
schampooing, n.m. shampoo
schisme, n.m. schism
scie, n.f. saw
science, n.f. science
science-fiction, n.f. science fiction
scientifique, adj. scientific
scier, vb. to saw
scinder, vb. divide
scintiller, vb. to twinkle
scission, n.f. cutting
scolaire, adj. scholstic. **système s.,** school system
scolastique, adj. scholastic
scrupule, n.m. scruple
scrupuleux, adj. scrupulous
scruter, vb. to scan, scrutinize
scrutin, n.m. ballot, poll
sculpter, vb. to carve
sculpteur, n.f. sculptor
sculpture, n.f. sculpture
se, pron. himself, herself, each other, oneself, themselves
séance, n.f. sitting, session; meeting
séant, adj. sitting, proper
seau, n.m. pail, bucket
sec m., sèche f. adj. dry
sécession, n.f. secession
sécher, vb. to dry
sécheresse, n.f. dryness, drought
second, n.f. second
secondaire, adj. secondary
seconde, n.f. second
seconder, vb. to support, help
secouer, vb. to shake, rouse
secourir, vb. to relieve, help
secours, n.m. help, relief; **premiers s.,** first aid
secousse, n.f. jar, shock
secret, adj. and n.m. secret
secrétaire, n.m.f. secretary

sécréter, vb. to secrete
sectaire, adj. sectarian
secte, n.f. sect
secteur, n.m. district, sector
section, n.f. section
sectionner, vb. to cut into sections
séculier, adj. lay
sécurité, n.f. safety
sédatif, adj. and n.m. sedative
sédentaire, adj. stationary
sédition, n.f. seditiion
séduction, n.f. seduction
séduire, vb. to seduce, attract, allure
séduisant, adj. attractive
segment, n.m. segment
ségrégation, n.f. segregation
seigle, n.m. rye
seigneur, n.m. lord, peer
seigneurie, n.f. lordship
sein, n.m. bosom, breast
seize, adj. and n.m. sixteen
seizième, adj. and n.m. sixteenth
séjour, n.m. stay
sel, n.m. salt
sélection, n.f. selection
selle, n.f. saddle
seller, vb. to saddle
selon, prep. according to
seltz, n.m. **eau de s.,** soda water
semailles, n.f., pl. sowing
semaine, n.f. weekly pay
semblable, adj. similar, alike
semblant, n.m. show; appearance
sembler, vb. to seem, appear
semelle, n.f. sole
semence, n.f. seed
semer, vb. to sow
semestre, n.m. semester
semeur, n.m. sower
sémillance, n.f. briskness
semoncer, vb. to lecture
sénat, n.m. senate
sénateur, n.m. senator
sénile, adj. senile
sénilité, n.f. senility
sens, n.m. meaning, direction; sense
sensation, n.f. sensation, feeling
sensationnel, adj. sensational

sensé, adj. sensible
sensibilité, n.f. sensitivity
sensible, adj. sensible, sensitive
sensitif, adj. sensitive
sensuel, adj. sensual
sentence, n.f. sentence
sentencieux, adj. sententious
senteur, n.f. smell
sentier, n.m. path
sentiment, n.m. feeling
sentimental, adj. sentimental
sentinelle, n.f. sentry
sentir, vb. to feel; smell
séparable, adj. separable
séparation, n.f. separation, parting
séparé, adj. separate
séparer, vb. to separate, segregate
septembre, n.m. September
septième, adj and n.m. seventh
septique, adj. septic
séquestrer, vb. to withdraw, remove
serein, adj. serene, placid
sérénade, n.f. serenade
sérénité, n.f. serenity
sergent, n.m. sergeant
série, n.f. series
sérieux, adj. serious, sober, grave; n.m. gravity
serin, n.m. canary
seringue, n.f. syringe
serment, n.m. oath
sermon, n.m. sermon
sermonner, vb. to lecture, preach
serpent, n.m. serpent, snake
serpenter, vb. to wind, wander
serre, n.f. greenhouse; claw
serré, adj. tight
serr-joint, n.m. clamp
serrer, vb. to tighten, squeeze, press, crowd, shake hands
serrure, n.f. lock
sérum, n.m. serum
servant, adj. serving; n.m. server
servante, n.f. maid
serviable, adj. helpful
service, n.m. service, favor
serviette, n.f. napkin; towel
servile, adj. menial

servir, vb. to serve

sevrage, n.m. weaning

serviteur, n.m. attendant, servant

servitude, n.f. slavery

session, n.f. session

seuil, n.m. threshold

seul, adj. alone, only, single

seulement, adv. only, solely

sève, n.f. sap

sévère, adj. sever, stern

sévérité, n.f. severity, rigor

sévir, vb. to punish, rage

sevrer, vb. to wean, withhold

sexe, n.m. sex

sexisune, n.m. sexism

sexiste, adj. sexist

sexuel, adj. sexual

seyant, adj. becoming

shoot, n.m. shot

short, n.m. shorts

shrapnel, n.m. shrapnel

shunt, n.m. shunt

si, conj. if whether, supposing

sicaire, n.m. hired assassin

siècle, n.m. century

siège, n.m. seat; siege

siéger, vb. to sit, convene, reside

sien, pron. le sien, la sienne, hers, his, its

sieste, n.f. siesta

siffler, vb. to whistle, hiss

sifflerie, n.f. hissing, whistling

sifflet, n.m. whistle

signal, n.m. signal

signalement, n.m. description, details

signaler, vb. to point out

signature, n.f. signature

signe, n.m. sign

signer, vb. to sign; se s., cross oneself

significatif, adj. significant, meaningful

signification, n.f. significance, meaning

signifier, vb. to signify, mean

silence, n.m. silence

silencieux, adj. noiseless, silent

silex, n.m. fling

silhouette, n.f. outline, profile

sillage, n.m. wake, course

sillon, n.m. furrow made with a plough

sillonner, vb. to plow

simagrée, n.f. pretence

similaire, adj. similar

simple, adj. plain, simple, mere

simplicité, n.f. simplicity

simplifier, vb. to simplify

simulation, n.f. simulation

simuler, vb. to pretend

simultané, adj. simultaneous

sincère, adj. candid, sincerity

singe, n.m. imitator

singularité, n.f. singularity; peculiar

singulier, adj. and n.m. singular; peculiar, strange

sinistre, n.m. disaster; adj. sinister

sinon, conj. otherwise

sinueux, adj. winding, sinuous

sirène, n.f. siren

sirop, n.m. syrup

siroter, vb. to sip

site, n.m. site

sitôt, adv. as soon as

situation, n.f. situation, office, position, location,

situer, vb. to situate, locate

six, adj. and n.m. six

sixième, adj. and n.m. sixth

ski, n.m. ski

smoking, n.m. dinner jacket, tux

sobre, adj. temperate, sober

sobriété, n.f. moderation, temperance

sobriquet, n.m. nickname

sociable, adj. sociable

social, adj. social

socialisme, n.m. socialism

socialiste, adj. and n.m.f. socaliste

société, n.f. society; company

sociologie, n.f. sociology

sociologiste, n.m. sociologist

soeur, n.f. sister

soie, n.f. silk goods

soif, n.f. thirst; avoir s., be thirsty

soigné, adj. trim; mal s., sloppy

soigner, vb. to tend, take care of, look

after

soir, n.m. evening; **ce s.,** tonight; **hier s.,** last night; **le s.,** at night

soirée, n.f. evening

soixantaine, adj. and n.m. about sixty

soixante-dix, adj. and n.m. seventy

sol, n.m. earth, soil, ground

solaire, adj. solar

soldat, n.m. soldier

solde, n.m. balance

sole, n.f. sole

soleil, n.m. sun, shunshine

solennel, adj. solemn

solenniser, vb. to solemnize

solennité, n.f. solemnity

solidariser, vb. **se s.,** to join together, unite

solidarité, n.f. joint responsibility

solide, adj. and n.m. solid

solidifier, vb. to solidify

solidité, n.f. solidity

soliloque, n.m. soliloquy

soliste, n.m. solosit

solitaire, adj. lonely, lonesome

solitude, n.f. solitude

solliciter, vb. to solicit, ask, apply

sollicitude, n.f. solicitude

soluble, adj. soluble

solution, n.f. solution

solvable, adj. solvent

sombre, adj. dark, somber, dim, gloomy

sombrer, vb. to sink

sommaire, n.m. summary

sommation, n.f. appeal, summons

somme, n.f. amount, sum; n.m. lap

sommeil, n.m. sleep

sommeiller, vb. to doze, slumber

sommer, vb. to summon

sommet, n.m. top, peak, summit

somnolence, n.f. drowsiness

somnolent, adj. drowsy, sleepy

somptueux, adj. lavish, sumptuous

son, n.m. sound, ring; bran; adj. his, hers, its

sonder, vb. to fathom; probe

songe, n.m. dream

songer à, vb. to think of, dream

songeur, adj. dreamy, thoughtful; n.m. dreamer

sonner, vb. to ring, sound, strike

sonnerie, n.f. ringing

sonnette, n.f. bell

sonore, adj. sonorous

sophiste, n.m. sophist

soprano, n.m. soprano

sorcier, n.m. wizard

sorcière, n.f. witch

sordide, adj. sordid

sort, n.m. lot

sorte, n.f. sort, kind

sortie, n.f. exit, way yout

sortilège, n.m. sorcery

sottise, n.f. foolishness

sou, n.m. cent; **sans le s.,** penniless

soubassement, n.m. basement

soubresaut, n.m. bound, jerk

souche, n.f. stub, stump

souci, n.m. care, worry, concern

soucieux, adj. anxious

soucoupe, n.f. saucer

soudain, adj. sudden

soudaineté, n.f suddenness

soude, n.f. soda

souder, vb. to solder, fuse

souffle, n.m. breath

souffler, vb. to blow

soufflet, n.m. bellows; blow, slap

souffleter, vb. to slap oneś face

souffrir, vb. to suffer, bear

sourfre, n.m. sulphur

souhait, n.m. wish

souhaiter, vb. to wish for

souiller, vb. to soil, defile

souillure, n.f. stain, dirt

soulager, vb. to relieve, alleviate

soûler, vb. to fill with food and drink

soulever, vb. to lift, raise, arouse

soulier, n.m. shoe

souligner, vb. to underline

soumettre, vb. to submit, subdue

soumis, adj. obedient, submissive

soumission, n.f. submission

soupape, n.f. valve

soupçon, n.m. suspicion

soupconneur, vb. to suspect	**spatule**, n.f. spatula
soupconneux, adj. suspicious	**spécial**, adj. special
soupe, n.f. soup	**spécialiser**, vb. to specialize
souper, n.m. supper	**spécialiste**, n.m.f. specialist
soupir, n.m. sigh	**spécialité**, n.f. specialty
soupirer, vb. to sigh	**spécifier**, vb. to specify
souple, adj. flexible	**spécifique**, adj. specific
souplesse, n.f. suppleness, pliability	**spécimen**, n.m. specimen
source, n.f. source; spring	**spectacle**, n.m. sight, show
sourcil, n.m. eyebrow	**spectaculaire**, adj. spectacular
sourciller, vb. to frown	**spectateur**, n.m. spectator
sourcilleux, adj. haughty, disdainful	**spectre**, n.m. ghost; spectrum
sourd, adj. deaf	**spéculation**, n.f. speculation
sourd-muet, n.m. deaf mute	**spéculer**, vb. to speculate
souricière, n.f. mouse trap	**sphère**, n.f. sphrer
sourire, n.m. and vb. smile	**spinal**, adj. spinal
souris, n.f. mouse	**spiral**, adj. spiral
sournois, adj. sly	**spirale**, n.f. spiral
sous, prep. under	**spirite**, n.m.f. spiritualist
souscription, n.f. subscription	**spiritisme**, n.m. spiritualism
souscrire, vb. to subscribe	**spirituel**, adj. spiritual; witty
sous-estimer, vb. to underestimate	**splendeur**, n.f. splendor
sous-louer, vb. to sublet	**splendide**, adj. splendid
sous-marin, n.m. submarine	**spontané**, adj. spontaneous
soussigné, adj. undersigned	**spontanéité**, n.f. spontaneity
sous-sol, n.m. basement	**sporadique**, adj. sporadic
sous-titre, n.m. subtitle	**sport**, n.m. sport
soustraction, n.f. subraction	**sportif**, adj. of sport
soustraire, vb. to subtract	**squelette**, n.m. skeleton
soustane, n.f. cassock	**stabiliser**, vb. to stabilize
soute, n.f. storeroom	**stabilité**, n.f. stability
soutenir, vb. to support, uphold, back up, maintain; claim	**stable**, adj. stable, steady
soutenu, adj. steady	**stage**, n.m. priod of probation
souterrain, adj. underground	**stagnant**, adj. stagnant
soutien, n.m. support	**stalle**, n.f. stall
soutien-gorge, n.m. brassiere	**stance**, n.f. stanza
souvenance, n.f. recall, recollection	**station**, n.f. stand, stop
souvenir, n.m. remberance, memory	**stationnaire**, adj. stationary
souvent, adv. often	**stationner**, vb. to park
souverain, n.m. ruler, sovereign	**statique**, adj. static
souveraineté, n.f. sovereignty	**statistique**, n.f. statistics
soyeux, adj. silky	**statue**, n.f. statue
spacieux, adj. spacious	**statuer**, vb. to decree, decide
spasme, n.m. spasm	**stature**, n.f. stature
	statut, n.m. statute
	sténographe, n.m.f. stenographer
	sténographie, n.f. stenography

stéréophonique, adj. sterophonic

stérile, adj. barren

stériliser, vb. to sterlize

stéthoscope, n.m. stethoscope

stigmatiser, vb. to mark, stigmatize

stimulant, n.m. stimulus

stimuler, vb. to stimulate

stipuler, vb. to stipulate

stoïque, adj. and n.m.f. stole

store, n. m. window shade, blind

stratagème, n.m. stratagem

stratégie, n.f. strategy

stratégique, adj. strategic

strict, adj. severe, strict

strier, vb. to mark, streak, make grooves

structure, n.f. structure

stuc, n.m. stucco

studieux, adj. studious

stupéfait, adj. astounded

stupéfiant, n.m. dope, narcotic

stupéfier, vb. to astound

stupeur, n.f. amazement

stupide, adj. stupid

stupidité, n.f. stupidity

style, n.m. style

styler, vb. to rain, teach

subdiviser, vb. to subdivide

subir, vb. to undergo

subit, adj. sudden

subjectif, adj. subjective

subjonctif, adj. and n.m. sub-junctive

subjuguer, vb. to subdue; overcome

sublime, adj. sublime, exalted

submerger, vb. to submerge, flood

subordonné, adj. and n.m. sub-ordinate

subreptice, adj. surreptitious

subséquent, adj. subsequent

subside, n.m. subsidy

subsister, vb. to subsist, live

substance, n.f. substance

substantiel, adj. substantial

substantif, n.m. noun

substituer, vb. to substitute

substitution, n.f. substitution

subtil, adj. subtle

subtillité, n.f. subtlety

subvention, n.f. grant, subsidy

subventionner, vb. to subsidize

subversif, adj. subversive

suc, n.m. juice

succéder à, vb. to succeed, follow

succès, n.m. success; hit

successeur, n.m. successor

successif, adj. successive

succession, n.f. succession

succion, n.f. suction

succursale, n.f. branch office

sucer, vb. to suck

sucre, n.m. sugar

sud, n.m. south

sudation, n.f. sweating

sud-est, n.m. southeast

sud-ouest, n.m. southwest

Suède, n.f. Sweden

Suédois, n.m. Swede

suédois, adj. and n.m. Swedish

suer, vb. to sweat

sueur, n.m. sweat

suffire, vb. to suffice

suffisance, n.f. adequacy, conceit

suffisant, adj. sufficient, adequate

suffixe, n.m. suffix

suffoquer, vb. to suffocate

suffrage, n.m. suffrage

suggérer, vb. to suggest

suggestion, n.f. suggestion

suicide, n.m. suicide

suicider, vb. se s., to kill oneself

suif, n.m. tallow

suniter, vb. to seep

Suisse, n.m. Swiss; n.f. Switzerland

suisse, adj. Swiss

suite, n.f. sequence; retinue

suivant, n.m. follower; adj. next, following, subsequent

suivre, vb. to follow; attend; **faire s.**, forward

sujet, n.m. subject; topic; adj. subject; **s. à**, liable to

sujétion, n.f. subjection, slavery

superbe, adj. superb, magnificent

superficie, n.f. surface

superficiel, adj. superficial, shallow

superflu, adj. superfluous
supérieur, adj. and n.m. higher,
  superior
supériorité, n.f. superiority
superlatif, adj. and n.m. superlative
superstar, n.m. superstar
superstitieux, adj. superstitious
superstition, n.f. superstition
suppléant, adj. and n.m. assistant, substitute
suppléer, vb. to substitute
supplément, n.m. supplement
supplémentaire, adj. extra; **heures
  s.s,** overtime
supplice, n.m. punishment, torture
supplier, vb. to beseech, supplicate
support, n.m. support, stand
supporter, vb. to support, bear, stand,
  endure
supposer, vb. to suppose, assume
supposition, n.f. assumption,
  supposition
suppôt, n.m. implement, tool, agent
suppression, n.f. suppression
supprimer, vb. to suppress, put down,
  take out
supputation, n.f. computation
supputer, vb. to compute
suprématie, n.f. supremacy
suprême, adj. supreme
sur, prep. on, upon. over
sûr, adj. safe, sure, secure
surabonder, vb. to be very abundant
suranné, adj. out-of-date
surcroît, n.m. addition
surdité, n.f. deafness
suret, adj. sour
sureté, n.f. safety, security,
  reliability
surface, n.f. surface, area
surgélateur, n.m. deep freeze
sugir, vb. to spring up, arise
surintendant, n.m. superintendent
sur-le-champ, adv. immediately, at
  once
surmener, vb. to overwork
surmonter, vb. to overcome, surmount
surnaturel, adj. and n.m. super-
  natural

surnom, n.m. nickname
surpasser, vb. to surpass
surplomber, vb. to overhang
surplus, n.m. surplus, excess
surprendre, vb. to surprise
surprise, n.f. surprise
sursaut, n.m. start
sursauter, vb. to give a start
sursis, n.m. delay, putting off
surveillance, n.f. supervision, watch
surveillant, n.m. superintendent
surveiller, vb. to supervise
survenir, vb. to happen
survie, n.f. survival
survivance, n.f. survival
survivre, vb. to survive
susceptible, adj. liable
suspect, adj. suspicious
suspecter, vb. to suspect
suspendre, vb. to suspend, sling
suspension, n.f. suspension
suspicion, n.f. suspicion
sustenter, vb. to sustain, bulwark,
  support, maintain
svelte, adj. slender, slim
sycomore, n.m. Sycamore
syllabaire, n.m. spelling book
syllable, n.f. syllable
sylvicole, adj. living in the woods
sylviculture, n.f. forestry
symbole, n.m. symbol, sign, emblem,
  creed
symboliser, vb. to symbolize
symétrie, n.f. symmetry
sympathie, n.f. sympathy; **avoir
  de la s. pour,** like
sympathique, adj. likeable
sympathisant, n.m. fellow traveler
sympathiser, vb. to sympathize
symphonie, n.f. symphony
symptôme, n.m. symptom
syndrome, n.m. syndrome
synonyme, n.m. synonym
synthèse, n.f. synthesis
synthétique, adj. synthetic
systématique, adj. systematic
système, n.m. system

tabac, n.m. tobacco
table, n.f. table
tableau, n.m. picture
tabler, vb. to count, on depend
tablette, n.f. tablet
tablier, n.m. apron
tabou, n.m. taboo
tabouret, n.m. stool
tache, n.f. spot, blot, smear
tâche, n.f. task; assignment
tacher, vb. to spot, stain, blot
tâcher, vb. to try
tacite, adj. silent
tact, n.m. tact
tacticien, n.m. tactician
tactique, adj. of tactics; n.f. tactics
taffetas, n.m. taffeta
taie, n.f. pillowcase
taillade, n.f. slash
taille, n.f. waist, figure, size
tailler, vb. to trim, cut
tailleur, n.m. tailor
taire, vb. to keep quiet
talent, n.m. ability, talent
talon, n.m. heel
talus, n.m. slope
tambour, n.m. drum
tambourin, n.m. tambourine
tamis, n.m. sieve
tampon, n.m. plug, pad
tamponner, vb. to plug; run together
tan, n.m. tan leather
tandis que, conj. whereas, while
tangible, adj. tangible
tant, adv. so many, so much; t. que, as long as
tante, n.f. aunt
tantième, n.m. part, percentage
tantôt, adv. presently, soon
tapage, n.m. din
tapageur, adj. rowdy
taper, vb. to pat, tap; type
tapis, n.m. carpet, rug
tapisserie, n.f. tapestry
tapissier, n.m. upholsterer
taquiner, vb. to tease
taquinerie, n.f. teasing
tard, adv. late

tarder, vb. to delay
tardif, adj. slow, tardy, late
tarif, n.m. scale of charges
tartan, n.m. plaid
tarte, n.f. pie
tartre, n.m. tartar
tas, n.m. heap, pile
tasse, n.f. cup
tasser, vb. to pack, fill up
tâter, vb. to feel
taupe, n.f. mole
taureau, n.m. bull
taux, n.m. rate
taverne, n.f. tavern
taxe, n.f. tax
taxer, vb. to tax, assess
taxi, n.m. cab, taxi
te, pron. you, yourself
technicien, n.m. technician
technique, n.f. technique; adj. technical
technologie, n.f. technology
teindre, vb. to dye
teint, n.m. complexion
teinte, n.f. tint, shade
teinter, vb. to tint, stain
teinturier, n.m. dry-cleaner
tel, adj. such
télégramme, n.m. telegram
télégraphe, n.m. telegraph
télégraphie, n.f. telegraphy
télégraphier, vb. to telegraph
téléphone, n.m. telephone
téléphoner, vb. to telephone
télescope, n.m. telescope
télescoper, vb. to crash
télévision, n.f. television
tellement, adv. so much
téméraire, adj. rash
témoignage, n.m. testimony
témoigner, vb. to testify
témoin, n.m. witness
tempe, n.f. temple
tempérament, n.m. temperament
tempérant, adj. temperate
température, n.f. temperature
tempéré, adj. temperate
température, n.f. temperature

tempérer, vb. to moderate, calm
tempête, n.f. storm, tempest
tempétueux, adj. tempestuous
temple, n.m. temple
temporaire, adj. temporary
temporiser, vb. to temporize, evade
temps, n.m. time, weather
tenance, adj. tenacious
ténacité, n.f. tenacity
tenailles, n.f., pl. tongs
tendance, n.f. tendency, trend
tendre, adj. tender, fond, loving; vb. tend, extend
tendresse, n.f. fondness, tenderness
tendu, adj. tense; uptight
ténèbres, n.f, pl. gloom, darkness
ténébreux, adj. dismal
teneur, n.m. t. de livres, bookkeeper
tenir, vb. to hold
tennis, n.m. tennis
ténor, n.m. tenor
tension, n.f. strin; stress
tentacule, n.m. tentacle
tentatif, adj. tentative
tentative, n.f. attempt
tente, n.f. tent; awning
tenter, vb. to tempt, try, attract
tenture, n.f. wallcovering
tenue, n.f. rig; conduct, manners
ténuité, n.f. tenuity, unimportance
térébenthine, n.f. turpentine
terme, n.m. term, period; end
terminaison, n.f. ending
terminer, vb. to end
terminologie, n.f. terminology
terne, adj. drab, dull, dim, dingy
ternir, vb. to tarnish, dull
terrain, n.m. grounds
terrasse, n.f. terrace
terrasser, vb. to conquer, heap up, embank; knock down
terre, n.f. ground, earth, land
terrestre, adj. earthly
terreur, n.f. terror, fright, fear
terrible, adj. terrible, awful
terrifier, vb. to terrify
territoire, n.m. territory
terroir, n.m. soil

terroriser, vb. to terrorize
tertre, n.m. mound
tesson, n.m. broken piece, fragment
testament, n.m. testament, will
tête, n.f. head
téter, vb. to suck
teton, n.m. breast
texte, n.m. text
textile, adj. textile
thé, n.m. tea
théâtral, adj. theatrical
théâtre, n.m. theater
théière, n.f. teapot
thème, n.m. theme
théologie, n.f. theology
théorie, n.f. theory
théorique, adj. theoretical
thermomètre, n.m. thermometer
thésauriser, vb. to hoard
thèse, n.f. thesis
thym, n.m. thyme
ticket, n.m. ticket, check, coupon
tiède, adj. lukewarm
tiédir, vb. to make or become cool
tien, pron. le tien, la tienne, yours
tiers, n.m. third
tige, n.f. stem, stalk
tigre, n.m. tiger
tilleul, n.m. linden, limetree
timbre, n.m. stamp; t-poste, postage stamp
timbrer, vb. to stamp
timide, adj. timid, shy, bashful
timidité, n.f. timidity
tintamarre, n.m. racket
tinter, vb. to ring, knell, tinkle
tirailleur, n.m. sharpshooter
tire, n.m. yank, pull
tirer, vb. to draw, pull; shoot
tiret, n.m. blank
tiroir, n.m. drawer
tisane, n.f. drink
tisser, vb. to weave
tisserand, n.m. weaver
tissu, n.m. web; cloth, fabric
titre, n.m. title, right
toast (-t), n.m. toast
toile, n.f. web; canvas; linen

toilette, n.f. toilet; dressing, dress

toison, n.f. fleece

toit, n.m. roof

toiture, n.f. roofing

tolérance, n.f. tolerance

tolérer, vb. to tolerate, bear

tomate, n.f. tomato

tombe, n.f. grave

tombeau, n.m. tomb

tombée, n.f. fall, decline

tomber, vb. to fall; **laisser t.,** drop

ton, n.m. tone, pitch

tondeuse, n.f. lawn mower

tondre, vb. to mow; shear

tonne, n.f. ton; barrel

tonneau, n.m. cask, barrel

tonner, vb. to thunder

topaze, n.f. topaz

torche, n.f. torch

tordre, vb. to twist, wrench, wring

torpille, n.f. torpedo

torrent, n.m. torrent

torride, adj. torrid

torse, n.m. torso

tort, n.m. wrong

tortiller, vb. to twist, wiggle

tortu, adj. crooked

tortue, n.f. turtle, tortoise

torture, n.f. torture

torturer, vb. to torture

tôt, adv. early, soon

totalisateur, n.m. adding machine

totaliser, vb. to total, add up

totalité, n.f. entirety

touchant, prep. concerning

touche, n.f. key

touffe, n.f. tuft, bunch

touffu, adj. bushy

toujours, adv. always, ever, yet

tour, n.m. turn; trick; stroll; **faire le t de,** go around

tourbe, n.f. rabble

tourbillon, n.m. whirl; **t. d'eau,** whirlpool

tourbilloner, vb. to whirl

tourelle, n.f. turret

touriste, n.m.f. tourist

tourment, n.m. torment

tourmenter, vb. to torment

tourne-disques, n.m. record player

tournée, n.f. round

tourner, vb. to turn, revolve

tournesol, n.m. sunflower

tournevis, n.m. screwdriver

tournoi, n.m. tournament

tournure, n.f. figure

tousser, vb. to cough

toutefois, adv. however

tout-puissant, adj. almighty

toux, n.f. cough

toxique, adj. toxic

tracasser, vb. to worry

trace, n.f. trace, track, footprint

tracer, vb. to outline, trace

tracteur, n.m. tractor

tradition, n.f. tradition

traditionnel, adj. traditional

traducteur, n.m. translator

traduction, n.f. translation

traduire, vb. to translate

trafic, n.m. traffic

tragédie, n.f. tragedy

tragique, adj. tragic

trahir, vb. to betray

trahison, n.f. treason

train, n.m. train

traînard, n.m. dawdler

traîne, n.f. train of a dress

traîneau, n.m. sled sleigh

traîner, vb. to drag, haul

traire, vb. to milk

trait, n.m. feature; draft; shot

traité, n.m. treaty

traitement, n.m. treatment

traiter, vb. to treat, deal

traître, n.m. traitor

traîtrise, n.f. treachery

trajet, n.m. crossing

trame, n.f. plan, plot

tramer, vb. to devise

tramway, n.m. streetcar

tranchant, adj. sharp, crisp

tranche, n.f. slice

tranchée, n.f. trench

trancher, vb. to cut

tranquille, adj. quiet
tranquilliser, vb. to make tranquil
tranquillité, n.f. quiet, stillness
transaction, n.f. transaction
transe, n.f. fright, fear
transférer, vb. to transfer
transformer, vb. to transform
transfuser, vb. to transfuse
transfusion, n.f. transfusion
transition, n.f. transition
transitoire, adj. transitory
transmettre, vb. to transmit, convey
transparent, adj. transparent
transpiration, n.f. perspiration
transpirer, vb. to perspire
transplanter, vb. to transplant
transport, n.m. transfer, transport, transportation; ecstasy
transporter, vb. to transport, transfer, convery
transposer, vb. to transpose
transsexuel, adj. transsexual
travail, n.m. work, job, labor
travailler, vb. to work
travailleur, n.m. worker, laborer; adj. industrious
travée, n.f. span
travers, n.m. breadth; **à t.,** across, through; **de t.,** awry
traversée, n.f. crossing
traverser, vb. to cross
traversin, n.m. bolster
travestir, vb. to disguise
trébucher, vb. to stumble, trip
treillis, n.m. denim
treize, adj. and n.m. thirteen
tremblement, n.m. trembling
trembler, vb. to tremble, quake, shake
trembloter, vb. to quiver
trémousser, vb. to flutter
trempe, n.f. temper, cast
tremper, vb. to soak, drench, temper
trente, adj. and n.m. thirty
trépasser, vb. to die
trépied, n.m. tripod, trivet
très, adv. very
trésor, n.m. treasure, treasury
trésorier, n.m. treasurer

tressaillement, n.m. thrill; start
tressaillir, vb. to thrill; start
tresse, n.f. braid
tresser, vb. to braid
tréteau, n.m. trestle
trêve, n.f. truce
triangle, n.m. triangle
tribade, n.f. Lesbian
tribu, n.f. tribe
tribulation, n.f. tribulation
tribut, n.m. tribute
tributaire, adj. tributary
tricher, vb. to cheat
tricherie, n.f. cheating
tricoter, vb. to knit
trier, vb. to sort
trimestre, n.m. term
trimestriel, adj. quarterly
triomphant, adj. triumphant
triomphe, n.m. triumph
triompher, vb. to triumph
triple, adj. and n.m. triple
triste, adj. sad
tristesse, n.f. sadness
trivial, adj. trivial
trivialité, n.f. triviality
troc, n.m. barter
trois, adj. and n.m. three
troisième, adj. third
trompe, n.f. horn
tromperie, n.f. deceit
trompette, n.f. trumpet
trompeur, adj. deceitful
tronc, n.m. trunk
trône, n.m. throne
trop, adv. too much; too
trophée, n.m. trophy
tropical, adj. tropical
tropique, n.m. tropic
troquer, vb. to barter, trade
trot, n.m. trot
trotter, vb. to trot
trottiner, vb. to trot, jog
trottoir, n.m. sidewalk
trou, n.m. hole
trouble, n.m. disturbance, riot
troublé, adj. anxious, worried
troubler, vb. to perturb

trouer, vb. to pierce
troupe, n.f. troop
troupeau, n.m. herd, flock. drove
troupier, n.m. soldier
trousseau, n.m. outfit
trousser, vb. to turn up
trouvaille, n.f. discovery; finding
trouver, vb. to find, discover
truc, n.m. trick; thing
truelle, n.f. trowel
truite, n.f. trout
truquer, vb. to fake
trust, n.m. trust
tu, pron., you
tuant, adj. exhausting, tiresome, killing
tub, n.m. tub
tuba, n.m. tuba
tube, n.m. tube, pipe
tuberculeux, adj. tuberculous
tuberculose, n.f. tuberculosis
tubulaire, adj. tubular
tubesque, adj. rough, coarse
tuer, vb. to slay; kill, slaughter
tuerie, n.f. slaughter, massacre
tueur, n.m. slayer, thug, killer
tuile, n.f. tile
tulipe, n.f. tulip
tuméfier, vb. to make swollen
tumeur, n.f. tumor
tumulte, n.m. turmoil, uproar, confusion
tunnel, n.m. tunnel
turbin, n.m. work
turbine, n.f. turbine
turbulence, n.f. tubulence
turc, adj. Turkish
turlutaine, n.f. a sentence or word that a person likes to repeat
turne, n.f. dirty, unorderly house
tunique, n.f. tunic
tunnel, n.f. tunnel
turc, m., **turque** f. adj. Turkish language
turnep, n.m. field turnip
Turquie, n.f. Turkey
turquin, adj. dark, deep blue
tutelle, n.f. protection

tuteur, n.m. guardian; trustee, protector
tutu, n.m. short ballet skirt
tuyau, n.f. pipe; hose; tube
tympan, n.m. eardrum
type, n.m. model, type, pattern; sample
typhus, n.m. typhus
typique, adj. typical, symbolical
tyran, n.m. tyrant
tyrannie, n.f. tyranny
tyranniser, vb. to tyrannize; oppress
tzigane, n. gypsy

U

ulcère, n.m. ulcer
ultfieur, adj. ulterior, further
ultime, adj. ultimate
umanime, adj. unanimous
umanimité, n.f. unanimity
unifier, vb. to unify
uniforme, adj. uniform
union, n.f. union
unique, adj. unique
unir, vb. to unite
unisexuel, adj. unisex
unisson, n.m. unison
unité, n.f. unit, unity
univers, n.m. universe
universel, adj. universal
université, n.f. university, college
urbain, adj. urban
urgence, n.f. urgency
urgent, adj. urgent, pressing
urticaire, n.m. hives
usage, n.m. use; custom
usager, adj. for daily use
user, vb. to make use of, wear out
usine, n.f. factory
ustensile, n.f. utensil
usuel, adj. usual
usure, n.f. wear and tear
utile, adj. helpful, useful
utilisation, n.f. use
utopie, n.f. utopia

vacance, n. vacancy
vacant, adj. vacant
vacarme, n.m. uproar, racket
vaccin, n.m. vaccine
vacciner, vb. to vaccinate, immunize
vache, n.f. cow; cow hide
vaciller, vb. to waver, flicker
vacuité, n.f. emptiness, vacuity
vagabond, adj. vagrant
vagabonder, vb. to roam, tramp
vague, n.f. wave; adj. vague
vaguer, vb. to wander
vaillant, adj. brave, gallant
vain, adj. idle, futile
vaincre, vb. to defeat
vainqueur, n.m. victor
vaisseau, n.m. ship
vaisselle, n.f. dishes
valeur, n.f. value, worth
valeureux, adj. brave, valorous
valide, adj. valid
valise, n.f. suitcase
vallée, n.f. valley
vallon, n.m. valley, vale
valoir, vb. to be worth
vaise, n.f. waltz
vandale, n.m.f. vandal
vanille, n.f. vanilla
vanité, n.f. conceit, vanity
vaniteux, adj. vain
vantard, adj. boastful
vapeur, n.m. steamship
vaporisateur, n.f. vaporizer, spray
variation, n.f. variation, change
varicelle, n.f. chicken-pox
varier, vb. to vary
variété, n.f. variety
variole, n.f. smallpox
vase, n.m. vase, vessel
vasectomie, n.f. vasectomy
vaseux, adj. slimy
vassal, n.f. vassal
vaste, adj. vast, spacious
veau, n.m. calf
végéter, vb. to vegetate
véhicule, n.m. vehicle
veille, n.f. eve, day before
veiller, vb. to watch over, sit up

veine, n.f. vein; luck
velours, n.m. velvet
velouté, adj. like velvet
velu, adj. hairy
vendange, n.f. vintage
vendeur, n.m. clerk, salesman
vendre, vb. to sell, sell out
vendredi, n.m. Friday
vénéneux, adj. poisonous
vénérer, vb. to venerate
vengeance, n.f. revenge, vengeance
venger, vb. to avenge
venimeux, adj. venomous
venin, n.m. venom
venir, vb. to come
vent, n.m. wind
vente, n.f. sale
venteux, adj. windy
ventilateur, n.m. fan, ventilator
ventiler, vb. to ventilate
ventre, n.m. belly, stomach
venue, n.f. advent, arrival
vêpres, n.f., pl. vespers
ver, n.m. worm
véracité, n.f. veracity
véranda, n.f. porch
verbe, n.m. verb
verbeux, adj. wordy, verbose
verdeur, n.f. sharpness, vigor
verdict, n.m. verdict
verge, n.f. rod; shank
verger, n.m. orchard
vérification, n.f. check, auditing
vérifier, vb. to check, confirm, verify
véritable, adj. genuine, real
vérité, n.f. truth
vermine, n.f. vermin
vernir, vb. to varnish
verre, n.m. glass
verrou, n.m. bolt
vers, n.m. verse; prep. toward, about
verser, vb. to pour, shed
versifier, vb. to versify
version, n.f. translation
vert, adj. green
vertical, adj. upright, vertical
vertige, n.m. dizziness
vertigineux, adj. dizzy

vertu, n.f. virtue
vertueux, adj. virtuous
verveux, adj. animated, lively
vessie, n.f. bladder
veste, n.f. jacket, coat
vestibule, n.m. hall, lobby
vestige, n.m. footprint
veston, n.m. coat
vêtement, n.m. garment; pl. clothes
vétéran, n.m. veteran
vétérinaire, n.m. veterinary
vêtir, vb. to clothe
véto, n.m. veto
veuf, n.m. widower
veuve, n.f. widow
vexation, n.f. vexation
vexer, vb. to vex
viaduc, n.m. viaduct
viande, n.f. meat
vibrant, adj. vibrant, vibrating
vibration, n.f. vibration
vibrer, vb. to vibrate
vicaire, n.m. vicar
vice, n.m. vice, defect
vice-roi, n.m. viceroy
vicieux, adj. vicious; wrong
victime, n.f. victim
victoire, n.f. victory
victorieux, adj. victorious
vidange, n.f. emptying, drain
vide, n.m. emptiness, vacuum,
  blank; adj. empty, void, vacant
vidéodisque, n.m. videodisc
vider, vb. to empty, drain
vie, n.f. life; livelihood
vieil, adj. old
vieillard, n.m. old man
vieille, n.f. old woman
vieillesse, n.f. old age
vieillir, vb. to age
vierge, n.f. virgin; virginal
vieux, adj. old
vif m., **vive** f. adj. lively, quick
  brisk, full of life
vigie, n.f. lookout
vigilance, n.f. vigilance
vigilant, adj. watchful
vigoureux, adj. vigorous

vigueur, n.f. vigor, force
vil, adj. vile
vilain, adj. ugly, wicked
village, n.m. village
ville, n.f. city, town
vin, n.m. wine
vinaigre, n.m. vinegar
vindicatif, adj. vindictive
violateur, n.m. violator
violation, n.f. violation
violemment, adj. violently
violence, n.f. violence
violent, adj. violent
violer, vb. to violate
violet, adj. purple, violet
violette, n.f. violet
violon, n.m. violin
vipère, n.f. viper
virgule, n.f. comma
viril, adj. manly
virilité, n.f. manhood
virtuel, adj. virtual
virtuouse, n.m.f. virtuoso
virus, n.m. virus
vis, n.f. screw
visa, n.m. visa
visage, n.m. face
vis-à-vis, adv. opposite,
  across from; facing
viser, vb. to aim at
visibilité, n.f. visibility
visible, adj. visible
visière, n.f. visor; keenness
vision, n.f. vision
visite, n.f. call, visit
visiter, vb. to visit
visiteur, n.m. visitor
visqueux, adj. viscous, sticky
visser, vb. to screw
visuel, adj. visual
vital, adj. vital
vitalité, n.f. vitality
vitamine, n.f. vitamin
vite, adv. quick, fast, swift
vitesse, n.f. speed, rate; gear
vitrail, n.m. stained-glass window
virtre, n.f. window, pane
vitrine, n.f. display case

vivacité, n.f. vivacity
vivant, adj. alive
vivement, adv. quickly, vividly
vivre, vb. to live
vocabulaire, n.m. vocabulary
vocal, adj. vocal
vocation, n.f. vocation
voeu, n.m. vow
vogue, n.f. bogue
voici, vb. to here is, behold
voie, n.f. track, road
voilà, vb. to there is; behold
voile, n.m. veil; sail
voiler, vb. to veil, hide
voilure, n.f. sails
voir, vb. to see. faire v., show
voirie, n.m. dump
voisin, n.m. neighbor; adj. nearby
voisinage, n.m. neighborhood
voisiner, vb. to act like a neighbor
voiture, n.f. car, carriage
voix, n.f. voice
vol, n.m. flight; robbery; ripoff
volage, adj. fickle
volaille, n.f. fowl, poultry
volatil, adj. volatile
volcan, n.m. volcano
volcanique, adj. volcanic
volée, n.f. flight, covey; herd
voler, vb. to fly; steal, rip off
volet, n.m. shutter, blind
voleur, n.m. thief, robber
vol frété, n.m. charter flight
volomtaire, n.m. volunteer
volonté, n.f. will
volontiers, adv. gladly, willingly
voltigement, n.m. flutter
voltiger, vb. to flutter; hover
volubilité, n.f. volubility
volume, n.m. volume
volumineux, adj. bulky
volupté, n.f. pleasure
vomir, vb. to vomit
vorace, adj. voracious
votant, n.m. voter
votre, adj. yours
vouer, vb. to vow, dedicate
vouloir, vb. to want, wish, require

vous, pron. you, yourself
voûte, n.f. vault
voûter, vb. to arch
voyage, n.m. journey, trip
voyager, vb. to travel
voyageur, n.m. traveler, passenger
voyelle, n.f. vowel
vrai, adj. true, real
vraisemblance, n.f. probability
vue, n.f. view, sight
vulgaire, adj. vulgar, coarse, rude
vulgarité, n.f. vulgarity

X

xérès, n.m. sherry (wine)
xylophone, n.m. xylophone

Y

y, adv. here, there, within
yacht, n.m. yachtnerable
yaourt, n.m. yogurt
yodler, vb. to yodel
yucca, n.m. yucca

Z

zèbre, n.m. zebra
zèle, n.m. zeal, warmth, ardour
zélé, adj. zealous
zénith, n.m. zenith
zéro, n.m. zero
zezayer, vb. to lisp
zibeline, n.f. sable
zigzaguer, vb. to zigzag
zodiaque, n.m. zodiac
zona, n.m. shingles
zone, n.f. area, zone
zoo, n.m. zoo
zoologiste, n. zoologist
zyeuter, v.t. to look at

a, art. un, m., une f.

aardvark, n. aardvark, m.

abacus, n. abaque m.

abandon, vb. abandonner

abandon, n. abandon m.

abandoned, adj. abandonné

abate, vb. diminuer

abatement, n. diminution f.

abbey, n. abbaye

abbreviate, vb. abréger

abbreviation, n. abréviation f.

abdicate, vb. abdiquer

abdomen, n. abdomen m.

abominal, adj. abdominal

abduct, vb. enlever

abductor, n. ravisseur m.

abettor, n. aide m. complice m.

abeyance, n. suspension f.

abide, vb. (tolerate) supporter; (remain) demeurer; **(a. by the law)** respecter la loi

ability, n. talent m.

abject, adj. abject

able, adj. capable; (to be able) pouvoir

able-bodied, adj. fort, robuste

ably, adv. capablement

aboard, adv. à bord

abode, n. demeure f.

abolish, vb. abolir

abolishment, n. abolissement m.

abominate, vb. abominer

abomination, n. abomination f.

abortion, n. avortement m.

abortive, adj. abortif, manqué

abound, vb. abonder (de or en)

about, adv. (approximately) à peu près; autour

above, adv. au-dessus; prep. au-dessus de; plus de

abrasive, adj. abrasif m.

abreast, adv. de front

abroad, adv. à l'étranger

abrupt, adj. (hasty) brusque

abscess, n. abcès m.

absence, n. absence f.

absent, adj. absent

absolute, adj. absolu

absolutely, adv. absolument

absolution, n. absolution f.

absolve, vb. absoudre

absorb, vb. absorber

absorbed, adj. absorbé

absorbent, adj. abosorbant m.

absorbing, adj. absorbant

absorption, n. absorption

abstinence, n. abstinence f.

abstract, adj. abstrait

absurd, adj. absurde

abundance, n. abondance f.

abundant, adj. abondant

abuse, n. abus m.

abusive, adj. (insulting) injurieux

abut, vb. aboutir (à)

abyss, n. abîme m.

academic, adj. académique

academy, n. académie f.

accede, vb. consentir

accelerate, vb. accélérer

accelerator, n. accélérateur m.

accent, n. accent m.

accept, vb. accepter

acceptance, n. acceptation f.

access, n. accès, abord m.

accessory, n. accessoire m.

accident, n. accident m.

accidental, adj. accidentel

acclaim, vb. acclamer

acclamation, n. acclamation f.

acclimate, vb. acclimater

accomodate, vb. (lodge) loger; (oblige) obliger

accompany, vb. accompagner

accomplish, vb. accomplir

accomplished, adj. accompli, achevé

accord, n. accord, rapport m.

accordance, n. accord m.

accordingly, adv. en conséquence

account, n. compte m.

accountant, n. comptable m.

accounting, n. comptabilité f.

accretion, n. accroissement m.

accumulate, v.t. accumuler

accumulation, n. entassement m.

accumulative, adj. (chose) qui s'accumule

accuracy, n. précision f.
accurate, adj. précis
accusative, n. and adj. accusatif m.
accuse, v.t. accuser
accustom, v.t. accoutumer
ace, n. as m.
acetate, n. acétate m.
acetylene, n. acétylène m.
ache, n. douleur f.
achieve, vb. exécuter
achievement, n. accomplissement m.
acid, adj. acide m.
acidity, n. acidité f.
acknowledge, vb. reconnaître
acne, n. acné f.
acorn, n. gland m.
acquaint, vb. informer (de)
acquaintance, n. connaissance f.
acquainted, adj. connu, familier (avec)
acquiesce(in), vb. acquiescer (à)
acquire, vb. acquérir
acquit, vb. acquitter
acre, n. arpten m., acre f.
acrid, adj. âcre
acrobat, n. acrobate
across, prep. à travers
act, n. acte m. vb. jouer
acting, n. jeu m.
action, n. action f.
active, adj. actif, agile, alerte
activity, n. activité f.
actor, n. acteur m.
actress, n. actrice f.
actual, adj. réel
actually, adv. réellement, en effet
actuate, vb. mettre en action, animer
acupuncture, n. acuponcture f.
acutely, adv. vivement
acuteness, n. finesse f.
adapt, v.t. adapter
adaptable, adj. adaptable
adaptability, n. faculté d'adaptation f.
adaptation, n. adaptation f.
adapter, n. qui adapte
add, v.t ajouter; additionner
adder, v. vipère f.
addict, n. personne adonnée à f.
addition, n. addition f.

additional, adj. additionnel
address, n. adresse m.
adenoid, adj. and n. adénoïde f.
adept, adj. habile adepte
adequacy, n. suffisance f.
adequate, adj. suffisant
adhere, vb. adhérer
adherent, n. adhérent m.
adhesion, n. adhésion f.
adieu, n. and adv. adieu
adjective, n. adjectif m.
adjoin, vb. adjoindre
adjourn, vb. ajourner
adjunct, n. and adj. adjoint,
  accessoire m.
adjust, vb. ajuster, arranger,
  régler
adjuster, n. ajusteur m.
adjustment, n. ajustement
  accommodement m.
administer, vb. administrer
administration, n. administration f.
administrative, adj. administratif
administrator, n. administrateur m.
admirable, adj. admirable
admiral, n. amiral m.
admiration, n. admiration f.
admire, vb. admirer
admirer, n. admirateur m.
admiringly, adv. avec admiration
admission, n. (entrance) entrée f.
admit, vb. laisser entrer
admittance, n. accès m.
admonish, vb. réprimander
adolescence, n. adolescence f.
adolescent, adj. and n. adolescent m., adolescente f.
adopt, vb. adopter
adoption, n. adoption f.
adorable, adj. adorable
adoration, n. adoration f.
adore, vb. adorer
adorn, vb. orner
adult, adj. and n. adulte m.f.
adulterer, n. adultère m.
adulteress, n. femme adultère f.
adultery, n. adultère m.
advance, v.t. avancer, faire

advanced, adj. avancé

advancement, n. avancement m.

advantage, n. avantage m.

advantageous, adj. avantageux

advent, n. venue f.; (eccles.) Avent m.

adventure, n. aventure f.

adventurer, n. aventurier m.

adventurous, adj. aventureux

adverb, n. adverbe m.

adverse, adj. adverse

advert, vb. faire allusion (à)

advertise, vb. annoncer

advertisement, n. annoncer

advertising, n. publicité f.

advice, n. conseil m.

advise, vb. conseiller

advocate, n. avocat m.

aerate, vb. aérer

aeration, n. aération f.

aerial, adj. aérien

aerie, n. aire f.

aesthetic, adj. esthétique

afar, adv. loin, de loin

affair, n. affaire f.

affect, vb. toucher, intéresser

affected, adj. maniéré

affecting, adj. touchant, émourvant

affection, n. affection f.

affiance, vb. fiancer

affidavit, n. déclaration par écrit sous serment attestation f.

affiliate, vb. affilier

affinity, n. affinité f.

affirm, vb. affirmer

affirmation, n. affirmation f.

affix, vb. apposer

afflict, vb. affliger (de)

affliction, n. affliction f.

affluence, n. affluence, opulence f.

affluent, adj. affluent, opulent

afford, vb. donner, fournir

affront, n. affront m.

afloat, adv. à flot

afraid, adj. effrayé pris de peur

Africa, n. l' Afrique f.

after, prep. après; sur, à la suite de

afternoon, n. après-midi m.f.

afterward, adv. ensuite

again, adv. encore

against, prep. contre

age, n. âge m.

ageless, adj. toujours jeune

agency, n. agence f.

agenda, n. ordre du jour, agenda m.

agent, n. agent m.

aggravate, vb. aggraver

aggravation, n. aggravation f., agacement m.

aggregate, adj. global

aggression, n. agression f.

aggressive, adj. agressif

aggressor, n. agresseur m.

aghast, adj. consterné

agitate, vb. agiter, exciter

agitator, n. agitateur m.

ago, adv. passé, il y a

agonized, v.t. torturer

agony, n. angoisse, agonie f.

agree, vb. être d'accord

agreeable, adj. agréable

agreeably, adv. agréablement

agreement, n. accord m.

agriculture, n. agriculture f.

ahead, adv. and interj. en avant

aid, n. aide, assistance f.

AIDS, n. (acaronym) - acquired immune deficiency syndrome - le SIDA (syndrome d'immuno-déficience acquise)

ail, vb. être souffrant

ailment, n. indisposition f.

aim, n. point de mire, but m.

air, n. air, vent m., brise f.

airbag, n. sac à air m.

airborne, adj. aéroporté

air-condition, vb. climatiser

air-conditioning, n. climatisation f.

aircraft, n. avion, les avions, m., pl.

air gun, n. fusil à vent

airliner, n. avion m.

air mail, n. poste aérienne f.

airplane, n. avion m.

air pollution, n. pollution de l'air f.

airport, n. aéroport m.

air pressure, n. pression d'air f.
airsickness, n. mal de l'air
airtight, adj. imperméable à l'air
airy, adj. ouvert à l'air; aéré
aisle, n. bas-côté m.
ajar, adv. entr'ouvert
akin, adj. allié (à). parent (de)
alarm, n. alarme, alerte f.
albino, n. albinos m.
album, n album m.
alcohol, n. alcool m.
alcoholic, adj. alcoolique
alert, adj. alerte
algebra, n. algèbre f.
alibi, n. alibi m.
alien, adj. etranger——————
align, vb. aligner
alike, adj. semblable; adv. également
alive, adj. vivant, envie
alkali, n. alcali m.
alkaline, adj. alcalin
all, adj. tout m. sg., toute
  f. sg., tous m., pl, toutes f., pl
  adv. and pron. tout; surtout; tout
  d'un coup
allay, vb. apaiser
allegation, n. allégation f.
allege, vb. alléguer
allegiance, n. fidélité f.
allergy, n. allergie f.
alleviate, vb. soulager
alley, n. ruelle f.
alliance, n. alliance f.
allied, adj. allié
alligator, n. alligator m.
allocate, vb. assigner
allot, vb. répartir
allotment, n. partage m.
allow, vb. permettre; admettre
allowance, n. allocation, ration
alloy, n. alliage m.
allure, vb. séduire
allusion, n. allusion f.
ally n. allié m.
almanac, n. almanach m.
almond, n. amande f.
aloft, adv. en haut, en l'air
alone, adj. seul, solitaire

along, adv. le long de
aloud, adv. à haute voix
alphabet, n. alphabet m.
alphabetical, adj. alphabétique
Alps, n. les Alpes f., pl.
already, adv. déja
also, adv. aussi
altar, n. autel m.
alter, vb. changer
alteration, n. modification f.
alternate, vb. alterner, faire
  alternativement
alternative, n. alternative f.
although, conj. bien que
altitude, n. altitude f.
altogether, adv. tout à fait
alum, n. alun m.
aluminium, n. aluminium m.
always, adv. toujours
amalgam, n. amalgame m.
amass, vb. amasser
amateur, n. amateur m.
amaze, vb. étonner
amazement, n. stupeur f.
amazing, adj. étonnant
ambassador, n. ambassadeur m.
amber, n. ambre m.
ambidextrous, adj. ambidextre
ambition, n. ambition f.
ambitious, adj. ambitieux
ambulance, n. ambulance f.
ambulatory, adj. ambulatoire
ambush, n. embuscade f.
amend, vb. amender
amenity, n. aménité f., agrément m.
America, n. l'Amérique f.
American, adj. américain, n.;
  Américain m.
amethyst, n. améthyste f.
amid, prep. au milieu de
amiss, adv. mal, en mauvaise part
amity, n. amitié f.
ammonia, n. ammoniaque f.
amnesty, n. amnistie f.
among, prep. parmi, entre
amount, n. somme, (quantity)
  quantité f.
ampere, n. ampère m.

amphibious, adj. amphibie
amphitheatre, n. amphithéâtre m.
ample, adj. ample
amplify, vb. amplifier
amputate, n. amputer
amputee, n. amputé m.
amuse, vb. amuser
an, art. un m., une f.
analysis, n. analyse f.
analyst, n. analyste m.
analyze, vb. analyser
anatomy, n. anatomie f.
ancestor, n. ancêtres m., pl.
ancestral, adj. d'ancêtres,
 héréditaire
ancestry, n. ancêtres m., pl.
anchor, vb. ancre f.
anchorage, n. mouillage, ancrage m.
anchovy, n. anchois m.
ancient, adj. ancien m.
and, conj. et
anecdote, n. anecdote f.
anemia, n. anémie f.
anesthetist, n. anesthésiste m.
anew, adv. de nouveau
angel, n. ange m.
anger, n. colère f.
angle, n. angle m.
angry, adj. fâché
anguish, n. angoisse f.
animal, n. and adj. animal m.
animate, vb. animer
animation, n. animation f.
animosity, n. animosité f.
anise, n. anis m.
ankle, n. cheville f.
annals, n., pl. annales f., pl.
annex, n. dépendance f.
annexation, n. annexation f.
annihilate, vb. anéantir
anniversary, n. anniversaire m.
annotate, vb. annoter
annotation, n. annotation f.
announce, vb. annoncer
announcement, n. annonce f.
announcer, n. annonciateur
annoy, vb. (vex) contrarie
annoyance, n. contrariété f.

annual, adj. annuel
annuity, n. annuité f.
annul, vb. annuler
anoint, vb. oindre
anonymous, adj. anonyme
another, adj. and pron. un autre m.,
 une autre f.
answer, vb. répondre; n. réponse f.
ant, n. fourmi f.
antagonize, vb. eveiller l'antagonisme
antarctic, adj. antarctique m.
antelope, n. antilope f.
antenna, n. antenne f.
anterior, adj. antérieur
anthem, n. hymne m.
anthrax, n. anthrax m.
antic, n. bouffonerie f.
anticipate, vb. anticiper; prévoir
anticipation, n. anticipation f.
antidote, n. antidote m.
antinomy, n. antinomie f.
antipathy, n. antipathie f.
antique, n. antique m.; (antique
 dealer) antiquaire m.
antiquity, n. antiquité f.
antiseptic, adj. and n. antiseptique m.
antisocial, adj. antisocial
antler, n. andouiller m.
anvil, n. enclume f.
anxiety, n. anxiété f.
anxious, adj. inquiet m.
any, adj. du, de la
anybody, pron. (somebody) quelq'un
anyhow, adv. de toute facon
anyone, pron. quelqu'un, chacun, qui
 que ce soit
anything, pron. quelque chose m.
anywhere, adv. n'importe où
apart, adv. à part
apartheid, n. ségrégation f.
apartment, n. logement m.
apathy, n. apathie f.
ape, n. singe m.
apex, n. sommet m.
apiece, adv. chacun
apologize, vb. s'excuser, faire des
 excuses
apology, n. excuses f., pl.

apostle, n. apôtre m.

appal, vb. épouvanter

apparatus, n. appareil m.

apparel, n. habillement, vêtement m.

apparent, adj. apparent

appeal, n. appel m.; vb. en appeler (de)

appear, vb. apparaître

appearance, n. apparition f.

appease, vb. apaiser, pacifier

appeaser, n. personne qui apaise

appendage, n. accessoire m.

appendectomy, n. appendéctomie f.

appendicits, n. appendicite f.

appendix, n. appendice m.

appetite, n. appétit m.

appetizer, n. apéritif m.

applaud, vb. applaudir

applause, n. applaudissements m., pl.

apple, n. pomme f.

applesauce, n. compote de pommes f.

appliance, n. appareil m.

applicant, n. postulant m.

application, n. demande f.

applied, adj. appliqué

apply, vb. appliquer (à), s'appliquer

appoint, vb. nommer; désigner

appointment, n. nomination f.

apposition, n. apposition f.

appraisal, n. évaluation f.

appraise, n. expert m.

appreciable, adj. appréciable

appreciate, vb. apprécier, estimer

appreciation, n. appréciation f.

apprehend, vb. saisir, arrêter

apprehension, n. arrestation f.

apprehensive, adj. intelligent

approach, n. approche f.

approbation, n. approbation f.

approval, n. approbation f.

approve, vb. approuver

approximate, adj. approximatif

approximately, adv. approximative-
ment, à peu pres

apricot, n. abricot m.

April, n. avril m.

apron, n. tablier m.

apt, adj. sujet, enclin, porté (à)

aptitude, n. aptitude f.

aquarium, n. aquarium m.

aquatic, adj. aquatique

aqueduct, n. aqueduc m.

aqueous, adj. aqueux

Arab, n. Arabe m.f. adj. arabe

Arabic, adj. and n. arabe m.

arbiter, n. arbitre m.

arbitrary, adj. arbitraire

arbitrate, vb. arbitrer

arbitration, n. arbitrage m.

arbitrator, n. arbitre m.

arbor, n. arbre m.

arc, n. arc m.

arcade, n. arcade f.

arch, n. arc m.; (of bridge) arche f.
adj. espiègle

archbishop, n. archevêque m.

archduke, n. archiduc m.

archer, n. archer m.

archery, n. tir à l'arc m.

architect, n. architecte m.

architecture, n. architecture f.

archives, n. archives f., pl.

archway, n. voûte f., passage
(sous une voûte) m.

arctic, adj. arctique

ardor, n. ardeur f.

area, n. aire; région, surface f.

area code, n. indicatif interurbain m.

arena, n. arène f.

argue, vb. argumenter

argument, n. argument m.; (dispute)
discussion f.

arid, adj. aride

arise, vb. s'élever; provenir de

aristocracy, n. aristocratie f.

aristocrat, n. aristocrate m.f.

arithmetic, n. arthimétique f.

ark, n. arche f.

arm, n. bras m.; arme f. vb. armer

arm-chair, n. fauteuil m.

armed forces, n. forces armées f., pl.

armful, n. brassée f.

armhole, n. emmanchure f.

armistice, n. armistice m.

armor, n. armure f.

armpit, n. aisselle f.

arms, n. armes f., pl.

army, n. armée f.

aroma, n. arome m.

aromatic, adj. aromatique

around, adv. autour; prep. autour de

arouse, vb. soulever; réveiller

arraign, vb. accuser, poursuivre en justice

arrange, vb. arranger, réler

arrangement, n. arrangement m.

array, vb. ranger

arrest, n. arrestation f.; arrêts m., pl.

arrival, n. arrivée f.

arrive, vb. arriver

arrogant, adj. arrogant

arrogate, vb. attributer injustement

arrow, n. flèche f.

arrowhead, n. pointe de flèche f.

arsenal, n. arsenal m.

arsenic, n. arsenic m.

arson, n. crime d'incendie m.

art, n. art m.; beauxarts

arterial, adj. artériel

artery, n. artère f.

artful, adj. artificieux; adroit

arthritis, n. arthrite f.

article, n. article m.

artillery, n. artillerie f.

artist, n. artiste m.

artistic, adj. artistique

artistry, n. habileté f.

as, adv. comme; aussi...que; conj. de facon à; pendant que

asbestos, n. asbeste m.

ascend, vb. monter

ascendancy, n. ascendant m.

ascendant, adj. ascendant, supérieur

ascertain, vb. s'assurer

ascetic, n. ascétique m.

ascribe, vb. attribuer

ash, n. cendre f.; (tree) frêne m.

ashamed, adj. honteux, confus

ashore, adv. à terre; débarquer

Asia, n. l'Asie f.

Asian, n. Asiatique m.f.; adj. asiatique

aside, adv. de côte

ask, vb. demander à; inviter

askance, adv. de travers, obliquement

asleep, adj. endormi

asparagus, n. asperges f., pl.

aspect, n. aspect m.

asphalt, n. asphalte m.

asphyxiate, vb. asphyxier

aspirant, n. aspirant m., candidat m.

aspiration, n. aspiration f.

aspirator, n. aspirateur m.

aspire, vb. aspirer

ass, n. âne m., ânesse f.

assail, vb. assaillir

assailant, n. assaillant m.

assassin, n. assassin m.

assassination, n. assassinat m.

assault, n. assaut m.

assay, n. essai m., vérification, épreuve f. vb. essayer

assemblage, n. assemblage m.

assemble, vb. assembler

assembly, n. assemblée f.

assert, vb. affirmer

assess, vb. evaluer, imposter

assets, n., pl. actif m.

assign, vb. assigner

assignable, adj. assignable, transférable

assignation, n. assignation f., rendezvous m.

assignment, n. attribution, assignation

assistance, n. aide f.

assistant, n. qui aide, auxiliaire

associate, vb. associe

association, n. association f.

assort, vb. assortir

assorted, adj. assorti

assortment, n. assortiment, m.

assume, vb. prendre sur soi

assuming, adj. prétentieux, arrogant

assumption, n. supposition f.

assurance, n. assurance f.

assure, vb. assurer

aster, n. aster m.

asterisk, n. astérisque m.

astern, adv. à l'arrière, sur l'arrière

asteroid, n. astéroïde m.

asthma, n. asthme m.

astonish, vb. étonner

astonishment, n. étonnement m.

astound, vb. étonner, ébahir	**auditor**, n. vérificateur m.
astride, adv. à califourchon	**auditorium**, n. salle f.
astringent, n. and adj. astringent m.	**auditory**, adj. auditif
astrology, n. astrologie f.	**August**, n. août m.
astronaut, n. astronaute m.	**aunt**, n. tante f.
astronomy, n. astronomie f.	**Australia**, n. l'Australie f.
at, prep. à, en, dans; contre	**authentic**, adj. authentique
atheist, n. athée	**authenticity**, n. authenticité f.
athlete, n. athlète m.	**author**, n. auteur m.
athletic, adj. athlétique	**authority**, n. authorité f.
Atlantic, adj. atlantique	**authorization**, n. autorisation f.
atlas, n. atlas m.	**authorize**, vb. autoriser
atomsphere, n. atmospère f.	**auto**, n. auto f.
atom, n. atome m.	**autobiography**, n. autobiographie f.
atomic, adj. atomique	**autogrpah**, n. autographe m.; vb.
atomic bomb, n. bombe atomique f.	autographier
atonement, n. expiation f.	**automatic**, adj. automatique
atrocity, n. atrocité f.	**automatically**, adv. automatiquement
atrophy, n. atrophie f.	**automobile**, n. automobile f.
attach, vb. attcher	**autopsy**, n. autopsie f.
attaché, n. attaché m.	**autumn**, n. automne m.
attachment, n. attachment	**auxiliary**, adj. auxiliaire m.
attack, n. attaque f.	**avail**, vb. servir
attain, vb. atteindre	**available**, adj. disponible
attainment, n. acquisition f.	**avenge**, vb. venger
attempt, n. tentative f.	**avenue**, n. avenue f.
attend, vb. soigner; servir; assister	**average**, n. moyenne f. adj. moyen
attendance, n. service m.; présence f.	**averse**, adj. opposé
attention, n. attention f.	**aversion**, n. aversion f.
attentive, adj. attentif	**avert**, vb. détourner
attest, vb. attester	**aviation**, n. aviation f.
attic, n. grenier m.	**aviator**, n. aviateur m.
attire, n. costume m.	**avid**, adj. avide
attitude, n. attitude f.	**avoid**, vb. éviter
attorney, n. avoué m.	**avow**, vb. avouer
attract, vb. attirer	**await**, vb. attendre
attraction, n. attraction f.	**awake**, vb. éveill
attractive, adj. attrayant	**award,**, n. prix m.; sentence f.; vb.
attribute, n. attribut m.	dècerner
attune, vb. accorder	**away**, adv. loin; absent
auction, n. enchère	**awful**, adj. terrible
auctioneer, n. commissairepriseur m.	**awhile**, adv. pendant quelque temps
audacity, n. audace f.	**awkward**, adj. gauche; embarrassant
audible, adj. intelligible	**awning**, n. tente f.
audience, n. auditoire m.	**axe**, n. hache f.
audit, vb. verifier (des comptes); n.	**axis**, n. axe m.
vérfication des comptes	**axle**, n. arbre, essieu
audition, n. audition f.	**azure**, n. azur m.

babble, vb. babiller
babe, n. enfant m.f.
baboon, n. babouin m.
baby, n. bébé m.
bachelor, n. célibataire m.
back n. dos m.; vb. reculer; adv. en arrière
backbone, n. épine dorsale f.
background, n. fond m.
backhand, adj. donné avec le revers de la main
backward, adv. en arrière
backwardness, n. état arriéré m.
backwater, n. eau stagnante f.
bacon, n. lard m.
bacterium n. bactérie f.
bad, adj. mauvais; mechant
baffle, vb. déconcerter
bag, n. sac m.; (suitcase) valise f.
baggage, n. bagage m.
bagpipe, n. cornemuse f.
bail, n. caution f. vb. vider
baliff, n. huissier m.
bait, n. appât m.
bake, vb. faire cuire au four
baker, n. boulanger m.
bakery, n. boulangerie f.
baking, n. cuisson f.
balance, n. équilibre, solde m.; balance f. vb. balancer, peser
balcony, n. balcon m.
baldness, n. calvitie f.
bale, n. balle f.
balk, vb. frustrer
ball, n. balle f., boule f., bal m.
ballad, n. romance f.; ballade f.
ballast, n. lest m.
ball bearing, n. roulements à billes m.
ballerina, n. ballerine f.
ballet, n. ballet m.
balloon, n. ballon m.
ballot, n. scrutin m.
balm, n. baume m.
balmy, adj. embaumé
balsam, n. baume m.
balustrade, n. balustrade f.
bamboo, n. bambou m.

ban, n. ban m. vb. metre au ban
banal, adj. banal
banana, n. banane f.
band, n. bande f.
bandage, n. bandeau m.
bandanna, n. foulard m.
bandbox, n. carton m.
bandit, n. bandit m.
bandsman, n. musicien m.
bandstand, n. kiosque á musique m.
baneful, adj. pernicieux
bang, vb. frapper violemment; n. coup m.
banish, vb. bannir
banishment, n. bannissement m.
banister, n. rampe, f.
bank, n. rivage m.
bankbook, n. livret de banque m.
banker, n. banquier m.
banking, n. banque f.
bank note, n. billet de banque m.
bankrupt, adj. failli, en faillite m.
bankruptcy, n. faillie f.
banner, n. bannière f.
banquet, n. banquet m.
banter, n. badinage m.; vb. badiner, railler
baptism, n. baptême m.
baptismal, adj. batismal
Baptist, n. Baptiste m.
baptistery, n. baptistère m.
baptize, vb. baptiser
bar, n. bar, barreau m.
barb, n. barbillon m.
barbarism, n. barbarie f., (gramm.) barbarisme m.
barber, n. coiffeur m.
barbiturate, n. barbiturate m.
bare, adj. nu; vb. découvrir
bareback, adv. à dos nu
barefoot, adv. nu-pieds
barely, adv. à peine
bareness, n. nudité f.
bargain, n. marché m.
bargain, vb. marchander
barge, n. chaland m.
bark, n. (tree) écorce f.; (dog) aboiement m.; vb. (dog) aboyer

barley, n. orge f.

barn, n. (grain) grange f.; (livestock) étable f.

barnacle, n. (shellfish) anatife m.; (goose) barnache f.

barometer, n. baromètre m.

barometric, adj. barométrique

baron, n. baron m.

baroness, n. baronne f.

baronial, adj. baronnial, seigneurial

baroque, adj. baroque m.

barrack, n. caserne f.

barrel, n. baril m.

barren, adj. stérile

barrenness, n. stérilité f.

barricade, n. barricade f.

barrier, n. barrière f.

barter, n. troc m.

base, n. base f.; adj. bas m.

baseball, n. base-ball m.

basement, n. sous-sol m.

bashful, adj. timide

bashfully, adv. timidement

bashfulness, n. timidité f.

basic, adj. fondamental

basin, n. cuvette f., bassin m.

basis, n. base f.

bask, vb. se chauffer

basket, n. panier m., corbeille f.

bass, n. basse f; (fish) bar m.

bassinet, n. bercelonnette f.

bassoon, n. basson m.

bastard, n. bâtard m.

baste, vb. arroser; (sewing) faufiler

bat, n. (animal) chauve-souris f.; (baseball) batte f.

batch, n. fournée f.

bate, vb. rabattre

bath, n. bain m.

bathe, vb. se baigner

bather, n. baigneur m.

baton, n. bâton m.

battalion, n. bataillon m.

batter, n. (cooking) pâte f.

battery, n. batterie

battle, n. bataille f.

battle, vb. lutter

battlefield, n. champ de bataile m.

battleship, n. cuirassé m.

bawl, vb. brailler

bayonet, n. baïonnette f.

bazaar, n. bazar m.

be, vb. être

beach, n. plage f.

beacon, n. phare m.

bead, n. perle f.

beak, n. bec m.

beaker, n. gobelet m., coupe f.

beam, n. putre f., rayon m.; vb. rayonner

beaming, adj. rayonnant

bean, n. haricot m.

bear, n. ours m.; vb. porter, supporter, enfanter

beard, n. barbe f.

bearer, n. porteur m.

bearing, n. maintien, coussinet, relèvement m.

beast, n. bête f.

beat, vb. battre; n. battement m.

beaten, adj. battu

beatify, vb. béatifier

beating, n. battement m., rossée f.

beau, n. galant m.

beautiful, adj. beau m.

beaver, n. castor m.

because, conj. parce que

beckon, vb. faire signe (à)

become, vb. devenir

becoming, adj. convenable

bed, n. lit m.

bedclothes, n. les draps et couvertures f., pl.

bedridden, adj. alité

bedroom, n. chambre à coucher f.

bedside, n. bord du lit m.

bedspread, n. dessus de lit m.

bedstead, n. bois de lit m.

bedtime, n. l'heure du coucher

bee, n. abeille f.

beef, n. boeuf m.

beehive, n. ruche f

beer, n. bière f.

beeswax, n. cire jaune f.

beet, n. betterave f.

beetle, n. scarabée m.
befit, vb. convenir à
befitting, adj. convenable
before, adv. en avant, avant; prep. devant, avant
beforehand, adv. d'avance
befriend, vb. seconder, aider
beg, vb. mendier, prier
beggar, n. mendiant m.
begin, vb. commencer
beginner, n. commençant m.
beginning, n. commencement m.
beguile, vb. tromper, séduire
behalf, n. de la part de, en faveur de
behave, vb. se conduire
behavior, n. conduite f.
behind, n. derrière m.
behold, vb. voir; interj. voici
beige, adj. beige m.
being, n. être m.
belated, adj. attardé
belch, vb. éructer
belfry, n. clocher, beffroi m.
Belgian, n. Belge m.f.; adj. beige
Belgium, n. Belgique f.
belief, n. croyance, confiance f.
believable, adj. croyable
believe, vb. croire
believer, n. croyant m.
bell, n. cloche, clochette f.
bellboy, n. chasseur m.
bellow, vb. mugir
bellows, n., pl. soufflet m.
belly, n. ventre m.
belongings, n., pl. effets m., pl.
beloved, adj. and n. chéri m.
below, prep. en aval, au-dessous de
belt, n. ceinture f.
bench, n. banc m.
bend, vb. plier, courber tourner
beneath, prep. sous, au-dessous
benediction, n. bénédiction f.
benefactor, n. bienfaiteur m.
beneficent, adj. bienfaisant
beneficial, adj. salutaire
beneficiary, n. bénéficiaire m.
benefit, n. bienfait, profit m.
benevolent, adj. bienveillant

benign, adj. bénin m. bénigne f.
bent, n. penchant m.
bequeath, vb. léguer
bequest, n. legs m.
bereave, vb. priver (de)
bereavement, n. privation f., perte f., deuil m.
berry, n. baie f.
beseech, vb. supplier, implorer
beside, prep. à côté de
besides, adv. en outre
besiege, vb. assiéger
best, adj. le meilleur; adv. le mieux
bestial, adj. bestial
bestir, vb. remuer
bestow, vb. accorder
bet, n. pari m.; vb. parier
betray, vb. trahir
betroth, vb. fiancer
betrothal, n. fiancailles f.,pl.
better, adj. en biseau; vb. biaiser
beverage, n. boisson f.
bewilder, vb. égarer
bewildering, adj. découtant
bewilderment, n. égarement m.
bewitch, vb. ensorceler
beyond, adv. au delà; prep. au delà de
biannual, adj. semestriel
bias, n. biais m.
bib, n. bavette f.
Bible, n. Bible f.
biblical, adj. biblique
bibliography, n. bibliographie f.
biceps, n. biceps m.
bicker, vb. se quereller, se chamailler
bicycle, n. bicyclette f.
bicyclist, n. cycliste m.
bid, n. enchère f., appel m.; vb. ordonner, inviter
bidder, n. enchérisseur m.
bide, vb. demeurer, attendre
bier, n. corbillard m., civière f.
bifocal, adj. bifocal
big, adj. grand
bigamy, n. bigamie f.
bigot, n. bigot m.
bigotry, n. bigoterie f.

bilateral, adj. bilatéral

bile, n. bile f.

bilingual, adj. bilingue

bilious, adj. bilieux

bill, n. addition, note f., billet m.

billet, n. (mil.) billet de logement m.

billiard, adj. de billard

billion, n. billion m.

billow, n. grande vague, lame f.

bi-monthly, adj. bimensuel

bin, n. coffre m.

bind, vb. lier; (books) relier

bindery, n. atelier de reliure m.

binding, n. (book) reliure f.; adj. obligatoire

binocular, adj. binoculaire

biochemistry, n. biochimie f.

biography, n. biographie f

biological, adj. biologique

biology, n. biologie f.

biped, n. bipède m.

bird, n. oiseau m.

birth, n. naissance f.

birth control, n. limitation des naissances f.

birthday, n. anniversaire m.

birthplace, n. lieu de naissance m.

birth rate, n. natalité f.

birthright, n. droit d'aînesse m.

biscuit, n. biscuit; petit four m.

bishop, n. évêque m.

bison, n. bison m.

bitch, n. chienne f.

bite, n. morsure f.; vb. mordre

biting, adj. mordant, piquant

bitterly, adv. amèrement, avec amertume

bitterness, n. amertume f.

bivouac, n. bivouac m.

biweekly, adj. and adv. (de) tous les quinze jours

black, adj. noir

blackberry, n. mûre

blackboard, n. tableau noir m.

blackmail, n. chantage m.

black-market, n. marché noir m.

blackout, n. blackout m.

blacksmith, n. forgeron m.

bladder, n. vessie f.

blade, n. lame f., brin m.

blame, n. blâme m.; vb. blâmer

blameless, adj. innocent, sans tache

blanch, vb. blanchir; pâlir

bland, adj. doux, aimable

blank, n. blanc m., vide m; adj. blanc m., blance f., vide

blanket, n. couverture f.

blast, n. (wind) rafale f.; (mine) explosion f.

blaze, n. flambée f.; vb. flamber

blazing, adj. enflammé, flamboyant

bleach, vb. blanchir

bleak, adj. morne

bleakness, n. froidure f.

bleed, vb. saigner

blemish, n. defaut m.

blend, n. mélange m.; vb. mêler

blended, adj. mélangé

bless, vb. bénir

blessed, adj. béni, saint

blessing, n. bénédiction f.

blight, vb. flétrir, détruire, nieller, brouir; n. brouissure f.

blind, n. store m.; adj. aveugle

blindness, n. cécité f.

blink, vb. clignoter

bliss, n. béatitude f.

blissful, adj. bienheureux

blissfully, adv. heureusement

blister, n. ampoule f.

blithe, adj. gai, joyeux

blizzard, n. tempête de neige f.

bloat, vb. boursoufle

block, n. bloc m.; vb. bloquer

blockade, n. blocus m.

blond, adj. and n. blond m.

blood, n. sang m.

bloodhound, n. limier m.

bloodless, adj. exsangue

bloodshed, n. effusion de sang f.

bloodshot, adj. injecté de sang

bloody, adj. sanglant

bloom, n. fleur f.; vb. fleurir

blooming, n. floraison f.; adj. fleurissant

blossom, n. fleur f.

blot, n. tache f.; vb. tacher
blotch, n. tache f.
blotchy, adj. tacheté
blouse, n. blouse f.
blow, n. coup m.; vb. souffler
blue, adj. bleu
blueprint, n. dessin négatif m.
bluff, n. bluff m.
blunder, n. bévue f.
blunt, adj. émoussé; brusque
bluntly, adv. brusquement
bluntness, n. brusquerie f.
blur, vb. barbouiller
blush, n. rougeur f.; vb. rougir
boar, n. sanglier m.
board, n. plance, pension f.
boast, vb. se vanter
boaster, n. vantard m.
boastful, adj. vantard m.
boat, n. bateau m.
boathouse, n. garage (à beaux) m.
bob, vb. (hair) couper court
bode, vb. présager
bodice, n. corsage m.
bodily, adj. corporel
body, n. corps m.
boil, vb. bouillir; intr., faire
  bouillir; n. furoncle m.
boiler, n. chaudière f.
boisterous, adj. bruyant
bold, adj. hardi
boldface, adj. caractères, impudent
boldly, adv. hardiment
boldness, n. hardiesse f.
bolster, n. traversin m.
bolt, n. verrou m.; vb. verrouiller
bomb, n. bombe f.
bombard, vb. bombarder
bombardier, n. bombardier m.
bond, n. lien m., obliation f.
bondage, n. servitude f.
bone, n. os m.
boneless, adj. sans os
bonfire, n. feu de joie m.
bonnet, n. chapeau m.
bonus, n. boni m.
bony, adj. osseux
book, n. livre m.

bookcase, n. bibliothèque f.
bookkeeper, n. teneur de livres m.
bookkeeping, n. comptabilité f.
booklet, n. opuscule m.
bookseller, n. libraire m.,
  bougquiniste m.
boon, n. bienfait m.
boor, n. rustre m.
boorish, adj. rustre
boost, vb. pousser
boot, n. bottine f.
bootblack, n. cireur m.
booth, n. baraque f., cabine f.
booty, n. butin m.
border, n. bord m., frontière f.
border-line, adj. touchant
bore, vb. forer, ennuyer
boredom, n. ennui m.
boring, adj. ennuyeux
born, adj. né; vb. naître
borrower, n. emprunteur m.
bosom, n. sein m.
boss, n. patron m.; vb. diriger
bossy, adj. autoritaire
botanical, adj. botanique
botany, n. botanique f.
botch, n. pustule f.; vb. ravauder
both, adj. and pron. tous les deux
bother, n. ennui m.
bothersome, adj. importun
bottle, n. bouteille f.
bottom, n. fond m.
bottomless, adj. sans fond
boulder, n. grosse pierre f.
boulevard, n. boulevard m.
bounce, vb. rebondir
bound, n. borne f., bound m.; vb.
  borner, bondir
boundary, n. frontière f.
boundless, adj. sans bornes,
  illimitè
bound, n. largesse, prim f.
bouquet, n. bouquet m.
bow, n. arc m., archet m., révérence f., avant m.
bowels, n., pl. entrailles f., pl.
bowl, n. bol m.; vb. jouer aux boules
box, n. boîte f.

boxer, n. boxeur m.

boxing, n. la boxe f.

boy, n. garcon m.

boycott, vb. boycotter

boyhood, n. enfance, adolescence f.

brace, vb. fortifier; n. vile-brequin m., paire f., couple m.

bracelet, n. bracelet m.

bracket, n. console f., crochet m.

brag, vb. se vanter

braid, n. tresse f.; galon m.; vb. tresser, natter

brain, n. cerveau m.; cervelle f.

brake, n. frein m.

bran, n. son m.

branch, n. branche f.

brand, n. marque f.

brandy, n. eau-de-vie f.

brass, n. cuivre jaune

brassiere, n. soutien-gorge m.

brat, n. marmot m.

bravado, n. bravade f.

brave, adj. courageux

bravery, adv. courageusement

brawl, n. rixe f.

bray, vb. braire

brazen, adj. effronté

Brazil, n. le Brésil m.

breach, n. infraction f.; (mil.) bréche f.

bread, n. pain m.

breadth, n. largeur f.

break, n. rupture f., interruption f.; vb. rompre, briser, casser

breakable, adj. fragile

breakage, n. cassure, rupture f.

breakfast, n. petit déjeuner m.

breast, n. poitrine f., sein m.

breath, n. haleine f., souffle m.

breathe, vb. respirer

breathless, adj. essoufflé

breathlessly, adv. en haletant

breed, vb. élever

breeder, n. éleveur m.

breeding, n. éducation f., élevage m.

breeze, n. brise (de houille) f.

breezy, adj. venteux, dégagé

brevity, n. brièveté f.

brew, vb. brasser, faire de la bière

brewery, n. brasserie f.

brick, n. brique f.

bridal, adj. nuptial

bride, n. nouvelle mariée f.

bridegroom, n. nouveau marié m.

bridesmaid, n. demoiselle d'honneur f.

bridge, n. pont m., passerelle f., bridge m.

bridle, n. bride f.

brief, adj. bref

brief case, n. serviette f.

briefly, adv. brièvement

briefness, n. brièveté f.

brigade, n. brigade f.

bright, adj. brillant

brighten, vb. faire briller

brightness, n. éclat m.

brilliance, n. brillant, éclat m

brilliant, adj. brillant

brim, n. bord m.

bring, vb. apporter, amener, porter

brink, n. bord m.

brisk, adj. vif

brisket, n. poitrine

briskly, adv. vivement

briskness, n. vivacité f.

bristle, n. soie f.

British, adj. britannique

brittle, adj. fragile

broad, adj. large

broadcast, adj. radiodiffusé

broadcaster, n. speaker m.

broadly, adv. largement

brocaded, adj. de brocart

broil, vb. griller

broiler, n. gril m.

broker, n. courtier m.

brokerage, n. courtage m.

bronchitis, n. bronchite f.

bronze, n. bronze m.

brooch, n. broche f.

brood, n. couvée f.; vb. couver

brook, n. ruisseau m.

broom, n. balai m.

broth, n. bouillon m.

brother, n. frère m.

brotherhood, n. fraternité f.

brotherly, adj. fraternel

brown, adj. brun

browse, vb. brouter; feuilleter

bruise, n. meurtrissure f.; vb. meurtrir

brunette, adj. and n. brune f.

brunt, n. choc m.

brush, n. brosse f.

brushwood, n. broussailles f.,pl.

brutality, n. brutalité f.

brutalize, vb. abrutir

brute, n. brute f.

bubble, n. bulle f.; vb. bouillonner

buck, n. daim, mâle m.

bucket, n. seau m.

buckle, n. boucle f.

bud, n. bourgeon m.; vb. bourgeonner

budge, vb. bouger

budget, n. budget m.

buffalo, n. buffle m.

buffet, n. buffet m.

buffoon, n. bouffon m.

bug, n. insecte m.

bugle, n. clairon m.

build, vb. bâtir

builder, n. entrepreneur m., construc- teur m.

building, n. bâtiment m.

bulb, n. ampoule f., bulbe m.

bulge, n. bosse f.

bulkhead, n. cloison étanche f.

bulky, adj. encombrant

bull, n. taureau m.

bulldog, n. bouledogue m.

bulldozer, n. machine à refouler f.

bullet, n. balle f.

bulletin, n. bulletin m.

bully, n. matamore m.

bulwark, n. rempart m.

bum, n. fainéant m.

bump, n. coup m., bosse f.; vb. cogner

bumper, n. pare-choc m.

bun, n. petit pain rond (au lait) m.

bunch, n. botte f.

bundle, n. paquet m.

bungle, vb. bousiller

bunion, n. oignon m.

bunk, n. couchette f.

bunny, n. lapin m.

bunting, n. drapeaux m., pl.

buoy, n. bouée f.

buoyant, adj. leger, flottant

burden, n. fardeau m.

burdensome, adj. onéreux

bureau, n. bureau m., commode f.

burglar, n. cambrioleur m.

burglarize, vb. cambrioler

burglary, n. vol avec effraction m., cambriolage m.

burial, n. enterrement m.

burly, adj. de forte carrure

burn, vb. brûler

burner, n. bec m., brûleur m.

burning, adj. brûlant

burrow, n. terrier m.

burst, vb. éclater

bury, vb. enterrer

bus, n. autobus m.

bush, n. buisson m.

bushel, n. boisseau m.

bushy, adj. buissonneux

busily, adv. activement

business, n. affaire f.; affaires f., pl.

businesslike, adj. pratique

busy, adj. occupé

but, conj. mais, sauf (except)

butcher, n. boucher m.

butler, n. maître d'hôtel m.

butt, n. bout m.

butter, n. beurre m.

buttercup, n. bouton d'or m.

butterfly, n. papillon m.

buttock, n. fesse f.

button, n. bouton m.

buttonhole, n. boutonnière f.

buttress, n. contrefort m.

buy, vb. acheter

buyer, n. acheteur m.

buzz, n. bourdonnement m.

buzzard, n. buse f.

by, prep. par, près de (near to)

bylaw, n. règlement local m.

by-pass, n. route d'évitement f.

by-product, n. sous-produit m.

bystander, n. spectateur, assistant m.

cab, n. taxi, fiacre m.
cabaret, n. cabaret m.
cabbage, n. chou m.
cabin, n. cabane, cabine f.
cable, n. cable m.; vb. câbler
cactus, n. cactus m.
cad, n. goujat m.
café, n. café m.
caffeine, n. caféine f.
cage, n. cage f.
cake, n. gâteau m.
calamity, n. calamité f.
calcium, n. calcium m.
calculable, adj. calculable
calculate, vb. calculer
calculus, n. calcul m.
calendar, n. calendrier m.
calf, n. veau m.
caliber, n. calibre m.
calico, n. calicot m.
call, n. appel m., visite f.; vb.
 appeler, faire visite à
calligraphy, n. calligraphie f.
calling, n. vocation, profession f.
callousness, n. insensibilité f.
callow, adj. blanc-bec
callus, n. callosité f.
calm, adj. calme; vb. calmer
calmly, adv. avec calme
calmness, n. tranquilité f.
caloric, adj. calorique
calore, n. calorie f.
calumniate, vb. calomnier
Calvary, n. Calvaire m.
calve, vb. vêler
calyx, n. calice m.
camel, n. chameau m.
camellia, n. camélia m.
cameo, n. camée m.
camera, n. appareil m.
camouflage, vb. camoufler
camp, n. camp, camping m.; vb.
 camper
campaign, n. campagne f.
camper, n. campeur m.
campus, n. terrains d'un collège or
 d'une université m., pl.
can, n. boîte f., bidon m.; vb. pouvoir

Canada, n. le Canada m.
canal, n. canal m.
canapé, n. canapé m.
canary, n. serin m.
cancel, vb. annuler, biffer
cancellation, n. annulation f.
cancer, n. cancer m.
candelabrum, n. candélabre m.
candid, adj. sincère
candidate, n. candidat m.
candidly, adv. franchement
candidness, n. candeur f.
candied, adj. candi
candle, n. bougie f.
candlestick, n. chandelier m.
candour, n. sincérité f
candy, n. bonbon m.
cane, n. canne f.
canine, adj. canin
canister, n. boîte à thé f.
canker, n. chancre m.
canned, adj. conservé en boites
cannery, n. conserverie f.
cannibal, n. cannibale m.f.
cannon, n. canon, m.
cannonade, n. canonnade f.
canny, adv. avisé, rusé
canoe, n. canot m.
canon, n. chanoine m., canon
 (rule) m.
canonical, adj. canonique
canonize, vb. canoniser
canopy, n. dais m.
can't, vb. ne pas pouvoir
cantaloup, n. melon m.,
 cantaloup m.
canteen, n. cantine f., bidon m
canter, n. petit galop f.; vb.
 aller au petit galop
canvas, n. toile f.
canvass, n. solicitation f.; vb.
 solliciter
canyon, n. gorge f., défilé m.
cap, n. bonnet m., casquette f.
capability, n. capacité f.
capable, adj. capable
capably, adv. capablement
capacity, n. capacité f.

cape, n. bond m., câpre f.; vb. bondir

capital, n. capital m., capitale f.

capitalism, n. capitalisme m.

capitalization, n. capitalisation f.

capitalize, vb. capitaliser

capon, n. capon m.

capsule, n. capsule f.

captain, n. capitaine m.

captivate, vb. captiver

captive, adj. and n. captif m.

captivity, n. captivité f.

capture, n. capture f.; vb. capturer

car, n. voiture f., wagon m.

carafe, n. carafe f.

caramel, n. caramel m.

carat, n. carat m.

caravan, n. caravane f.

caraway, n. carvi, cumin m.

carbohydrate, n. carbohydrate m.

carbon, n. carbone m.

carbon dioxide, n. acide carbonique m.

carbon monoxide, n. oxyde de carbone m.

carbon paper, n. papier carbone m.

carburetor, n. carburateur m.

card, n. carte f.

cardboard, n. carton m.

cardiac, adj. cardiaque

cardigan, n. gilet de tricot m.

cardinal, n. cardinal m.

care, n. souci m.; attention f.; prendre soin de.; vb soucier de

career, n. carrière f.

carefree, adj. insouciant

careful, adj. soigneux

carefully, adv. soigneusement

carefulness, n. soin m., attention f.

careless, adj. insouciant

caress, n. caresse f.; vb. caresser

cargo, n. cargaison

caries, n. carie f.

carillon, n. carillon m.

carload, n. voiturée f.

carnal, adj. charnel

carnation, n. incarnat m.

carol, n. noël m.

carpenter, n. charpentier m.

carpet, n. tapis m.

carpeting, n. pose de tapis f.

carriage, n. voiture f., maintien m., transport m.

carrier, n. porteur m., messager m.

carrot, n. carotte m.

carrousel, n. carrousel m.

carry, vb. porter, continuer, exécuter

cart, n. charrette f.

cartel, n. cartel m.

carter, n. charretier m.

cartilage, n. cartilage m.

carton, n. carton m.

cartoon, n. dessin satirique m.

carve, vb. sculpter; découper

carver, n. découpeur m., sculpteur m.

carving, n. découpage m., sculpture f.

cascade, n. cascade f.

case, n. cas m., cause f., caisse f., eui m., en tout cas (in any case)

cash, n. espèces f., pl.; (C.O.D.) livraison contre remboursement f.

cashier, n. caissier m.

cashmere, n. cachemire m.

casino, n. casino m.

cask, n. tonneau m.

casket, n. cassette f.

casserole, n. casserole f.

cassette, n. cassette f.

cast, n. coup m., trempe f., distribution f., moulage m.

castaway, n. naufragé m., rejeté m.

caste, n. caste f.

caster, n. fondeur m.

castle, n. château m.

castoff, adj. abondonné

casual, adj. casuel, insouciant

casualness, n. nonchalance f.

casualties, n. pertes f., pl.

cat, n. chat m., chatte f.

cataclysm, n. cataclysme m.

catacomb, n. catacombe f.

catalogue, n. catalogue m.

cataract, n. cataracte f.

catastrophe, n. catastrophe f.

catch, vb. attraper, saisir	**centerpiece,** n. pièce de milieu f.
catcher, n. qui attrape	**centigrade,** adj. centigrade
catchy, adj. facile à retenir	**centigrade thermometer,** n.
categorical, adj. catégorique	thermomètre centigrade m.
category, n. catégorie f.	**central,** adj. central
cater, vb. pourvoir (à)	**centralize,** vb. centraliser
caterpillar, n. chenille f.	**century,** n. siècle m.
catgut, n. corde à boyau f.	**ceramic,** adj. céramique
cathedral, n. cathédrale f.	**ceramics,** n. céramique f.
Catholicism, n. catholicisme m.	**cereal,** adj. and n. céréale f.
catsup, n. sauce piquante f.	**cerebral,** adj. cérébral
cattle, n. bétail m., bestiaux m., pl.	**ceremonial,** adj. and n. céré-
cattleman, n. éleveur de bétail m.	monial m.
cauliflower, n. chou-fleur m.	**ceremony,** n. cérémonie f.
cause, n. cause f.	**certain,** adj. certain
causeway, n. chaussée f.	**certainly,** adv. certainement
caution, n. prudence f.	**certainty,** n. certitude f.
cautious, adj. prudent	**certificate,** n. certificat m.;
cavalier, adj. and n. cavalier m.	acte de naissance
cavalry, n. cavalerie f.	**certification,** n. certification f.
cave, n. caverne f.	**certified,** adj. certifié, diplôme,
cavern, n. caverne f.	breveté
caviar, n. caviar m.	**certifier,** n. qui certifie
cavity, n. cavité f.	**certify,** vb. certifier
cease, vb. cesser (de)	**certitude,** n. certitude f.
cedar, n. cèdre m.	**cervical,** adj. cervical
ceiling, n. plafond m.	**cervix,** n. cervix m.
celebrant, n. célébrant	**cessation,** n. cessation, suspension f.
celebrate, vb. célébrer	**cession,** n. cession f.
celebration, n. célébration f.	**cesspool,** n. fosse d'aisances f.
celebrity, n. célébrité f.	**chafing dish,** n. réchaud m.
celery, n. céleri m.	**chagrin,** n. chagrin m.
celestial, adj. céleste	**chain,** n. chaîne f.
celibacy, n. célibat m.	**chair,** n. chaise f., fauteuil m.
cell, n. cellule f.	**chairman,** n. président m.
cellar, n. cave f.	**chairperson,** n. président m.,
cellophane, n. cellophane f.	présidente f.
cellular, adj. cellulaïre	**chairwoman,** n. présidente f.
cellulose, n. cellulose f.	**chalice,** n. calice m.
cement, n. ciment m.; vb. cimenter	**chalk,** n. craie f.
cemetery, n. cimetière m.	**challenge,** vb. défier, contester
censor, n. censeur m.; vb. censurer	**challenger,** n. qui fait un défi,
censorship, n. censure f.	prétendant m.
censure, n. censure f.	**chamber,** n. chambre f.
census, n. recensement m.	**chamberlain,** n. chambellan m.
cent, n. cent	**champ,** vb. ronger, mâcher
center, n. centre m.	**champion,** n. champion m.
centerfold, n. pages centrales f., pl.	**championship,** n. championnat m.

chance, n. chance f., par hasard m.

chancel, n. sanctuaire, choeur m.

chancellor, n. chancelier m.

chandelier, n. lustre m.

change, n. chagement m.

changeable, adj. changeant

changer, n. changeur m.

channel, n. canal m.

chant, n. chant m.; vb. chanter

chaos, n. chaos m.

chap, n. gercure f., gars m.

chapel, n. chapelle f.

chaperon, n. duègne f.; chaperon m.

chaplain, n. aumônier m.

chapter, n. chapitre m.

character, n. caractère, personnage, rôle m.

characterize, vb. caractériser

charcoal, n. charbon (m.) de bois

charge, n. charge f. prix, soin m.; vb. charger, charger de; demander

charger, n. grand plat, cheval de bataille m.

charitable, adj. charitable

charitably, adv. charitablement

charity, n. charité f.

charm, n. charme m. vb. charmer

charmer, n. charmeur, enchanteur m.

charming, adj. charmant

charred, adj. carbonisé

chart, n. carte f.; grapique m.

chase, n. chasse f.; vb. chassser

chaser, n. chasseurm., ciseleur m.

chasm, n. abime m.

chassis, n. chassis m.

chaste, adj. chaste

chastise, vb. châtier

chastity, n. chasteté f.

chat, n. causette f.; vb. causer

chateau, n. château m.

chattel, n. bien, meuble m.

chatter, n. vavardate m.; vb. vavarder

chatterbox, n. vavard m.

chauffeur, n. chauffeur m.

cheap, adj. bon marché, de peu de valeur

cheapen, vb. déprécier

cheapness, n. bon marché m.,

bas prix m., basse qualité f.

cheat, vb. tromper, tricher

cheater, n. tricheur, trompeur m.

check, n. frein m., vérification f., ticket m., addition f., chèque

checker, n. enregistreur m., contrôleur m.

cheek, n. joue f.

cheerfully, adv. gaiement, de bon coeur

cheerfulness, n. gaieté f., bonne humeur f.

cheerless, adj. triste, morne, sombre

cheery, adj. gai, joyeux

cheese, n. fromage m.

cheesecloth, n. gaze f.

chemical, adj. chimique

chemically, adv. chimiquement

chemist, n. chimiste m.f.

chemistry, n. chimie f.

chemotherapy, n. chimiothérapie f.

chenille, n. chenille f.

cherish, vb. chérir

cherry, n. cerise f.

chess, n. échecs m., pl.

chessman, n. pièce f.

chest, n. coffre m., poitrine f.

chestnut, n. châtaigne f.

chevron, n. chevron m.

chew, vb. mâcher

chic, adj. chic

chick, n. poussin m.

chicken, n. poulet m.

chicken-pox, n. varicelle f.

chicle, n. chiclé m.

chief, n. chef m.; adj. principal

chiefly, adv. surtout, principalement

chieftain, n. chef de clan m.

chiffon, n. chiffon m.

chilblain, n. engelure f.

child, n. enfant m.f.

childbirth, n. enfantement m.

childhood, n. enfance f.

childish, adj. enfantin

childlessness, n. puérilité f., enfantillage m.

childlike, adj. comme un enfant,

en enfant
Chile, n. le Chili m.
chili, n. piment m.
chill, n. froid m., frisson m.
 vb. refroidir
chilly, adj. un peu froid
chime, n. carillon m.; vb. carillonner
chimney, n. cheminée f.
chimpanzee, n. chimpanzé m.
chin, n. menton m.
China, n. la Chine f.
china, n. porcelaine f.
chinchilla, n. chinchilla m.
chintz, n. perse f.
chip, n. éclat m., frites f., pl.
chipmunk, n. tamias m.
chiropractor, n. chiropracteur m.
chirp, vb. pépier, gazouiller
chisel, vb. ciseler; n. ciseau m.
chivalry, n. chevalerie f.
chive, n. ciboulette f.
chlorine, n. chlore m.
chocolate, n. chocolat m.
choice, n. choix m.
choir, n. choeur m.
choke, vb. étouffer
choker, n. foulard m.
choose, vb. choisir
chop, n. côtelette f.; vb. couper
chopper, n. couperet m.
chopstick, n. baguette f., bâtonnet m.
choral, adj. choral
chord, n. accord m.
chorus, n. choeur m.
christen, vb. baptiser
christening, n. baptême m.
Christian, adj. and n. chrétien m.
Christianity, n. christiansime m.
Chirstmas, n. Noël m.
chronic, adj. chronique
chronicle, n. chronique f.
chronological, adj. chronologique
chrysalis, n. chrysalide f.
chrysanthemum, n. chrysanthème m.
chubby, adj. joufflu
chuckle, vb. rire tout bas
chum, n. camarade, copain m.
chummy, adj. familier, intime

chunk, n. gros morceau m.
chunky, adj. en gros morceaux
church, n. église f.
churchman, n. homme d'église m.,
 ecclésiastique m.
churchyard, n. cimetière m.
churn, vb. baratter
chute, n. glissière f.
chutney, n. chutney m.
cicada, n. cigale f.
cider, n. cidre m.
cigar, n. cigare m.
cigarette, n. cigarette f.
cilla, n. cils m., pl.
ciliary, adj. ciliaire
cinch, n. c'est facile
cinchona, n. quinquina m.
cinder, n. cendre f.
cinema, n. cinéma m.
cinematic, adj. cinematographique
cinnamon, n. cannelle f.
cipher, n. chiffre m., zéro m.
circle, n. cercle m.; vb. entourer (de)
circuit, n. circuit m.
circular, adj. circulaire
circulation, n. circulation f.
circulator, n. circulateur m.
circumcise, vb. circoncire
circumcision, n. circoncision f.
circumference, n. circonférence f.
circumscribe, vb. circonscrire
circumstance, n. circonstance f.,
 moyens m., pl.
circus, n. cirque m.
citation, n. citation f.
cite, vb. citer
citizen, n. citoyen m.
citizenry, n. touse les citoyens m., pl.
citizenship, n. droit de cité
citric acid, n. acide citrique m.
city, n. ville f., cité f.
civic, adj. civique
civil, adj. civil, poli, (civil servant)
 fonctionnaire m.
civilization, n. civilisation f.
civilize, vb. civiliser
clad, adj. habilié, vêtu
claim, n. demande f., droit m.; vb.

demander

clairvoyance, n. clairvoyance f.

clairvoyant, n. voyant m.

clam, n. palourde f., mollusque m.

clamber, vb. grimper

clammy, adj. visqueux, moite

clamor, n. clameur f.

clamorous, adj. bruyant

clan, n. clan m., clique f.

clap, vb. (applaud) applaudir

clapboard, n. bardeau m.

clapper, n. claqueur m., battant (of a bell) m.

claque, n. claque f.

claret, n. vin rouge de Bordeaux m.

clarify, vb. (lit.) clarifier; (fig.) éclaircir

clarinet, n. clarinette f.

clarion, n. clairon m.

clarity, n. clarté f.

clash, vb. choquer, s' entrechoquer; n. choc m.

clasp, n. agrafe, étreinte f.; vb. agrafer, étreindre

class, n. classe f.

classification, n. classification f.

classify, vb. classifier, classer

classroom, n. salle de classe f.

clatter, n. burit m.

clause, n. clause f.

claw, n. griffe f.

claw-hammer, n. marteau à dent m.

clay, n. argile, glaise f.

clean, adj. propre; vb. nettoyer

clean-cut, adj. net, fin

cleanse, vb. nettoyer, curer

cleanser, n. chose qui nettoie f., détersif, cureur m.

clear, adj. clair, net, lucide

clearing, n. éclaircissement m.

clearly, adv. clairement, nettement

clearness, n. clarté f., neteté f.

cleat, n. fer m., (naut.) taquet m.

cleavage, n. fendage m., scisson f.

cleaver, n. fendeur m., fendoir m., couperet m.

cleft, n. fente f.

clemency, n. clémence f.

clench, vb. serrer

clergy, n. clergé m.

clergyman, n. ecclésiastique m.

clerical, adj. clerical, de bureau

clerk, n. employé m., commis m.

clever, adj. habile

cleverness, n. adresse f.

clew, n. fil m.

cliché, n. cliché m.

click, n. cliquetis m., déclic m.; vb. cliqueter

client, n. client m.

cliff, n. falaise f.

climax, n. comble m.

climb, n. montée f.; vb. monter, grimper

climber, n. grimpeur m., ascensioniste m.

clinch, vb. river; conclure

cling, vb. s'accrocher

clinic, n. clinique f.

clip, vb. couper; n. pince f.

clipping, n. coupure f.

clique, n. clique f.

clock, n. (large) horloge f., (small) pendule f.

clockwise, adv. dans le sens des aiguilles d'une montre

clockwork, n. mouvement d'horlogerie m.

clod, n. motte de terre f.

clog, b. entraver

clone, n. reproduction exacte f.

close, adj. clos, bien fermé

closely, adv. de près, étroitement

closeness, n. proximité, exactitude f.

closet, n. cabinet, boudoir m.

clot, n. caillot m.

cloth, n. étoffe f.

clothe, vb. vêtir, habiller

clothes, n. habits m., pl.

clothespin, n. pince f.

clothier, n. drapier m. tailleur m.

clothing, n. vêtements m., pl.

cloud, n. nuage m.

cloudburst, n. rafale de pluie f.

cloudless, adj. sans nuage

cloudy, adj. nuageux, couvert

clout, n. morceau m., piece f.

clove, n. clou de girofle m.

clover, n. trèfle m.

clown, n. bouffon m.

cloy, vb. rassasier

club, n. massues f., cercle m.

clubfoot, n. pied bot m.

clue, n. fil m.

clumsy, adj. gauche

cluster, n. groupe m., grappe f., bouquet m.; vb. se grouper

clutch, n. griffe f., embrayage m.

clutter, vb. encombrer

coach, n. carrosse m., voiture f.

coal, n. charbon m., houille f.

coalition, n. coalition f.

coarse, adj. grossier

coarseness, n. gorssièreté f.

coast, n. côte f.

coastal, adj. de la côte, littoral

coaster, n. caboteur m., dessous de carage m.

coast guard, n. garde-côtes m.

coat, n. habit; m. couche f.

coating, n. couche f., enduit m., étoffe pour habits f.

coax, vb. cajoler

cobalt, n. cobalt m.

cobblestone, n. pierre du pavé f.

cobra, n. cobra m.

cobweb, n. toile d'araignée f.

cocaine, n. cocaine f.

cockroach, n. blatte f.

cocky, adj. suffisant

cocoa, n. cacao m.

cocoon, n. cocon m.

cod, n. morue f.

coddle, vb. dorloter

code, n. code m.

codeine, n. codéine f.

codfish, n. morue f.

coerce, vb. contraindre

coffee, n. café m.

coffin, n. cercueil m.

cog, n. dent f.

coherent, adj. cobérent

coiffure, n. coffure f.

coil, n. couleau m.

coin, n. pièce de monnaie

coincide, vb. coïncider

coincidence, n. coïncidence f.

coincident, adj. coïncident

colander, n. passoire f.

cold, n. froid m., rhume m.

cold-blooded, adj. de sang froid

coldness, n. froideur f.

collaborate, vb. collaborer

collapse, vb. s'effrondrer, s'affaisser

collar, n. col m.; (dog) collier m.

collarbone, n. clavicule f.

collate, vb. collationner, comparer

collation, n. collation f., comparaison f., repas froid m.

colleague, n. collègue m., f.

collect, vb. rassembler

collection, n. collection, collecte f.

collective, adj. collectif

collectively, adv. collectifement

collector, n. collectionneur m., contrôleur m.

college, n. collège m., université f.

collegiate, adj. de collège, collégial

collide, vb. se heurter

collision, n. collision f.

collusion, n. collusion f., connivence f.

colon, n. deux points m., pi.

colonel, n. colonel m.

colonial, adj. colonial

colonist, n. colon m.

colonization, n. colonisation f.

colonize, vb. coloniser

colony, n. colonie f.

color, n. couleur f.

colored, adj. coloré, de couleur, colorie

colorful, adj. coloré, pittoresque

coloring, n. coloris m., couleur f.

colossal, adj. colossal

colt, n. poulain m.

colter, n. coutre m.

column, n. colonne f.

coma, n. com m.

comb, n. peigne m.

combat, n. combat m.

combination, n. combinaison f.

combustible, adj. and n. combustible m.

combustion, n. combustion f.

come, vb. venir; arriver; recontrer; partir; revenir; descendre; entrer

comedian, n. comédien m.

comedy, n. comédie f.

comely, adj. avenant

comet, n. comète f.

comfort, n. consolation f., confort m.

comfortable, adj. commode, confortable

comforter, n. consolateur m.

comfortless, adj. sans consolation, inconsolable, désolé

coming, n. venue, arrivée, approche f.

comma, n. virgule f.

command, n. commandement m.

commandeer, vb. réquisitioner

commemorate, vb. commémorer

commemorative, adj. commémoratif

commence, vb. commencer

commencement, n. commencement, début

commend, vb. recommander, louer

commendable, adj. louable, recommandable

comment, n. commentaire m.

commerce, n. commerce m.

commercial, adj. commercial

commission, n. commission; perpétration f.

commissioner, n. commissaire m.

commit, vb. commettre

commitment, n. engagement m.

committee, n. comité m.

commodity, n. produit m., commodité f., denrée f.

common, adj. commun, vulgaire

commonly, adv. communément, ordinairement

commonplace, n. lieu-commun m.

commonwealth, n. état m.

communicate, vb. communiquer

communication, n. communication f.

communion, n. communion f.

community, n. communauté f.

commuter, n. voyageur de banlieue m.

compact, adj., serré, compact

compactness, n. compacité f.

companion, n compagnon m., compagne f.

companionship, n. camaraderie f.

company, n. compagnie f.

comparable (with,) adj. comparable (à)

comparatively, adv. comparativement, relativement

compare, vb. comparer

comparison, n. comparaison f.

compartment, n. compartiment m.

compass, n. (naut.) boussole f.; (geom.) compas m.

compassion, n. compassion f.

compassionate, adj. compatissant

compatible, adj. compatible

compel, vb. forcer

compensate, vb. compenser

compensation, n. compensation f.

compete, vb. rivaliser

competence, n. compétence f.

competent, adj. capable

competently, adv. convenablement, avec compétence

competition, n. concurrence f.

competitor, n. concurrent m.

compile, vb. compiler

complacency, n. contentement m.

complacent, adj. content de soi-même

complacently, adv. avec un air (un ton) suffisant

complain, vb. se plaindre

complainer, n. plaignant m., réclameur m.

complainingly, adv. d'une manière plaignante

complaint, n. plainte f.

complement, n. complément m.

complete, adj. complet

completely, adv. complètement, tout à fait

completeness, n. état complet m., perfection f.

completion, n. achèvement m.

complex, adj. and n. complexe m.

complexion, n. teint m.

complexity, n. complexité f.

compliance, n. acquiescement m.

complaint, adj. complaisant, accommodant

complicate, vb. compliquer

complicity, n. complicité f.

compliment, n. compliment m.

complimentary, adj. flatteur, de félicitations

component, adj. and n. composant m.

comport, vb. s'accorder (avec)

compose, vb. composer

composer, n. compositeur m.

composite, adj. composé

composition, n. composition f.

compost, n. compost m., terreau m.

composure, n. calme m., tranquilité f., slang-froid m.

compound, n. composé m., composition f.

comprehend, vb. comprendre

comprehensible, adj. compréhensible, inteligible

comprehension, n. compréhension f.

comprehensive, adj. compréhensif

compress, n. compresse f.

compressed, adj. comprimé

compression, n. compression f.

compressor, n. compresseur m

comprise, vb. comprendre

compromiser, n. comprometteur m.

compulsion, n. contrainte f.

compulsive, adj. coercitif, obligatoire

compulsory, adj. obligatoire

compunction, n. componction f.

computation, n. supputation f.

compute, vb. supputer

computer, n. ordinateur m.

computerize, vb. informatiser

computer science, n. informatique f.

comrade, n. camarade m.f.

concave, adj. concave

conceal, vb. cacher

concede, vb. concéder

conceivably, adv. d'une manière concevable

conceive, vb. concevoir

concentrate, vb. concentrer

concept, n. concept m.

conception, n. conception f.

concern, n. affxiété, intérêt, soin, souci m.

concerning, prep. concernant

concert, n. concert m.

concession, vb. concession f.

concise, adj. concis

concisely, adv. avec concision, succinctement

conciseness, n. concision f.

conclave, n. conclave m.

conclude, vb. conclure

conclusion, n. conclusion f.

conclusive, adj. concluant

concord, n. concorde f.

concordat, n. concordat m.

concourse, n. councours m., affluence f.

concrete, n. béton m.

concur, vb. concourir, être d'accord

concurrence, m. assentiment m.

concurrent, adj. concourant

condemn, vb. condamner

condemnable, adj. condamnable

condensation, n. condensation f.

condense, vb. condenser

condenser, n. condenseur m.

condiment, n. condiment m., assaisonnement m.

condition, n. condition f.

conditional, adj. and n. conditionnel m.

conditionally, adv. conditionanellement

condolence, n. condoléance f.

condominium, n. condominium m.

conducive, adj. favorable

conduct, n. conduite f.

conductivity, n. conductivité f.

conductor, n. conducteur, receveur (d'orchestre) m.

conduit, n. conduit, tuyau m.

cone, n. cône m.

confection, n. confection f.; (sweet) bonbon m.

confectioner, n. confiseur m.

confectionery, n. confiserie f.

confederate, adj. and n. confédéré m.

confer, vb. conférer

conference, n. entretien m.

confess, vb. avouer

confession, n. confession f.

confessional, n. confessional m.

confessor, n. confesseur m.

confetti, n. confetti m.

confidant, n. confident m.

confidence, n. confiance f.

confident, adj. confiant

confidently, adv. avec confiance

confine, vb. confiner; limiter

confirm, vb. confirmer

confirmation, n. confirmation f.

confirmed, adj. invétéré, incorrigible

confiscate, vb. confisquer

conflagration, n. conflagration f., incendie m.

conflict, n. conflit m.

conform, vb. conformer

conformation, n. conformation, conformité f.

conformer, n. conformiste m.

conformist, n. conformiste m.

conformity, n. conformité f.

confront, vb. confronter

confuse, vb. confondre

confusion, n. confusion f.

congenial, adj. sympathique, convenable

congential, adj. congénital

congestion, n. (med.) congestion f.; (traffic) encombrement m.

congratulate, vb. féliciter de

congratulation, n. félicitation f.

congregate, vb. rassembler

congregation, n. assemblée f.

congress, n. congrès m.

conjecture, n. conjecture f.

conjunction, n. conjonction f.

conjunctive, adj. conjonctif

connect, vb. joindre

connection, n. connexion f.

conquer, vb. conquérir

conqueror, n. conquérant m.

conquest, n. conquête f.

conscience, n. conscience f.

conscious, adj. conscient

consciously, adv. sciemment, en parfaite connaissance

consciousness, n. conscience f.

conscript, adj. and n. conscrit m.

conscription, n. conscription f.

consecrate, vb. consacrer

consecration, n. consécration f.

consecutive, adj. consécutif

consecutively, adv. consécutivement, de suite

consensus, n. consensus m., assentiment général m.

consent, n. consentement m.

consequence, n. conséquence f.

consequent, adj. conséquent

consequential, adj. conséquent, logique

consequently, adv. par conséquent

conservation, n. conservation f.

conservatism, n. conservatisme m.

conservative, adj. conservateur

conservatively, adv. d'une manière conservatrice

conservatory, n. conservatoire m.

conserve, vb. conserver

consider, vb. considérer

considerable, adj. considérable

considerably, adv. considérablement

considerate, adj. plein d'égards

considerately, adv. avec égards, avec indulgence

consideration, n. considération f.

considering, prep. vu que, attendu que

consign, vb. consigner

consignment, n. expédition, consignation f.

consistency, n. consistance f.

consistent, adj. consistant

consolation, n. consolation f.

console, vb. consoler

consolidate, vb. consolider

consonant, n. consonne f.

conspicuous, adj. en évidence
conspiracy, n. conspiration f.
conspirator, n. conspirateur m.
conspire, vb. conspirer
constant, adj. constant
constipation, n. constipation f.
constituent, adj. constituant
constitute, vb. constituer
constitution, n. constitution f.
constrain, vb. contraindre
constraint, n. contrainte f.
constrict, vb. resserrer
construct, vb. construire
construction, n. construction f.
constructive, adj. constructif
constructor, n. constructeur m.
consul, n. consul m.
consult, vb. consulter
consultation, n. consultation f.
consume, vb. consumer
consumer, n. consommateur m.
consummate, adj. consommé
consumption, n. consommation;
 (med.) phtisie f.
consumptive, adj. poitrinaire,
 tuberculeux
contact, n. contact m.
contagious, adj. contagieux
contain, vb. contenir
container, n. récipient m.
contaminated, adj. contaminé
contemplation, n. contemplation f.
contemplative, adj. contemplatif
contemporary, adj. contemporain
contempt, n. mépris m.
contemptuous, adj. méprisant
contend, vb. lutter, soutenir
contender, n. compétiteur m.,
 concurrent m.
content, n. contentement m.
contention, n. contention, lutte f.
contentment, n. contentement m.
contest, n. lutte f., concours m.
contestant, n. concurrent m.
context, n. contexte m.
contiguous, adj. contigu
continent, adj. and n. continent m.
continental, adj. continental

contingency, n. contingence f.
contingent, adj. contingent
continuation, n. continuation f.
continue, vb. continuer
continuous, adj. continu
continouously, adv. continû-
 ment, sans interruption
contort, vb. tordre, défigurer
contour, n. contour m.
contraband, n. contrebande f.
contraception, n. procédés
 anticonceptionnels m., pl.
contract, n. contrat m.
contracted, adj. contracté, res-
 serré
contraction, n. contraction f.
contractor, n. entrepreneur m.
contradict, vb. contredire
contradictable, adj. qui peut
 être contredit
contradiction, n. contradiction f.,
 démenti m.
contraption, n. machin m.
contrast, n. contraste m.
contribute, vb. contribuer
contribution, n. contribution f.
contributor, n. contribuant m.
contributory, adj. contribuant
contrite, adj. contrit, pénitent
contrition, n. contrition f.
contrive, vb. inventer, imaginer,
 arranger
control, n. autorité f.
controllable, adj. vérifiable,
 gouvernable
controller, n. contrôleur m.
controversy, n. controverse f.
contusion, n. contusion f.
convalescence, n. convalescence f.
convalescent, adj. convalescent
convenience, n. convenance f.,
 commodité f.
convenient, adj. commode
convent, n. couvent m.
conventional, adj. conventionnel
converge, vb. converger
convergent, adj. convergent
conversation, n. conversation f.

converse, vb. converser
convert, vb. convertir
converter, n. convertisseur m.
convertible, adj. convertible,
 convertissable
convex, adj. convexe
convey, vb. transporter, transmettre
conveyance, n. transport m.
convict, n. forcat m.; vb. condamner
conviction, n. conviction,
 persuasion f.
convince, vb. convaincre
convincing, adj. convaincant
convicingly, adv. d'une manière
 confaincante
convival, adj. jovial, joyeux
convocation, n. convocation f.
convoy, n. convoi m.
convulsion, n. convulsion f.
convulsive, adj. convulsif
cook n. cuisinier m.; vb. cuire, intr.
 faire cuire
cookbook, n. livre de cuisine m.
cookie, n. gâteau sec m.
cool, adj. frais m., fraîche f.
cooler, n. rafraîchissoir m.
coolness, n. fraîcheur f.
co-operate, vb. coopérer
co-operation, n. coopération f.
co-operative, n. coopérative f. adj.
 coopératif
co-ordinate, vb. coordonner
co-ordination, n. coordination f.
cop, n. flic m.; vb. attraper, pincer
copier, n. machine à copier f.
copious, adj. copieux
copper, n. cuivre m.
copy, n. copie f.; vb. copier
copyright, n. droit d'auteur m., pl.
coquette, n. coquette f.
coral, n. corail m., pl. coraux
cord, n. corde f.
cordial, adj. and n. cordial m.
cordiality, n. cordialité f.
cordially, adv. cordialement
cordon, n. cordon m.
corduroy, n. velours côtelé m.
core, n. coeur m.

cork, n. liège, bouchon m.
corkscrew, n. tire-bouchon m.
corn, n. maïs m.
cornea, n. cornée f.
corner, n. coin m.
cornerstone, n. pierre angulaire f.
cornet, n. cornet m.
cornice, n. corniche f.
coronary, adj. coronaire
coronation, n. couronnement m.
coroner, n. coroner m.
coronet, n. (petite) couronne f.
corporal, n. (mil.) caporal m.
corporate, adj. de corporation
corporation, n. corporation f.
corps, n. corps m.
corpse, n. cadavre m.
corpulent, adj. corpulent, gros
corpuscle, n. corpuscule m.
corral, n. corral m.
correct, adj. correct; vb. corriger
correction, n. correction f.
corrective, adj. de correction,
 correctif
correctly, adv. correctment, justement
correctness, n. correction f.
correlate, vb. être en corrélation;
 intr. mettre en corrélation
correspond, vb. correspondre
correspondence, n correspondance f.
correspondent, n. correspondant m.
corridor, n. couloir m.
corrode, vb. corroder
corrosion, n. corrosion f.
corrugate, vb. rider, plisser
corrupt, adj. corrompu; vb. corrompre
corruptible, adj. corruptible
corruption, n. corruption f.
corruptive, adj. corruptif
corsage, n. corsage m.
corset, n. corset m.
corvette, n. corvette f.
cosmetic, adj. and n. cosmétique m.
cosmic, adj. cosmique
cosmopolitan, adj. and n. cosmopolite m.f.
cosmos, n. cosmos m.

cost, n. coût; vb. coûter
costly, adj. coûteux
costume, n. costume m.
costumer, n. costumier m.
cost, n. prix, frais m.
cottage, n. chaumière f.
cotton, n. coton m.
cottonseed, n. graine de coton f.
couch, n. divan m.
cough, n. toux f.; vb. tousser
could, vb. pouvait, pourrait
council, n. conseil m.
councilman, n. conseiller m.
counsel, n. conseil m.; vb. conseiller
counselor, n. conseiller m.
count, n. compte, comte m.; vb.
 compter
counter, n. comptoir m.; adv. à
 l'encontre de
counteract, vb. neutraliser
counteraction, n. action contraire f.
counterfeit, adj. faux m., fausse f.; vb.
 contrefaire
counterpart, n. contre-partie f.
countess, n. comtesse f.
countless, adj. innombrable
country, n. pays m., campagne,
 patrie f.
county, n. comté m.
coupé, n. coupé m.
couple, n. couple f.; vb. coupler
coupon, n. coupon m.
courage, n. courage m.
courageous, adj. courageux
courier, n. courrier m.
course, n. cours m., bien entendu
 route f., service m.
court, n. cour f.; vb. faire la
 cour à
courteous, adj. courtois
courtesy, n. courtoisie f.
courthouse, n. palais de jusitice m.
courtier, n. courtisan m.
courtroom, n. salle d'audience f.
courtship, n. cour f.
cousin, n. cousin m., cousine f.
covenant, n. pacte m.
cover, vb. couvrir, voiler, déguise;

cacher
coverage, n. couverture f.
covering, n. couvertue f., enveloppe f.
covet, vb. convoiter
cow, n. vache f.
coward, n. lâche m.
cower, vb. se blottir
cowhide, n. peau de vache f.
coy, adj. timide
cozy, adj. confortable
crab, n. crabe m.
crab apple, n. pomme sauvage f.
crack, vb. fendre, fêler, casser; n.
 fente, fissure f.
cracked, adj. fendu, fêlé
cracker, n. biscuit m.
cracking, n. craquement,
 claquement m.
crackup, n. crach m.
cradle, n. berceau m.
craft, n. habileté f., métier m.,
 embarcation f.
craftsman, n. artisan m.
craftsmanship, n. habilté,
 technique f.
crafty, adj. rusé, astucieux
cram, vb. remplir, farcir
cramp, n. crampe f., crampon m.
cranberry, n. canneberge, airelle f.
crane, n. grue f.
cranium, n. crâne m.
crank, n. manivelle f.
cranky, adj. d'humeur difficile
crash, n. faire un grand fracas
crate, n. caisse f.
crater, n. cratère m.
craven, adj. lâche, poltron
craving, n. désir ardent, besoin
 impérieux m.
crawl, vb. ramper, se trainer
crayon, n. pastel m.
crazed, adj. fou, dément
crazy, adj. fou m. folle f.
cream, n. crème f.
creamy, adj. crémeux, de crème
crease, n. pli m.; vb. frois ser
create, vb. créer
creation, n. création f.

creative, adj. créateur m., créatrice f.

creator, n. créateur m., créatrice f.

creature, n. créature f.

credible, adj. croyable

credit, n. crédit; honneur m.

creditable, adj. estimable

creditably, adv. honorablement

creditor, n. créancier m.

creed, n. croyance f.; credo m.

creek, n. ruisseau m.

creep, vb. ramper; se glisser

cremate, vb. incinérer

crematory, n. crématorium m.

crepe, n. crêpe m.

crescent, n. croissant m.

crest, n. crête, f.

crew, n. équipage m., équipe f.

crib, n. lit d'enfant m., mangeoire f.

cricket, n. (insect) grillon m.

crier, n. crieur, huissier m.

crime, n. crime m.

criminal, adj. criminel

criminology, n. criminologie f.

crimson, adj. and n. cramoisi m.

cringe, vb. faire des courbettes, se lapir, s'humilier

crinkle, n. pli m., sinuosité f.

cripple, n. estropié m.; vb. estropier

crisis, n. crise f.

crisp, adj. cassant, croquant, croustillant

crispness, n. frisure f.

crisscross, adj. and adv. entre-croisé

critic, n. critique m.

critical, adj. critique

criticism, n. critique f.

criticize, vb. critiquer

critique, n. critique f.

croak, vb. coasser, croasser

crochet, vb. broder au crochet; crochet n.

crock, n. pot de terre m.

crockery, n. faïence f.

crocodile, n. crocodile m.

crone, n. vieille femme f.

crony, n. vieux camarade,

compère m.

crook, n. escroc, voleur m.

crooked, adj. tortu

croon, vb. chantonner, fredonner

crop, n. récolte f.

croquette, n. croquette f.

cross, n. croix f.; adj. maussade; vb. croiser, se signer, rayer

crossbreed, n. race croisée f.

cross-examine, vb. contre-examiner

cross-eye, adj. louche

cross-fertilization, n. croisement m.

cross-purpose, n. opposition, contradiction f.; malentendu m.

cross section, n. coupe en travers f.

crossword puzzle, n. mots croisés m., pl.

crotch, n. fourche f., fourchet m.

crouch, vb. s'accroupir

croup, n. croupe f.; (med.) croup m.

croupier, n. croupier m.

crouton, n. croûton m.

crow, n. corneille f.; chant du coq m.

crowd, n. foule f.

crowded, adj. encombré

crown, n. couronne f., calotte f., sommet m.; vb. couronner

crucial, adj. crucial

crucifix, n. crucifix m.

crucifixion, n. crucifixion f.; crucifiement m.

crucify, vb. crucifier

crude, adj. grossier, imparfait, fruste

cruel, adj. cruel

cruise, n. croisière f.

cruiser, n. croiseur m.

crumbs, n. miette, mie f.

crumble, vb. émietter

crunch, vb. croquaer broyer

crusade, n. croisade f.

crush, vb. écraser

crust, n. croûte f.

crutch, n. béquille f.

cry, n. cri m.; vb. crier, pleurer

crying, adj. criant

cryosurgery, n. cryochirurgie f.

crypt, n. crypte f.

crystal, n. cristal m.

crysallize, vb. cristalliser
cub, n. petit m.
Cuba, n. le Cuba m.
Cuban, n. Cubain m.; adj. cubain
cube, n. cube m.
cubic, adj. cubique
cubicle, n. compartiment m., cabine f.
cubic measure, n. mesures de volume f., pl.
cubism, n. cubisme m.
cucumber, n. concombre m.
cud, n. bol alimentaire m.; panse, chique f.
cuddle, vb. serrer
cue, n. réplique f.; mot m.
cuff, n. poignet m.
cuisine, n. cuisine f.
culinary, adj. culinaire, de cuisine
cull, vb. cueillir, recuellir
culprit, n. accusé m., accusée f.
cult, n. culte m.
cultivate, vb. cultiver; adj. cultivable
cultivated, adj. cultivé
cultivation, n. culture f.
cultivator, n. cultivateur m.
cultural, adj. cultural, agricole, culturel
culture, n. culture f.
culvert, n. ponceau, petit aqueduc
cumbersome, adj. encombrant
cunning, n. ruse, adresse, finesse f.
cup, n. tasse, coupe f.; gobelet, godet m.
cupful, n. tasse, pleine tasse f.
cupboard, n. armoire f.
cupel, n. coupelle f.
Cupid, n. Cupidon m.
curable, adj. guérissable, curable
curator, n. conservateur, administrateur m.
curb, n. gourmette f.; bord, frein m. vb. mettre la gourmette à
curd, n. lait caillé, caillé m.; vb. cailler, figer
curdle, vb. cailler
cure, n. guérison f.; remède m.; vb. guérir
curfew, n. courvre-fue m.

curio, n. curiosité f.
curiosity, n. curiosité f.; antiaqaire m.
curious, adj. curieux
curl, n. boucle f.; vb. friser
curling, n. frisure
curly, adj. risé, bouclé
currant, n. groseille f.
currency, n. monnaie f.
current, adj. and n. courant m.
currently, adv. couramment
curriculum, n. programme d'é-tudes, plan d'études m.
curry, n. cari m.
curse, n. malédiction f.; juron m., fléau m.; vb. maudire; hurer
cursed, adj. maudit
cursor, n. curseur m.
curt, adj. brusque, bref, sec
curtail, vb. raccourcir
curtain, n. rideau m.; courtine f.
curve, n. courbe f.; vb. courber
cushion, n. clussin m.
cuspidor, n. crachoir m.
custard, n. crème f.
custodian, n. gardien m.
custody, n. garde, détention f.
custom, n. coutume f.
customary, adj. habituel
customer, n. client m.
cute, adj. gentil m., gentille f.
cuticle, n. cuticule f.
cutlery, n. coutellerie f.
cutlet, n. côtelette f.
cutthroat, n. coupe-jarret m.
cutting, n. incision f.; adj. incisif, tranchant
cutty, adj. court
cycle, n. cycle m.; vb. faire de la bicyclette
cyclist, n. cycliste m.
cyclone, n. cyclone m.
cylinder, n. cylindre m.
cynic, n. cynique m.
cynical, adj. cynique
cypress, n. cyprès m.
cyst, n. kyste m.
Czech, adj. tchèque

dab, n. coup léger m.; tape f.;
 vb. toucher légèrement

dad, n. papa m.

daffodil, n. narcisse m.

daily, adj. quotidient, journalier

dainty, adj. délicat, friand

dairy, n. laiterie f.

daisy, n. marguerite f.

dam, n. digue f.

damage, n. dommage m.; vb.
 endommager

damp, adj. humide

dampen, vb. humecter

dance, n. danse f.; vb. danser

dandruff, n. pellicules f., pl.

danger, n. danger m.

dangerous, adj. dangereux

dangle, vb. intr. pendiller

Danish, adj. and n. danois m.

dare, vb. oser

dark, adj. sombre

darken vb. obscurcir

darling, adj. and n.; chéri m.

dart, n. dard m.; pince f.

dash, n. fougue f.; trait m.; vb. lancer,
 détruire, se précipiter

data, n. données f., pl.

data processing, n. élaboration f.

date, n. date f.; rendezvous m.

daughter, n. fille f.

daughter-in-law, n. belle-fille f.

daunt, vb. intimider

dauntless, adj. intrépide, in-
 domptable

dawn, n. aube f.

day, n. jour m.; journée f.

daylight, n. lumière du jour f.

daylight-saving time, n. l'heure d'éte f.

daze, vb. étourdir

deacon, n. diacre m.

dead, adj. mort

dead end, n. cul de sac m.;
 impasse f.

deadline, n. ligne de délimi-
 tation f.

deadlock, n. impasse f.

deadly, adj. mortel

deaf, adj. sourd

deafen, vb. assourdir

deaf-mute, adj. sourd-muet

deafness, n. surdité f.

dealer, n. marchand m.

dean, n. doyen

dear, adj. and n. cher m.

dearly, adv. chèrement

death, n. mort f.

deathless, adj. impérissable

deathly, adj. mortel

debacle, n. débâcle f.

debase, vb. avilir

debatable, adj. discutable

debate, n. débat m.

debater, n. orateur parlementaire, argumentateur m.

debentue, n. obligation f.

debiliate, vb. débiliter, affaiblir

debit, n. débit m.

debonair, adj. courtois et jovial

debris, n. débris m., pl.

debt, n. dette f.

debtor, n. débiteur m.

debunk, vb. dégonfler

debut, n. deut m.

debutante, n. débutante f.

decade, n. période de dix ans f.

decadence, n. décadence f.

decaffeinated, adj. décaféiné

decanter, n. carafe f.

decay, n. décadence f.

deceased, adj. dunt

deceit, n. tromperie f.

deceitful, adj. trompeur

deceive, vb. tromper

deceiver, n. imposteur

December, n. décembre m.

decency, n. décence f.

decent, adj. décent

deception, n. tromperie, duperie f.

deceptive, adj. décevant, tromppeur

decide, vb. décider

decided, adj. décidé, prononcé

decimal, adj. décimal

decimate, vb. décimer

decipher, vb. déchiffrer

decision, n. décision f.

decisive, adj. décisif

deck, n. pont, paquet m.

declaim, vb. déclamer

declare, vb. déclarer

decline, vb. décliner

decompose, vb. décomposer

decor, n. décor m.

decorate, vb. décorer

decoration, n. décoration f.

decorative, adj. décoratif

decorator, n. décorateur m.

decoy n. leurre m.; vb. leurrer

decrease, n. diminution f.; vb. diminuer

dedication, n. dédicace f.

deduce, vb. déduire

deduct, vb. déduire

deduction, n. déduction

deed, n. action f.; (law) acte notarié m.

deep, adj. profond

deepen, vb. approfondir

deeply, adv. profondément

deer, n. cerf m.

deface, vb. défigurer

default, n. défaut m.

defeat, n. défaite f.; vb. vaincre

defect, n. défaut m.

defection, n. défection f.

defective, adj. défectueux

defend, vb. défendre

defendant, n. défendeur m.

defender, n. défenseur m.

defense, n. défense f.

defenseless, adj. sans défense

defensive, adj. défensif

defer, vb. différer, déférer

deference, n. déférence f.

defiant, adj. de défi

deficiency, n. insuffisance f.

deficient, adj. insuffisant

deficit, n. deficit m.

defile, vb. souiller

define, vb. définir

definite, adj. défini

definitely, adv. d'une manière derminée

definition, n. définition f.

definitive, adj. définitif

deflate, vb. dégonfler

deflation, n. dégonflement m.

deflect, vb. faire dévier, détourner

deform, vb. déformer

deformity, n. difformité f.

defraud, vb. frauder

defray, vb. payer

defrost, vb. déglacer

defroster, n. déglaceur m.

deft, adj. adroit

defy, vb. défier

degenerate, vb. dégénérer

degrade, vb. dégrader

degree, n. degré m.

dehydrate, vb. déshydrater

deify, vb. déifier

deign, vb. daigner

dejected, adj. abattu

dejection, n. abattement m.

delay, n. retard m.; vb. retarder

delegate, n. délégué m.; vb. déléguer

delegation, n. délégation f.

delete, vb. rayer, vigger

deliberate, adj. délibéré; vb. délibérer

deliberately, adv. de propos délibéré

deliberation, n. délibération f.

deliberative, adj. délibératif

delicacy, n. délicatesse f.

delicate, adj. délicate

delicious, adj. délicieux

delight, n. délices f., pl.; vb. enchanter

delightful, adj. charmant

delinquency, n. délit m.

delinquent, adj. and n. délinquant m.

delirious, adj. délirant

deliver, vb. délivrer

deliverance, n. délivrance f.

delivery, n. accouchement, débit m.; livraison, distribution f.

delude, vb. tromper

delusion, n. illusion f.

deluxe, adv. de luxe

demand, n. demande f.; vb. demander

demean, vb. comporter

demeanor, n. maintien m.

demerit, n. démérite m.

demise, n. décès m., mort f.

demobilize, vb. démobiliser

democracy, n. démocratie f.

democrat, n. démocrate m.f.

democratic, adj. démocratique

demolish, vb. démolir

demonstrate, vb. dontrer

demonstration, n. démonstration f.

demonstrative, adj. démonstratif

demonstrator, n. démonstrateur m.

demoralize, vb. démoraliser

demote, vb. réduire à un grade inférieur

demure, adj. posé, d'une modestie affectee

den, n. antre, repaire m.

denial, n. dénégation f.; refus m.

Denmark, n. Danemark m.

denominator, n. dénominateur m.

denote, vb. dénoter

denounce, vb. dénoncer

dense, adj. dense, bête

density, n. densité f.

dent, n. bosselure f.

dental, adj. dentaire, dental

dentist, n. dentiste m.

denture, n. dentier, râtelier m.

denude, vb. dénuder

deny, vb. nier

deodorant, n. désodorisant m.

deodorize, vb. désodoriser, désinfecter

depart, vb. partir, s'en aller, quitter

department, n. département, ministère, grand magasin m.

deparmental, adj. départemental

departure, n. départ m.

dependability, n. confiance que l'on inspire f.

dependable, adj. digne de confiance

dependence, n. dépendance, confiance f.

dependent, adj. dépendant

depict, vb. peindre

depiction, n. description f.

deplorable, adj. déplorable

deplore, vb. déplorer

deport, vb. déporter

deportation, n. déportation f.

depose, vb. déposer

deposit, n. dépôt m.; vb. déposer

depositor, n. déposant m.

deprecate, vb. désapprouver, s'opposer à

depreciate, vb. déprécier

depress, vb. abaisser, abattre

depression, n. dépression, crise f.; abattement m.

depth, n. profoundeur f.

deputy, n. délégué, député m.

derail, vb. défailler

derange, vb. déranger

derive, vb. dériver

dermatology, n. dermatologie f.

derrick, n. grue f.

descend, vb. descendre

descendant, n. descendant m.

descent, n. descente f.

describe, vb. décrire

description, n. description f.

desert, n. désert, mérite m.; vb. déserter

deserter, n. déserteur m.

desertion, n. abandon m.; désertion f.

deserve, vb. mériter

deserving, adj. méritoire, de mérite

design, n. dessein, projet m.; vb. dessiner

designate, vb. désigner

designation, n. désignation f.

designer, n. dessinateur m.

designing, adj. intrigant, artificieux

desirable, adj. désirable

desire, n. désir m.; vb. désirer

desist, vb. cesser

desk, n. bureau, pupitre m.

desolate, adj. désolé

despair, n. désespoir m.; vb. désespérer

desperate, adj. désespéré

despicable, adj. méprisable

despise, vb. mépriser

despite, prep. en dépti de

despondent, adj. découragé

despot, n. despote m.

desser, n. desser m.

destination, n. destination f.

destine, vb. destiner

destiny, n. destin m.
destitute, adj. dénué, indigent
destitution, n. destitution f.
destroy, vb. détruire
destroyer, n. destructeur,
contre-torpilleur m.
destructible, adj. destructible
destruction, n. destruction f.
destructive, adj. destructif
detach, vb. détacher
detachment, n. détachement m.
detail, n. détail m.
detain, vb. retenir, détenir
detect, vb. découvrir
detection, n. découverte f.
detective, n. agent de la
police secrète, roman policier m.
detention, n. détention f.
detergent, n. détersif m.
deteriorate, vb. détériorer
determine, vb. déterminer
determined, adj. déterminé
deterrent, n. and adj. préventif m.
detest, vb. détester
detour, n. détour m.
devastate, vb. dévaster
develop, vb. développer
developer, n. révélateur m.
development, n. développement m.
device, n. expédient m.
devil, n. diable m.
devise, vb. combiner, tramer
devote, vb. consacrer
devotee, n. dévot m.; dévote f.
devotion, n. dévotion f.;
dévouement m.
devour, vb. dévorer
devout, adj. dévot
dew, n. rosée f.
dexterity, n. destérité f.
dexterous, adj. adroit
diabetes, n. diabète m.
diagnose, vb. diagnostiquer
diagnosis, n. diagnose f.
diagnostic, adj. diagnostique
diagonally, adv. diagonalement
diagram, n. diagramme m.
dial, n. cadran m.; vb. composer

dialect, n. dialecte m.
dialogue, n. dialogue m.
diameter, n. diamètre m.
diamond, n. diamant m.
diaper, n. couche f.
diaphragm, n. diaphragme m.
diarrhea, n. diarrhée f.
diary, n. journal m.
dice, n. dés m., pl.
dictaphone, n. machine à dicter f.
dictate, vb. dicter
dictation, n. dictée f.
dictator, n. dictateur m.
dictorial, adj. dictatorial
dictatorship, n. dictature f.
diction, n. diction f.
dictionary, n. dictionnaire m.
die, n. dé m.; vb. mourir
diet, n. régime m.
dietary, adj. diététique
dietetics, n. diététique f.
dietitian, n. diététicien m.
difference, n. différence f.
different, adj. différent
differential, adj. différentiel
difficult, adj. difficile
difficulty, n. difficulté f.
diffuse, adj. diffus
diffusion, n. diffusion f.
dig, vb. bêcher, creuser
digest, vb. digérere
digestible, adj. digestible
digestion, n. digestion f.
digestive, adj. and n. digestif m.
digital, adj. digital
digitalis, n. digitaline f.
dignified, adj. plein de dignité
dignify, vb. honorer, élever
dignity, n. dignité f.
digress, vb. faire une digression
digression, n. digression f.
dilate, vb. dilater
dilatory, adj. dilatoire, lent,
négligent
dilemma, n. dilemme m.
dilettante, n. dilettante, amateur m.
diligence, n. diligence f.
diligent, adj. diligent

dill, n. aneth m.

dilute, vb. diluer

dim, adj. faible, terne

dime, n. un dixième de dollar m.

dimension, n. dimension f.

diminish, vb. diminuer

dimness, n. faiblesse, obscurité f.

dimple, n. fossette f.

dine, vb. diner

dingy, adj. défraîchi; terne

dinner, n. diner m.

dinosaur, n. dinosaurien m.

dip, vb. plonger

diptheria, n. diphtérie f.

diploma, n. diplôme m.

diplomacy, n. diplomatie f.

diplomat, n. diplomate m.

diplomatic, adj. diplomatique

dipper, n. cuiller à pot f.

dire, adj. affreux

direct, vb. diriger, addresser; adj. direct

direction, n. direction f.; instructions f., pl.

directly, adv. directement

directness, n. rectitude, ranchise f.

director, n. directeur m.

directory, n. annuaire m.

dirt, n. saleté f.

dirty, adj. sale

disabiltiy, n. incapacité f.

disable, vb. mettre hors de combat

disabled, adj. invalide

disadvantage, n. désavantage m.

disagree, vb. être en désaccord

disagreeable, adj. désagréable

disagreement, n. désaccord m.

disappear, vb. disparaître

disapperance, n. disparition f.

disappoint, vb. désappointer

disappointment, n. désappointe-ment m.

disapproval, n. désapprobation f.

disapprove, vb. désapprouver

disarmament, n. désarmement m.

disarray, n. désarroi, désordre m.

disassemble, vb. démonter, déassembler

disaster, n. désastre m.

disavow, vb. désavouer

disband, vb. congédier

disbelieve, vb. ne pas croire, refuser de croire

discern, vb. discerner

discerning, adj. judicieux, éclaire

discharge, n. décharge f.; (mil.) congé m.; vb. décharger; congédier

discipline, n. discipline f.

disclaim, vb. désvouer, nier

disclaimer, n. désavouer m.

disclose, vb. révéler

disco, adj. disco

discolor, vb. décolorer

discomfiture, n. féfaite, déroute f.

discomfort, n. malaise m.

disconnect, vb. désunir

discontent, n. mécontentement m.

discontented, adj. mécontent

discontinue, vb. discontinuer

discord, n. discorde f.

discordant, adj. discordant, en désaccord

discotheque, n. discothèque f.

discount, n. escompte m.; remise f.

discourage, vb. décourager

discouragement, n. découragement m.

discourse, n. discours m.

discourteous, adj impoli

discourtesy, n. impolitesse f.

discover, vb. découvrir

discovery, n. découverte f.

discreditable, adj. déshono-rant, peu honorable

discrepancy, n. contradiction f.

discretion, n. discrétion f.

discriminate, vb. distinuer

discrimination, n. discernement, jugement m.

discuss, vb. discuter

discussion, n. discussion f.

disdain, n. dédain m.

disdainful, adj. dédaigneux

disease, n. maladie f.

disembark, vb. débarquer

disenchantment, n. désenchan-tement m.

disengage, vb. dégager

disentangle, vb. démêler

disfavor, n. défaveur f.

disfigure, vb. defigurer, enlai dir

disgrace, n. disgrâce f.

disgraceful, adj. honteux

disgruntled, adj. mécontent, de mauvaise humeur

disguise, n. déguisement m.

dish, n. plat m.; vb. (to do the dishes) laver la vaisselle

dishonest, adj. malhonnête(té)

dishonor, n. déshonneur m.

dishonorable, adj. déhonorant

disinfect, vb. désinfecter

disinfectant, n. désinfectant m.

disinherit, vb. déshériter

disjointed, adj. désarticulé, disloqué

disk, n. disque m.

dislike, n. aversion f.; vb. ne pas aimer

dislocate, vb. disloquer

dislodge, vb. déloger

disloyal, adj. infidele

dismay, n. consternation f.

dismember, vb. démembrer

dismiss, vb. congédier

dismount, vb. descendre

disobedience, n. désobéissance f.

disobey, vb. désobéir à

disorder, n. désordre m.

disorderly, adj. désordonné

disown, vb. désavouer

disparate, adj. disparate

disparity, n. inégalité f.

dispatch, n. expédition, promptitude, dépêche f.

dispatcher, n. expéditeur m.

dispel, vb. dissiper

dispensable, adj. dont on peut se passer

dispense, vb. distribuer, dispenser

dispersal, n. dispersion f.

disperse, vb. disperser

displace, vb. déplacer

displacement, n. déplacement m.

display, n. exposition f.; étalage m.; vb. étaler

displease, vb. déplaire à

disposal, n. disposition f.

dispose, vb. disposer

disposition, n. disposition, f.; caractère m.

disproportion, n. disproportion f.

disprove, vb. réfuter

disputable, adj. contestable, disputable

dispute, n. discussion, dispute f.

disqualify, vb. disqualifier

disregard, n. insouciance f.

disrespect, n. irrevérence f.

disrespectful, adj. irrespectueux

disrobe, vb. déshabiller, dévêtir

disrupt, vb. faire éclater, rompre

dissatisfaction, n. mécontentement m.

dissatisfy, vb. mécontenter

dissect, vb. disséquer

disservice, n. mauvais service rendu m.

dissimilar, adj. dissemblable

dissipate, vb. dissiper

dissipated, adj. dissipé

dissociate, vb. déassocier, dissocier

dissolute, adj. dissolu

dissolution, n. dissolution f.

dissolve, vb. dissoudre

dissonant, adj. dissonant

distance, n. distance f.

distant, adj. distant

distaste, n. dégoût m.

distasteful, adj. désagréable

distend, vb. dilater, gonfler

distill, vb. distiller

distillery, n. distillerie f.

distinct, adj. distinct

distinction, n. distinction f.

distinctive, adj. dinstinctif

distinctly, adv. distinctement

distinguish, vb. distinguer

distinguished, adj. distingué

distract, vb. distraire; affoler

distracted, adj. affolé, bouleversé

distraction, n. distraction; folie f.

distraught, adj. affolé, éperdu

distress, n. détresse f.; vb. affliger

distribute, vb. distribuer

distribution, n. distribution f.

distributor, n. distributeur m.

district, m. contrée f.

distrust, n. méfiance f.

disturb, vb. défanger

disturbance, n. défangement m.

ditch, n. fossé m.

diver, n. plongeur m.

divergence, n. divergence f.

diverse, adj. divers

diversion, n. divertissement m.

diversity, n. diversité f.

divert, vb. détourner, divertir

divide, vb. diviser

divided, adj. divisé, séparé

divine, adj. divin

divinity, n. divinité f.

divisible, adj. divisible

division, n. division f.

divorce, n. divorce m.; vb. divrocer

dizziness, n. vertige m.

dizzy, adj. pris de vertige

do, vb. faire

docile, adj. docile

dock, n. bassin m.

docket, n. registre, bordereau m.

doctor, n. docteur m.

doctrine, n. doctrine f.

document, n. document m.

documentary, adj. documentaire

dodge, vb. esquiver, éluder

doe, n. daine f.

dog, n. chien m.

doghouse, n. chenil m.

doleful, adj. lugubre

doll, n. poupée f.

dollar, n. dollar m.

dolphin, n. dauphin m.

domain, n. domaine m.

dome, n. dôme m.

domestic, adj. domestique

domicile, n. domicile m.

dominance, n. dominance,
 prédominance f.

dominate, vb. dominer

domination, n. domination f.

dominion, n. domination f.

donate, vb. donner

donation, n. donation f.

done, vb. fait

donkey, n. âne m.

doom, vb. condamner

door, n. porte f.; concierge m.f.

dormitory, n. dortoir m.

dosage, n. dosage m.

dose, n. dose f.

dot, n. point m.

double, adj. and n. double m.

double-breasted, adj. croisé

doubt, n. doute m.

doubtful, adj. douteux

doubtless, adv. sans doute

dough, n. pâte f.

doughnut, n. pet de nonne m.

dove, n. colombe f.

down, n. duvet m.

downfall, n. chute f.

downhill, n. descente f.

downpour, n. averse f.

downright, adv. tout à fait

downstairs, adv. en bas

downtown, adv. en ville

downy, adj. duveteux

doze, vb. sommeiller

dozen, n. douzaine f.

drab, adj. gris, terne

draft, n. dessin, courant d'air m. (mil.)
 conscription f.

draftsman, n. dessinateur m.

drafty, adj. plein de courante d'air

drag, vb. traîner

dragnet, n. drague, seine f.;
 chalut m.

dragon, n. dragon m.

drain, vb. drainer

drainage, n. drainage m.

dram, n. drachme, goutte f.

drama, n. drame m.

dramatic, adj. dramatique

dramatist, n. dramaturge m.

dramatize, vb. dramatiser

drape, vb. draper

drapery, n. draperie f.

drastic, adj. drastique

draught, n. traction f.; trait m.

draw, vb. dessiner

drawbridge, m. pont-levis m.

drawer, n. tiroir m.

drawing, n. dessin m.

dray, n. camion m.

drayman, n. camionneur m.

dread, n. crainte f.

dreadful, adj. affreux

dream, n. rêve m.

dreamer, n. rêveur m.

dreamy, adj. rêveur m., rêveuse f.

dreary, adj. morne

dredge, vb. draguer

drench, vb. tremper

dress, vb. habiller, vêtir, parer, orner

dresser, n. commode f.

dressing, n. toilette f.; pansement m.

dressmaker, n. couturière f.

drier, n. sécheur, dessécheur m.

drift, vb. dériver

driftwood, n. bois flottant m.

drill, n. foret, exercice m.; vb. forer

drink, n. boisson f.; vb. boire

drip, vb. dégoutter

drive, n. promenade en voiture f.

driver, n. chauffeur m.

drizzle, n. bruine f.; vb. bruiner

droop, vb. pencher

drop, n. goutte f.; vb. laisser tomber

dropsy, n. hydropisie f.

drought, n. sécheresse f.

drove, n. troupeau m.

drown, n. noyer

drowse, vb. s'assoupir

drowsy, adj. somnolent

drudge, vb. s'éreinter

drug, n. drogue f.

druggist, n. pharmacien m.

drum, n. tambour, tympan m.

drummer, n. tambour m.

drunk, adj. ivre

drunkard, n. ivrogne m.

dry, adj. sec m.; sèche f.

dryness, n. sécheresse f.

dual, adj. double

duck, n. canard m.

duct, n. conduit m.

ductile, adj. ductile

duel, n. duel m.

duelist, n. duelliste m.

duet, n. duo m.

duke, n. duc m.

dull, adj. ennuyeux

dullard, n. lourdaud m.

dullness, n. monotonie f.

dumb, adj. muet m., muette f.

dummy, n. mannequin m., mort m.

dump, n. voirie f.

dumping, n. boulette (de pâte) f.

dum, vb. importuner, talonner

dunce, n. crétin m.

dune, n. dune f.

dungeon, n. cachot m.

duplex, adj. double

duplicate, n. double m.; vb. faire le double de

duplication, n. duplication f.

duplicity, n. duplicité f.

durable, adj. durable

durability, n. durabilité f.

duration, n. durée f.

duress, n. contrainte, coercition f.

during, prep. pendant

dusk, n. crépuscule m.

dusky, adj. sombre

dust, n. poussière f.; vb. épousseter

dusty, adj. poussiéreux

Dutch, adj. and n. hollandais m.

Dutchman, n. Hollandais m.

dutiful, adj. respectueux, fidèle

dutifully, adv. ave soummission

duty, n. devoir, dorit m.; être de service

duty-free, adj. exempt de droits

dwarf, adj. and n., nain m.

dwell, vb. demeurer

dwindle, vb. diminuer

dye, n. teinture f.

dyer, n. teinturier m.

dynamic, adj. dynamique

dynamics, n. dynamique f.

dynamite, n. dynamite f.

dynamo, n. dynamo f.

dynasty, n. dynastie f.

dyslexia, n. dyslexie f.

dyspepsia, n. dyspepsie f.

dyspeptic, adj. dyspeptique

each, adj. chaque; pron. chacun m.

eager, ad. ardent, vif

eagerness, n. empressement m.

eagel, n. aigle m.; (mil.) aigle f.

ear, n. oreille f.

eardrum, n. tympan m.

earl, n. comte m.

early, adj. matinal, premier

earn, vb. gagner

earnest, adj. sérieux

earphone, n. casque m.

earring, n. boucle d'oreille f.

earth, n. terre f.

earthly, adj. terrestre

earthquake, n. tremblement de terre

ease, n. aise f.; avec facilité

easel, n. chevalet m.

easily, adv. largement, facilement

easiness, n. aisance, facilité f.

east, n. est m.

Easter, n. Pâques m.

eastern, adj. de l'est, oriental

eastward, adv. vers l'est

easy, adj. facile, aise

eat, vb. manger

ebb, n. reflux, déclin m.

ebony, n. ébène m.

eccentric, adj. excentrique

eccentricity, n. excentricité f.

ecclesiastic, adj. and n. ecclésiastique m.

ecclesiastical, adj. ecclésiastique

echelon, n. échelon m.

echo, n. écho m.

eclipse, n. éclipse f.

ecological, adj. écologique

ecology, n. écologie f.

economic, adj. économique

economical, adj. économe

economics, n. éconoimie politque f.

economist, n. économiste m.

economize, vb. économiser

economy, n. économie f.

ecstasy, n. extase f.; transport m.

eczema, n. eczéma m.

edge, n. bord, fil m.

edging, n. pose, bordure f.

edgy, adj. d'un air agacé

edibile, adj. comestible

edict, n. edit m.

edition, n. édition f.

editor, n. éditeur, rédacteur m.

editorial, n. article de fond m.

educate, vb. elever, instruire

education, n. éducation f.

educator, n. éducateur m.

eel, n. anguille f.

effect n. effet m.; vb. effectuer

effective, adj. efficace, effectif

effectivenss, n efficacité f.

efficacy, n. efficacité f.

efficiency, n. compétence f.; rendement m.

efficient, adj. capable

effort, n. effort m.

effortless, adj. sans effort

effusive, adj. démonstratif

egg, n. oeue m.; (boiled) oeuf á la coque; (fried) oeuf sur le plat; (hard-boiled) oeuf dur

eggplant, n. aubergine f.

Egypt, n. l Égypte m.

Egyptian, n. Égyptien m.; adj. égyptien

eight, adj. and n. huit m.

eighteen, adj. and n. dix-huit m.

eighteenth, adj. and n. dix-huitième, m.f.

eight, adj. and n. huitième m.f.

eighty, adj. and n. quatrevingts m.

either, pron. l'un ou l'autre m.; conj. ou, soit

eject, vb. rejeter, émettre

ejection, n. expulsion, éjection f.

elaborate, adv. minutieux.; vb. élaborer

elapse, vb. s'écouler

elastic, adj. and n. élastique m.

elasticity, n. élasticité f.

elate, vb. exalter, transporter

elated, adj. exalté

elbow, n. coude m.

elder, adj. and n. aïné m.

elderly, adj. d'un certain âge

elect, vb. élire

election, n. élection f.

elective, adj. électif

electorate, n. électorat m., les votants m., pl.

electric, electrical, adj. électrique

electrician, n. électricien m.

electricity, n. électricité f.

electrocute, vb. électrocuter

electron, n. électron m.

electronics, n. électronique f.

elegance, n. élégance f.

elegant, adj. élégant

elegiac, adj. élégiaque

elegy, n. élégie f.

element, n. élément m.

elementary, adj. élémentaire

elephant, n. éléphant m.

elevate, vb. élever

elevation, n. élévation f.

elevator, n. ascenseur m.

eleven, adj. and n. onze m.

eleventh, adj. and n. onzième m.f.

elf, n. elfe m.

elfin, adj. d'elfe

elicit, vb. tirer, faire jaillir

eligibility, n. éligibilité f.

eligible, adj. éligible

eliminate, vb. éliminer

elimination, n. élimination f.

elixir, n. élixir m.

elk, n. élan m.

elm, n. orme m.

elope, vb. s'enfuir

eloquence, n. éloquence f.

eloquent, adj. éloquent

eloquently, adv. d'une manière éloquente

else, adj. autre, quelqu'un d'autre.,

elsewhere, adv. ailleurs

elucidate, vb. élucider, éclaircir

elude, vb. éluder

elusive, adj. évasif, insaisissable

emaciated, adj. émacié

emancipate, vb. émanciper

emancipation, n. émancipation f.

emasculate, vb. émasculer

embalm, vb. embaumer

embankment, n. levée f.

embargo, n. embargo m.

embark, vb. embarquer

embarrass, vb. embarrasser

embarrassing, adj. embarrassant

embarrassment, n. embarras m.

embassy, n. ambassade f.

embellish, vb. embellir

embellishment, n. embellissement m.

ember, n. braise f., charbon ardent m.

embezzle, vb. détourner

embitter, vb. aigrir, envenimer

emblazon, vb. blasonner

emblem, n. emblème m.

embody, vb. incarner, incorporer

emboss, vb. graver en relief, travailler en boasse

embrace, n. reinte f.

embroider, vb. broder

embroidery, n. broderie f.

embryo, n. embryon m.

emerald, n. émeraude f.

emerge, vb. émerger

emergency, n. circonstance critique f.

emery, n. émeri m.

emigrant, n. émigrant m.

emigrate, vb. émigrer

emigration, n. émigration f.

eminence, n. éminence f.

emit, vb. émettre

emolument, n. traitement m.

emotion, n. émotion f.

emotional, adj. émotif, émotionnable

emperor, n. empereur m.

emphasis, n. force f.; accent m.

emphasize, vb. mettre en relief

emphatic, adj. énergique

empire, n. empire m.

employ, vb. employer

employee, n. employé m.

employer, n. patron m.

employment, n. emploi m.

empress, n. impératrice f.

emptiness, n. vide m.

empty, adj. vide, à vide

emulate, vb. émuler

enable, vb. mettre à même (de)

enact, vb. ordonner, arrêter

enactment, n. promulgation f.; acte législatif m.

enamel, n. émail m.

encephalitis, n. encéphalite f.

enchant, vb. enchanter

enchanting, adj. ravissant

enchantment, n. enchantement m.

enclose, vb. enclore, clore

enclosure, n. action de clore, clôture

encompass, vb. entourer

encounter, vb. rencontrer f.

encourage, vb. encourager

encouragement, n. encouragement m.

encroach, vb. empiéter

encyclopedia, n. encyclopédie f.

end, n. fin, extrémité f.; bout, but, objet m.

endanger, vb. mettre en danger

endear, vb. rendre cher

endearment, n. charme, attrait m.

endeavor, n. effort m.; vb. tâcher, essayer

endemic, adj. endémique

ending, n. terminaison, désinence f.

endless, adj. sans fin, perpétuel

endorse, vb. endosser, appuyer

endorsement, n. endossement, approbation m.

endowment, n. dotation, fondation f.

endurance, n. résistance f.

endure, vb. supporter

enduring, adj. durable

enema, n. lavement m.

enemy, adj. and n ennemi m.

energetic, adj. énergique

energy, n. énergie f.

enfold, vb. envelopper

enforce, vb. imposer, exécuter

enforcement, n. exécution f.

enfranchise, vb. affranchir, accorder le droit de vote

engage, vb. engager, retenir, prendre, louer

engaged, adj. fiancé, occupé

engagement, n. engagement m.; fiancailles f., pl.

engaging, adj. attrayant, séduisant

engine, n. machine, locomotive f.; moteur m.

engineer, n. ingénieur, mécanicien m.; (mil.) soldat du génie m.

engineering, n. génie m.

England, n. l'Angleterre f.

English, adj. and n. anglais m.

engrave, vb. graver

engraver, n. graveur m.

engraving, n. gravure f.

enhance, vb. rehausser

enjoy, vb. jouir de, s'amuser

enjoyable, adj. agréable

enjoyment, n. jouissance f.

enlarge, vb. agrandir

enlargement, n. agrandissement m.

enlarger, n. agrandisseur, amplificateur m.

enligthen, vb. éclairer

enlightenment, n. éclaircissement m.

enlist, vb. enrôler

enmity, n. inimitié f.

enormous, adj. enorme

enough, adj. and adv. assez

enrage, vb. faire enrager

enrich, vb. enrichir

ensemble, n. ensemble m.

entail, vb. entraîner, imposer

entangle, vb. empêtrer

enter, vb. entrer dans

enterprise, n. enteprise f.

enterprising, adj. entreprenant

entertain, vb. amuser, recevoir

entertainment, n. hospitalité

enthusiasm, n. enthousiasme m.

entice, vb. attirer

entire, adj. entier

entirely, adv. entièrement

entitle, vb. donner droit à, intituler

entrails, n. entrailles f., pl.

entrance, n. entrée f.

entrap, vb. attraper, prendre au piège

entreat, vb. supplier

entry, n. entrée, inscrihon f.

enumerate, vb. énumérer

enunication, n. énonciation f.

envelop, vb. envelopper

envelope, n. enveloppe f.
enviable, adj. enviable
envious, adj. envieux
environment, n. milieu m.
envoy, n. envoyé m.
envy, n. envie f.; vb. envier
epic, n. épopée f.; adj. épique
epilepsy, n. épliepsie f.
epilogue, n. épilogue m.
epoch, n. époque f.
equable, adj. uniforme, régulier
equal, adj. égal, être à la hauteur de
equality, n. égalité f.
equalize, vb. égaliser
equate, vb. égaler, mettre en equation
equation, n. équation f.
equator, n. équateur m.
equilibrium, n. équilibre m.
equip, vb. équiper
equipment, n. equipment m.
equitable, adj. équitable, juste
equity, n. équité f.
equivalent, adj. and n. équivalent m.
era, n. ère f.
eradicate, vb. défaciner
erase, vb. effacer
eraser, n. gomme f.
erect, adj. droit
erection, n. érection, construction f.
erectness, n. attitude droite f.
erode, vb. éroder, ronger
erosion, n. érosion f.
erosive, adj. érosif
erotic, adj. érotique
err, vb. errer
errand, n. course f.
errant, adj. errant
erratic, adj. irrégulier, excentrique
erring, adj. égaré dévoyé
erroneous, adj. erroné
error, n. erreur f.
erudite, adj. érudit
erudition, n. érudition f.
erupt, vb. entrer en éruption
eruption, n. éruption f.
escalate, vb. escalader
escalator, n. escalier roulant m.
escape, n. fuite f.; vb. échapper

escort, n. (mil.) escorte f.; cavalier m.
esculent, adj. comestible
esoteric, adj. ésotérique
especial, adj. spécial
espionage, n. espionnage m.
espouse, vb. éspouser, embrasser
Eskimo, n. Esquimau m.
esquire, n. écuyer m.
essay, n. essai m.; épreuve f.
essence, n. essence f.
essential, adj. essentiel
essentially, adv. essentiellement
establish, vb. établir
establishment, n. établissement m.
estate, n. état, rang m.; propriété f.
esteem, n. estime f.; vb. estimer
estimate, n. estimation, évaluation f.
estimation, n. jugement m.
estrange, vb. aliéner
etching, n. gravure à l'eau-forte f.
eternal, adj. éternel
eternity, n. éternité f.
ether, n. éther m.
ethical, adj. moral
ethics, n. éthique f.
Ethiopia, n. l' Ethiopie f.
ethnic, adj. ethnique
etiquette, n. étiquette f.
eucalyptus, n. eucalyputs m.
eugenic, adj. eugénésique
eugneics, n. eugénisme m.; eugénique f.
Europe, n. l'Europe f.
European, adj. Européen m.
euthanasia, n. euthanasie f.
evacuate, vb. évacuer
evade, vb. éluder
evaluate, vb. évaluer
evaluation, n. évaluation f.
evangelist, n. évangéliste m.
evaporate, vb. évaporer
evaporation, n. évaporation f.
evasion, n. subterfuge f.
eve, n. veille f.
even, adj. égal, régulier
evening, n. soir m.; soirée f.
event, n. événement, cas m.

eventful, adj. plein d'événements

ever, adv. toujours; jamais

evergreen, adj. toujours vert

everlasting, adj. eternel, perétuel

every, adj. chaque, tous les m.; toutes les f.

everybody, everyone, pron. tout le monde

everyday, adj. de tous le jours, journalier

everything, n. tout m.

everywhere, adv. partout

evict, vb. évincer, expulser

eviction, n. éviction, expulsion f.

evidence, n. évidence, preuve f.

evident, adj. évident

evidently, adv. évidemment

evil, n. mal m.

evoke, vb. évoquer

evolution, n. évolution f.

evolve, vb. évoluer, développer

ewe, n. agnelle f.

exact, adj. exact

exacting, adj. exigeant

exactly, adv. exactement

exaggerated, adj. exagéré

exaggeration, n. exagération f.

exalt, vb. exalter, élever

exaltation, n. exaltation f.

examination, n. examen m.

examine, vb. examiner

example, n. exemple m.

exasperate, vb. exaspérer

exasperation, n. exaspération f.

exceed, vb. excéder

exceedingly, adv. extrêmement

excel, vb. exceller

excellence, n. excellence f.

excellent, adj. excellent

except, vb. excepter, exclure; prep. excepté, sauf

exception, n. exception f.

exceptional, adj. exceptionnel

excerpt, n. extrait m.

excess, n. excès, excédent, surpoids m.

excessive, adj. excessif

exchange, n. échange, troc m.

exchangeable, adj. échangeable

excise, n. contribution indirecte, régie f.

excitable, adj. émotionnable, excitable

excite, vb. exciter

excitement, n. agitation f.

exclaim, vb. s'écrier

exclamation, n. exclamation f.

exclude, vb. exclure(de)

exclusion, n. exclusion f.

exclusive, adj. exclusif, sélect

excommunicate, vb. excommunier

excortate, vb. excorier, écorcher

excruciating, adj. atroce, affreux

exculpate, vb. disculper, exonérer

excursion, n. excursion f.

excusable, adj. excusable

excuse, n. excuse f.

execute, vb. exécuter

execution, n. exécution f.

executive, adj. and n. exécutif m.

executor, n. exécuteur m.

exemplify, vb. expliquer par des exemples

exempt, adj. exempt; vb exempter

exercise, n. exercice m.; vb. exercer

exert, vb. employer, s'efforcer de

exertion, n. effort m.

exhale, vb. exhaler

exhaust, n. échappement m.; vb. épuiser

exhaustion, n. épuisement m.

exhaustive, adj. complet, approfondi

exhibit, vb. exposer, montrer

exhibition, n. exposition f.

exhilarate, vb. égayer

exhort, vb. exhorter

exhortation, n. exhortion f.

exhume, vb. exhumer

exile, n. exil, exilé m.; vb. exiler

exist, vb. exister

existence, n. existence f.

existent, adj. existant

exit, n. sortie f.

exodus, n. exode m.

exorcise, vb. exorciser

exotic, adj. exotique

expand, vb. étendre, déployer

expanse, n. étendue f.

expansion, n. expansion f.

expansive, adj. expansif

expatriate, vb. expatrier

expect, vb. s'attendre à, attendre

expectancy, n. attente f.

expectation, n. attente, espérance f.

expediency, n. convenance f.

expedient, n. expédient m.

expedite, vb. activer, accélérer

expedition, n. expédition f.

expel, vb. expulser

expend, vb. dépenser, épuiser

expenditure, n. dépense f.

expense, n. dépnse f.; frais m., pl.

expensive, adj. coûteux, cher

experienced, adj. expérimenté

experiment, n. expérience f.

experimental, adj. expérimental

expert, adj. and n. expert m.

expiate, vb. expier

expiration, n. expiration f.

expire, vb. expirer

explain, vb. expliquer

explanation, n. explication f.

explanatory, adj. explicatif

explicit, adj. explicite

explode, vb. éclater

exploitation, n. exploitation f.

exploration, n. exploration f.

exploratory, adj. exploratif

explore, vb. explorer

explorer, n. explorateur m.

explosion, n. explosion f.

explosive, adj. and n. explosif m.

exponent, n. interprète m.

export, n. exportation f.; vb. exporter

expose, vb. exposer

exposition, n. exposition

exposure, n. exposiiton f.

expound, vb. exposer

express, adj. exprès; vb. exprimer

expression, n. expression f.

expressive, adj. expressif

expressly, adv. expressément

expressman, n. agent de

messageries m.

expropriate, vb. exproprier

expulsion, n. expulsion f.

expunge, vb. effacer, rayer

exquisite, ajd. exquis

extant, adj. existant

extend, vb. étendre, prolonger

extension, n. extension f.

extensive, adj. étendu

extensively, adv. d'une manière étendue

extent, n. étendue f.

extenuate, vb. exténuer, atténuer

exterior, adj. and n. extérieur m.

exterminate, vb. exterminer

extermination, n. extermination f.

external, adj. externe

extinct, adj. éteint

extinction, n. extinction f.

extinguish, vb. éteindre

extirpate, vb. extirper

extol, vb. vanter

extort, vb. extorquer

extortion, n. extorsion f.

extra, adj. supplémentaire, en sus, extraordinaire

extract, n. extraire

extraction, n. extraction, origine f.

extraordinary, adj. extraordinaire

extravagance, n. extravagance, prodigalité f.

extravagant, adj. extravagant, prodigue

extravaganza, m. oeuvre fantaisiste f.

extreme, adj. and n. extrême m.

extremity, n. extrémite f.

exuberant, adj. exubérant

exude, vb. exsuder

exult, vb. exulter

exultant, adj. exultant, joyeux

eye, n. oiel m.; yeux m., pl.

eyeball, n. bulbe de l'oeil m.

eyebrow, n. sourcil m.

eyeglass, n. lorgnon m.

eyeglasses, n. lunettes f., pl.

eyelash, n. cil n.

eyelid, n. paupière f.

eyesight, n. vue f.

eyewitness, n. temoin oculaire m.

fable, n. fable f.

fabric, n. construction f.

fabricate, vb. fabriquer

fabulous, adj. fabuleux

face, n. figure f.; vb. faire
face à

facet, n. facette f.

facial, adj. facial

facing, n. revêtement, revers m.

facsimile, n. fac-similé m.

fact, n. fait m.; en effet (in fact)

faction, n. faction f.

factual, adj. effectif, positif

fad, n. marotte f.

fade, vb. se faner, se décolorer,
s'évanouir

fail, vb. manquer, faillir

faint, adj. faible, défaillant

fair, n. foire m.; adj. beau m., belle f.;
blond, juste; passable

fairly, adj. honnêtement,
impartialement

fairness, n. honnêteté f.

faith, n. foi f.

faithful, adj. fidèle

fake, vb. truquer

faker, n. truqueur m.

falcon, n. faucon m.

fall, n. chute f.; (month) automme m.

fallen, adj. tombé déchu

fallout, n. pluie radioactive f.

fallow, adj. en jachère

false, adj. faux m.; fausse f.

falsehood, n. mensonge m.

fame, n. renommée f.

familiar, adj. familier

familiarity, n. familiarité f.

familiarize, vb. familiariser

family, n. famille f.

famished, adj. affamé

famous, adj. célèbre

fan, n. éventail, ventilateur m.

fancy, n. fantaisie f.; vb. se figurer

fanfare, n. fanfare f.

fantastic, adj. fantastique

fantasy, n. fantaisie f.

far, adv. loin, jusqu'ici, autant que,
beaucoup, de beaucoup

faraway, adj. lointain

fare, n. prix m.; chère f.; vb. aller

farewell, interj. and n. adieu m.

far-fetched, adj. forcé

farm, n. ferme f.

farmer, n. fermier m.

farmhouse, n. maison de ferme f.

farming, n. culture f.

far-sighted, adj. clairvoyant

farther, adj. plus éloigné; adv. plus
loin

fascinate, vb. fasciner

fashion, n. mode, manière f.

fast, n. jeûne m.,; adj. rapide, en
avance, en avance; vb. jeûner; adv.
vite, ferme

fasten, vb. attacher

fastening, n. attache f.

fat, adj. gras m.; grasse f.

fatal, adj. fatal, mortel

fatality, n. fatalité f.

fatally, adv. fatalement, mortellement

fate, n. destin m.

father, n. père m.

fatherhood, n. paternité f.

father-in-law, n. beau-père m.

fatherless, adj. sans père

fatherly, adj. paternel

fatigue, n. fatigue f.

fatten, vb. engraisser

fatty, adj. graisseux

faucet, n. robinet m.

fault, n. faute f.; défaut m.

faultless, adj. sans défaut

faulty, adj. défectueux

favor, n. faveur f.; vb. favoriser

favorable, adj. favorable

favored, adj. favorisé

favorite, adj. and n. favori, m.;
favorite f.

fawn, n. faon m.

fear n. crainte, peur f.; vb. craindre,
avoir peur de

fearful, adj. craintif; effrayant

fearless, adj. intrépide

feasible, adj. faisable

feast, n. fête f.; festin m.

feather, n. plume f.

feathered, adj. emplumé
feature, n. trait m.
February, n. février m.
federal, adj. fédéral
federation, n. fédération f.
fedor, n. chapeau mou m.
fee, n. honoraires m.pl.; frais m., pl.
feeble, adj. faible
feed, n. nourriture f.; vb. nourrir
feel, vb. sentir, tâter
feeling, n. sentiment m.
feline, adj. félin
fell, adj. funeste
fellow, n. homme, garçon, compagnon m.
fellowship, n. camaraderie, bourse universitaire f.
felon, n. criminel m.
felony, n. crime m.
felt, n. feutre m.
female, n. femme, femelle f.; adj. féminin, femelle
feminine, adj. féminin
femininity, n. féminéité f.
fence, n. clôture f.; vb. enclore, fair de l'escrime
fencing, n. escrime f.
fender, n. garde-boue; garde-feu m.
fern, n. fougère f.
ferry, n. passage en bac; bac m.
fertile, adj. fertile
fertility, n. fertilité f.
fertilization, n. fertilisation f.
fertilize, vb. fertiliser
fervent, adj. fervent
festival, n. fête f.
festive, adj. de fête
festoon, n. feston m.; vb. festonner
fetal, adj. foetal
fetch, vb. aller chercher, apporter
fetching, adj. attrayant
fete, vb. fêter
fetter, n. lien m.; chaîne f.; vb. enchaîner
fetus, n. foetus m.
feud, n. inimitié f.; fief m.
feudalism, n. régime féodal m.
fever, n. fièvre f.

feverish, adj. fiévreux, fébrile
feverishly, adv. fébrilement, fiévreusement
few, adj. peu de, quelques
fiancé, n. fiancé m.
fiasco, n. fiasco m.
fiat, n. décret m.
fib, n. petit mensonge m.
fiber, n. fibre f.
fickle, adj. volage
fiction, n. fiction f.; romans m., pl.
fictional, adj. de romans
fictitious, adj. fictif, imaginaire
fiddle, n. violon m.; vb. jouer du violon
fidelity, n fidélité f.
field, n. champ m.
fiendish, adj. diabolique, infernal
fierce, adj. féroce
fiery, adj. ardent
fiesta, n. fête f.
fife, n. fifre m.
fifteen, adj. and n. quinze m.
fifteenth, adj. and n. quinzième m.
fifth, adj. and n. cinquième m.
fifty, adj. and n. cinquante m.
fig, n. figue f.
fight, n. combat m.; lutte, dispute f.; vb. combattre, se disputer
fighter, n. combattant m.
figment, n. invention f.
figurative, adj. figuré
figuratively, adj. au figuré
figure, n. figure, tournure f.; chiffre m. vb. figurer, calculer
figured, adj. à dessin
figurehead, n. homme de paille m.
filament, n. filament m.
flich, vb. escamoter
file, n. lime, file, liasse f.; archives f., pl.; classeur m.
fill, vb. remplir
filling, n. remplissage m.
film, n. film m.; pellicule f.
filter, n. filtre m.; vb. filtrer
fin, n. nageoire f.
final, adj. final
finale, n. finale m.
finally, adv. finalement, enfin

finance, n. finance f.; vb. financer
financial, adj. financier
find, vb. trouver
fine, n. amende, belle f.; fin.; vb.
  mettre à l'amende; adj. beau m.
finery, n. parure f.
finesse, n. finesse f.; vb. finasser
finger, n. doigt m.
fingernail, n. ongle m.
fingerprint, n. empreinte digitale f.
finish, vb. finir
finite, adj. fini
Finland, n. la Finlande f.
Finn, n. Finladais, Finnois m.
fire, n. feu, incendie m.
fire alarm, n. avertisseur d'incendie m.
firearm, n. arme à feu f.
fire escape, n. échelle de sauvetage f.
fire extinguisher, n. extincteur m.
fireman, n. pompier m.
fireplace, n. cheminée f.
fireproof, adj. à l'épreuve du feu
firewood, n. bois de chauffage m.
fireworks, n. feu d'artifice m.
firm, n. maison de commerce f.
firmness, n. fermeté f.
first, adj. premier; adv. d'abord
first aid, n. premiers secours m., pl.
first-class, adj. de premier ordre
first-hand, adj. de première main
fiscal, adj. fiscal
fish, n. poisson m.; vb. pêcher
fisherman, n. pêcheur m.
fishing, n. pêche f.
fist, n. poing m.
fit, n. accès m.; adj. convenable,
  capable, propre à
fitful, adj. agité, irrégulier
fitness, n. convenance, santé
  physique f.; à-propos m.
fitting, n. convenable, à propos, juste
five, adj. and n. cinq m.
fix, vb. fixer, attacher, établir, arrêter
fixed, adj. fixe
fixture, n. meuble à demeure
flabby, adj. flasque
flag, n. drapeau m.; dalle f.
flagon, n. flacon m.

flagpole, n. mât de drapeau m.
flagrant, adj. flagrant
flagrantly, adv. d'une manière
  flagrante
flair, n. flair m.
flamboyant, adj. flamboyant
flame, n. flamme f.; vb. flamboyer
flaming, adj. flamboyant
flamingo, n. flamant m.
flank, n. flanc m.
flannel, n. flanelle f.
flap, n. coup, battant m.; patte f.;
  vb. battre
flare, vb. flamboyer
flash, n. éclair m.
flashlight, n. flash m.
flashy, adj. voyant
flask, n. gourde f.
flat, n. appartement m.; adj. plat m.
flatness, n. égalité f.; aplatissement m.
flatten, vb. aplatir
flatter, vb. flatter
flattery, n. flatterie f.
flaunt, vb. parader, étaler
flavor, n. saveur f.; arome m.
flavoring, n. assaisonnement m.
flavorless, adj. fade
flaw, n. défaut m.
flawless, adj. sans défaut, parfait
flawlessly, adv. d'une manière
  impeccable
flax, n. lin m.
flea, n. puce f.
flee, vb. s'enfuir
fleece, n. toison f.
fleecy, adj. laineux, moutonneux
fleet, n. flotte f.
fleeting, adj. tugitif
flesh, n. chair f.
flexibility, n. flexibilité f.
flexible, adj. flexible
flicker, vb. trembloter, vaciller
flier, n. aviateur m.
flight, n. vol m.; fuite f.
flinch, vb. reculer, broncher
fling, vb. jeter
flint, n. pierre à briquet; silex m.
flirt, vb. flirter

flirtation, n. flirt m.

float, vb. flotter

flock, n. troupeau m.; vb. accourir

flog, vb. fouetter

flood, n. inondation f.

floodlight, n. lumière à grand flots f.

floor, n. plancher, parquet, carreau m.

flooring, n. plancer, parquet m.

flop, n. coup mat m.

floral, adj. floral

florist, n. fleuriste m.f.

flounder, n. flet m.

flour, n. fairne f.

flourish, vb. prospérer

flow, vb. couler

flower, n. fleur f.

flowerpot, n. pot à fleurs m.

flue, n. tuyau de cheminée m.

fluency, n. facilité f.

fluent, adj. courant

fluid, adj. and n. fluide m.

flunk, vb. coller, recaler

flourescent lamp, n. lampe flourescente f.

flurry, n. agitation f.

flush, n. rougeur, chasse f.

flute, n. flûte f.

flutter, n. voltigement m. palpiter

fly, n. mouche f.

foam, n. écume f.

focal, adj. focal

focus, n. foyer m.

foe, n. ennemi m.

fog, n. brouillard m.

foggy, adj. brumeux

foil, n. feuille f.

foist, vb. fourrer

fold, n. pli m.

folder, n. prospectus m.

foilage, n. feuillage m.

folio, n. in-folio m.

folk, n. gens m.f., pl.

folklore, n. folk-lore m.

follow, vb. suivre

follower, n. disciple m.

folly, n. folie f.

fond, adj. tendre; vb. aimer

fondant, n. fondant m.

fondle, vb. caresser

fondly, adv. tendrement

fondness, n. tendresse f.

food, n. nourriture f.

fool, n. sot, bête m.; sotte f.

foot, n. pied m.

footage, n. métrage m.

football, n. fottball, ballon m.

footing, n. pled, point d'appui m.

footnote, n. note f.

footprint, n. empreinte de pas f.

footstep, n. pas m.

footstool, n. tabouret m.

footwork, n. jeu de pieds m.

for, prep. paour; conj. car

forage, n. fourrage m.; vb. fourrager

forbear, vb. s'abstenir de, montrer de la patience

forbearance, n. patience f.

forbid, vb. défendre (à)

forbidding, adj. rébarbatif

force, n. force f.

forced, adj. force

forceful, adj. énergique

forcefulness, n. énergie, vigueur f.

forceps, n. forceps m.

forcible, adj. forcé

ford n. gué m.; vb. traverser à gué

forearm, n. avant-bras m.

forebears, n. ancêtres m., pl.

forecast, n. prévision f.; vb. prévoir

forecastle, n. gailard m.

foreclose, vb. exclure, forclore

forefather, n. ancêtre m.

forefinger, n. index m.

foregone, adj. décidé d'avance

foreground, n. premier plan m.

forehead, n. front m.

foreign, adj. étranger

foreigner, n. étranger m.

foreleg, n. jambe antérieure f.

foremost, adj. premier

forensic, adj. judiciaire

foresee, vb. prévoir

foresight, n. prévoyance f.

forest, n. forêt f.

forestall, vb. anticiper, devancer

forester, n. forestier m.

foretell, vb. prédire

forever, adv. pour toujours

forevermore, adv. à jamais

forfeit, vb. forfaire

forfeiture, n. perte par confiscation, forfaiture f.

forge, n. forge f.; vb. forger, contrefaire

forger, n. faussaire, falsificateur m.

forgery, n. faux m.

forget, vb. oublier

forgetful, adj. oublieux

forgive, vb. pardonner (à)

forgiveness, n. pardon m.

forgo, vb. renoncer à

fork, n. fourchette, fourche f.

forlorn, adj. désespéré; abandonné

formal, adj. formel

formally, adv. formellement

format, n. format m.

formation, n. formation f.

formative, adj. formatif, formateur

former, adj. précédent; pron. le premier

formerly, adv. autrefois, jadis, auparavant

formula, n. formule f.

forsake, vb. abandonner

fort, n. fort m.

forth, adv. en avant

forthcoming, adv. à venir

forthwith, adv. sur-le-champ

fortitude, n. courage m.

fortress, n. forteresse f.

fortunate, adj. heureux

fortune, n. fortune f.

forty, adj. and n. quarante m.

forward, adj. en avant, avancé, hardi

forwardness, n. empressement m.; effronterie f.

fossil, n. fossile m.

foster, vb. nourrir

foul, adj. sale, malpropre, dégoûtant

found, vb. fonder

foundation, n. foundation f.; fondement m.

founder, n. foundateur m.

fountain, n. fontaine f.

four, adj. and n. quatre m.

four-in-hand, n attelage à quatre m.

fourscore, adj. quatre-vingts

foursome, n. à quatre

fourteen, adj. and n. quatorze m.

fourth, adj. and n. quatrième m.

fowl, n. volaille f.

fox, n. renard m.

foxglove, n. digitale f.

foxhole, n. renardière f.

foxy, adj. rusé

foyer, n. foyer m.

fraction, n. fraction m.

fracture, n. fracture f.

fragile, adj. fragile

fragment, n. fragment m.

fragmentary, adj. fragmentaire

fragrance, n. parfum m.

fragrant, adj. parfumé

frail, adj. frêle

frailty, n. faiblesse f.

frame, n. cadre m.; structure f.

frame-up, n. coup monté m.

framework, n. charpente f.

France, n. la France f.

franchise, n. droit de vote m.

frank, adj. franc m.; franche f.

frankincense, n. encens m.

frankly, adv. franchement

frankness, n. franchsie f.

frantic, adj. frénétique

fraternal, adj. fraternel

fraternally, adv. fraternellement

fraternity, n. fraternité f.

fraud, n. fraude f.; imposteur m.

fraudulent, adj. frauduleux

fraudulently, adv. frauduleusement

fraught, adj. chargé(de), plein, gros

fray, n. bagarre f.

freak, n. caprice, phénomène m.

freckle, n. tache de rousseur f.

freckled, adj. taché de rousseur

free, adj. libré; gratuit; vb. libérer, affranchir

freedom, n. liberté f.

freeze, vb. geler

freezer, n. glacière f.; congélateur m.

freight, n. fret m.

French, adj. and n. français m.

frenzy, n. frénésie f.

frequency, n. fréquence f.

frequent, adj. fréquent, fréquenter

frequently, adv. fréquemment

fresco, n. fresque f.

fresh, adj. frais, récent, nouveau m.

freshen, vb. refraichir

freshman, n. étudiant de première année m.

freshness, n. fraîcheur f.

fret, n. fermentation

fretful, adj. chagrin

fretfulness, n. irritabilité f.

friction, n. friction f.

Friday, n. vendredi m.

friend, n. ami m.; amie f.

friendless, adj. sans amis

friendliness, n. disposition amicale f.

friendly, adj. amical

friendship, n. amitié f.

frighten, vb. effrayer

frigid, adj. glacial

frill, n. volant m.

frilly, adj. froncé, ruché

frisky, adj. folâtre

frivolous, adj. frivole

frog, n. grenouille f.

frolic, vb. folâtrer

from, prep. de, depuis

front, n. front, devant m.

frontage, n. étendue de devant f.

fronteir, n. frontière f.

frost, n. gelée f.

frosting, n. glacage m.

frosty, adj. gelé, glacé

frown, vb. forncer les sourcils

frowzy, adj. mal tenu, peu soigné

frozen, adj. gelé

frugal, adj. frugal

frugalty, n. frugalité f.

fruit, n. fruit m.

fruitful, adj. fructueux fructification f.

fruitless, adj. infructueux

frustrate, vb. faire échouer

frustration, n. frustration f.

fry, vb. frire, faire frire

fryer, n. casserole f.

fuchsia, n. fuchsia m.

fudge, n. travail bâclé m.

fuel, n. combustible m.

fugitive, adj. fugitif

fugue, n. fugue f.

fulfill, vb. accomplir

fulfillment, n. accomplissement m.

full, adj. plein

fullback, n. arrière m.

fully, adv. pleinement

fumble, vb. tâtonner

fume, n. fumée f.

fumigage, vb. desinfecter

fumigator, n. fumigateur m.

fun, n. amusement m.; plaisanterie drôlerie f.

function, n. fonction f.

fund, n. fonds m.

fundamental, adj. fondamental

funeral, n. funérailles f., pl.

fungus, n. fongus m.

funnel, n. entonnoir m.; cheminée f.

funny, adj. drôle

fur, n. fourrure f.

furious, adj. furieux

furlong, n. furlong m.

furnace, n. fourneau m.

furnish, vb. fournir, meubler

furniture, n. meubles m., pl.

furred, adj. fourré

furrier, n. fourreur m.

furrow, n. sillon m.

furry, adj. qui ressemble à la fourrure

further, adv. plus éloigné

furthermore, adv. en outre

fury, n. furie f.

fuse, vb. fondre

fuselage, n. fuselage

fusion, n. fusion f.

fuss, n. faire des histoires

fussy, adj. difficile

futile, adj. futile, vain, frivole

future, n. avenir m.

fuzz, n. duvet, flou m.

gab, vb. jaser

gabardine, n. gabardine f.

gable, n. pignon m.

gadget, n. truc m.

gag, n. blague, bobard f., bâilon m.; vb. bâilonner

gain, n. gain m.; vb. gagner

gainful, adj. profitable, rémunérateur

gait, n. allure f.

gala, n. fête de gala f.

galaxy, n. galaxie, assemblée brillante f.

gale, n. grand vent m.

gall, n. fiel m.; écorchure f.

gallant, adj. vailant, galant

gall bladder, n. vésicule du fiel f.

galley, n. galère, cuisine, galée f.

gallon, n. gallon m.

gallows, n. potence f.

gallstone, n. calcul biliaire m.

galore, adv. à foison, à profusion

galosh, n. galoche f.

galvanize, vb. galvaniser

gamble, n. jeu de hasard m.

gambler, n. joueur m.

gambling, n. jeu m.

gambler, n. joueur m.

gambling, n. jeu

gambol, n. gambade f.; vb. gamboler

game, n. jeu, gibier m.

gamely, adv. courageusement, crânement

gameness, n. courage m.; crânerie f.

gander, n. jars m.

gang, n. bande, équipe f.

gangling, adj. dégingandé

gangrene, n. gangrène f.

gangrenous, adj. gangreneux

gangster, n. gangster m.

gangway, n. passage, passavant m.

gap, n. ouverture f.

garage, n. garage m.

garb, n. vêtement, costume m.; vb. vêtir, habiller

garbage, n. ordures f., pl.

garble, vb. tronquer, altérer

garden, n. jardin m.

gardener, n. jardinier m.

gardenia, n. gardénia m.

gargle, n. gargarisme m; vb. se gargariser

gargoyle, n. gargouille f.

garsih, adj. voyant

garland, n. guirlande f.

garlic, n. ail m.

garment, n. vêtement m.

garner, vb. mettre en grenier

garnet, n. grenat m.

garnish, vb. garnir

garnishee, n. tiers-saisi m.

garnishment, n. saisie-arrêt f.

garret, n. mansarde f.

garrison, n. garnison f.

garrote, n. garrotte f.; vb. garrotter

garrulous, adj. bavard, loquace

garter, n. jarretière f.

gas, n. gaz m.

gaseous, adj. gazeux

gash, n. coupure, entaille f.; vb. couper, entailler

gasket, n. garcette f.

gasless, adj. sans gaz

gas mask, n. masque à gaz m.

gasoline, n. essence f.

gasp, vb. sursauter, haleter

gassy, adj. gazeux, bavard

gastric, adj. gastrique

gastric juice, n. suc gastrique m.

gastritis, n. gastrite f.

gastronomically, adv. d'une manière gastronomique

gastronomy, n. gastronomie f.

gate, n. porte, barriére, grille f.

gateway, n. porte, entrée f.

gather, vb. rassembler, recueillir

gathering, n. rasemblement m.

gaudy, adj. voyant

gaunt, adj. décharné

gauntlet, m. gantelet m.

gauze, n. gaze f.

gavel, n. marteau m.

gawky, adj. dégingandé

gaze, vb. regarder fixement

gazette, n. gazette f.

gear, n. appareil, engrenage m.;

gearing, n. engrenage m.

gearshift, n. changement de vitesse m.

gelatin, n. gélatine f.

gelding, n. animal châtré m.

gem, n. pierre précieuse f.

gender, n. genre m.

gene, m. déterminant d'hérédité m.

general, adj. and n. général m.

generalize, vb. généraliser

generally, adv. généralement

generate, vb. engendrer, générer

generation, n. génération f.

generic, adj. gémérique

generous, adj. généreux

generously, adv. généreusement

genetic, adj. génétique

genetics, n. génétique f.

genial, adj. sympathique

genially, adv. affablement

genital, adj. génital

genitals, n. organes génitaux m., pl.

genius, n. génie m.

genteel, adj. de bon ton

gentle, n. gentil m.; adj. doux m., douce f.

gentleman, n. monsieur m.

gentleness, n. douceur f.

gently, adv. doucement

gentry, n. petite noblesse f.

genuine, adj. véritable

genuinely, adv. véritablement

genuineness, n. authenticité f.

genus, n. genre m.

geography, n. géographie f.

geometry, n. géométrie f.

geranium, n. géranium m.

germ, n. germe m.

German, n. Allemand m.; allemand m. adj. allemand

German measles, n. rougeole bénigne f.

Germany, n. l' Allemagne f.

germicide, n. microbicide m.

germinage, vb. germer

gestate, vb. enfanter

gestation, n. gestation f.

gesticulate, vb. gesticuler

gesticulation, n. gesticulation f.

gesture, n. geste m.

get, vb. obtenir, recevoir, prendre, devenir, arriver, entrer, descendre

getaway, n. fuite f.

geyser, n. geyser m.

ghastly, adj. horrible

ghost, n. revenant m.

ghoul, n. goule f.; vampire m.

giant, n. géant m.

gibberish, n. baragouin m.

gibbon, n. gibbon m.

gibe, n. raillerie f.; vb. railler

giblet, n. abatis m.

giddy, adj. étourdi

gift, n. don, cadeau m.

gifted, adj. doué

gigantic, adj. géant, gigantesque

giggle, vb. rire nerveusement, glousser

glid, vb. dorer

gill, n. ouïes f.,pl.

gilt, n. dorure f.; adj. doré

gimlet, n. vrille f.

gin, n. genièvre m.

ginger, n. gingembre m.

gingersnap, n. biscuit au gingembre m.

gingham, n. guingan m.

giraffe, n. girafe f.

gird, vb. ceindre

girder, n. support m.

girdle, n. gaine f.

girl, n. fille, jeune fille f.

girlish, adj. de jeune fille

gist, n. fond m.; essence f.

give, vb. donner, rendre, céder, distribuer, renoncer à

given, adj. donné

giver, n. donneur m.

gizzard, n. gésier m.

glace, adj. glacé

glacial, adj. glaciaire

glacier, n. glacier m.

glad, adj. heureux

glade, n. clairère, éclaircie f.

gladly, adv. volontiers

gladness, n. joie f.

glamour, n. éclat m.

glance, n. coup d'oeil m.

gland, n. glande f.

glare, n. clarté f.; regard enflammé m.;
vb. briller, jeter des regards

glaring, adj. éclatant, flagrant,
voyant, manifeste

glass, n. verre m.

glasses, n. lunettes f., pl.

glassful, n. verre m.; verrée f.

glassware, n. verrerie f.

glassy, adj. vitreux

glaucoma, n. glaucome m.

glaze, n. lustre m.; vb. vitrer

glazier, n. vitrier m.

gleam, n. lueur f.; vb. luire

glee, n. allégresse f.

gleeful, adj. joyeux, allègre

glen, n. vallon, ravin m.

glide, vb. glisser, planer

glider, n. planeur m.

glimpse, vb. entrevoir

glitter, vb. étinceler

globe, n. globe m.

globular, adj. globulaire, globuleux

globule, n. globule m.

gloom, n. ténèbres f., pl.; tristesse f.

gloomy, adj. sombre

glorify, vb. glorifier

glorious, adj. glorieux, radieux

glory, n. gloire f.

gloss, lustre, vernis m.; glose f.;
vb. lustrer, glacer

glossary, n. glossaire m.

glossy, adj. lustré, glacé

glove, n. gant m.

glow, n. lumière, chaleur f.

glowing, adj. embrasé, rayonnant

glowingly, adv. en termes chaleureux

glucose, n. glucose m.

glue, n. colle forte f.; vb. coller

glum, adj. maussade

glumness, n. air maussade m.;
tristesse f.

glutinous, adj. glutineux

glutton, n. gourmand m.

gluttonous, adj. gourmand, goulu

glycerin, n. glycérine f.

gnarl, n. loupe f.; noeud m.

gnash, vb. grincer

gnat, n. moucheron m.

gnaw, vb. ronger

go, vb. aller

goal, n. but m.

goat, n. chèvre f.

goatee, n. barbiche f.

goatskin, n. peau de chèvre f.

gobble, n. avaleur, dindon m.; vb.
gober, avaler

goblet, n. gobelet m.

goblin, n. gobelin, lutin m.

God, n. Dieu m.

godchild, n. filleul m.

goddess, n. déesse f.

godfather, n. parrain m.

godless, adj. athée, impie,
sans Dieu

godlike, adj. comme un dieu;
divin

godly, adj. dévot, pieux, saint

godmother, n. marraine f.

goiter, n. goitre m.

gold, n. or m.

golden, adj. d'or

goldenrod, n. solidage m.

goldsmith, n. orfèvre m.

golf, n. golf m.

gondola, n. gondole f.

gone, adj. disparu, parti

gonorrhea, n. gonorrhée f.

good, n. bien m.; adj. bon m., bonne f.

good-bye, n. and interj. adieu m.

good-hearted, adj. qui a bon
coeur, compatissant

good-humored, adj. de bonne
humeur, plein de bonhomie

good-natured, adj. au bon naturel,
accommodant

goodness, n. bonté f.

good will, n. bonne volonté f.

goose, n. oie f.

gooseberry, n. groseille verte f.

gore, n. chanteau, soufflet m.; vb.
corner

gorge, n. gorge f.

gorgeous, adj. splendide

gorilla, n. gorille m.

gory, adj. sanglant, ensanglanté
gospel, n. évangile m.
gossip, n. bavardage m.; vb. bavarder
Gothic, adj. gothique
gouge, n. gouge f.; vb. gouger
gourmet, n. gourmet m.
govern, vb. gouverner
governess, n. gouvernante f.
government, n. gouvernement m.
governmental, adj. gouvernemental
governor, n. gouvernant m.
gown, n. robe f.
grab, vb. saisir
grace, n. grâce f.
graceful, adj. graceiux
gracefully, adv. avec grâce
gracious, adj. gracieux
grackle, n. mainate m.
grade, n. grade m.; qualité f.; vb.
   classer
gradually, adv. graduellement
graduate, vb. raduer, prendre ses
   grades
graft, n. corruption f.
grail, n. graal m.
grain, n. grain m.
gram, n. gramme m.
grammar, n. grammaire f.
grammar school, n. école primaire f.
grammatical, adj. grammatical
grand, adj. grandiose
grandchild, n. petit-fils m.; petite-fille f.
granddaughter, n. petite-fille f.
grandee, n. grand m.
grandeur, n. grandeur f.
grandfather, n. grand-père m.
grand jury, n. jury d'accusation m.
grandly, adv. grandement, magnifi-
   quement
grandmother, n. grand'mère f.
grandson, n. petit-fils m.
grandstand, n. grande tribune f.
granite, n. granit m.
granny, n. bonne-maman f.
gran, n. concession f, subvention f.;
   vb. accorder; admettre

granule, m. granule m.
grape, n. raisin m.
grapefruit, n. pamplemousse f.
grapevine, n. treille f.
graph, n. courbe f.
graphic, adj. graphique, pittoresque
graphite, n. graphite m.
grasp, n. prise f.; vb. saisir
grass, n. herbe f.
grasshopper, n. sauterelle f.
grate, n. grille f.
grateful, adj. reconnaissant
gratify, vb. contenter, satisfaire
grating, n. grille f.; vb. grincant,
   discordant
gratitude, n. gratitude f.
gratuity, n. pourboire m.
grave, n. tombe f.; adj. grave
gravel, n. gravier m.
gravely, adv. gravement, sérieusement
gravestone, n. pierre sépulcrale,
   tombe f.
graveyard, n. cimetière m.
gravitate, vb. graviter
gravitation, n. gravitation f.
gravity, n. gravité f.
gravure, n gravure f.
gravy, n. jus m.
gray, adj. gris
grayish, adj. grisâtre
graze, vb. paître
grazing, n. graisse f.; vb. graisser
great, adj. grand
greatness, n. grandeur f.
Greece, n. la Grèce f.
greediness, n. gourmandise f.
greedy, adj. gorumand
Greek, n. Grec m.; adj. grec m.,
   grecque f.
green, adj. vert
greenhouse, n. serre f.
greet, vb. saluer
greeting, n. salutation f.; accueil m.
gregarious, adj. grégaire
grenade, n. grenade f.
greyhound, n. lévrier m.
grid, n. gril m.
griddle, n. gril m.

gridiron, n. gril m.

grief, n. chagrin m.

grievance, n. grief m.

grieve, vb. affliger, chagriner

grievous, adj. douloureux

grill, n. gril m.; vb. griller

grim, adj. inistre

grimace, n. grimace f.

grime, n. saleté, noirceur f.

grin, n. large sourire m.

grind, vb. moudre, aiguiser

grip, n. prise f.

gripe, vb. saisir, empoigner, grogner

grisly, adj. hideux, horrible

gristle, n. cartilage m.

grit, n. grès, sable m.

groan, n. gémissement m.; vb. gémir

grocer, n. épicier m.

grocery, n. épicerie f.

groin, n. aine f.

groom, n. palefrenier, nouveau marié m.

groove, n. rainure f.

grope, vb. tâtonner

gross, adj. gros m.; grosse f.

grossness, n. grossièreté, énormite f.

grostesque, adj. and n. grotesque m.

grouch, n. maussaderie f.

ground, n. terre f.

grouse, n. tétras m.; vb. grogner

grove, n. bocage, bosquet m.

grovel, vb. ramper, se vautrer

grow, vb. croitre, grandir, devenir, cultiver

growl, vb. grogner

grown, adj. fait, grand

grownup, adj. and n. grand m., adulte m.f.

growth, n. croissance f.

growl, vb. grogner

grown, adj. fait

grown-up, adj. fait, grand

growth, n. croissance f.

grub, n. larve f.; ver blanc m.

gruel, n. gruau m.

gruesome, adj. lugubre, terrifiant

grumble, adj. bourru, morose; n. grondeur

grumbling, n. murmure m.

grunt, n. grogenement m.

guarantee, n. garantie f.; vb. garantir

guaranty, n. garantie f.

guard, n. garde f.; vb. garder

guarded, adj. prudent, circonspect, réserve

guardian, n. gardien m.

guardsman, n. garde m.

guava, n. goyave f.

guerrilla, n. guérilla f.

guess, n. conjecture f.

guesswork, n. conjecture

guest, n. invité m.

guidance, n. direction f.

guide, n. guide m.

guidebook, n. guide m.

guidepost, n. poteau indicateur m.

guilt, n. culpabilité f.

guiltly, adv. criminellement

guiltless, adj. innocent

guilty, adj. coupable

guinea pig, n. cobaye m.

guitar, n. guitare f.

gulch, n. ravin m.

gulf, n. golfe m.

gull, n. mouette f.

gulp, n. goulée f.

gum, n. gomme f.

gun, n. canon m.

gunboat, n. canonnière f.

gunman, n. partisan armé, voleur arme, bandit m.

gunshot, n. portée de fusil f.

gush, n. jaillissement m.

gusto, n. goût m., délectation, verve f.

gut, n. boyau, intestin m.

gutter, n. gouttière f.

guzzle, vb. ingurgiter, boire avidement

gym, n. gymnase m.

gymnasium, n. gymnase m.

gymnast, n. gymnaste m.

gymnastic, adj. gymnastique

gymnastics, n. gymnastique f.

gynecology, n. gynécologie f.

gypsy, n. gitane m.f.

habeas corpus, n. habeas corpus m.

habiliment, n. habillement m.

habit, n. coutume, habitude f.

habitat, n. habitat m.

habitation, n. habitation f.

habitual, adj. habituel

hack, vb. hacher, tailler en pièces

haddock, n. aigle fin m.

hail, n. grêle f; vb. grêler

hailstorm, n. tempète de grêle f.

hair, n. cheveux m., pl.; chevelure f.

haircut, n. coupe de cheveux f.

hairdo, n. coiffure f.

hairpin, n. épingle à cheveux f.

hale, adj. sain

half, n. motié f.

halfback, n. demi-arrière m.

halfway, adv. à mi-chemin

half-wit, n. niais, sot m.

halibut, n. flétan m.

hall, n. salle f.; vestibule m.

hallow, vb. sanctifier

halloween, n. la veille de la

hallway, n. vestibule m.

halo, n. auréole f.

halt, n. halte f.

halter, n. licou m.; longe, corde f.

halve, vb. diviser en deux, partager en deux

ham, n. jambon m.

hammer, n. marteau m.

hammock, n. hamac m.

hamper, n. pannier m.

hamstring, vb. couper le jarret à, couper les moyens à

hand, n. main f.

handcuff, n. menotte f.; vb. mettre les menottes à

handful, n. poitnée f.

handicap, n. handicap, désavan-tage m.

handicraft, n. métier m.

handiwork, n. main-d'oeuvre f.

handkerchief, n. mouchoir m.

handle, n. manche m.; vb. manier

handmade, adj. fait à la main, fabriqué à la main

handmaid, n. servante f.

hand organ, n. orgue portatif, orgue de Barbarie m.

handout, n. aumône f.; compte rendu, communiqué à la presse m.

handsome, adj. beau m.; belle f.

handwriting, n. écriture f.

handy, adj. adroit, commode, sous la main

hang, vb. pendre

hanging, n. suspension, pendaison f.

hangman, n. bourreau m.

hangnail, n. envie f.

hang-over, n. reste, reliquat m.

hank, m. écheveau m.; torchette f.

hanker, vb. désirer vivement, convoiter

haphazard, adv. au hasard

happen, vb. arriver, se trouver

happening, n. événement m.

happily, adv. heureusement

happiness, n. bonheur m.

happy, adj. heureux

harass, vb. harceler, tracasser

harbor, n. asile, port m.

hard, adj. dur, difficile; adv. fort

harden, vb. durcir

hardly, adv. durement, à peine

hardness, n. dureté, difficulté f.

hardship, n. privation f.

hardware, n. quincaillerie f.

hardy, adj. robuste

hare, n. lièvre m.

harelip, n. bec-de-lièvre m.

harem, n. harem m.

hark, vb. prêter l'oreille à

harlot, n. prostituée, fill de joie f.

harm, n. mal m.

harmful, adj. nuisible

harmless, adj. inoffensif

hamronic, adj. harmonique

harmonious, adj. harmonieux

harmonize, vb. harmoniser

harmony, n. harmonie f.

harness, n. harpon m.

harrow, vb. herser, tourmenter

harry, vb. harceler

harsh, adj. rude

harshness, n. rudesse f.

harvest, n. moisson f.

hash, n. hachis m.

hasn't, vb. n'a pas

hassle, vb. harceler

haste, n. hâte f.

hasten, vb. hâter

hasty, adj. précipité

hat, n. chapeau m.

hatch, vb. couver

hatchery, n. établissement de pisiculture m.

hatchet, n. hachette f.

hate, vb. haïr, détester

hateful, adj. odieux

hatred, n. haine f.

haul, vb. trîner

haunt, vb. hanter

have, vb. avoir

haven't, n. n'ont pas

havoc, n. ravage m.

hawk, n. faucon m.

hawker, n. colporteur, marchand ambulant m.

hay, n. foin m.

hay fever, n. fièvre des foins f.

hayloft, n. fenil, grenier m.

haystack, n. meule de foin f.

hazard, n. hasard m.

haze, n. petite brume

hazel, n. noisetier, coudrier m.

hazy, adj. brumeux, nébuleux

he, pron. il; lui, celui

head, n. tête f.

headache, n. mal de tête m.

headband, n. bandeau m.

headgear, n. garniture de tête, coiffure f.

heading, n. rubrique f.

headlight, n. phare, projecteur m.

headmaster, n. directeur, principal m.

head-on, adj. and adv. de front

headquarters, n. (mil.) quartier général m.

headstone, n. pierre angulaire f.

heady, adj. capiteux, emporté

heal, vb. guérir

health, n. santé f.

healthful, adj. salubre

healthy, adj. sain

heap, n. tas m.

hear, vb. entendre

hearing, n. audition, ouïe f.

hearse, n. corbillard m.

heart, n. coeur m.

heartache, n. chagrin m.; peine de coeur f.

heartbreak, n. déchirement de coeur m.

heartbroken adj. qui a le coeur brisé

heartburn, n. brûlures d'estomac, aigreur f., pl.

heartsick, adj. qui a la mort dans l'âme

hearty, adj. cordial

heat, n. chaleur f.

heated, adj. chaud, chauffé, animé

heatstroke, n. coup de chaleur m.

heavenly, adj. céleste, divin

heavy, adj. lourd

heavyweight, n. poids lourd m.

Hebrew, n. hébreu m.

heckle, vb. embarrasser de questions

hectare, n. hectare m.

hedge, n. haie f.

hedgehog, n. hérisson m.

heed, n. attention f.

heel, n. talon m.

hefty, adj. fort, solide, costaud

heifer, n. génisse f.

height, n. hauteur f.

heir, n. héritier m.

heirloom, n. meuble de famille m.

helicopter, n. hélicoptère m.

helium, n. hélium m.

hell, enfer m.

hello, interj. allô (au téléphone)

helm, n. gouvernail, timon m.

helmet, n. casque m.

help, n. aide, assistance f.; secours m.

helper, n. aide m.f.

helpful, adj. serviable, utile

helping, n. portion, secourable f.

helpless, adj. délaisse, impuissant

hem, n. ourlet m.; vb. ourler

hemisphere, n. hémisphère m.

hemlock, n. ciguë f.

hemoglobin, n. hémoglobine f.

hemorrhoid, n. hémmorroïde f.

hemp, n. chanvre m.

hen, n. poule f.

hence, adv. d'ici, de là

henceforth, adv. désormais

henchman, n. homme de confiance, acolyte, satellite m.

henna, n. henné m. teindre au henné

her, adj. son, sa, ses

herald, n. héraut m.

heraldic, adj. héraldique

herb, n. herbe f.

herd, n. troupeau m.

here, adv. ici, voici

hereabout, adv. ici; voici, que voici

hereafter, adv. dorénavant

hereby, adv. par ce moyen, par ceci

hereditary, adj. héréditaire

herein, adv. cienclus

heretic, n. hérétique m.f.

heritage, n. héritage, patrimoine m.

hermit, n. ermite m.

hernia, n. hernie f.

hero, n. héros m.

heroic, adj. héroïque

heroin, n. héroïne f.

heroism, n. héroïsme m.

heron, n. héron m.

herpes, n. herpès m.

herring, n. hareng m.

herringbone, n. arête de hareng f.

hers, pron. le sien m.; la sienne f.

herself, pron. le sien m.; la sienne f.

hertz, n. hertz m.

hesitancy, n. hésitation, incertitude f.

hesitant, adj. hésitant, irrésolu

hesitate, vb. hésiter

hesitation, n. hésitation f.

heterosexual, adj. hétérosexuel

hew, vb. couper, tailler

hexagon, n. hexagone m.

hiatus, n. lacune f.

hibernate, vb. hiberner, hiverner

hibernation, n. hibernation f.

hiccup, n. hoquet m.

hickory, n. noyer blanc d'Amerique m.

hide, vb. cacher; n. peau f.

hideous, adj. hideux

high, adj. haut

highbrow, n. intellectuel m.

high fidelity, n. haute fidélité f.

highland, n. haute terre f.

highlight, n. clou m.

highly, adv. extrèmement

high-minded, adj. à l'esprit élevé, généreux

high school, n. lycée m.

high tide, n. marée haute f.

highway, n. grande route f.

hijacker, n. pirate de l'air m.

hike, n. aller à pied

hilarious, adj. hilare

hill, n. colline f.

him, pron. le, lui, celui

himself, pron. lui-même

hinder, vb. gêner, empêcher

hindquarter, n. arrière-main, arrière-train m.

hindrance, n. empêchement, obstacle m.; entrave f.

Hindu, n. Hindou m.; adj. hindou

hinge, n. gond m.

hip, n. hanche f.

hippopotamus, n. hippopotame m.

hire, vb. louer, engager

his, adj. son m., sa f., ses pl.; pron. le sien m.; la sienne f.

Hispanic, adj. hispanique

historian, n. historien m.

historic, adj. historique

historical, adj. historique

history, n. histoire f.

hit, n. coup, succès m.; vb. frapper

hitch, n. anicroche f.; vb. accrocher

hither, adv. ici.; adj. le plus rapproché

hive, n. ruche f.

hives, n. éruption, varicelle, pustuleuse, urticaire f.

hoard, n. amas m.; vb. amasser; thésauriser

hoarse, adj. enroué

hoax, n. mystification f.

hobo, n. vagabond m., clochard m., ouvrier ambulant m.

hock, n. jarret m.

hockey, n. hockey m.

hod, n. auge f.

hog, n. proc m.

hoist, n. treuil m.; grue f.; vb. hisser

hold, n. prise, cale f.; vb. tenir, contenir, retainir, arrêter, détenir

holdup, n. arrêt m., coup à main arméem.; suspension f.

hole, n. trou m.

holiday, n. jour, de fête m.

holiness, n. sainteté f.

Holland, n. les Pays-Bas m., pl.

hollow, adj. and n. creux m.

holly, n. houx m.

holocaust, n. holcauste m.

hologram, n. hologramme m.

holster, n. étui m.

holy, adj. saint

Holy Spirit, n. Saint-Esprit m.

homage, n. hommage m.

home, n. maison f.; foyer domestique, chez-soi m.

homeland, n. patrie f.

homeless, adj. sans foyer, sans asile, sans abri

homely, adj. laid

homemade, adj. fait à la maison

homesick, adj. nostalgique

homestead, n. ferme f.; bien de famille m.

homework, n. ravail fait à la maison m.; devoirs m., pl.

homocide, n. homicide m.

homonym, n. homonyme m.

homosexual, n. and adj. homosexuel m.

Honduras, n. l' Honduras m.

hone, vb aiguiser, faffiler

honest, adj. honnête

honestly, adv. honnêtement, de bonne foi

honesty, n. honnêteté f.

honey, n. miel m.

honeybee, n. abeille domestique f.

honeycomb, n. rayon de miel m.; vb. cribler, affouiller

honeymoon, n. lune de miel f.

honeysuckle, n. chèvre-feuille m.

honor, n. honneur m.

honorable, adj. honorable

honorary, adj. honoraire

hood, n. capuchon m.; capote f.

hoof, n. sabot m.

hook, n. cro, homeçon m.

hooked, adj. crochu, recourbé

hoop, n. cercle m.

hoot, n. ululation f.

hop, n. houblon m. vb. sautiler

hope, n. espérance f., espoir

hopeful, adj.. plein d'espoir

hopeless, adj. désespéré

hoplessness, n. désespoir, état désespéré m.

hopscotch, n. marelle f.

horde, n. horde f.

horizon, n. horizon m.

horizontal, adj. horizontal

hormone, n. hormone f.

horn, n. corne f.; cor m.

hornet, n. frelon m.

horoscope, n. horoscope m.

horrendous, adj. horrible, horripilant

horrible, adj. horrible

horrid, adj. affreux

horrify, vb. horrifier

horror, n. horreur f.

horse, n. cheval m.

horsepower, n. puissance en chevaux f.

horseradish, n. raifort m.

horseshoe, n. fer à cheval m.

horsewhip, n. cravache f.

hose, n. tuyau m.; bas m., pl.

hosiery, n. bonneterie f.

hospitable, adj. hospitalier

hospital, n. hôpital m.

hospitality, n. hospitalité f.

hospitalization, n. hospitalisation f.

hospitalize, vb. hospitaliser

host, n. hôte m.

hostage, n. otage m.

hostel, n. hôtellerie, auberge f.

hostess, n. hôtesse f.

hostile, adj. hostile

hot, adj. chaud

hot dog, n. saucisse chaude

hotel, n. hôtel m.

hound, n. chien de chasse m.

hour, n. heure f.

hourglass, n. sablier m.

hourly, adv. à chaque heure

house, n. maison, chambre f.

housefly, n. mouche domestique f.

household, n. famille f.; ménage m.

housekeeper, n. gouvernante f.

housewife, n. ménagère f.

housework, n. ménage m.

hover, vb. planer

hovercraft, n. aéroglisseur m.

how, adv. comment; de quelle façon; (how much) combien

however, adv. de quelque manière que, quelque...que

howl, vb. hurler

hub, n. moyeu, centre m.

huckleberry, n. airelle f.

huddle, n. tas confus, fouillis m.

hue, n. couleur f.

huff, n. emportement m., accès de colère m.

hug, n. étreinte f.

huge, adj. énorme

hulk, n. carcasse f., ponton m.

hull, n. coque f.; corpos m.

hullabaloo, n. vacarme m.

hum, vb. bourdonner, fredonner

human, humane, adj. humain

humanism, n. humanisme m.

humanitarian, adj. humanitaire

humanities, n. humanités f., pl.

humanity, adv. humainement

humble, adj. humble

humbug, n. blague, tromperie, fumisterie f.

humid, adj. humide

humidify, vb. humidifier

humidor, n. boîte à cigares f.

humiliate, adj. humilier

humiliation, n. humiliation f.

humility, v. humilité f.

humor, n. humour m.; humeur f.

humorous, adj. humoristique, drôle

hump, n. bosse f.

humus, n. humus, terreau m.

hunch, n. bossef, pressentiment m.; vb. arrondir, voûter

hunchback, n. bossu m.

hundred, adj. and n. cent m.

hundredth, n. and adj. centième m.

Hungarian, n. Hongrois m.; hongrois f. (language) hongrois m.

Hungary, n. l'Hongrie f.

hunger, n. faim f.

hungry, adj. affamé

hunk, n. gros morceau m.

hunt, vb. chasser

hunter, n. chassuer m.

hunting, n. chasse f.

hurl, vb. lancer

hurricane, n. ouragan m.

hurry, n. hâte, précipitation, confusion f.

hurt, vb. faire du mal; n. mal m.

hurtle, vb. se choquer, se heurter

husband, n. mari m.

hush, n. calme, silence m.

husky, adj. cossu, rauque, enroué

hustle, vb. bousculer, (se)presser

hut, n. cabane f.

hutch, n. huche f.; clapier m.

hybrid, n. hybride m.

hydrant, n. prise d'eau, bouche d'incendie f.

hydraulic, adj. hydraulique

hydrogen, n. hydrogène m.

hyena, n. hyène f.

hygiene, n. hygiène f.

hymn, n. hymne, hymne m.f.

hymnal, n. hymnaire, receuil d'hymnes m.

hypen, n. trait d'union m.

hyphenate, vb. mettre un trait d'union à

hypnotism, n. hypnotisme m.

hynotoize, vb. hynotiser

hysteria, n. hystérie f.

I, pron. je, moi

iamble, adj. iambique

Iberia, n. l' Ibérie f.

ice, n. glace f.

ice cream, n. glace f.

icing, n. glacé m.

icon, icone f.

idea, n. idée f.

ideal, adj. and n. idéal m.

identical, adj. identique, même

identification, n. identification f.

ideology, n. idéologie f.

idiocy, n. idiotie f.

idiom, n. idiome, idiotisme m.

idiot, adj. and n. idiot m.; imbécile m.f.

idle, adj. désoeuvré, paresseux

idleness, n. oisiveté f.

idol, n. idole f.

idyl, idylle f.

idylic, adj. idyllique

if, conj. si

ignorance, n. ignorance f.

ignorant, adj. ignorant

ignore, vb. feindre d'ignorer

ill, n. mal; adj. malade

illegal, adj. illégal

illegitimate, adj. illégitime

illicit, adj. illicite

illiteracy, n. analphabétisme m.

illiterate, adj. illettré

illness, n. maladie f.

illogical, adj. illogique

illuminate, vb. illuminer

illumination, n. illumination, enluminure f.

illusion n. illusion f.

illusive, adj. illusoire

illustrative, adj. explicatif, qui éclaircit

illustrious, adj. illustre

ill will, adj. mauvais vouloir m.; malveillance f.

image, n. image f.

imagery, n. images f., pl.; language figuré m.

imaginative, adj. imaginatif

imagine, vb. imaginer

imam, n. imam m.

imbecile, n. imbécile m.

imitate, vb. imiter

imitation, n. imitation f.

immanent, adj. immanent

immature, adj. pas mûr, prématuré

immediate, adj. immédiate

immense, adj. immense

immerse, vb. immerger, plonger

immigrant, n. immigrant, immigré m.

immigrate, vb. immigrer

imminent, adj. imminent

immobile, adj. fixe, immobile

immoral, adj. immoral

immortal, adj. and n. immortel m.

immunity, n. exemption, immunité f.

immunize, vb. immuniser

impact, n. choc, impact m.

impale, vb. empaler

impart, vb. donner, communiquer, transmettre

impartial, adj. impartial

impatience, n. impatience f.

impatient, adj. impatient

impede, vb. entraver, empêcher

impediment, n. entrave, empêchement f. obstacle m.

impel, vb. pousser, forcer

impenetrable, adj. impénétrable

impenitent, adj. impénitent

imperative, n. impératif m.; adj. urgent, impérieux

imperceptible, adj. imperceiptible

imperfect, adj. and n. imparfait m.

imperial, adj. impérial

impersonate, vb. personnifier, représenter

impertinence, n. impertinence f.

impervious, adj. impénétrable

impetuous, adj. impétueux

impetus, n. élan m.; vitesse, acquise f.

implacable, adj. implacable

implant, vb. inculquer, implanter

implement, n. outil m.

implicate, vb. impliquer, entremêler

implication, n. implication f.

implicit, adj. implicite

implied, adj. implicite, tacite

implore, vb. implorer

imply, vb. impliquer

impolite, adj. impoli

imoponderable, adj. impondérable

import, n. portée, signification f.

importance, n. importance f.

important, adj. important

importation, n. imporation f.

importune, vb. importuner

impose, vb. imposer

imposition, n. imposition f.

impossible, adj. impossible

impotence, n. impuissance f.

impotent, adj. impuisant

impoverish, vb. appauvrir

impregnate, vb. imprégner, féconder

impressrio, n. imprésario m.

impress, vb. imprimer(à)

impression, n. impression f.

impressive, adj. impressionnant

imprison, emprisonner

improbable, adj. improbable

impromptu, adv. adj. and n.
 impromptu m

improper, adj. inconvenant

improve, vb améliorer

improvement, n. amélioration f.

improvise, vb. improviser

impugn, vb. attaquer, contester, impugner

impulse, n. impulsion f.

impulsion, n. impulsion f.

impunity, n. impunité f.

impure, adj. impur

impurity, n. impureté f.

impute, vb. imputer

in, prep. en, dans, à, par, pour

inadvertent, adj. inattentif,
 négligent

inalienable, adj. inaliénable

inaugural, adj. inaugural

incandescence, n. incandescence f.

incandescent, adj. incandescent

incapacitate, vb. rendre incapable

incarcerate, vb. incarcérer

incarnate, vb. incarner

incendiary, n. incendiaire m.

incense, n. encens m.

incentive, n. stimulant, aiguillon m.

inception, n. commencement m.

incest, n. inceste m.

inch, n. pouce m.

incident, n. incident m.

incinerator, n. incinérateur m.

incipient, adj. naissant

incision, n. incision, entaille f.

incisive, adj. incisif, tranchant

incisor, n. incisive f.

incite, vb. inciter, instiguer

incline, vb. incliner

include, vb. renfermer

inclusive, adj. inclusif

incognito, adj. and adv. incognito

income, n. revenu m.

incomparable, adj. incomparable

inconvenience, n. inconvénient m.

incorporate, vb. incorporer

incorrigible, adj. incorrigible

increase, n. augmentation f.

incredible, adj. incroyable

incredulous, adj. incrédule

incriminate, vb. incriminer

incumbent, n. titulaire, bénéficiaire m.

incur, vb. encourir

incurable, adj. incurable

indeed, adv. en effet

indefatigable, adj. infatigable,
 inlassable

indefinite, adj. indéfini

indefinitely, adv. indéfiniment

indelible, adj. indélébile, inef-
 façable

indemnity, n. garantie, indemnité, f.;
 dédommagment m.

indent, vb. denteler, découper, entailer

independence, n. indépendance f.

independent, adj. indépendant

in-depth, adj. profond

index, n. index m.

India, n. l'Inde f.

indicate, vb. indiquer

indication, n. indication f.

indicative, adj. and n. indicatif m.

indicator, n. indicateur m.

indict, vb. accuser, inculper

indifference, adj. indifférent

indigenous, adj. indigène

indigent, adj. indigent, pauvre

indigestion, n. dyspepsie, indigestion f.

indignant, adj. indigné

indignity, n. indignité f.; affront m.

indirect, adj. indirect

indiscreet, adj. indiscret

indiscretion, n. imprudence f.

indispensable, adj. indispensable

indisposed, adj. souffrant

individual, n. individuel, isolé

indoctrinate, vb. endoctriner

indolent, adj. indolent, paresseux

indorse, vb. endosser, sanctionner

induce, vb. persuader, produire

induct, vb. installer, conduire

inductive, adj. inductif

indulge, vb. contenter, favoriser

indulgent, adj. indulgent

industry, n. industrie, assiduité f.

ineligible, adj. inéligible

inept, adj. inepte, mal à propos

inert, adj. inerte, apathique

inertia, n. inertie f.

inevitable, adj. inévitable

inexplicable, adj. inexplicable

infallible, adj. infaillible

infamous, adj. infâme

infamy, n. infamie f.

infance, n. enfance f.

infant, n. enfant m.f.; bébé m.

infantile, adj. enfantin, enfantile

infantryman, n. soldat d'infanterie m.

infatuated, adj. infauté, entiché

infect, vb. infecter

infection, n. infection f.

infectious, adj. infectieux

infer, vb. duire

inference, m. inférence f.

inferior, adj. and n. inférieur m.

infernal, adj. infernal

inferno, n. enfer m.

infest, vb. infester

infidelity, n. infidélité f.

infiltrate, vb. infiltrer

infinite, adj. and n. infini m.

infinity, n. infinité f.

infirm, adj. infirme, faible, maladif

inflame, vb. enflammer

inflate, vb. gonfler

inflict, vb. infliger

infliction, n. infliction; peine f.

influenca, n. influence f.

influential, adj. influent

influenze, n. grippe, influenza f.

inform, vb. informer

information, n. renseignements m., pl.

infringe, vb. enfreindre, violer

infuriate, vb. rendre furieux

ingenious, adj. ingénieux

ingredient, n. ingrédient m.

inhabit, vb. habiter

inhale, vb. inhaler, aspirer

inherent, adj. inhérent

inherit, vb. hériter

inhibit, vb. arrêter, empêcher

inhuman, adj. inhumain, barbare

inimical, adj. enemi, hostile, défavorable

inimitable, adj. inimitable

iniquity, n. iniquité f.

initial, n. initiale f.

initiate, vb. commencer, initier

initiation, n. commencement, début m.; initiation f.

initiative, n. initiative f.

inject, vb. injecter

injection, n. injection f.

injure vb. nuire blesser, abimer

injurious, adj. nuisible, injurieux

injury, n. person préjudice m.; blessure f.

injustice, n. injustice f.

ink, n. encre f.

inland, adj. and n. intérieur m.

inmate, n. habitant, pensionnaire m.

inn, n. auberge f.

innocence, n. innocence f.

innocent, adj. innocent

innocuous, adj. inoffensif

innovation, n. innovation f.

innumerable, adj. innombrable

inoculate, vb. inoculer

inquest, n. enquête f.

inquire, vb. se renseigner
insane, adj. fou m.; folle f.
insanity, n. folie, démence f.
inscribe, vb. inscrire, graver
inscription, n. inscription f.
insect, n. insecte m.
inseparable, adj. inséparable
insert, vb. insérer
inside, n. dedans m.
insidious, adj. insidieux
insight, n. perspicacité, pénétration f.
insignia, n. insignes m., pl.
insignificant, adj. insignifiant
insinuate, vb. insinuer
insinuation, n. insinuation f.
insipid, adj. insipide, fade
insist, vb. insister
insistence, n. insistance f.
insistent, adj. qui insiste, importun
insolence, n. insolence f.
insolent, adj. insolent
insomnia, n. insomnie f.
inspect, vb. examiner, inspecter
inspection, n. inspection f.
inspector, n. inspecteur m.
inspiration, n. inspiration f.
inspire, vb. inspirer
install, vb. installer
instance, n. exemple m.
instant, n. instant m.
instantaneous, adj. instantané
instantly, adv. à l'instant
instead, adv. au lieu de cela
instigate, vb. instiguer
instill, vb. instiller, faire pénétrer, inculquer
instinct, n. instinct m.
instinctive, adj. instinctif
institute, vb. instituer
instruct, vb. instruire
instruction, n. instruction f.
instructor, n. (mil.) instructeur, m.; chargé de cours m.
instrument, n. instrument m.
insufficient, adj. insuffisant
insular, adj. insulaire
insulate, vb. isoler
insulation, n. isolement m.

insulin, n. insuline f.
insult, vb. insulter
insuperable, adj. insurmontable
insurance, n. assurance f.
insure, vb. assurer
insurgent, adj. and n. insurgé m.
intact, adj. intact
integral, adj. intégrant
integrate, vb. intégrer, compléter, rendre entier
integrity, n. intégrité f.
intellect, n. esprit; intellect m.
intellectual, adj. and n. intellectuel m.
intelligent, adj. intelligent
intelligible, adj. intelligible
intend, vb. avoir l'intention de
intense, adj. intense
intensive, adj. intensif
intention, n. intention f.
intercede, vb. intervenir, intercéder
intercept, vb. intercepter, capter
interdict, vb. interdire, prohiber
interest, n. intérêt m.
interesting, adj. intéressant
interface, n. entreface f.
interfere, vb. intervenir
interim, adv. entre temps, en attendant
interject, vb. lancer, émettre
interjection, n. interjection f.
interlude, n. intermède, interlude m.
intermarry, vb. se marier
interment, n. enterrement m.
intermittent, adj. intermittent
intern, n. interne m.
internal, adj. interne
international, adj. international
interne, n. interne m.
interpret, vb. interpréter
interpretation, n. interprétation f.
interpreter, n. interprète m.f.
interrogate, n. interroger, questionner
interrogation, n. interrogation f.
interrupt, vb. interrompre
intersect, vb. entrecouper, intersecter
intersection, n. intersection f.
intersperse, vb. entremêler, parsemer

interval, n. intervalle m.

intervene, vb. intervenir

intervention, n. intervention f.

interview, n. entrevue f.

intestine, n. intestin m.

intimacy, n. intimité f.

intimate, adj. intime

intimidate, vb. indimider

into, prep. en, à, dans

intonation, n. intonation f.

intone, vb. entonner, psalmodier

intoxicate, vb. enivrer

intravenous, adj. intraveineux

intrepid, adj. intrépide, brave,
 courageux

intricate, adj. compliqué

intrigue, n. intrigue f.

intrinsic, adj. intrinsèque

introduce, vb. introduire

introspection, n. introspection f;
 recueillement m.

introver, n. introverti m.

intrude (on), vb. importuner

intruder, n. intrus m.

intuition, n. intuition f.

inundate, vb. inonder

invade, vb. envahir

invader, n. envahisseur m.

invalid, adj. and n. infirme m.f.

invariable, adj. invariable

invasion, n. invasion f.

invective, n. invective f.

invent, vb. inventer

invention, n. invention f.

inventor, n. inventeur m.

invest, vb. investir, placer

investigation, n. investigation f.

investment, n. placement m.

invidious, adj. odieux, haïssable,
 ingrat

invigorate, vb. fortifier, vivfier

invincible, adj. invincible

invisible, adj. invisible

invitation, n. invitation f.

invite, vb. inviter

invocation, n. invocation f.

invoice, n. facture f.

invoke, vb. invoquer

involuntary, adj. involontaire

involve, vb. impliquer, entraîner

iodine, n. iode m.

Iraq, n. l'Irak m.

irate, adj. en colère, furieux

Ireland, n. l'Irlande f.

iris, n. iris m.

Irish, adj. irlandais

irk, vb. ennuyer

iron, n. fer m.

irony, n. ironie f.

irrational, adj. irrationnel, abusrde

irrefutable, adj. irréfutable, irrécusable

irregular, adj. irrégulier

irrelevant, adj. non pertinent,
 hors de propos

irresistible, adj. irrésistible

irresponsible, adj. irresponsable

irreverent, adj. irrévérent, irré-
 vérencieux

irrevocable, adj. irrévocable

irrigate, vb. irriguer, arroser

irrigation, n. irrigation f.

irritability, n. irritabilité f.

irritant, n. irritant m.

irritate, vb. irriter

Islam, n. Islam m.

island, n. île f.

isolate, vb. isoler

isolation, n. isolement m.

isosceles, adj. isoscèle

Israel, n. l'Israël m.

issuance, n. délivrance f.

issue, n. issue, question, émission f.;
 résultat m.

it, pron. il m.; elle f.; le m., la f.,
 lui

Italy, n. l'Italie f.

itch, n. démangeaison f.

item, n. articlé; détail m.

itinerant, adj. ambulant

its, adj. son m.; sa f.; ses
 pl.; pron. le sien m.; la
 sienne f.

itself, pron. lui-même m.; elle-
 même f.

ivory, n. ivoire m.

ivy, n. lierre m.

jab, n. coup de pointe, coup sec m.

jackal, n. chacal m.

jackass, n. âne, idiot m.

jacket, n. veston m.; jaquette f.

jacknife, n. couteau de poche m.

jade, n. rosse, haridelle f.

jaded, adj. surmené, éreinté

jaged, adj. déchiqueté, entaillé

jaguar, n. jaguar m.

jail, n. prison f.

jailer, n. gardien, geôlier m.

jam, n. foule, presse, confiture f.

jamb, n. jambage, chambranle m.

janitor, n. concierge, portier m.

January, n. janvier m.

Japan, n. le Japon m.

Japanese, n. Japonais

jar, n. pot, son discordant m.

jargon, n. jargon m.

jasmine, n. jasmin m.

jaundice, n. jaunisse f.

jaunt, n. petite excursion, balade f.

javelin, n. javelot m.; javeline f.

jaw, n. mâchoire f.

jay, n. geai m.

jazz, n. jazz m.

jealous, adj. jaloux

jealousy, n. jalousie f.

jeans, n. jeans m., pl.

jeer, n. raillerie, moquerie, huée f.

jelly, n. gelée f.

jellyfish, n. méduse f.

jeopardize, vb. exposer au danger, mettre en danger, hasarder

jeopardy, n. danger m., péril m.

jerk, n. saccade f.

jerky, adj. saccadé, coupé

jersey, n. jersey, tricot de laine m.

Jerusalem, n. Jérusalem m.

jester, n. railleur, farceur, bouffon m.

Jesus, n. Jésus m.

jet, n. jet, jet d'eau m.

jettison, n. jet à la mer m.

jetty, n. jetée f.; môle m.

Jew, n. Juif m.; Jive f.

jewel, n. bijou m.

jeweler, n. bijoutier, jouaillier m.

jewelry, n. bijouterie f.

Jewish, adj. juif m.; jive f.

jib, n. loc m.

jiffy, n. instant, clin d'oeil m.

jig, n. gigue f.; calibre, gabarit m.

jilt, vb. délaisser

jingle, n. tintement m., cliquetis m.

jinx, n. porte-malheur m.

jittery, adj. trés nerveux

job, n. travail; emploi m.

jobber, n. intermédiaire, marchandeur m.

jockey, n. jockey m.

jocular, adj. facétieux, jovial

jocund, adj. enjoué

jodhpurs, n. pantation d'équita- tion m.

jog, n. coup, cahot m.; secousse f.

joggle, n. petite secousse f.

join, vb. joindre, se jondre à

joiner, n. menuisier m.

joint, n. joint m.; adj. commun

jointly, adv. ensemble, conjointement

joist, n. solive, poutre f.

joke, n. plaisanterie f.; vb. plaisanter

joker, n. farceur, blagueur, joker m.

jolly, adj. joyeux

jolt, n. cahot, choc m.; secousse f.; vb. cahoter, secouer, ballotter

jonquil, n. jonquille f.

jostle, vb. coudoyer

journal, n. journal m.

journalism, n. journalisme m.

journalist, n. journaliste m.

journey, n. voyage m.; vb. voyager

journeyman, n. compagnon m.

jovial, adj. jovial, gai

jowl, n. mâchoire f.

joy, n. joie f.

joyful, adj. joyeux

jubilant, adj. réjoui, jubilant, exultant

jubilee, n. jubilé m.

Judaism, n. judaïsme m.

judge, n. juge m.

judgement, n. jugement m.

judicial, adj. judiciaire

judiciary, adj. judiciaire

judicious, adj. judicieux, sensé

jug, n. cruche f.

juggle, vb. jongler

jugular, adj. jugulaire

juice, n. jus m.

juicy, adj. juteux

July, n. juillet m.

jumble, n. brouillamini, fouillis m.

jump, n. saut m.; vb. sauter

junction, n. jonction f.; embranchement m.

juncture, n. jointure, jonction, conjoncture f.

June, n. juin m.

jungle, n. jungle, brousse f.

junior, adj. and n. cadet, subalterne m.

juniper, n. genévrier, genièvre m.

junk, n. rebut m.

junket, n. jonchée f.; festin m.

jurisdiction, n. juridiction f.

jurist, n. juriste, légiste m.

juror, n. juré, membre du jury m.

jury, n. jury m.

just, adj. juste

justice, n. justice f.

justifiable, adj. justifiable, justifié

justification, n. justification f.

justify, vb. justifier

jut, vb. faire saillie

jute, n. jute m.

juvenile, adj. juvénile

K

kale, n. chou m.

kaleidoscope, n. kaléidoscope m.

kangaroo, n. kangourou m.

karat, n. carat m.

karate, n. karaté m.

keen, adj. aiguisé, aigu, pénétrant

keep, vb. tenir, garder, continuer à

keeper, n. gardien m.

keepsake, n. souvenir m.

keg, n. caque f.; barillet m.

kennel, n. chenil m.

kerchief, n. fichu, mouchoir m.

kernel, n. grain m.; amande f.

kerosene, n. pétrole m.

ketchup, n. sauce piquante à

kettle, n. bouilloire f.

key, n. clef, clé f.

keyhole, n. entrée de clef f.

khaki, n. kaki m.

kick, n. coup de pied m.

kid, n. gosse m.f., chevreau m.

kidnap, vb. enlever de vive force

kidnaper, n. auteur de l'enlévement m.

kidney, n. rein, rognon m.

kidney bean, n. haricot nain m.

kill, vb. tuer

killer, n. tueur, meurtrier m.

kiln, n. four, séchoir m.

kilocycle, n. kilocycle m.

kilowatt, n. kilowatt m.

kilt, n. kilt m.

kimono, n. kimonoi m.

kin, n. parent m.

kind, n. genre m.

kindergarten, n. jardin dénfants m.

kindle, vb. allumer

kindling, n. allumage m.

kindness, n. bonté f.

kindred, n. parenté f.

kinetic, adj. cinétique

king, n. roi m.

kiss, n. baiser m.; vb. baiser, embrasser

kitchen, n. cuisine f.

kite, n. cer-volant m.

kitten, n. petit chat m.

knack, n. tour de main m.

knapsack, n. havresac m.

knead, vb. pétrir, malaxer

knee, n. genou m.

kneecap, n. genouillère f.

knife, n. couteau m.

knock, n. coup m.

knot, n. noeud m.

know, vb. savoir, connaître

knowing, adj. intelligent, instruit

knowledge, n. connaissance f.

knuckle, n. articulation du doigt, jointure

kodak, n. kodak m.

Korea, n. la Corée f.

kosher, adj. cachir, cacher

label, n. étiquette m.

labor, n. travail m.; ouvriers m., pl.

laboratory, n. laboratoire m.

laborer, n. travailleur m.

laborious, adj. laborieux

labor union, n. syndicat m.

laburnum, n. cytise m.

labyrinth, n. labyrinthe m.

lac, n. gomme-laque

lace, n. dentelle f.; cordon, point, lacet m.

lacerate, vb. lacérer, déchirer

laceration, n. lacération f.

lack, n. manque, besoin, défaut m.; vb. manquer de

lackadaisical, adj. affecté, minaudier, apathique

lacking, adj. manquant (de)

laconic, adj. laconique

lacquer, n. laque m.

lacrosse, n. crosse canadienne f.

lactic, adj. lactique

lactose, n. lactose f.

lacy, adj. de dentelle

lad, n. garçon, jeune homme

ladder, n. échelle f.

lade, vb. charger (de), jeter

lady, n. dame f.

lading, n. chargement m.

ladle, n. cuiller à pot

lady, n. dame f.

ladybug, n. coccinelle f.

lag, n. repris de justice

lagoon, n. lagune f.

laid, adj. vergé

laid-back, adj. décontracté

lair, n. tanière f.; repaire m.

laissez faire, n. laissez faire m.

laity, n. les laïques m., pl.

lake, n. lac m.

lamb, n. agneau m.

lamb's wool, n. laine d'agneau

lambent, adj. qui effleure, qui rayonne doucement

lame, adj. boiteux

lament, vb. se lamenter, pleurer

lamentable, adj. lamentable, déplorable

lamentation, n. lamentation f.

laminate, vb. laminer, écacher

lamp, n. lampe f.

lamplighter, n. allumeur m.

lamp post, n. lampadaire m.

lampoon, n. pasquinade f.

lance, n. lance f.

lancer, n. lancier m.

land, n. terre f.

landholder, n. propriétaire, foncier m.

landing, n. débarquement, mise à terre m.

landlord, n. propriétaire m.f.

landmark, n. borne f.

landscape, n. paysage m.

landslide, n. éboulement m.

landward, adv. vers la terre

lane, n. senteir m.; ruelle f.

language, n. langue f.; langage m.

languid, adj. languissant

languish, vb. languir

languor, n. langueur f.

lank, adj. grand et maigre

lanolin, n. lanoline f.

lantern, n. lanterne f.

lap, n. genoux m., pl.

lapel, n. revers m.

lapin, n. lapin m.

lapse, n. laps m.; faute f.

larceny, n. larcin, vol m.

lard, n. saindoux m.

large, adj. grand

largely, adv. en grande partie

largo, n. largo m.

lariat, n. lasso m.

lark, n. aloutette f.

larkspur, n. pied d'alouette, delphinium m.

larva, n. larve f.

laryngitis, n. laryngite f.

larynx, n. larynx m.

lascivious, adj. lascif

laser, n. laser m.

lash, n. lanière f.; coup de fouet m.

lass, n. jeune fille f.

lassitude, n. lassitude f.

lasso, n. lasso m.

last, adj. dernier, enfin
lasting, adj. durable
latch, n. loquet m.
latchet, n. cordon de soulier m.
late, adj. and adv. tard, en retard, feu,
  dernier
lately, adv. dernièrement
latecomer, n. retardataire
latent, adj. latent, caché
lateral, adj. latéral
lath, n. latte f.
lathe, n. tour m.
lather, n. mousse, écume f.
Latin, n. Latin, latin m.
latitude, n. latitude f.
latrine, n. latrine f.
latten, n. fer-blanc, laiton
latter, adj. and pron. dernier
lattice, n. treillis m.
laud, vb. louer
laudable, adj. louable
laudanum, n. laudanum m.
laudatory, adj. élogieux
laugh, n. rire m.
laughable, adj. risible
laugher, n. rieur m.
laughing, adj. rieur, enjoué
laughter, n. rire m.
launch, vb. lancer, mettre à la mer
launder, vb. blanchir
laundry, n. buanderie f.
laundryman, n. blanchisseur m.
laureate, adj. and n. lauréat m.f.
laurel, n. laurier m.
lava, n. lave f.
lavatory, n. lavabo m.
lave, vb. laver, baigner
lavender, n. lavande f.
lavish, adj. prodigue, somptueux
lavishly, adv. prodigalement
lavishness, n. prodigalité f.
law, n. loi f.; droit m.
lawful, adj. légal
lawless, adj. sans loi
lawn, n. pelouse f.
lawsuit, n. procès m.
lawyer, n. avocat, avoué,
  jurisconsulte m.

lax, adj. lâche, mou, relâche
laxative, n. laxatif m.
laxity, n. relâchement m.
lay, vb. poser
layer, n. couche f.
layman, n. laïque m.
lazy, adj. paresseux
lead, n. plomb m.; mine f.
leaden, adj. de plomb
leader, n. chef m.
leaf, n. feuille f.
leaflet, n. feuillet m.
leafy, adj. feuillu
league, n. ligue, lieue f.
leak, n. fuite f., voie d'eau f.
leakage, n. fuite d'eau f.
leaky, adj. qui coule, qui fait eau
lean, vb. s'appuyer, s'incliner,
  pencher, incliner; adj maigre
leap, vb. sauter
leap year, n. année bissextile f.
learn, vb. apprendre
learned, adj. savant, docte
learning, n. science, instruction f.
lease, n. bail m.
leash, n. laisse, attache f.
least, n. permission f.
leaven, n. levain m.; vb. faire lever
lecherous, adj. lascif, libertin
lecture, n. conférence f
lecturer, n. conférencier m
ledge, n. bord m.
ledger, n. grand livre m.
leech, n. sangsue f.
leek, n. poireau m
leeward, adj. and adv. sous le
  vent
left, adj. and n. gauche f.; à gauche
leftist, n. gaucher m.
leg, n. jambe, patte f.
legacy, n. legs m.
legal, adj. légal
legality, n. légalité f.
legalization, n. légalisation
legalize, vb. rendre egal
legally, adv. légalement
legate, vb. léguer
legation, n. légation

legend, n. légende f.
legendary, adj. légendaire
legible, adj. lisible
legion, n. légion f.
legionary, adj. de légion
legislate, vb. faire les lois
legislation, n. législation f.
legislator, n. législateur m.
legislature, n. législature f.
legitimate, adj. légitime
legume, n. légume m.
leisure, n. loisir m.
leisurely, adv. à loisir
lemon, n. citron m.
lemonade, n. limonade f.
lend, vb. prêter
lenght, n. longueur, durée f.
lengthen, vb. allonger
lengthwise, adv. en long
lengthy, adj. assez long
lenient, adj. indulgent
lens, n. lentille f.; objectif m.
Lent, n. carême m.
Lenten, adj. le carême
lentil, n. lentile f.
lento, adv. lento
leopard, n. léopard m.
leper, n. lépreux m.
leprosy, n. lèpre f.
lesbian, n. lesbienne f.
lesion, n. lesion f.
less, adj. moindre; moins de
lesser, adj. moindre
lesson, n. leçon f.
lest, conj. de peur que
let, vb. laisser, louer
letdown, n. décaption f.
lethal, adj. mortel
lethargic, adj. léthargique
lethargy, n. léthargie f.
letter, n. lettre f.
letterhead, n. en-tête de lettre m.
lettuce, n. laitue f.
levee, n. lever m.
level, adj. égal
lever, n. levier m.
levity, n. légèreté f.
levy, n. levée f.

lewd, adj. impudique
lexicon, n. lexique m.
liability, n. responsibilité f.
liable, adj. responsable de sujet à
liar, n. menteur m.
libation, n. libation f.
libel, n. diffamation f.
libelous, adj. diffamatoire
liberal, adj. libéral, généreux
liberalism, n. libéralisme m.
liberality, n. libéralité f.
liberate, vb. libérer
libertine, n. libre-penseur m.
liberty, n. liberté f.
libidinous, adj. libidneux
libido, n. libido m.
librarian, n. bibliothécaire m.
library, n. bibliothèque f.
libretto, n. livret m.
licnese, n. permis m.; patente f.
licentious, adj. licencieux
lick, vb. lécher
licorice, n. réglisse f.
lid, n. couvercle m.
lie, n. mensonge m.; vb. mentir
lien, n. privilège m.
lieutenant, n. lieutenant m.
life, n. vie f.
lifeguard, n. garde du corps m.
life insurance, n. assurance sur
  la vie f.
lifeless, adj. sans vie
life preserver, n. appareil de
  sauvetage m.
lifetime, n. vie f.; vivant m.
lift, vb. lever
ligament, n. ligament m.
ligature, n. ligature f.
light, n. lumière f.; adj. léger, clair
lighten, vb. alléger, éclairer
lighthouse, n. phare m.
lightly, adv. légèrement
lightness, n. légèreté f.
lightning, n. éclair m.
lignite, n. lignite m.
likable, adj. agréable
like, adj. pareil; même, égal; vb. aimer
  bien, trouver bon

likelihood, n. probabilité f.

likely, adj. probable

liken, vb. comparer

likeness, n. ressemblance f.

likewise, adv. de même

lilac, n. lilas m.

lily, n. lis, muguet m.

limb, n. membre m.; grosse branche f.

limber, adj. souple, flexible

limbo, n. limbes m., pl.

lime, n. chaux, lime f.

limelight, n. lumière oxhydrique f.

limestone, n. pierre à chaux f.;
calcaire m.

limit, n. limite f.

limitation, n. limitation f.

limitless, adj. sans limite

limousine, n. limousine f.

limp, adj. flasque

limpid, adj. limpide

linden, n. tilleul m.

line, n. ligne f.

lineage, n. lignée, race f.

lineal, adj. linéaire

linen, n. toile f.; linge m.

linger, vb. s'attarder

lingerie, n. lingerie f

liniment, n. liniment m.

lining, n. doublure f.

link, n. chaînon, anneau m.

linoleum, n. linoléum m.

linseed, n. graine de lin f.

lint, n. charpie f.

lion, n. lion m.

lip, n. lèvre f.

liquefy, vb. liquéfirer

liqueur, n. liqueur f.

liquid, adj. and n. liquide m.

liquidate, vb. liquider

liquidation, n. liquidation f.;
acquittement m.

liquor, n. boisson alcoolique f.

lisle, n. fil d'Ecosse m.

lisp, vb. zézayer; n. zézaiement m.

list, n. liste f.

listen, vb. écouter

listless, adj. inattentif

litany, n. litanie f.

literacy, n. degré d'aptitude
à lire et à écrire m.

literal, adj. litéral

literary, adj. littéraire

literate, adj. lettré

literature, n. littérature f.

lithe, adj. flexible, pliant

lithograph, vb. lithographier

lithography, n. lithographie f.

litiant, n. plaideur m.

litigation, n. litige m.

litmus, n tournesoil m.

litter, n. litière f.; fouillis m.

little, n. and adv. peu m.; adj. petit

liturgical, adj. liturgique

liturgy, n. liturgie f.

live, vb. vivre

lively, adj. vif m.; vive f.

liven, vb. animer, activer

liver, n. foie m.

livery, n. livrée f.

livestock, n. bétail m.

livid, adj. livide, blême

lizard, n. lézard m.

llama, n. lama m.

lo, interj. voilà

load, n. charge f.; fardeau m.

loaf, n. pain m.

loafer, n. fainéant m.

loam, n. terre grasse f.

loan, n. prêt, emprunt m.

loath, adj. fâché, peiné; vb. détester

loathing, n. dégoût m.

loathsome, adj. dégoûtant

lobby, n. vestibule m.

lobe, n. lobe m.

lobster, n. homard m.

local, adj. local

locale, n. localité, scène f.

locality, n. localité f.

localize, vb. localiser

location, n. placement m.

lock, n. serrure, mèche f.

locker, n. armoire f.

locket, n. médaillon m.

lockjaw, n. tétanos m.

locksmith, n. serrurie m.

locomotive, n. locomotive f.

lode, n. filon m.

lodge, vb. loger

lodger, n. locataire m.

lodging, n. logement m.

loft, n. grenier m.

lofty, adj. élevé, hautain

log, n. bûche f.; loch m.

loge, n. loge f.

logic, n. logique f.

logical, adj. logique

loins, n. reins m., pl.

loiter, vb. fiâner

lollipop, n. sucre d'orge m.

London, n. Londres m.

lone, adj. solitaire, délaissé

lonely, adj. isolé

loneliness, n. solitude f.

long, adj. long m.; longue f.

longevity, n. longévité f.

loom, n. métier m.

loop, n. boucle f.

loophole, n. meurtrière f.

loose, adj. lâche

loosen, vb. desserrer

loot, n. butin m.

lop, vb. élaguer, ébrancher

loquacious, adj. loquace

lord, n. seigneur, lord m.

lordship, n. seigneurie f.

lose, vb. perdre

loss, n. perte f.

lot, n. sort, terrain m.

lotion, n. lotion f.

lottery, n. loterie f.

lotus, n. lotus, lotos m.

loud, adj. fort, bruyant

lounge, n. sofa, hall m.

louse, n. pou m.

lout, n. rustre m.

louver, n. auvent m.

lovable, adj. aimable

love,n. amour m.

lovely, adj. beau m.; belle f.

lover, n. amoureux m.

low, adj. bas m.; basse f.

lower, vb. baisser

lowly, adj. humble

loyal, adj. loyal

loyalist, n. loyaliste m.

loyalty, n. loyauté f.

lozenge, n. pastille f.

lubricant, n. lubrifiant m.

lubricate, vb. lubrifier

lucid, adj. lucide

luck, n. chance f.

lucky, adj. heureux

lucrative, adj. lucratif

ludicrous, adj. risible

lug, vb. traîner, tirer

luggage, n. bagages m., pl.

lukewarm, adj. tiède

lull, n. moment de calme m.

lullaby, n. berceuse f.

lumbago, n. lumbago m.

lumber, n. bois de charpente m.

luminous, adj. lumineux

lump, n. masse f.

lumpy, adj. grumeleux

lunacy, n. folie f.

lunar, adj. lunaire

lunatic, n. aliéné m.

lunch, n. déjeuner m.

luncheon, n. déjeuner m.

lung, n. poumon m.

lunge, n. embardée f.

lure, vb. leurrer; attirer

lurid, adj. blafard, sombre

lurk, vb. se cacher

luscious, adj. délicieux

lush, adj. luxuriant

lust, n. luxure f.

luster, n. lustre m.

lustful, adj. lascif, sensuel

lustrous, adj. brillant, lustré

lusty, adj. vigoureux

lute, n. luth m.

Lutheran, adj. luthérien

luxuriant, adj. exubérant

luxurious, adj. luxueux

luxury, n. luxe m.

lying, n. mensonge m.

lymph, n. lymphe f.

lynch, vb. lyncher

lyre, n. lyre f.

lyric, adj. lyrique

lyricism, n. lyrisme m.

macaroni, n. macaroni m.

machine, n. machine f.

machinery, n. machiniste m.

machismo, n. phallocratie f.

macho, adj. phallocrate

mackerel, n. maquereau m.

mad, adj. fou m.; folle f.

madam, n. madame f.

made, adj. fait, fabriqué

mafia, n. mafia f.

magazine, n. revue f.

magic, n. magie f.

magistrate, n. magistrat m.

magnanimous, adj. magnanime

magnate, n. magnat m.

magnesium, n. magnésium m.

magnet, n. aimant m.

magnificance, n. maginificence f.

magnificent, adj. magnifique

magnify, vb. grossir

magnitue, n grandeur f.

mahogany, n. acajou m.

maid, n. bonne f.

maiden, adj. de jeune fille

mail, n. courrier m.

mailman, n. facteur m.

maim, vb. estropier, mutiler

main, adj. principal

mainland, n. continent m.

maintain, vb. maintenir, soutenir

maintenance, n. entretien m.

maize, n. maïs m.

majestic, adj. majestueux

majesty, n. majesté f.

major, n. commandant m.

majority, n. majorité f.

make, n. fabrication f. vb. faire, fabriquer

maker, n. fabricant m.

malady, n. maladie f.

malaria, n. malaria f.

male, adj. and n. mâle m.

malevolent, adj. maleveillant

malice, n. méchanceté f.

malicious, adj. méchant

malign, vb. calomnier

malignant, adj. malin m.; maligne f.

malleable, adj. malléable

malnutirition, n. sousalimentation f.

malpractice, n. méfait m.

malt, n. malt m.

mammal, n. mammifère m.

man, n. homme m.

manage, vb. diriger, mener, conduire

management, n. direction f.

manager, n. directeur, ménager m.

mandate, n. mandat m.

mandatory, adj. obligatoire

mandolin, n. mandoline f.

mane, n. crinière f.

maneuver, n. manoeuvre f.

manganese, n. manganèse m.

manger, n. mangeoire f.

mangle, vb. mutiler

manhood, n. virilité f.

mania, n. manie, folie f.

maniac, adj. and n. fou m.; folie f.

manicure, n. manucure m.f; soin des ongles m.

manifest, adj. manifeste

manifesto, n. manifeste m.

manifold, adj. divers, multiple

manipulate, vb. manipuler

mankind, n. genre humain m.

manly, adj. viril

manner, n. manière f.; moeurs f., pl.

mannerism, n. maniérisme, m.; affectation f.

mansion, n. château, hôtel m.

mantel, n. manteau m.; tablette f.

manual, adj. and n. manuel m.

manufacture, n. manufacture f.; produit m.

manufacturer, n. fabricant m.

manure, n. fumier m.

manuscript, adj. and n. manuscrit m.

many, adj. beacoup de, bien

map, n. carte géographique f.

maple, n. érable m.

mar, vb. gâter

marble, n. marbre m.

march, n. march f.; vb. marcher

March, n. mars m.

mare, n. jument f.

margarine, n. marge f.

marine, n. marine f.; fuslier marin m.; adj. marin, de mer

mariner, n. marin m.

marionette, n. marionnette f.

marital, adj. matrimonial

maritime, adj. maritime

market, n. marché m.

market place, n. place due marché f.

marmalade, n. confiture f.

marquee, n. marquise f.

marquis, n. marquis m.

marriage, n. mariage m.

married, adj. marié

marrow, n. moelle f.

marry, vb. épouser, se marier

marsh, n. marais m.

marshal, n. maréchal m.

martial, adj. martial

martyr, n. martyr m.

marvel, n. merveille f.; vb. s'étonner de.

marvelous, adj. merveilleux

mascara, n. mascara m.

mascot, n. mascotte f.

masculine, adj. masculin

mash, n. purée f.

mask,, n. masque m.; vb. masquer

mason, n. maçon m.

masquerade, n. mascarade f., bal masqué m.

mass, n. masse f.

massacre, n. massacre m.; vb. massacrer

massage, n. massage m.

masseur, n. masseur m.

massive, adj. massif

mass metting, n. réunion f.

mast, n. mât m.

master, n. maître m.; vb. maîtriser

masterpiece, n. chef-d'oeuvre m.

mastery, n. maîtrise f.

masticate, vb. mâcher

mat, n. paillasson m.

match, n. allumette f.; égal, mariage m.; vb. assortir

material, n. matière; étoffe f.; adj. matériel

maternal, adj. maternel

maternity, n. maternité f.

mathematical, adj. mathématique

mathematics, n. mathématiques f., pl.

matinee, n. matinée f.

matriarch, n. femme qui porte les chausses f.

matrimony, n. mariage m.

matron, n. matrone f.

matter, n. matière, affaire f.; suiet m.; vb. importer

mattress, n. matelas m.

mature, adj. mûr.; vb. mûrir

maturity, n. maturité, échéance f.

maudlin, adj. larmoyant

mausoleum, n. mausolée m.

maxim, n. maxime f.

maximum, n. maximum m.

may, vb. pouvoir

May, n. mai m.

maybe, adv. peut-être

mayhem, n. mutilation f.

mayonnaise, n. mayonnaise f.

mayor, n. maire m.

maze, n. labyrinthe m.

me, pron. me, moi

meadow, n. prée m.; prairie f.

meager, adj. maigre

meal, n. repas m.; farine f.

mean, n. moyenne f.; moyens m.,pl.; moyen m.; adj. humble, avare; vb. vouloir dire, se proposer

meaning, n. sens m.

meantime adv. sur ces entrefaites

measles, n. rougeole f.

measure, n. mesure f.; vb. mesurer

measurement, n. mesurage m.

meat, n. viande f.

mechanic, n. mécanicien m.

mechanical, adj. mécanique

mechanism, n. mécanisme m.

mechanize, vb mécaniser

medal, n. médaille f.

meddle, vb. se mêler

media, n. organes de communication m., pl.

median, n. médian
mediate, vb. agir en médiateur
medical, adj. médical
medicate, vb. médicamenter
medicine, n. médecine m.
medieval, adj. médiéval
mediocre, adj. médiocre
mediocrity, n. médiocrité f.
meditate, vb. méditer
meditation, n. méditation f.
medium, n. milieu, intermédiaire,
 médium m.
medley, n. mélange m.
meek, adj. doux m.; douce f.
meekness, n. douceur f.
meet, vb. rencontrer, faire
 la connaissance de; faire face à
meeting, n. réunion f.
megahertz, n. mégahertz m.
megaphone, n. mégaphone m.
melancholy, n. mélancolie f.
mellow, adj. moelleux
melodous, adj. mélodieux
melodrama, n. mélodrame m.
melody, n. mélodie f.
melon, n. melon m.
melt, vb. fondre
meltdown, n. fusion f.
member, n. membre m.
membrane, n. membrane f.
memnto, n. mémento m.
memoir, n. mémoire m.
memorable, adj. mémorable
memorandum, n. mémorandum m.
memorial, n. souvenir, monument m.;
 adj. commémoratif
memorize, vb. apprendre par
 coeur
memory, n. mémoire f.
menace, n. menace; vb. menacer
menagerie, n. ménagerie f.
mend, vb. raccommoder, corriger
mendacious, adj. menteur
mendicant, n. and adj. mendiant m.
menial, adj. servile
menstruation, n. menstruation f.
menswear, n. habillements
 masculins m., pl.

mental, adj. mental
mentality, n. mentalité f.
menthol, n. menthol m.
mention, n. mention f.; vb.
 mentionner, il n'y a pas de quoi
menu, n. menu m.
mercantile, adj. mercantile
merchandise, n. marchandise f.
merchant, n. négociant m.; adj.
 marchand
merciful, adj. miséricordieux
merciless, adj. impitoyable
mercury, n. mercure m.
mercy, n. miséricorde f.; à la merci de
mere, adj. simple
merely, adv. simplement
merge, vb. fusionner
merger, n. fusion f.
merit, n. mérite m.; vb. mériter
meritorious, adj. méritant, méritoire
mermaid, n. sirène f.
merriment, n. gaieté f.
merry, adj. gai
mesh, n. maille f.
mesmerize, n. magnétiser
mess, n. fouillis, gâchis m.; (mil.)
 popote f.; vb. gâcher
message, n. message m.
messenger, n. messager m.
messy, adj. malpropre
metabolism, n. métabolisme m.
metal, n. métal m.
metallic, adj. métallique
metamorphosis, n. métamorphose f.
metaphysics, n. métaphysique f.
meteor, n. météore m.
meter, n. mètre, compteur m.
method, n. méthode f.
meticulous, adj. méticuleux
metric, n. métrique
metropolis, n. métropole f.
metroplitan, adj. métropolitain
mettle, n. ardeur f.
mezzanine, n. mezzanine f.
microbe, n. microbe m.
microfiche, n. microfiche f.
microfilm, n. microfilm m.
microform, n. microforme f.

microphone, n. microphone m.
microscope, n. microscope m.
microscopic, adj. microscopique
mid, adj. du milieu, moyen
middle, n. milieu m.
midget, n. nain m.
midnight, n. minuit m.
midriff, n. diaphragme m.
midwife, n. sage-femme f.
mien, n. mine f.; air m.
might, n. puissance f.
mighty, adj. puissant
migrate, vb. emigrer
migration, n. migration f.
mild, adj. doux m.; douce f.
mildew, n. rouille f.
mile, n. mille m.
mileage, n. kilométrage m.
military, adj. militaire
milk, n. lait m.
milkman, n. laitier m.
mill, n. moulin m.; filature,
usine f.; vb. moudre, fourmiller
miller, n. meunier m.
millimeter, n. millimètre m.
milliner, n. modiste f.
million, n. million m.
mince, vb. hacher
mind, n. eprit, avis m.; envie f.; vb.
faire attention à, écouter, s'occuper
de, prendre garde, garder, n'importe
mindful, adj. attentif
mine, n. mine f.; pron. le mien m.; la
mienne f.
miner, n. mineur m.
mineral, adj. and n. minéral m.
mingle, vb. mêler
minature, n. miniature f.
miniaturize, vb. miniaturiser
minimize, vb. réduire au minimum
minimum, n. minimum m.
mining, n. exploitation minière,
pose de mines f.
minister, n. ministre m.
ministry, n. ministère m.
mink, n. vison m.
minnow, n vairon m.
minor, adj. and n. mineur m.

minority, n. minorité f.
minstrel, n. ménestrel m.
mint, n. la monnaie f.; vb. frapper
minute, n. minute f.; adj. minusculé;
minutieux
miracle, n. miracle m.
miraculous, adj. miraculeux
mirage, n. mirage m.
mire, n. boue f.; bourbier m.
mirror, n. miroir m.
mirth, n. gaieté f.
misappropriate, vb. détourner,
dépréder
misbehave, vb. se mal conduire
miscellaneous, adj. divers
mischief, n. mal m.; malice f.
misconstrue, vb. mal interpréter,
tourner en mal
misdemeanor, n. délit m.
miser, n. avare m.f.
miserable, adj. malheureux, misérable
misery, n. misère f.
misfortune, n. malheur m.
misgiving, n. doute m.
mishap, n. mésaventure f.
mislead, vb. romper, égarer
misplace, vb. mal placer
mispronounce, vb. mal prononcer, estropier
miss, vb manquer, vous me manquez
Miss, n. mademoiselle f.
missile, n. projectile, m.
mission, n. mission f.
missionary, adj. and n. mis-
sionnaire m.f.
mist, n. brume f.
mistake, n. erreur f.; vb. comprendre
mal, se tromper
mister, n. monsieur m.
mistletoe, n. gui m.
mistreat, vb. maltraiter
mistress, n. maîtresse f.
misty, adj. brumeux
misunderstand, vb. mal comprendre
misuse, vb. faire
mauvais usage; maltraiter
mite, n. denier m.; obole f.

mitigate, vb. adoucir

mitten, n. moufle f.

mix, vb. mêler

mixture, n. mélange m.

mix-up, n. émbrouillement m.

moan, n. gémissement m.

moat, n. fossé m.

mob, n. foule, populace f.

mobile, adj. mobile

mobilization, n. mobilisation f.

mobilize, vb. mobiliser

mock, vb. se moquer de, singer

mockery, n. moquerie f.

mod, adj. à la mode

mode, n. mode m.

model, n. modèle m.

moderate, adj. modéré; vb. modérer

modern, adj. moderne

modest, adj. modeste

modesty, n. modestie f.

modify, vb. modifier

modish, adj. à la mode

modulate, vb. moduler

moist, adj. moite

moisten, vb. humecter

moisture, n. humidité f.

molar, n. and adj. molaire f.

molasses, n. mélasse f.

mold, n. moule m.; moisissure f.; vb. mouler

moldy, adj. moisi

mole, n. taupe f.; grain de beauté m.

molecule, n. molécule f.

molest, vb. molester

mollify, vb. adoucir, apaiser

molten, adj. fondu, coulé

moment, n. moment m.

momentary, adj. momentané

momentous, adj. important

monastery, n. monastère m.

Monday, n. lundi m.

monetary, adj. monétaire

money, n. argent m.; monnaie f.

mongre. n. métis m.

monitor, n. moniteur m.

monk, n. moine m.

monkey, n. singe m.

monologue, n. monologue m.

monopoly, n. monopole m.

monotone, n. monotone m.

monotonous, adj. monotone

monotony, n. monotonie f.

monsoon, n. mousson f.

monster, n. monstre m.

monstrosity, n. monstruosité f.

monstrous, adj. monstrueux

month, n. mois m.

monument, n. monument m.

monumnetal, adj. monumental

mood, n. humeur f.; mode m.

moon, n. lune f.

moonlight, n. clair de lune m.

moor, n. lande f.

mooring, n. amarrage m.

moot, adj. discutable

mop, n. balai à laver m.

moped, n. cyclomoteur m

moral, n. morale f., moralité f.

morale, n. moral m.

moralist, n. moraliste m.f.

morality, n. moralité, morale f.

morally, adv. moralement

morbid, adj. morbide

more, adj. and adv. plus, plus de

moreover, adv. de plus

mores, n. moeurs f., pl.

morgue, n. morgue f.

morning, n. matain m.; matinée f.

moron, n. idiiot

morose, adj. morose

morsel, n. morceau m.

mortal, adj. and n. mortel m.

mortar, n. mortier m.

mortgage, n. hypothèque f.

mortify, vb. mortifier

mortuary, adj. mortuaire

Moslem, adj. and n. musulman m.

mosquito, n. moustique m.

moss, n. mousse f.

most, n. le plus.; adj. le plus, la plupart.

moth, n. mite f.

mother, n. mère f.

mother-in-law, n. belle-mère f.

motif, n. motif m.

motion, n. mouvement, signe m.

motionless, adj. immobile
motivate, vb. motiver
motive, n. motif m.
motor, n. moteur m.
motorist, n. automobiliste m.
motto, n. devise f.
mound, n. tertre m.
mount, n. mont m.; monture f. vb. monter
mountain, n. montagne f.
mountaineer, n. montagnard m.
mountainous, adj. montagneux
mourn, vb. pleurer
mournful, adj. triste
mourning, n. deuil m.
mouse, n. souris f.
mouth, n. bouche f.
movable, adj. mobile
move, vb. mouvoir, remuer, bouger, émouvoir
movement, n. mouvement m.
mow, vb. faucher, tondre
much, adj. pron, and adv. beaucoup; (too much) trop, (so much) tant
mucilage, n. mucilage m.
muck, n. fumier n.
mucous, adj. muqueux
mud, n. boue f.
mud-bank, n. de vase m.
muddle, vb. brouiller, troubler
muddler, n. brouillon m.
muddy, adj boueux
muff, n. manchon m.
muffin, n. petit pan m.
muffle, vb. emmitoufler
mug, n. gobelet, pot m.
mulberry, n. mûre f.
mulch, n. paillis m.
mule, n. multet m.
mull, n. cap promontoire m.
muller, n. molette
multiple, adj. multiple m.
multiply, vb. multiplier
multitude, n. multitude f.
mum, n. maman f.; adj. muet
mumble, vb. marmotter
mummer, n. mime
mummy, n. momie, maman f.

mumps, n. oreilons m., pl.
munch, vb. mâcher
mundane, adj. mondain
mungoose, n. mangouste f.
municipal, adj. municipal
munificent, adj. munificent
munition, n. munition f.
mural, n. peinture murale f.
murder, n. meurtre m.
murderer, n. meutrtrier m.
murmur, n. murmure m.; vb. murmurer
muscle, n. muscle m.
muse, n. muse f.; vb. méditer
museum, n. musée m.
mush, n. brouillage m.
mushroom, n. champignon m.
music, n. musique f.
musical, adj. musical, musicient
musician, n. musicien m.
Muslim, adj. and n. musulman m.
muslin, n. mousseline f.
must, vb. devoir, falloir
mustache, n. moustache f.
muster, vb. rassembler
musty, adj. moisi, suranné
mutation, n. mutation f.
mute, adj. muet
mutilitate, vb. mutiler
mutiny, vb. mutinerie f.
mutter, vb. grommeler
mutton, n. mouton m.
mutual, adj. mutuel
muzzle, n. muselière f.
my, adj. mon m.; ma f.; mes pl.
myopia, n. myopie f.
myuriad, n. myriade f.
myrtle, n. myrte m.
myself, pron. moi-même, moi
mystagogue, n. mystagogue m.
mystery, n. mystère m.
mystic, adj. mystique, initié, magicien
mystical, adj. mystique
mystify, vb. mystifier
myth, n. mythe m.
mythical, adj. mythique
mythology, n. mythologie f.

nab, vb. happer, pincer, saisir

nag, vb. gronder

nail, n. ongle, clou m.

nail-brush, n. brosse à ongles f.

nail-file, n. lime à ongles f.

naïve, adj. naïf; m. naïve f.

naked, adj. nu, à nu

name, n. nom m.

named, adj. nommé désigné

nameless, adj. sans nom, anonyme

name-plate, n. plaque f.

namesake, n. homonyme m.

nanny, n. bonne d'enfant

nap, n. peitit somme m.

nape, n. nuque f.

napkin, n. serviette f.

napkin ring, rond de serviett m.

narcissus, n. narcisse m.

narcotic, adj. and n. narcotique m.

narrate, vb. raconter

narration, narration f.

narrative, n. récit, narré m.

narrator, n. narrateur m.

narrow, adj. étroit

narrow minded, adj. à l'esprit étroit

nasal, adj. nasal, du nez

nasty, adj. désagréable

natal, adj. natal

nation, n. nation f.

national, national m.

nationalism, n. nationalisme m.

nationalist, n. nationaliste m.

nationalize, vb. nationaliser

native, n. natif m.; indigène m.f.

nativity, n. naissance f.

natural, adj. naturel

naturalism, n. naturalisme m.

naturalist, n. naturaliste m.

naturalize, vb. naturaliser

naturalness, n. naturel m.

nature, n. nature f.

naught, n. néant, rien

naughty, adj. méchant

nausea, n. nausée f.

nauseous, adj. nauséeux

nauseousness, n. nature
nauséabonde f.

nautical, adj. marin, nautique

naval, adj. naval

nave, n. nef f.

navel, n. nombril m.

navigable, adj. navigable

navigate, vb. naviguer

navigation, n. navigation f.

navigator, n. navigateur m.

navy, n. marine f.

nay, adv. non, bien plus

near, adj. proche.; adv. prés.

nearly, adv. de près, presque

nearness, n. proximité

near-sighted, adj. myope

neat, adj. propre, soigné

neatness, n. propreté f.

nebula, n. nébuleuse f.

nebulous, adj. nébuleux

necessary, adj. nécessaire

necessitate, vb. nécessiter

necessity, n. nécessité f.

neck, n. cou, goulot m.

necklace, n. collier m.

nectar, n. nectar m.

need, n. besoin m.

needful, adj. nécessaire

needfully, adv. nécessairement

needle, n. aiguille f.

needle point, n. pointe d'aiguille f.

needless, adj. inutile

needlessness, n. inutilité f.

needs, adv. nécessairement

needy, adj. nécessiteux

nefarious, adj. infame

negative, adj. négatif

neglect, n. négligence f.

negligee, n. négligée f.

negligent, adj. négligent

negligible, adj. négligeable

negotiate, vb. négocier

negotiation, n. négociation f.

neigh, vb. hennir

neighbor, n. voisin, prochain m.

neighborhood, n. voisinage m.

neither, adj. and pron. ni l'un ni
l'autre

neon, n. néon m.

neophyte, n. néophyte m.

neoplasm, n. néoplasme m.
nephew, n. neveu m.
nepotism, n. népotisme m.
Neptune, n. Neptune m.
nerve, n. nerf m.; audace f.
nerve cell, n. cellule nerveuse f.
nerve racking, adj. horripilant
nervous, adj. nerveux
nest, n. nid m.
nest egg, n. nichet m.
nesting, adj. nicheur
nestle, vb. se nicher
net, n. filte m.; adj. net m.; nette f.
Netherlands, (the) n. les Pays Bas
 m., pl. Hollande f.
network, n. réseau m.
neuraliga, n. névralgie f.
neurology, n. neurologie f.
neurotic, adj. and n. nevrosé m.
neuter, adj. neutre
neutral, adj. and n. neutre m.
neutralize, vb. neutraliser
neutron, n. neutron m.
never, adv. jamais
nevertheless, adv. néanmoins
new, adj. nouveau m.; nouvelle f.; neuf
 m.; neuve f.
newel, adj. tout flambant neuf
news, n. nouvelle f.; nauvellas f., pl.
newsboy, n. vendeur de journaux m.
newscast, n. journal parlé m.;
 informations f., pl.
newspaper, n. journal m.
newsreel, n. film d'actualité m.
New Testament, n. le Nouveau
 Testament m.
new year, n. nouvel an m.
next, adj. prochain; adv. ensuite
nexus, n. connexion f.
nib, n. bec m.; pointe f.
nibble, vb. grignoter
nice, adj. bon, agréable
niceness, n. goût agréable m.
nick, n. entaille f.
nickel, n. nickel m.
nickname, n. surnom m.
nicotine, n. nicotine f.
niece, n. nièce f.

nifty, adj. pimpant
night, n. nuit f.; soir m.
night cap, n. bonnet de nuit
night club, n. boite de nuit f.;
 établissement de nuit m.
nightgown, n. chemise de nuit f.
nightingale, n. rossignol m.
nightly, adv. tous les soirs,
 toutes le nuits
nightmare, n. cauchemar m.
nimble, adj. agile
nine, adj. and n. neuf m.
nineteen, adj. and n. dix-neuf m.
ninety, adj. and n. quatrevingt-dix m.
ninth, adj. and n. neuvième m.
nip, n. pincement m.; pince f.
nipple, n. mamelon m.
nitrogen, n. nitrogène m.
no, adj. and adv. non, pas, ne...pas de
nob, n. caboche f.
nobility, n. noblesse f.
noble, adj. noble
nobleman, n. gentilhomme m.
nobleness, n. noblesse f.
nobly, adv. noblement
nobody, pron. personne
nocturnal, adj. nocturne
nocturnally, adv. nocturnement
nod, n. signe de la tête m.
node, n. noeud m.
nohow, adv. en aucune façon
noise, n. bruit m.
noiseless, adj. silencieux
noisome, n. puant, fétide
noisy, adj. bruyant
nomad, n. nomade m.f.
nominal, adj. nominal
nominate, vb. nommer, désigner
nomination, n. nomination,
 présentation f.
nominee, n. personne nommée f.;
 candidat choisi m.
nonability, n. inhabilité
non acceptance, n. nonacceptation f.
nonaligned, adj. non-aligné
nonchalant, adj. nonchalant
noncombatant, adj. and n. non-
 combattant m.

noncommissioned, adj. sans brevet

noncommittal, adj. qui n'engage à rien

nondescript, adj. indéfinissable

none, pron. aucun

nonentity, n. nullité f.

non-proliferation, n. non-proli-fértion m.

non-resident, n. and adj. non-résident m.

nonsense, n. absurdité f.

non-stop, adj. sans arrêt

noodles, n. nouilles f., pl.

nook, n. coin m.; recoin m.

noon, n. midi m.

noonday, n. midi m.

noose, n. noeud coulant m.

nor, conj. ni; ni...ne

norm, n. norme f.

normal, adj. normal

normality, n. normalité f.

normalize, vb. normaliser

normally, adv. normalement

north, n. nord m.

northeast, n. nord-est m.

northern, adj. du nord

North Pole, n. pôle Nord m.

northwest, n. nord-ouest m.

Norway, n. la Norvège f.

Norwegian, n. Norvégien m.

nose, n. nez m.

nosebleed, n. saignement de nez m.

nose dive, n. vol piqué m.

nosalgia, n. nostalgie f.

nostalgic, adj. nostalgique

nostril, n. narine f.; naseau m.

nostrum, n. panacée f.; remède de chariatan m.

nosy, adj. fouinard

not, adv. pas, non pas, ne...pas, non

notability, n. notabilité f.

notable, adj. and n. notable m.

notary, n. notaire m.

notation, n. notation

notch, n. coche, encoche

note, n. note f.; billet m.

notebook, n. carnet m.

noted, adj. célèbre

notepaper, n. papier à notes m.

noteworthy, adj. remarquable, mémorable

nothing, pron. rien

notice, n. avis, préavis m.; attention f.; vb. remarquer

noticeable, adj. remarquable, apparent

notification, n. notification f.

notify, vb. avertir

notion, n. idée f.

notoriety, n. notoriété f.

notorious, adj. notoire

notwithstanding, adv. tout de même

noun, n. substantif, nom m.

nourish, vb. nourrir

nourishment, n. nourriture f.

novel, n. roman m.

novelist, n. romancier m.

novelty, n. nouveauté f.

November, n. novembre m.

novice, n. novice m.f.

now, adv. maintenant, à présent

nowhere, adv. nulle part

nozzle, n. ajutage m.

nuance, n. nuance f.

nuclear, adj. nucléaire

nude, adj. nu; n. le nu m.

nugget, n. pépite f.

nuisance, n. ennui m.; peste f.

null, adj. nul

number, n. nombre, chiffre m.

numerical, adj. numérique

numerous, adj. nombreux

nun, n. religieuse f.

nuncho, n. nonce m.

nuptial, adj. nuptial

nurse, n. garde-malade m.f.

nursery, n. chambre des enfants, pépinière f.

nurture, n. nourriture f.; vb. nourrir

nut, n. noix f.; écrou m.

nutcracker, n. casse-noix m.

nutrition, n. nutrition f.

nutritious, adj. nutritif

nutshell, n. coquille de noix f.

nylon, n. nylon m.

nymph, n. nymphe f.

oak, n. chêne m.

oar, n. rame f.

oasis, n. oasis f.

oath, n. serment, juron m.

oatmeal, n. farine d'avoine f.

oats, n. avoine f.

obodurate, adj. obstiné teu

obedience, n. obéissance f.

obedient, adj. obéissant

obeisance, n. salut m.

obelisk, n. obélisque m.

obey, vb. obéir à

obituary, n. nécrologe m.

object, n. objet m.

objection, n. objection f.

objectionable, adj. répréhensible

objective, adj. and n. objectif m.

obligation, n. obligation f.

obligatory, adj. obligatoire

oblige, vb. obliger

oblivion, n. oubli m.

obnoxious, adj. odieux

obscene, adj. obscène

obscure, adj. obscur

obsequious, adj. obsequieux

observance, n. observance f.

observation, n. observation f.

observe, vb. observer

observer, n. observateur m.

obsession, n. obsession f.

obsolete, adj. désuet

obstacle, n. obstacle m.

obstetrician, n. accoucheur m.

obstinate, adj. obstiné

obstroperous, adj. tapageur

obstruct, vb. obstruer

obstruction, n. obstruction f.

obtain. vb. obtenir

obtrude, vb. mettre en avant

obviate, vb. prévenir, éviter

obvious, adj. évident

occasion, n. occasion f.

occasional, adj. de temps en temps

occult, adj. occulte

occupant, n. occupant m.

occupation, n. occupation f.;
métier m.

occupy, vb. occuper

occur, vb. avoir lieu, se présenter à l'esprit

occurrence, n. occurrence f.

ocean, n. océan m.

octagon, n. octogone m.

octave, n. octave f.

October, n. octobre m.

octopus, n. poulpe m.

ocular, adj. oculaire

oculist, n. oculiste f.

odd, adj. impair, dépariellé,
bizarre

oddity, n. singularité f.

odds, n. inégalité, cote f.

odious, adj. odieux

odor, n. odeur f.

of, prep. de

off, adv. à...de distance, trompu;
prep. de

offend, vb. offenser, enfreindre la loi

offender, n. offenseur, délinquant m.

offense, n. offense f.; délit m.

offensive, n. offensive f.; adj. offensif,
offensant

offer n. offre f.; vb. offrir

offering, n. offre, offrande f.

office, n. office, bureau m.; fonctions
f., pl.

officer, n. (mil) officier, fonctionnaire m.

official, adj. officiel

officiate, vb. officier

officious, adj. officieux

offshore, adv. au large

offspring, n. descendant m.

often, adv. souvent

oil, n. huile f.

oilcloth, n. toile cirée f.

oily, adj. huileux

ointment, n. onguent m.

okay, interj. très bien

old, adj. vieux m.

old-fashioned, adj. démodé

Old Testament, n. l'Ancien
Testament m.

olfactory, adj. olfactif

oligarchy, n. oligarchie f.

olive, n. olivier m.; olive f.

omelet, n. omelette f.

omen, n. présage m.

ominous, adj. de mauvais augure

omission, n. omission f.

omit, vb. omettre

omnibus, n. omnibus m.

omnipotent, adj. omnipotent,
 tout-puissant

on, prep. sur

once, adv. une fois, autrefois

one, adj. un, seul m.

one-sided, adj. unilatéral

onion, n. oignon m.

only, adj. seul; adv. seulement

onslaught, n. assaut m.

onward, adj. and adv. en avant

opal, n. opale f.

opaque, adj. opaque

open, adj. ouvert; vb. ouvrir

opening, n. ouverture f.

opera, n. opéra m.

opera glasses, n. jumelles f., pl.

operate, vb. opérer; actionner

operatic, adj. d'opéra

operation, n. opération f.;
 fonctionnement m.

operator, n. opérateur m.

operetta, n. opérette f.

opinion, n. opinion f.

opponent, n. adversaire m.f.

opportunism, n. opportunisme m.

opportunity, n. occasion f.

oppose, vb. (put in opposition)
 opposer; (resit) s'opposer à

opposite, adj. opposé, adv.
 vis-à-vis; prep. en face de

opposition, n. oppositon f.

oppress, vb. opprimer

oppression, n. oppression f.

oppressive, adj. oppressif;
 (heat, etc.) accablant

optic, adj. optique

optician, n. opticien m

optimism, n. optimisme m

optismistic, adj. optimiste

option, n. option f.

optional, adj. facultatif

optometry, n. optométrie f.

opulent, adj. opulent, riche

or, conj. ou, (negative) ni

oracle, n. oracle m.

oral, adj. oral

orange, n. orange f.

orangeade, n. orangeade f.

oration, n. discours m.

orator, n. orateur m.

oratory, n. art oratoire m.

orbit, n. orbite f.

orchard, n. verger m.

orchestra, n. orchestre m.

orchid, n. orchidée f.

ordain, vb. ordonner

ordeal, n. épreuve f.

order, n. ordre m.; commande f.; vb.
 ordonner, commander

orderly, adj. ordonné

ordinance, n. ordannance f.

ordinary, adj. and n. ordinaire m.

ordination, n. ordinatiion f.

ore, n. minerai m.

organ, n. orgue m.; organe m.

organdy, n. organdi m.

organic, adj. organique

organism, n. organisme m.

organist, n. organiste m.f.

organization, n. organisation f.

organize, vb. organiser

orgy, n. orgie f.

orient, vb. orienter

Orient, n. Orient m.

Oriental, n. Oriental m.; adj. oriental

orientation, n. orientation f.

origin, n. origine f.

original, adj. original, originel

originality, n. originalité f.

ornament, n. ornement m.

ornamental, adj. ornemental

ornate, adj. orné

ornithology, n. ornithologie f.

orphan, n. orphelin m.

orphanage, n. orphelinat m.

orthodox, adj. orthodoxe

orthopedics, n. orthopédie f.

osmosis, n. osmose f.

ostensible, adj. prétendu

ostentation, adj. plein d'ostentation

ostracize, vb. ostraciser

ostrich, n. autruch f.

other, adj. and pron. autre

otherwise, adv. autrement

ought, vb. devoir

ounce, n. once f.

our, adj. notre (possessive)

ours, pron. le nôtre m.

ourself, pron. nous-même, nous

oust, vb. évincer

ouster n. éviction f.

out, adv. dehors

outbreak, n. commencement m.

outburst, n. éruption f.

outcast, n. paria m.

outcome, n. résultat m.

outdoors, adv. dehors

outer, adj. extérieur

outfit, n. équipement m.

outgrowth, n. conséquence f.

outing, n. promenade f.

outlandish, adj. bizarre

outlaw, vb. proscrire

outlet, n. issue f.

outline n. contour m.

out-of-date, adj. suranné

output, n. rendement m.

outrage, n. outrage m.

outrageous, adj. outrageant

outrank, vb. occuper un rang
supérieur

outright, adv. complètement

outrun, vb. dépasser

outside, adv. dehors; prep. en
dehors de

outskirts, n. extrémité m.; bords f., pl.

outspread, vb. étendre, déployer

outstanding, adj. non payé

outstay, vb. rester plus longtemps
que

outstretched, adj. étendue, tendu

outwalk, vb. marcher plus vite que

outward, adj. extérieur, du dehors

outwardly, adv. extérieurement

outwardness, objectivité f.

outwear, durer plus longtemps que

oval, adj. and n. ovale m.

ovation, n. ovation f.

oven, n. four m.

over, prep. sur, au-dessus de, au
delà de; plus de; adv. partout

overbearing, adj. arrogant

overcoat, n. pardessus m.

overcome, vb. vaincre, succomber à

overdue, adj. arriéré, échu

overflow, vb. déborder

overhaul, vb. examiner en détail, remettre au point

overhead, adj. général; adv. en haut

overkill, n. exagération rhétorique f.

overlook, vb. avoir vue sur, négliger

overnight, adv. pendant la nuit

overpower, vb. subjuguer, accabler

overrule, vb. décider contre

overrun, vb. envahir

oversee, vb. surveiller

oversight, n. inadvertance f.

overstuffed, adj. rembourré

overt, adj. manifeste

overtake, vb. rattraper, arriver à

overtax, vb. surtaxer, surcharger
pressurer

overthrow, vb. renverser

overtime, n. heures supplé-
mentaires f., pl.

overtone, n. harmoniques m., pl.

overtop, vb. s'élever au-dessus de

overture, n. ouverture f.

overturn, vb. renverser

overview, n. vue d'ensemble f.

overweight, n. excédent m.

overwhelm, vb. accabler (de)

owe, vb. devoir

owing, adj. dû

owl, n. hibou m.

own, adj. propre; vb. posséder

owner, n. propriétaire m.f.

ox, n. boeuf m.

oxide, oxyde m.

oxygen, n. oxygène m.

oxygen mask, n. masque
d'oxygène m.

oyster, n. huître f.

ozone, n. ozone m.

pace, n. pas m.; allure f.; vb.
 arpenter
pacific, adj. pacifique
pacify, vb pacifier
pack, n. paquet m.; bande f.; vb.
 emballer, entasser
package, n. paquet m.
pact, n. pacte, contrat m.
paddle, n. pagaie f.
pagan, adj. and n. païen m.
page, n. (of a book) de livre
pageant, n. spectacle m.
pail, n. seau m.
pain, n. douleur, peine f.
pair, n. apire f.
pajamas, n. pyjama m.
palace, n. palais m.
palate, n. palais m.
pale, adj. pâle
pallid, adj. pâle, blème
paltry, adj. mesquin
pamper, vb. choyer
pamphlet, n. brochure f.
pan, n. casserole f.
panacea, n. panacée f.
pane, n. vitre f.
panel, n. panneau m.
pang, n. angoisse f.
panic, n. panique f.
pant, vb. haleter
pantomime, n. pantomime m.
pantry, n. office f.
pants, n. pantalon m.
paper, n. papier m.
par, n. pair m.; égalité f.
parable, n. parabole f.
parade, n. parade f.
paradox, n. paradoxe m.
paraffin, n. paraffine f.
paragraph, n. alinéa m.
paralyze, vb. paralyser
paramedic, n. assistant médical m.
parameter, n. paramètre m.
paramount, adj. souverain
paraphrase, vb. paraphraser
parasite, n. parasite m.
parcel, n. paquet; colis postal m.
parch, vb. dessécher

parchment, n. parchemin m.
pardon, n. pardon m.
pare, vb. peler (fruit)
parent, n. père m.; mère f.;
 parents (parents) m., pl.
parentage, n. naissance f.
parenthesis, n. parenthèse f.
park, n. parc m.; vb. stationner
parley, n. conférence f.; pourparler m.
parliament, n. parlement m.
parlor, n. petit salon m.
parochial, adj. paroissial, de clocher
parody, n. parodie f.
parole, n. parole f.
parrot, n. perroquet m.
parsley, n. persil m.
parson, n. pasteur m.
part, n. partie, part f.; vb. diviser,
 partager, se séparer
partial, adj. partiel, partial
participate, vb. participer
particle, n. particule f.
partition, n. partage m.; cloison f.
partner, n. associé m.
party, n. parti, groupe m.;
 réception f.
pass, vb. passer, passer par
passage, n. passage m.
passenger, n. voyageur, air
 passager m.
passion, n. passion f.
passive, adj. and passif m.
passport, n. passeport m.
pastime, n. passe-temps m.
pastor, n pasteur m.
pastry, n. pâtisserie f.
pasture, n. pâturage m.
pasty, adj. empâte, pâteux
pat, vb. taper
patch, n. pièce f.; vb. rapiécer
patent, n. brevet d'invention m.
paternal, adj. paternel
paternity, n. paternité f
path, n. sentier m.
pathetic, adj. pathétique
pathology, n. pathologie f.
pathos, n. pathétique m.
patience, n. patience f.

patient, n. malade m.f.; adj. patient
patio, n. patio m.
patriarch, n. patriarche m.
patriot, n. patriote m.f.
patrol, n. patrouille f.
patrolman, n. agent, patrouilleur m.
patron, n. protecteur, client m.
pattern, n. modèle, dessin m.
pause, n. pause f.
paver, vb. paver
pavement, n. pavé, trottoir m.
pavillion, n. pavillon m.
pay, n. salaire m.; vb. payer
payment, n. payement m.
pea, n. pois m.
peace, n. paix f.
peach, n. pêche f.
peak, n. sommet, m.
peal, n. retentissement m.; vb. sonner, retentir
peanut, n. arachide f.
pear, n. poire f.
pearl, n. perle f.
peasant, n. paysan m.
peck, vb. becqueter
peculiar, adj. particulier, singulier
pecuniary, adj. pécuniaire
pedagogue, n. pedagagoue m.
pedagogy, n. pagogie f.
pedal, n. pédale f.
pedant, n. pédant m.
peddle, vb. colporter
pedestal, n. piédestal m.
pedestrian, n. piéton m.
pediatrician, n. pédiatre m.
pedigree, n. généalogie f.
peel, n. pelure f.; vb. peler
pen, n. plume f.
penalty, n. peine f.
penance, n. pénitence f.
pencil, n. crayon m.
pending, prep. pendant
penetrate, vb. énétrer
penetration, n. pénétration f.
peninsula, n. peninsule f.
penitent, adj. pénitent, contrit
penny, n. sou m.
pension, n. pension f.

pensive, adj. pensif
people, n. gens m.f, pl; peuple m.
pepper, n. poivre m.
perambulator, n. voiture d'enfant f.
perceive, vb. apercevoir
percent, pour cent
percentage, n. pourcentage m.
perceptible, adj. perceptible
perception, n. perception f.
perch, n. perchoir m.; perche f.
perdition, n. perte f.
peremptory, adj. péremptoire
perennial, adj. perpétuel, vivace
perfect, adj. parfait
perfection, n. perfection f.
perform, vb. accomplir, jouer
perfume, n. parfum m.
perhaps, adv. peut-être
peril, n. péril m.
perilous, adj. périlleux
perimeter, n. périmètre m.
period, n. période f.; point m.
periphery, n. périphérie f.
perish, vb. périr
perishable, adj. périssable
perjury, n. parjure m.
permanent, adj. permanent
permeate, vb. filtrer
permission, n. permission f.
permit, n. permis m.; vb. permettre
pernicious, adj. pernicieux
perpetrate, vb. perpétrer
perpetual, adj. perpétuel
perplex, vb. mettre dans la perplexité
persecute, vb. persécuter
persecution, n. persécution f.
perseverance, n. persévérance f.
persevere, vb. persévérer
persist, vb. persister
person, n. personne f.
personage, n. personnage m.
personality, n. personnalité f.
personnel, n. personnel m.
perspective, n. perspective f.
perspiration, n. transpiration f.
perspire, vb. transpirer
persuade, vb. persuader

pertain, vb. appartenir
pertinent, adj. pertinent
perturb, vb. troubler
pervade, vb. pénétrer
perverse, adj. entêté
pessimism, n. pessimisme m.
pestilence, n. pestilence f.
pet, n. animal familier m.
petal, n. pétale m.
petition, n. pétition f.
petroleum, n. pétrole m.
phantom, n. fantôme m.
pharmacy, n. pharmacie f.
phase, n. phase f.
phenomenal, adj. phénoménal
philosopher, n. philosophe m.
philosophy, n. philosophie f.
phobia, n. phobie f.
phonograph, n. phonographe m.
photocopy, n. photocopie f.
phrase, n. phrase f.
physical, adj. physique
physician, n. médecin m.
piano, n. piano m.
picnic, n. pique-nique m.
picture, n. tableau m., film m.
pie, n. tarte f.
piece, n. morceau m.
pier, n. jetée f.; quai m.
pierce, vb. percer
piety, n. piété f.
pigeon, n. pigeon m.
pile, n. pieu, tas m.; vb. entasser
pilgrim, n. pèlerin m.
pill, n. pilule f.
pillar, n. pilier m.
pillow, n. oreiller m.
pilot, n. pilote m.
pin, n. épingle f.; vb. épingler
pinch, vb. pincer
pine, n. pin m.; vb. languir
pineapple, n. ananas m.
pink, adj. and n. rose m.
pinnacle, n. pinacle m.
pint, n. pinte f.
pious, adj. pieux
pipe, n. tuyau m.; pipe f.
piquant, adj. piquant

pirate, n. pirate m.
pistol, n, pistolet m.
piston, n. piston m.
pit, n. fosse f.
pitcher, n. cruche f.; lanceur m.
pitiful, adj. pitoyable
pity, n. pitié f; dommage m.; vb.
  plaindre
pivot, n. pivot, axe m.
pizza, n. pizza f.
place, n. endroit, lieu m.; vb. mettre
placid, adj. placide
plague, n. peste f.; fléau m.
plaid, n. plaid, tartan m.
plain, n. plaine f.; adj. clair, simple,
  quelconque
plaintiff, n. demandeur m.
plan, n. plan m.; vb. faire le plan de
plane, n. plan
planet, n. planète f.
plant, n. plante f.; vb. planter
plantation, n. plantation f.
planter, n. planteur m.
plasma, n. plasma m.
plaster, n. plâtre m.
plastic, adj. plastique
plate, n. plaque, assiette f.
plateau, n. plateau m.
platform, n. plate-forme f.; quai m.
platter, n. plat m.
plausible, adj. plausible
play, n. jeu m.; piece de theâtre f.; vb.
  jouer, jouer à, jouer de
playmate, n. camarade de jeu m.f.
playwright, n. dramaturge m.
plea, n. défense, excuse f.
plead, vb. plaider, alléguer
pleasant, adj. agréable
please, vb. plaire à, contenter, s'il
  vous plaît
pleasure, n. plaisir m.
pleat, n. pli m.
pledge, n. gage, engagement m.
plenty, n. abondance f.
pliable, adj. pliable
pliers, n. pinces f., pl.
plight, n. état m.
plot, n. intrigue f.; complot m.

plow, n. charrue f.; vb. labourer
pluck, n. courage m.
plum, n. prune f.
plume, n. panache m.
plump, adj. grassouillet
plunge, n. plongeon m.; vb. plonger
plural, adj. and. pluriel m.
plus, n. plus m.
pneumonia, n. pneumonie f.
poach, vb. pocher
pocket, n. poche f.
poem, n. poésie, poème f.
poet, n. poète m.
poetry, n. poésie f.
poignant, adj. poignant
point, n. point m.
poise, n. équilibre m.
poison, n. poison m.; vb. empoisonner
Poland, n. la Pologne f.
polar, adj. polarie
pole, n. pôle m.; perche f.
police, n. police f.
policeman, n. agent de police m.
polish, vb. polir, cirer
polite, adj. poli
politics, n. politique f.
poll, n. scrutin m.
pollute, vb. polluer
pomp, n. pompe f.
pond, n. étang m.
ponder, n. refléchir
pony, n. poney m.
pool, n. mare, piscine f.
poor, adj. pauvre
popular, adj. populaire
population, n. population f.
porch, n. véfanda f.
pore, n. pore m.; vb. s'absorber dans
pork, n. porc m.
pornography, n. pornographie f.
porous, adj. preux
port, n. port, bâbord, porto m.
portable, adj. portatif
portfolio, n. portefeuille m.
portion, n. portion f.
portrait, n. portrait m.
portray, vb. peindre, dépeindre
Portugal, n. le Portugal m.

pose, n. pose f.
position, n. position f.
positive, n. positif m.
possess, vb. posséder
possession, n. possession f.
possibility, n. possibilité f.
possible, adj. possible
possibly, adv. il est possible
post, n. poste f.; poteau, poste m.
postage, n. affranchissement m.
postal, adj. postal
post card, n. carte postale f.
posterior, adj. postérieur
posterity, n. postérité f.
post office, n. bureau de poste m.
postpone, vb. remettre
posture, n. posture f.
pot, n. pot m.; marmite f.
potato, n. pomme de terre f.
potent, adj. puissant
potential, adj. and n. potentiel m.
pottery, n. poterie f.
pouch, n. sac m.
poultry, n. volaille f.
pound, n. livre f.
pour, vb. verser, tomber à verse
poverty, n. pauvreté f.
powder, n. poudre f.
practical, adj. pratique
practiccally, ad. pratiquement
practice, n. exercice m.; habitude, pratique f.; vb. pratiquer
practiced, adj. expérimenté
prairie, n. savane f.
praise, n. éloge m.; vb. louer
prank, n. fredaine f.
pray, vb. prier
prayer, n. prière f.
preach, n. prêcher
preacher, n. prédicateur m.
precaution, n. précaution f.
precede, vb. précéder
precept, n. précepte m.
precious, adj. précieux
precipice, n. précipice m.
precise, adj. précis
precision, n. précision f.
preclude, vb. empêcher

precocious, adj. précoce
predict, vb. prédire
predispose, vb. prédisposer
preface, n. préface f.
prefer, vb. préférer
preferable, adj. préférable
preference, n. préférence f.
prefix, n. préfixe m.
pregnant, adj. enceinte
prejudice, n. préjugé m.
preliminary, adj. préliminaire
prelude, n. prélude m.
premature, adj. prématuré
premeditate, vb. préméditer
premier, n. premier ministre m.
première, n. première f.
premise, n. lieux m., pl.; prémisse f.
premium, n. prix m.
preparation, n. préparation f.;
  préparatifs m., pl.
prepare, vb. préparer
preponderant, adj. prépondérant
preposition, n. préposition f.
preposterous, adj. absurde
prerequisite, n. nécesité préalable f.
prescribe, vb. prescrire
prescription, n. prescription,
  ordannance f.
presence, n. présence f.
presently, adv. tout à l'heure
preserve, n. confiture f.; vb. préserver
preside, vb présider
president, n. président m.
press, n. presse f.; vb. presser
pressure, n. pression f.
prestige, n. prestige m.
presume, vb. présumer
presumptuous, adj. présomptueux
pretend, vb. prétendre, simuler
pretense, n. faux semblant m.
prentionious, adj. préntentieux
pretext, n. prétexte m.
pretty, adj. joli
prevail, vb. prévaloir
prevalent, adj. répandu
prevent, vb. empêcher, prévenir
prevention, n. empêchement m.
preventive, adj. préventif

previous, adj. antérieur
prey, n. proie f.
price, n. prix m.
priceless, adj. inestimable
prick, n. piqûre f.
pride, n. orgueil m.
priest, n. prêtre m.
prim, adj. affecté
primary, adj. premier, primaire
prime, n. combine m.; adj. premier, de
  première qualite
primitive, adj. primitif
prince, n. prince m.
principal, adj. principal
principle, n. principe m.
print, n. empreinte, impression,
  épreuve f.; vb. imprimer
priority, n. priorité f.
prism, n. prisme m.
prison, n. prison f.
privacy, n. retraite f.
private, adj. particullier prive
privation, n. privation f.
prize, n. prix m.
probability, n. probabilité f.
probable, adj. probable
probe, vb. sonder
problem, n. problème m.
procedure, n. procédé m.
proceed, vb. procéder, avancer
process, n. procédé m.
proclaim, vb. proclamer
procure, vb. procurer
prodigal, adj. and n. prodigue m.
prodigy, n. prodige m.
produce, vb. produire
product, n. produit m.
production, n. production f.
productive, adj. productif
profane, adj. profane
profess, vb. professer
professional, adj. professionnel
professor, n. professeur m.
proficient, adj. capable
profile, n. profil m.
profit, n. profit m.
profound, adj. profond
profuse, adj. profus, prodigue

program n. programme m.

progress, n. progrès m.; marche f.

prohibit, vb. défendre

prohibition, n. défense f.

prohibitive, adj. prohibitif

project, n. projet m.; vb. projeter, faire saillie

proliferation, n. prolifération f.

prolong, vb. prolonger

prominent, adj. saillant

promiscuous, adj. sans distinction

promise, n. promesse f.

promote, vb. promouvoir, encourager

prompt, adj. prompt

pronounce, vb. prononcer

pronunciation, n. prononciation f.

proof, n. preuve, épreuve f.

prop, n. appui

propagate, vb. propager

proper, adj. propre, convenable

property, n. propriété f.

prophecy, n. prophétie f.

prophesy, vb. prophétiser

prophet, n. prophète m.

proportion, n. proportion f.

proportionate, adj. proportionné

proposal, n. proposition, demande en mariage f.

propose, vb. proposer

proposition, n. proposition, affaire f.

proprietor, n. propriétaire m.f.

proscribe, vb. proscrire

prose, n. prose f.

prosecute, vb. poursuivre

prospect, n. perspective f.

prospective, adj. en perspective

prosper, vb. prospérer

prosperity, n. prospérité f.

prosperous, adj. prospère

prostrate, adj. prosterné

protect, vb. protéger

protégé n. protégé m.

protein, n. protéine f.

protest, n. protestation f.; protêt m.; vb. protester

protocol, n. protocole m.

protrude, vb. saillir

prove, vb. prouver, éprouver

proverb, n. proverbe m.

provide, vb. pourvoir, fournir

province, n. province f.

provision, n. provision f.

provocation, n. provocation f.

provoke, vb. provoquer, irriter

prowl, vb. rôder

proximity, n. proximité f.

prudence, n. prudence f.

prudent, adj. prudent

prune, n. pruneau m.

psalm, n. psaume m.

psychiatry, n. psychiatrie f.

psychology, n. psychologie f.

public, n. public m.; adj. public m.; publique f.

publication, n. publication f.

publish, vb. publier

pudding, n. pouding m.

puddle, n. flaque f.

pull, vb. tirer

pulp, n. pulpe f.

pulpit, n. chaire f.

pulsate, vb. battre

pulse, n. pouls m.

pump, n. pompe f.; vb. pomper

pumpkin, n. potiron m.

punctual, adj. ponctuel

punctuate, vb. ponctuer

puncture, n. piqûre f.

punish, vb. punir

punishment, n. punition f.

pupil, n. élève m.f.; pupille f.

puppet, n. marionnette f.

purchase, n. achat m.; vb. acheter

pure, adj. pur

puree, n. purée f.

purge, vb. purger

purpose, n. but m.

purse, n. bourse f.

pursue, vb. poursuivre

pursuit, n. poursuite, occupation f.

push, n. poussée f.; vb. pousser

put, vb. mettre

puzzle, n. problème m.; vb. embarrasser

pyramid, n. pyramide f.

python, n. pythonisse f.

quack, n. charlatan, empirique m.
quackery, n. charlatanisme m.
quackish, adj. de charlatan
quad, cadrat m.
quadrangle, n. quadrilatère m.
quadraphonic, adj. quadriphonique
quaestor, n. questeur m.
quag, n. fondrière f.
quail, n. caille f.
quaint, adj. étrange
quake, vb. trembler
Quaker, n. Quakeresse f.;
  Quakeress n.
quaking, n. tremblement m.
quakingly, adv. en tremblant
qualifiable, adj. qualifiable
qualification, n. réserve; compétence, qualification f.
qualify, vb. qualifier, modifier
qualifying, adj. qualificatif
quality, n. qualité f.
qualm, n. scrupule m.
quandary, n. embarras m.
quantitative, adj. quantitatif
quantity, n. quantité f.
quantum, n. montant, quantum m.
quarantine, n. quarantaine f.
quarrel, n. querelle f.
quarreller, n. querelleur m.
quarrelling, n. querelle f.
quarry, n. carrière f.
quart, n. quart de gallon m.
quartan, n. fièvre quarte f.
quarter, n. quart, quartier m.
quarterly, adj. trimestriel
quartern, n. quart de pinte m.
quartet, n. quatuor m.
quartz, n. quartz m.
quasar, n. quasar m.
quaver, vb. chevroter
quavering, n. trille, tremolo m.;
  cadence f.
quay, n. quai m.; vb. garnir de quais
queasiness, n. nausées f., pl.
queasy, adj. sujet à des nausées
queen, n. reine f.
queen bee, n. reine-abeille f.
queer, adj. bizarre, étrange, drôle

quell, vb. réprimer
queller, n. personne qui réprime f.
quench, vb. éteindré; étancher
quenchable, adj. extinguible
quencher, n. personne f.
querulous, adj. plaintiff, maussade
querulously, adv. d'un ton dolent en
  se plaignant
query, n. question f.
quest, n. recherche f.
question, n. question f.; vb. interroger,
  mettre en doute
questionable, adj. douteux
questionary, n. questionnaire m.
questioner, n. questionneur m.
questioning, n. questions f., pl.
question mark, n. point
  d'interrogation m.
questionnaire, n. questionnaire m.
quibble, n. argutie, chicane f.
quick, adj. rapide, vif; adv. vite
quicken, vb. accélérer
quickening, adj. vivifiant, qui ranime
quiet, n. tranquillité f.; adj. tranquille
quietness, n. tranquillement
quill, n. (for writing) plume d'oie f.
quilling, n. tuyautage m.
quilt, n. courtepointe f.
quilting, adj. quinaire
quiaine, n. quinine f.
quint, n. quinte f.
quintain, n. quintaine f.
quinte, n. quinte f.
quip, n. mot piquant m.
quirk, n. sarcasme m.
quit, vb. quitter, abandonner
quite, adv. tout à fait
quitter, n. personne qui quitte f.
quiver, vb. trembler
quivering, n. tremblement m.
quiz, n. petit examen m.; vb. examiner
quizzing, n. raillerie f.
quoin, n. coin m.
quoit, n. palet m.
quorum, n. quorum m.
quota, n. quote-part f.; contingent m.
quotation, n. citation, cote f.
quote, vb. citer

rabbi, n. rabbin m.

rabbit, n. lapin

rabble, n. tourbe f.

rabid, adj. enragé

rabies, n. rage, hydrophobie f.

race, n. (people) race f.; vb. lutter à la course

race-track, n. piste f.

rack, n. râtelier, (torture) chevalet de torture m.

racket, n. (tennis) raquette f.; (noise) tintamarre m.

racoon, n. raton laveur m.

racy, adj. qui a un goût de terroir

radar, n. radar m.

raddle, n. ocre rouge f.

radiance, n. éclat m.

radiant, adj. radieux

radiate, vb. irradier

radiation, n. rayonnement m.

radical, adj. and n. radical m.

radicular, adj. radiculaire

radio, n. télégraphie sans fil f.

radioactive, adj. radio-actif

radish, n. radis m.

radium, n. radium m.

radius, n. rayon m.

raffle, n. loterie, tombola f.

rag, n. chiffon m.

ragamuffin, n. gueux, polisson

rage, n. rage, fureur f.

ragged, adj. en haillons

ragweed, n. ambrosie f.

raid, n. (police) descente f.

rail, n. barre f.

railroad, n. chemin de fer m.

railway, n. chemin de fer m.

raiment, n. vêtement m.

rain, n. pluie f.; vb. pleuvoir

raincoat, n. imperméable m.

rainfall, n. chute de pluie f.

rainy, adj. pluvieux

raise, vb. (bring up,) élever; (lift) lever; cultiver

raisin, n. raisin sec m.

rake, n. râteau m.; vb. râteler

raking, n. ratissage m.

rally, n. ralliement, rassemblement m.

ram, n. bélier m.

ramification, n. ramification f.

rammer, n. pilon m.

ramp, n. rampe f.

rampart, n. rempart m.

ramrod, n. baguette f.

ramshackle, adj. qui tombe en ruines

ranch, n. ranch m.

rancid, adj. rance

random, n. hassard m.

range, n. étendue, portée f.

rank, n. rang m.; vb. ranger

ransack, vb. fouiller; (pillage) saccager

ransom, n. rançon f.

rant, n. déclamation extravagante f.

rap, n. coup m.; vb. frapper

rapid, adj. and n. rapide m.

rapper, n. frappeur, râfleur d'antiquités m.

rapture, n. ravissement m.

rare, adj. rare

rarely, adv. rarement

rascal, n. coquin m.

rask, n. éruption f.; adj. téméraire

raspberry, n. framboise f.

rat, n. rat m.

rate, n. taux m.; vitesse f.

rather, adv. plutôt

ratify, vb. ratifier

ration, n. ration f.

rational, adj. raisonnable

rattle, n. (toy) hochet, (noise) fracas m.; vb. faire claquer

rave, vb. délirer; (rave about) s'extasier sur

raven, n. corbeau m.

raw, adj. cru

ray, n. rayon m.

rayon, n. rayonne f.

razor, n. rasoir m.

reach, n. portée f.; vb. atteindr; étendre, arriver à

react, vb. réagir

reaction, n. reaction f.

reactionary, adj. réactionnaire

read, vb. lire

reader, n. (person) lecteur m.

readily, adv. promptement
ready, adj. prêt
real, adj. réel
realist, n. réaliste m.f.
reality, n. réalité f.
realization, n. réalisation f.
realize, vb. s'apercevoir de, réaliser
really, adv. vraiment
realm, n. royaume m.
reap, vb. moissonner
rear, n. queue f.; adj. situé à l'arrière
reason, n. raison,; vb. raisonner
reasonable, adj. rasonnable
reassure, vb. rassurer
rebate, n. rabais m.
rebel, adj. and n. rebelle m.f
rebellion, n. rébellion f.
rebellious, adj. rebelle
rebirth, n. renaissance f.
rebound, n. rebond m.
rebuke, n. réprimande f.; vb. réprimander
rebuttal, n. réfutation f.
recall, vb. (remember) se rappeler
reced, vb. s'éloigner
receipt, n. quittance f.
receive, vb. recevoir
receiver, n. (phone) récepteur m.
recent, adj. récent
receptacle, n. réceptacle m.
reception, n. réception f.; accueil m.
receptive, adj. réceptif
recess, n. recoin m.; vacances f., pl.; récréation f.
recipe, n. recette f.
reciprocate, vb. payer de retour
recite, vb. réciter
reckless, adj. téméraire
reckon, vb. compter
reclaim, vb. défricher
recline, vb. reposer
recognition, n. reconnaissance f.
recognize, vb. reconnaître
recoil, vb. reculer
recollect, vb. se rappeler
recommend, vb. recommander
recommendation, n. recommanda-

tion f.
recompense, n. récompense f.
reconcile, vb. réconcilier
record, n. registre, antécédents m.; mention f.; vb. enregistrer
recount, vb. raconter
recover, vb. recouvrer, se rétablir
recovery, n. recouvrement, rétablissement m.
recruit, n. recrue f.; vb. recruter
rectangle, n. rectangle m.
rectify, vb. rectifier
recuperate, vb. recouvrer se rétablir
recur, vb. revenir
recycle, vb. recycler
red, adj. and n. rouge m.
redeem, vb. racheter
redemption, n. rachat m.
redress, n. justice f.; vb. redresser, téparer, faire justice à
reduce, vb. réduire
reed, n. roseau m.; (music) anche f.
reef, n. récif m.
reel, n. bobine f.
refer, vb. référer
referee, n. arbitre m.
reference, n. référence f.
refill, vb. remplir
refine, vb. raffiner
reflect, vb. réfléchir
reflection, n. réflexion f.
reform, n. réforme f.; vb. réformer
reformation, n. réforme f.
refractory, adj. réfractaire
refrain from, vb. se retenir de
refresh, vb. rafraîchir
refreshment, n. rafraîchissement m.
refrigerator, n. frigidaire m.
refuge, n. refuge m.
refugee, n. réfugié m.
refund, n. remboursement m. vb. rembourser
refusal, n. refus m.
refuse, n. rebut m.; vb. refuser
refute, vb. réfuter
regain, vb. regagner
regal, adj. royal
regard, n. égard m.; amitiés f., pl.; vb.

regarder
regent, adj. and n. régent m.
regime, n. régime m.
regiment, n. régiment m.
region, n. région f.
register, n. registre m.; vb. enregistrer, recommander
regret, n. regret m.; vb. regretter
regular, adj. régulier
regularity, n. régularité f.
regulate, vb. régler
regulation, n. réglement m.
regulator, n. régulateur m.
rehabilitate, vb. réhabiliter
rehearse, vb. répéter
reign, n. règne m.; vb. régner
rein, n. rêne f.
reindeer, n. renne m.
reinforce, vb. renforcer
reinforcement, n. renfort m.
reject, vb. rejeter
rejoice, vb. réjouir
rejoin, vb. rejoindre; (reply) répliquer
relapse, n. rechute f.
relate, vb. raconter, se rapporter (à) (relate to); entrer en rapport avec
relation, n. relation f.; (relative) parent m.
relative, n. parent m.; adj. relatif
relax, vb. relâcher
relay, n. relais m.; vb. relayer
release, n. délivrance f.; vb. libérer
relent, vb. se laisser attendrir
relevant, adj. pertinent
reliability, n. sûreté f.
reliable, adj. digne de confiance
reliant, adj. confiant
relic, n. relique f.
relief, n. (ease) soulagement, (help) secours, (projection) relief m.
relieve, vb. (ease) soulager, secourir
religion, n. religion f.
religious, adj. religieux
relish, n. goût m.; vb. goûter
reluctant, adj. peu disposé (à)
rely (upon), vb. compter (sur)
remain, vb. rester
remainder, n. reste m.

remark, n. remarque f.; vb. remarquer
remarkable, adj. remarquable
remedy, n. remède m.; vb. rémédier à
remember, vb. se souvenir de
reminisce, vb. raconter ses souvenirs
remit, vb. remettre
remnant, n. reste, vestige, coupon m.
remorse, n. remords m.
remote, adj. éloigné, vague
removal, n. enlèvement m.
remove, vb. enlever
rend, vb. déchirer
render, vb. rendre
renew, vb. renouveler
renewal, n. renouvellement m.
renounce, vb. renoncer à, répudier
renovate, vb. renouveler
renown, n. renommée f.
rent, n. réparation f.; vb. réparer
repay, vb. rendre, (refund) rembourser
repeat, vb. répéter
repel, vb. repousser
repent, vb. se repentir
repertoire, n. répertoire m.
repetition, n. répétition f.
replace, vb. replacer; (take the place of) remplacer
reply, n. réponse f.; vb. répondre
report, n. rapport m.; vb. rapporter
repose, n. repos m.
represent, vb. représenter
representation, n. représentation f.
repress, vb. réprimer
reprimand, n. réprimande f.
reproduce, vb. reproduire
reproduction, n. reproduction f.
reproof, n. réprimande f.
reprove, vb. réprimander
reptile, n. reptile m.
republic, n. république f.
republican, adj. and n. républicain m.
repulsive, adj. répulsif
reputation, n. réputation f.
repute, n. renom m.; vb. réputer
request, n. requête f.; vb. demander
require, vb. exiger

requirement, n. exigence f.
requisite, adj. nécessaire
requisition, n. réquisition f.
rescue, n. délivrance f.; vb. délivrer
research, n. recherche f.
resemble, vb. ressembler à
resent, vb. être froissé de
reservation, n. réserve
reserve, n. réserve f.; vb. réserver
reservoir, n. réservoir m.
reside, vb. résider
residence, n. résidence f.
resident, n. habitant m.; adj. résidant
resign, vb. résigner; se démettre (de)
resignation, n. résignation, démission f.
resist, vb. résister (à)
resistance, n. résistance f.
resolute, adj. résolu
resolution, n. résolution f.
resolve, vb. résoudre
resonant, adj. résonnant
resound, vb. résonner
resource, n. ressource f.
respect, n. repsect, (reference) rapport m.; vb. respecter
respectable, adj. respectable
respectful, adj. respectueux
respective, adj. respectif
respiration, n. respiration f.
respite, n. répit m.
respond, vb. répondre
response, n. réponse f.
responsibility, n. responsabilité f.
responsible, adj. responsable
rest, n. repos, (remainder) reste m.; les autres m.f., pl.; vb. se reposer
restaurant, n. restaurant m.
restful, adj. qui repose
restrain, vb. contenir
restraint, n. contrainte f.
restrict, vb. restreindre
result, n. résultat m.; vb. résulter
resume, vb. reprendre
résumé, n. résumé m.
resurrect, vb. ressusciter
retail, n. détail m.
retain, vb. retenir

retaliate, vb. user de représailles
retard, vb. retarder
reticent, adj. réservé
retire, vb. se retirer
retort, n riposte f.
retreat, n. retraite f.; vb. se retirer
retrieve, vb. recouvrer
reunion, n. réunion f.
reveal, vb. révéler
revel, vb. s'ébattre
revelation, n. révélation f.
revenue, n. revenu m.
revere, vb. révérer
reverend, adj. révérend
reverent, adj. respectueux
reverie, n. rêverie f.
revert, vb. revenir
review, n. revue f.
revise, vb. réviser
revoke, vb. révoquer
revolt, n. révolte f.; vb. se révolter
revolution, n. révolution f.
revolutionary, adj. révolutionnaire
revolve, vb. tourner
revolver, n. revolver m.
reward, n. récompense f.; vb. récompenser
rheumatism, n. rhumatisme m.
rhinoceros, n rhinocéros m.
rhubarb, n. rhubarbe f.
rhyme, n. rime f.; vb. rimer
rhythm, n. rythme m.
rhythmical, adj. rythmique
rib, n. côte f.
ribbon, n. ruban m.
rice, n. riz m.
rich, adj. riche
rid, vb. débarrasser
riddle, n. énigme f.
ride, n. promenade f.; vb. (horse) aller à cheval; (vehicle) aller en voiture
rider, n. cavalier m.
ridge, n. crête f.
ridiculous, adj. ridicule
rifle, n. fusil m.
right, n. droit m.; adj. (correct, proper) juste; avoir raison bien

righteous, adj. juste

rigid, adj. rigide

rigor, n. rigueur f.

rigorous, adj. rigoureux

rim, n. bord m.; (wheel) jante f.

ring, n. anneau m.; (ornament) bague f.; (circle) cercle

rip, n. fente f.; vb. fendre

ripe, adj. mûr

ripple, n. ride f.; vb. rider

rise, n. (increase) augmentation f.; (rank) avancement m.; vb. se lever

risk, n. risque m.; vb. risquer

rite, n. rite m.

ritual, adj. rituel

river, n. fleuve m.

rivet, n. rivet m.

road, n. route f.

roam, vb. errer

roast, n. rôti m.; vb. rôtir

rob, vb. voler

robber, n. vol m.

robe, n. robe f.

robin, n. rouge-gorge m.

robot, n. automate m.

robust, adj. robuste

rock, n. rocher m.; vb. balancer; (child) bercer

rocket, n. fusée f.

rocky, adj. rocheux

rod, n. verge f.

rodent, adj. and n. rongeur m.

rogue, n. coquin m.

roguish, adj. coquin

role, n. rôle m.

Roman, n. Romain m.; adj. romain

romance, n. roman de chevalerie m.

romantic, adj. romanesquer; romantique

romp, n. tapage m.; vb. batifoler

roof, n. toit m.

room, n. place, chambre, salle f.

root, n. racine, (source) source f.; vb. enraciner

rope, n. corde f.

rosary, n. rosaire m.

rose, n. rose f.

rosin, n. colophane f.

rosy, adj. de rose

rot, n. pourriture f.; vb. pourrir

rotary, adj. rotatoire

rotate, vb. tourner

rotation, n. rotation f.

rouge, n. rouge m.

rough, adj. rude; (sea weather) gros m.; grosse f.

round adj. round, l'aller et le retour m.; n. rond m.; (circuit) tournée f.

rouse, vb. (wake) reveiller, secouer

rout, n. (mil.) déroute f.

route, n. route f.

routine, n. routine f.

rove, vb. errer (par)

rover, n. rôdeur m.

row, n. rang m.; dispute f.; vb. ramer

rowdy, adj. tapageur

royal, adj. royal

rub, vb. frotter

rubber, n. caoutchouc m.

ruby, n. rubis m.

ruddy, adj. rouge

rudiment, n. rudiment m.

rue, vb. regretter

ruffian, n. bandit m.

ruffle, n. fraise f.; vb. froncer

rug, n. tapis m.

ruler, n. souverain m.; règle f.

rum, n. rhum m.

Rumania, n. la Roumanie f.

rumba, n. rumba f.

rumble, vb. gronder

rumor, n. rumeur f.

run, vb. courir, marcher, déteindre, couler, s'enfuir

rung, n. échelon m.

rupture, n. rupture f.

rural, adj. rural

rush, n. (haste) hâte, ruée f.; coup, jonc m.; vb. se précipiter

Russia, n. la Russie f.

rust, n. rouille f.; vb. rouiller

rustle, n. (leaves) bruissement m.

rusty, adj. rouillé

rut, n. ornière f.

ruthless, adj, impitoyable

rye, n. seigle m.

Sabbath, n. sabbat m.

saber, n. sabre m.

sable. n. zibeline f.

sabotage. n. sabotage m.; vb. saboter

saboteur, n. saboteur m.

saccharin, n. saccharine f.

sachet, n. sachet m.

sack, n. sac m.; vb. saccager

sacrament, n. sacrement m.

sacred, adj. sacré

sacrifice, n. sacrifice m.; vb. sacrifier

sacrilege, n. sacrilège m.

sad, adj. triste

sadden, vb. attrister

saddle, n. selle f.; vb. seller

sail, n. voile f.; vb. faire voile

sailor, n. marin m.

saint, adj. and n. saint m.

salad, n. salade f.

salary, n. appointements m., pl.

sale, n. vente f.

saliva, n. salive f.

salmon, n. saumon m.

salt, n. sel m.; vb. saler

salute, n. salut m.; vb. saluer

salvage, n. sauvetage m.

salvation, n. salut m.

salve, n. onguent m.

sample, n. échantillon m.

sanatorium, n. sanatorium m.

sanctify, vb. sanctifier

sanction, n. sanction f.

sanctuary, n. sanctuaire m.

sand, n. sable m.

sandal, n. sandale f.

sandwich, n. sandwich m.

sane, adj. sain d'esprit

sanity, n. santé d'esprit f.

sap, n. sève f.

sapphire, n. saphir m.

sarcasm, n. sarcasme m.

sardine, n. sardine f.

satellite, n. satellite m.

satin, n. satin m.

satire, n. satire f.

satisfaction, n. satisfaction f.

satisfactory, adj. satisfaisant

saturate, vb. saturer

Saturday, n. samedi m.

sauce, n. sauce f.

saucer, n. soucoupe f.

sausage, n. saucisse f.

savage, adj. and n. sauvage m.f.

savior, n. sauveur m.

savor, n. saveur f.

saw, n. scie f.; vb. scier

say, vb. dire

scab, n. croûte, gale f.

scald, vb. échauder

scalp, n. cuir chevelu m.; vb. scalper

scan, vb. (examine) scruter

scandal, n. scandale m.

scar, n. cicatrice f.

scarce, adj. rare

scare, vb. effrayer; n. panique f.

scarf, n. écharpe f.

scathing, adj. cinglant

scatter, vb. éparpiller

scenario, n. scénario m.

scene, n. scène f.

scenery, n. (landscape) paysage m.

scent, n. parfum m.; odeur f.; vb.
flairer, sentir

schedule, n. plan m.

scheme, n. plan m.

scholar, n. savant m.

scholarship, n. (school) bourse f.

school, n. école f.

sciatica, n. sciatique f.

science, n. science f.

scientist, n. homme de science m.

scissors, n. ciseaux m., pl.

scoff at, vb. se moquer de

scold, vb. groner

scoop out, vb. évider

scorch, vb. roussir

Scotland, n. l'Ecosse f.

scour, vb. nettoyer

scourge, n. fléau m.

scout, n. éclaireur, boy-scout m.

scowl, vb. se renfrogner

scramble, vb. avancer péniblement

scream, n. cri m.; vb. crier

screen, n. écran m.; (folding screen)
paravent m.

screw, n. vis f.; vb. visser

scribble, vb. griffonner
scroll, n. rouleau m.
scrub, vb. frotter
scruple, n. scrupule m.
scrupulous, adj. scrupuleux
scrutinize, vb. scruter
sculptor, n. sculpteur m.
sculpture, n. sculpture f.
scythe, n. faux f.
sea, n. mer f.
seam, n. couture f.
seaport, n. port de mer m.
search, n. recherche f.; vb. chercher
season, n. saison f.; vb. assaisonner
seat, n. siège m.; vb. asseoir
secondary, adj. secondaire
secret, adj. and n. secret m.
secretary, adj. secrétaire m.f.
sect, n. secte f.
section, n. section f.
sedative, adj. and n. sédatif m.
seduce, vb. séduire
see, vb. voir
seek, vb. chercher
seem, vb. sembler
segment, n. segment m.
segregate, vb. séparer
seize, vb. saisir
seldom, adv. rarement
select, vb. choisir
self, n. moi m.; personne f.
selfish, adj. égoiste(me)
sell, vb. vendre
semantics, n. sémantique f.
semester, n. semestre m.
semicircle, n. demi-cercle m.
seminary, n. séminaire m.
senate, n. sénat m.
senator, n. sénateur m.
senile, adj. sénile
sensation, n. sensation f.
sense, n. sens m.
sensitive, adj. sensible
sentiment, n. sentiment m.
September, n. septembre m.
serenade, n. sérénade f.
serene, adj. serein
sergeant, n. sergent m.

serious, adj. serieux
sermon, n. sermon m.
serpent, n. serpent m.
serum, n. sérum m.
serve, vb. servir
srvice, n. service, (church) office m.
session, n. session f.
seven, adj. and n. sept m.
seventeen, adj. and n. dix-sept m.
seventh, adj. and n. septième m.
sever, vb. séparer, couper
several, adj. and pron. plusieurs
sever, adj. sévère
sew, vb. coudre
sex, n. sexe m.
sexton, n. saacristain m.
shadow, n. ombre f.
shaggy, adj. poilu, hirsute
shallow, adj. peu profond
shame, n. honte f.
shameful, adj. honteux
shampoo, n. shampooing m.
shape, n. forme f.; vb. former
share, n. part, (finance) action f.;
  vb. partager
shark, n. requin m.
sharp, adj. (cutting) tranchant; (clever)
  fin; (piercing) perçant; (music) dièse
shatter, vb. briser
shave, vb. raser
shawl, n. châle m.
she, pron. elle
sheaf, n. (grain) gerbe f.
sheath, n. étui m.
shed, n. hangar m.; vb. verser
sheep, n. mouton m.
sheet, n. (bed) drap m.; (paper,
  metal) feuille f.
shelf, n. rayon m.
shelter, n. abri m.; vb. abriter
shepherd, n. berger m.
sherbet, n. sorbet m.
sherry, n. xérès m.
shield, n. bouclier m.
shine, vb. briller, intr. (shoes) cirer
ship, n. navire, vaisseau m.
shipment, n. envoi m.
shirk, vb. esquiver

shirt, n. chemise f.

shiver, n. frisson m.; vb. frissonner

shock, n. choc m.; vb. choquer

shoe, n. soulier m.

shore, n. rivage m.

short, adj. court

shot, n. coup m.

should, vb. devoir (in conditional)

shoulder, n. épaule f.

shout, n. cri m.; vb. crier

shove, vb. pousser

shovel, n. pelle f.

shower, n. averse f.

shrewed, adj. sagace

shriek, n. cir perçant m.

shrill, adj. aigu

shrimp, n. crevette f.

shrine, n. châsse f.

shrink, vb. rétrécir

shroud, n. linceul m.

shudder, n. frisson m.; vb. frissonner

shun, vb. fuir

shut, vb. fermer

shy, adj. timide

sick, adj. malade

side, n. côte f.

siege, n. siège m.

sieve, n. tamis m.

sift, vb. cribler

sigh, n. soupir m.; vb. soupirer

signature, n. signature f.

significant, adj. significatif

signify, vb. signifier

silence, n. silence m.

silent, adj. silencieux

silk, n. soie f.

silken, adj. de soie

silver, n. argent m.; adj. d'ártent

similar, adj. semblable

simple, adj. simple

simply adv. simplement

simultaneous, adj. simultané

sin, n. péché m.; vb. pécher

since, adv. prep. depuis; conj. (time) depuis que; (cause) puisque

sincere, adj. sincère

sincerity, n. sincérité f.

singer, n. chanteur m.

single, adj. (one) seul; (particular) particulier; (not married) célibataire

singular, adj. and n. singulier m.

sinner, n. pécheur m.; pécheresse f.

sinus, n. sinus m.

sip, vb. siroter

sir, n. monsieur m.

sirloin, n. aloyau m.

sister, n. soeur f.

sister-in-law, n. belle-soeur f.

sit, vb. (sit down) s'asseoir; (be seated) être assis

site, n. emplacement m.

situate, vb. situer

situation, n. situation f.

six, adj. and n. six m.

sixteen, adj. and n. seize m.

sixth, adj. and n. sixième m.

size, n. grandeur, (person) taille, (shoes, gloves) pointure f.

skate, n. patin m.

skeleton, n. squelette m.

sketch, n. croquis m.; vb. esquisser

ski, n. ski m.; vb. faire du ski

skill, n. adresse f.

skim, vb. (milk) écrémer; (book) feuilleter; (surface) effleurer

skin, n. peau f.; vb. écorcher

skip, vb. sauter

skirt, n. jupe f.

sky, n. ciel m.

slab, adj. lache; n) dalle, plaque f.

slacken, vb. (slow up) ralentir; (loosen) relâcher

slacks, n. pantalon m.

slander, n. calomnie f.; vb. calomnier

slang, n. argot m.

slant, n. inclinaison, pente f.

slap, n. claque f.

slate, n. ardoise f.

slave, n. esclave m.f.

slay, vb. tuer

sled, n. traineau m.

sleet, n. neige à moitié fondue f.

sleeve, n. manche f.

sleigh, n. traneau m.

slender, adj. mince, svelte

slice, n. tranche f.

slight, adj. léger, mince
slim, adj. svelte
slit, n. fente f.; vb. fendre
slope, n. pente f.; vb. incliner
slot, n. fente f.
slow, adj. lent, tardif
slowness, n. lenteur f.
sluggish,m adj. paresseux
slumber, vb. sommeiller
sly, adj. (crafty) fusé
small, adj. petit
smart, adj. (clever) habile, (stylish)
élégant; vb. cuire
smash, vb. briser
smear, n. tache f.; vb. salir
smell, n. odeur f.; vb. sentir
smelt, n. éperlan, m; vb. fondre
smile, n. vb. sourire m.
smite, vb. frapper
smoke, n. fumée f.; vb. fumer
smolder, vb. couver
smooth, adj. lisse; vb. lisser
smother, vb. étouffer
snack, n. cass-croute m.
snag, n. obstacle caché m.
snail, n. escargot m.
snake, n. serpent m.
snare, n. piège m.
snarl, vb. grogner
snatch, vb. saisir
sneak, vb. se glisser furtivement
sneer, vb. ricaner; n. rire
snob, n. snob m.
snow, n. neige f.; vb. neiger
snug, adj. confortable
so, adv. si; tellement; (thus)
ainsi
soak, vb. tremper
soap, n. savon m.
soar, vb. prendre son essor
sociable, adj. sociable
social, adj. social
sock, n. chaussette f.
socket, n. douille f.
sod, n. motte f.
sofa, n. canapé m.
soft, adj. doux m., douce f. (yielding)
mou m., molle f.

soil, n. terrori m.; vb. souiller
sojours, n. séjour m.; vb. séjourner
solace, n. consolation f.
solar, adj. solaire
soldier, n. soldat m.
sole, n. (shoe) semelle, (fish) sike f.
solicit, vb. solliciter
solid, adj. and n. solide n.
solitary, adj. solitaire
solitude, n. solitude f.
solution, n. solution f.
solve, vb. résoudre
somber, adj. sombre
some, adj. quelque m. or f.
somebody, someone, pron. quelqu'un
something, pron. quelque chose m.
somewhat, adv. quelque peu
somewhere, adv. quelque part
son, n. fils m.
song, n. chant m.; chanson f.
son-in-law, n. gendre m.
soon, adv. bientôt, tôt
soot, n. suie f.
soothe, vb. calmer
sophisticated, adj. blasé
soprano, n. soprano m.
sordid, adj. sordide
sore, adj. douloureux, endolori,
susceptible
sorrow, n. douleur f.
sorrowful, adj. affligé, triste
sorry, adj. fâché, désolé
sort, n. sorte f.; vb. trier
soul, n. âme f.
sound, adj. en bon état, bon; vb.
sonner, retentir
soup, n. potage n.
sour, adj. aigre
source, n. source f.
south, n. sud m.
southeast, n. sud-est m.
southern, adj. du sud
souvenir, n. souvenir m.
sow, vb. semer
space, n. espace m.
spacious, adj. spacieux
spade, n. bêche f.; (cards) pique m.
Spain, n. l'Espagne f.

span, n. empan m.; (bridge) travée f.

spank, vb. fesser

spanking, n. fessée f.

spark, n. étincelle f.

sparkle, vb. étinceler

spasm, n. spasme m.

speak, vb. parler

speaker, n. (public) orateur m.

special, adj. spécial

species, n. espèce f.

specify, vb. spécifier

speciment, n. spécimen m.

spectacle, n. spectacle m.

spectator, n. spectateur m.

speculate, vb. spéculer

speed, n. vitesse f.

spend, vb. (money) dépenser; (time) passer

sphere, n. sphère f.

spice, n. épice f.

spider, n. araignée f.

spill, vb. répandre

spin, vb. (thread) filer; tourner

spinach, n. épinards m., pl.

spine, n. épine dorsale f.

spirit, n. esprit m.

spiritual, adj. spirituel

spit, n. crachat m., salive f.

spite, n. dépit m.

splash, vb. éclabousser

splendid, adj. splendide

splendor, n. splendeur f.

split, vb. fendre

spoil, n. butin m.; vb. gâter

sponge, n. éponge f.

sponsor, n. (law) garant m.

spontaneous, adj. spontané

spool, n. bobine f.

spoon, n. cuiller f.

sporadic, adj. sporadique

sport, n. sport, (fun) jeu m.

spouse, n. époux m.; épouse f.

spout, n. bec m.; vb. jailir

sprain, n. entorse f.

sprawl, vb. s'étaler

spead, n. étendue f.; vb. étendre

sprightly, adj. éveillé

sprinkle, vb. asperger

spry, adj. alerte

spur, n. éperon m.; vb. éperonner

spurious, adj. faux m.

spurn, vb. repousser

spurt, n. jet m.; vb. jaillir

squad, n. escouade f.

squadron, n. escardron m.

squalid, adj. misérable

squall, n. rafale f.

squander, vb. gaspiller

square, n. (geom.) carré m.; adj. carré

squat, vb. s'accroupir

squeak, vb. crier

squeeze, vb. serrer, presser

squirrel, n. écureuil m.

squirt, vb. seringuer

stab, vb. poignarder

stability, n. stabilité f.

stable, n. écurie f.; adj. stale

staff, n. bâton, (personnel) personnel m.

stage, n. estrade, scène, phase f.

stagflation, n. staglation f.

stagger, vb. (totter) chanceler

stagnant, adj. stagnant

stain, n. tache f.; vb. (spot) tacher; (color) teinter

stairs, n. escalier m.

stale, adj. (bread) rassis

stalk, n. tige f.

stall, n. (stable, church) stalle f.

stamina, n. vigueur f.

stammer, vb. gégayer

stampede, n. sauve-qui-peut n.

star, n. étoile, (movie) vedette f.

starch, n. amidon m.

stare, vb. regarder fixement

stark, adj. pur

starvation, n. faim f.

starve, vb. intr. mourir de faim

state, n. état m.; vb. déclarer

statement, n. déclaraton f.

statesman, n. homme d'état m.

static, adj. statique

stationary, adj. stationnaire

stationery, n. papeterie f.

statistics, n. statistique f.

statue, n. statue f.

stay, vb. rester

steady, adj. ferme, soutenu

steak, n. bifteck m.

steal, vb. voler

steam, n. vapeur f.

steep, adj. raide

steeple, n. clocher m.

stem, n. (plant) tige f.

stenographer, n. sténographe m.f.

stenography, n, sténographie f.

sterile, adj. stérile

stern, adj. sévère

stethoscope, n. stéthoscope m.

stew, n. ragoût m.

stick, n. bâton m.; vb. (paste) coller

stiff, adj. raide

stifle, vb. étouffer

stimulant, n. stimulant m.

stimulate, vb. stimuler

stimulus, n. stimulant m.

stingy, adj. mesquin

stitch, n. (sewing) point m.; (knitting) maille f.; vb. coudre

stole, n. étole f.

stomach, n. estomac m.

stone, n. pierre f.

stool, n. excabeau m.

stoop, vb. se pencher

stop, n. arrêt m.; vb. arrêter, (prevent) empêcher (de); (cease) cesser

storm, n. orage m.; tempête f.

stormy, adj. orageux

story, n. histoire f.; (floor) étage m.

stouts, adj. gros m. grosse f.

stove, n. fourneau m.

straight, adj. and adv. droit

straighten, vb. redresser

strait, n. (geographical) détroit m.

strand, n. plage f.

strange, adj. étrange

stranger, n. étranger m.

strangle, vb. étrangler

strap, n. courroie f.

strategic, adj. stratégique

strategy, n. stratégie f.

straw, n. paille f.

strawberry, n. fraise f.

stray, adj. égaré

streak, n. raie f.; vb. rayer

street, n. rue f.

strength, n. force f.

strengthen, vb. fortifier

strenuous, adj. énergique

stress, n. force, tension f.; (gramm.) accent m.; vb. accentuer

stretch, vb. étendre

stretcher, n. brancard m.

strict, adj. strict

stride, n. enjambée f.

strife, n. lutte f.

string, n. ficelle, (music) corde f.

strip, n. bande f.; vb. dépouiller

stripe, n. bande f.; (mil.) galon m.

strive, vb. s'efforcer (de)

stroke, n. coup m.; vb. caresser

stroll, n. tour m.

strong, adj. fort

structure, n structure f.

struggle, n. lutte f.; vb. lutter

stub, n. souche f.

stubborn, adj. opiniâtre, obstiné, têtu

student, n. étudiant m.

studio, n. atelier m.

study, n. étude f.; (room) cabine de travail m.; vb. étudier

stumble, vb. trébucher

stump, n. (tree) souche f.

stum, vb. étourdir

stunt, n. tour de force m.

stupid, adj. stupide

stupidity, n stupidité f.

sturdy, adj. virgoureux

stutter, vb. bégayer

style, n. style m.

stylish, adj. élégant

subconscious, adj. subconscient

subdue, vb. subjuguer

sublimate, vb. sublimer

sublime, adj. sublime

submerge, vb. submerger

submission, n. soumission f.

submit, vb. soumettre

subsequent, adj. subséquent

subsidy, n. subvention f.

substance, n. substance f.

substitute, n. remplaçant m.; vb. substituer

subtle, adj. subtil

subract, vb. soustraire

suburb, n. faubourg m.

subversive, adj. subversif

subway, n. métro (politain) m.

success, n. succés m.

succession, n. succession

successive, adj. successif

successor, n. successeur m.

succumb, vb. succomber

such, adj. tel, pareil

suck, vb. sucer

suction, n. succion f.

sudden, adj. soudain

sue, vb. poursuivre

suffer, vb. souffrir

suffice, vb. suffire

sufficient, adj. suffisant

sugar, n. sucre m.

suggest, vb. suggérer

suggestion, n. suggestion f.

suit, n. (law) procès, (clothes) complet m.; (cards) couleur f.; vb. convenir (à)

suitable, adj. convenable

suitcase, n. valise f.

sum, n. somme f.

summer, n. été m.

sumn, n. soleil m.

sunburn, n. hâle m.

Sunday, n. dimanche m.

sunny, adj. ensoleillé

sunshine, n. soleil m.

superb, adj. superbe

superfluous, adj. superflu

superintendent, n. surveillant m.

superior, adj. and n. supérieur m.

supersede, vb. remplacer

superstition, n. superstition f.

superstitious, adj. superstitieux

supervise, vb. surveiller

supper, n. souper m.

supplement, n. supplément m.

suppose, vb. supposer

suppress, vb. supprimer

suppression, n. suppression f.

supreme, adj. suprême

sure adj. sûr

surface, n. surface f.

surge, n. houle f.

surgeon, n. chirurgien m.

surgery, chirurgie f.

surpass, vb. surpasser

surplus, n. surplus m.

surprise, n. surprise f.; vb. surprendre

surround, vb. entourer

survive, vb. survivre

suspect, vb. soupconner

suspend, vb. suspendre

suspense, n. incertitude f.

suspension, n. suspension f.

sujspicion, n. soupcon m.

sustain, vb. soutenir

swamp, n. marais m.

swan, n. cygne m.

swarm, n. essaim m.

sway, n. (rule) domination, (motion) oscillation f. ; vb. gouverner

swear, n. jurer

sweat, n. sueur f.; vb. suer

Sweden, n. la Suède f.

sweet, adj. doux m., douce f.; sucré

swell, vb. bonfler, enfler

swollen, vb. enfler, s'enfler

swerve, vb. s'écarter, se détourner

swift, adj. rapide

swiss, vb. nager

swine, n. cochon m.

swing, vb. balancer

Switzerland, n. la Suisse f.

sword, n. épée f.

syllable, n. syllable f.

symbol, n. symbole m.

sympathetic, adj. compatisstant

sympathy, n. compassion f.

symphony, n. symphonie f.

symptom, n. symptôme m.

syndicate, n. syndicat m.

syndrome, n. syndrome m.

synonym, n. synonyme m.

synthetic, adj. synthétique

syrup, n. sirop m.

system, n. système m.

systemtaic, adj. systématique

tabernacle, n. tabernacle m.

table, n. table f.

tablecloth, n. nappe f.

tablespoon, n. cuiller à bouche f.

tablet, n. tablette f.

tabular, adj. arrangé en tableaux

tack, n. (nail) brouqette f.; vb. clouer

tacking, n. cloutage m.

tackle, n. attirail m.

tackler, n. plaqueur m.

tacky, adj. collant, visqueur

tact, n. tact m.

tactful, adj. plein de tact

tactless, adj. sans tact

tadpole, n. têtard m.

taffeta, n. taffetas m.

tag, n. étiquette f.

tail, n. queue f.

tailor, n. tailleur m.

take, vb. prendre; (lead) conduir

tale, n. conte m.

talent, n. talent m.

talk, n. conversation f.; vb. parler

talkative, adj. bavard

tall, adj. grand

tame, adj. (animal) apprivoisé

tamper, vb. toucher à

tan, n. (leather) tan m.; (skin) hâle m.

tangible, adj. tangible

tangle, n. embrouillement m.

tank, n. réservoir, (mil.) char (d'assaut) m.

tap, n. (water) robinet m.; (knock) petit coup m.; vb. frapper legèrement

tape, n. ruban m.

tapestry, n. tapisserie f.

tar, n. goudron m.

target, n. cible f.

tariff, n. tarif m.

tarnish, vb. ternir

task, n. tâche f.

taste, n. goût m.; vb. goûter

tasty, adj. savoureux

tavern, n. taverne f.

tax, n. impôt m.; vb. imposer

taxi, n. taxi m.

taxpayer, n. contribuable m.

tea, n. thé m.

teach, vb. enseigner; (to do) apprendre à

teacher, n. instituteur, (school) professeur m.

team, n. (animals) attelage m.,; (people) équipe f.

tear, n. larme, (rip) déchirure f.; vb. déchirer

tease, vb. taquiner

teaspoon, n. cuiller à thé f.

technical, adj. technique

technique n. technique f.

tedious, adj. ennuyeux

telegram, n. télégramme m.

telephone, n. téléphone m.; vb. téléphoner

telescope, n. téléscope m.

television, n. télévision f.

tell, vb. dire; (story, etc.) raconter

teller, n. (bank) caissier m.

temper, n. (humor) humeur f.; (anger) colère, (metals) trempe f.

temperament, n. tempérament m.

temperence, n. tempérance f.

temperature, n. température f.

tempest, n. tempête f.

temple, n. temple m.; (forehead) tempe f.

temporary, adj. temporaire

tempt, vb. tenter

temptation, n. tentation f.

ten, adj. and n. dix m.

tenant, n. locataire m.f.

tendency, n. tendance f.

tender, adj. tendre

tendon, n. tenon m.

tennis, n. tennis m.

tenor, n. (music) ténor m.

tense, adj. tendu

tent, n. tente f.

tentative, adj. tentatif, expérimental

tenth, adj. and n. dixième m.

term, n. terme m.; (school) trimestre m.; (conditions) conditions f., pl.

terrace, n. terrasse f.

terrible, adj. terrible

terrify, vb. terrifier

territory, n. territoire m.

terror, n. terreur f.

test, n. épreuve f.; vb. mettre à l'épreuve

testament, n. testament m.

testify, vb. témoigner (de); (declare) affirmer

testimony, n. témoignage m.

text, n. texte m.

textile, adj. textile

texture, n. texture f.

than, conj. que; de (between numbers)

thank, vb. remercier, merci

that, (those, pl.) adj. ce cet m., cette f., ces, pl.; demonstrative pron. celui-là m., celle-là f., ceux-là m., pl.; conj. que; (purpose) pour que

the, art. le m., la f., les, pl.

theater, n. théâtre m.

theft, n. vol m.

their, adj. leur, leurs pl.

theirs, pron. le leur m., la leur f., les leurs pl.

them, pron. eux m., pl. elles f.; pl.; les (direct), leur (indirect)

theme, n. thème m.

themselves, pron eux-mêmes m., elles-mêmes f.; (reflexive) se

then, adv. alors; (after that) ensuite

theology, n. théologie f.

theory, n. théorie f.

therapy, n. thérapie f.

there, adv. là, y, il, en cela

therefore, adv. donc

thermometer, n. thermomètre m.

they, pron. ils m., elles f.

thick, adj. épais

thicken, vb. épaissir

thief, n. voleur m.

thigh, n. cuisse f.

thimble, n. dé m.

thin, adj. mince

thing, n. chose f.

third, n. tiers m.; adj. troisième

thirst, n. soif f.

thirsty, adj. avoir soif

thirteen, adj. and n. treize m.

thirty, adj. and n. trente m.

this, sg. (these, pl.) adj. ce, cet m., cette f., ces pl.; demonstrative pron. celui-ci m.f., ceux-ci m., pl., celles-ci f.,pl.

thorough, adj. complet, entier

though, conj. quoique

thought, n. pensée f.

thoughtful, adj. pensif

thousand, adj. and n. mille m.

thread, n. fil m.

threat, n. menace f.

threaten, vb. menacer

three, adj. and n. trois m.

thrift, n. économie f.

thrill, n. tressaillement m.; vb. tressaillir, intr.; faire frémir

thrive, vb. prospérer

throat, n. gorge f.

throne, n. trône m.

through, prep and adv. à travers, avoir fini

throughout, adv. partout

throw, vb. jeter

thumb, n. pouce m.

thunder, n. tonnerre m.; vb. tonner

Thursday, n. jeudi m.

thus, adv. ainsi

tickle, vb. chatouiller

tide, n. marée f.

tie, n. lien m.; cravate f.; vb. attacher; (bind) lier; (knot) nouer

tiger, n. tigre m.

tight, adj. serré

tighten, vb. serrer

tile, n. (roof) tuile f.

till prep. jusqu'à; conj. jusqu'à ce que

timber, n. (building) bois de construction m.

time, n. temps m.; (occasion) fois f.; (clock) heure f.; (what time is it?) quelle heure est-il?

timid, adj. timide

timidity, n. timidité f.

tin, n. étain m.

tint, n. teinte f.

tiny, adj. tout petit

tip, n. (money) pourboire m.; (end) bout m.

tire, n. (car, etc.) pneu(matique) m.; vb. fatiguer

tired, adj. fatigué

tissue, n. tissu m.

title, n. titre m.

to, prep à, de

tobacco, n. tabac m.

today, adv. aujourd'hui

toe, n. orteil m.

together, adv. ensemble

toilet, n. toilette f.

token, n témoignage, (coin) jeton m.

tolerance, n. tolérance f.

tolerant, adj. tolérant

tolerate, vb. tolérer

tomato, n. tomate f.

tomb, n. tombeau m.

tomorrow, adv. demain

ton, n. tonne f.

tone, n. ton m.

tongue, n. langue f.

tonic, adj. and n. tonique m.

tonight, adv. cette nuit; (evening) ce soir

tonsil, n. amygdale f.

too, adv. trop; (also) aussi

tool, n. outil m.

tooth, n. dent m.

toothache, n. mal de dents m.

toothbrush, n. brosse á dents f.

top, n. (mountain, etc.) sommet, (table) dessus m.

topic, n. sujet m.

torment, n. tourment m.; vb. tourmenter

torture, n. torture f.; vb. torturer

toss, vb. (throw) jeter, s'agiter

total, adj. and n. total m.

touch, n. (touching) attouchement, (sense) toucher, (contact) contact m. pointe f.; vb. toucher

tough, adj. dur

tour, n. tour m.

tourist, n. touriste m.f.

tournament, n. tournol m.

tow, vb. remorquer

toward, prep. (place, time) vers; (feelings, etc.) envers

towel, n. serviette f.

tower, n. tour f.

town, n. ville f.

toy, n. jouet m.

trace, n. trace f.

track, n. piste f.; (railroad) voie f.

tract, n. (space) étendue f.

tractor, n. tracteur m.

trade, n. commerce, (job) métier m.; vb. commercer

trader, n. commercant m.

tradition, n. tradition f.

traditional, adj. traditionnel

traffic, n. circulation f.

tragedy, n. tragédie f.

tragic, adj tragique

trail, n. trace f.

train, n. train m.; (dress) traîne f.; (retinue) suite f.; vb. (sports) entraîner

traitor, n. traitre m.

tramp, n. (steps) bruit de pas; (person) chemineau m.

tranquil, adj. tranquille

tranquility, n. tranquillité f.

transaction, n. opération f.

transfer, n. transport m.; (ticket) billet de correspondance m.; vb. transférer

transform, vb. transformer

transfusion, n. transfusion f.

translate, vb. traduire

translation, n. traduction f.

transmit, vb. transmettre

transparent, adj. transparent

transport, n. transport m.; vb. transporter

trap, n. piège m.; vb. prendre au piège

trash, n. (rubbish) rebut m.

travel, n. voyage m.; vb. voyager

traveler, n. voyageur m.

tray, n. plateau m.

tread, vb. marcher

treasure, n. trésor m.

treasurer, n. trésorier m.

treasury, n. trésor m.

treat, vb. traiter

treatment, n. traitement m.

treaty, n. traité m.

tree, n. arbre m.

tremble, vb. trembler

tremendous, adj. terrible

trench, n. tranchée f.

trend, n. tendance f.

trespass, vb. empiéter

trial, n. (law) procès m.; (test) épreuve f.

triangle, n. triangle m.

tribulation, n. tribulation f.

tributary, n. (river) affluent m.; adj tributaire

trick, n. ruse f.; vb. duper

tricky, adj. astucieux

trifle, n. bagatelle f.

trigger, n. détente f.

trim, adj. soigne.; vb. (put in order) arranger; (adorn) garnir; tailer

trinket, n. breloque f.

trip, n. voyage m.; vb. trébucher

triple, adj. and n. triple m.

trite, adj rebattu

triumph, n. triomphe m.

trivial, adj. trivial

trophy, n. trophée m.

tropic, n. tropique m.

trot, n. trot m.; vb. intr. trotter

trouble, n. (misfortune) malheur m.; (difficulty) difficulté f.; dérangement m.; vb. (worry) inquiéter, déranger

troublesome, adj. gênant

trousers, n. pantalon m.

trousseau, n. trousseau m.

trout, n. truite f.

truce, n. trève f.

truck, n. camion m.

true, adj vrai

truly, adv. vraiment

trumpet, n. trompette f.

trunk, n. (clothes) malle f.; (body, tree) tronc m.

trust, n. confiance f.; (business) trust m.; vb. se confier à; (entrust) confier

trustworthy, adj. digne de confiance

truth, n. vérité f.

truthful, adj. sincère

try, vb. essayer; (law) mettre en jugement

tub, n. baignoire f.

tube, n. tube m.

tuberculosis, n. tuberculose f.

tuck, n. (fold) pli m.; vb. plisser, serrer

Tuesday, n. mardi m.

tug, n. (boat) remorqueur m.; vb. (pull) tirer

tuition, n. (prix de l') enseignement m.

tumble, vb (fall) tomber

tumor, n. tumeur f.

tuna, n. thon m.

tune, n. air m.; (concord harmony) accord m.; vb. accorder

tunnel, n. tunnel m.

turf, n. gazon m.

Turk, n. Turc m., Turque f.

turkey, n. dindon m.

Turkey, n. la Turquie f.

turmoil, n. tumulte m.

turn, n. tour m.; (road) détour m.; vb. tourner

turnip, n. navet m.

turret, n. tourelle f.

turtle, n. tortue f.

tutor, n. précepteur m.

twelfth, adj. and n. douzième m.

twelve, adj. and n. douze m.

twenty, adj. and n. vingt m.

twice, adv. deux fois

twig, n. brindile f.

twilight, n. crépuscule m.

twin, adj. and n. jumeau m., jumelle f.; jumeaux m., pl., jummelles f., pl.

twine, n. ficelle f.

twinkle, vb. scintiller

twist, vb. tordre

two, adj. and n. deux m.

type, n. type m.; (printing) caractère m.; vb. taper à la machine

typical, adj. typique

typist, n. dactylo(graphe) m.f.

tyranny, n. tyrannie f.

tyrant, n. tyran m.

udder, n. mamelle f.

ugliness, n. laideur f.

ugly, adj. laid

ulcer, n. ulcère m.

ulterior, adj. ultérieur

ultimate, adj. dernier

umbrella, n. parapluie m.

umpire, n. arbitre m.f.

unable, adj. incapable; (u.to) dans l'impossibilité de

unanimous, adj. unanime

uncertain, adj. incertain

uncle, n. oncle m.

unconscous, n. inconscient m. ; adj. (aware) inconscient; (faint) sans connaissance

uncover, vb. découvrir

under, prep. sous.; adv. au-dessous,

underestimate, vb. sous-estimer

undergo, vb. subir

underground, adj. souterrain

underline, vb. souligner

underneath, adv. en dessous

undershirt, n. gilet de dessous m.

understand, vb. comprendre

undertake, vb. entreprendre

undertaker, n. entrepreneur de pompes funèbres m.

underwear, n. vêtements de dessous m., pl.

undo, vb. défaire

undress, vb. déshabiller

uneasy, adj. gêné

uneven, adj. inégal

unexpected, adj. nattendu

unfair, adj. injuste

unfit, adj. peu propre (à)

unfold, vb. déplier

unforgettable, adj. inoubliable

unfortunate, adj. malheureux

unhappy, adj. malheureux

unicorn, n. licorne f.

unidentified, adj. peu idiomatique

uniform, adj. and n. uniforme m.

uniformity, n. uniformité f.

uniformly, adv. uniformément

unify, vb. unifier

union, n. union f.

unique, adj. unique

unisex, adj. unisexuel

unit, n. unité f.

unite, vb. unir

United Nations, n. Nations Unies f., pl.

United States, n. les États-Unis m., pl.

unity, n. unité f.

universal, adj. universel

universe, n. univers m.

university, n. université f.

unleaded, adj. sans plomb

unless, conj. à moins que...ne

unlike, adj. dissemblable

unload, vb. décharger

unlock, vb. ouvrir

untie, vb. dénouer

until, conj. jusqu'à ce que

unusual, adj. insolite

up, prep. vers le haut de, au haut

uphold, vb. soutenir

upholster, vb. tapisser

upon, prep. sur

upper, adj. supérieur

upright, adj. droit

uproar, n. vacarme m.

upset, vb. renverser

upstairs, adv. en haut

uptight, adj. tendu

upward, adj. dirigé en haut; adv. en montant

urge, vb. (beg) prier

urgency, n. urgence f.

urgent, adj. urgent

us, pron. nous

use, n. usage m.; vb. employer, se servir de

useful, adj. utile

useless, adj. inutile

usher, n. huissier m.

usual, adj. usuel

utensil, n. ustensile m.

utilize, vb. utiliser, se servir de

utmost, n. le plus, tout son possible; adj. (greatest) le plus grand

utter, adj. absolu; vb. prononcer; (cry) pousser

utterance, n. emmission f.

uvula, n. luette, uvule f.

vacancy, n. vide m., vacance f.	veto, n. véto m.
vacant, adj. vide	vibrate, vb. vibrer
vacate, vb. quitter, évacuer	vibration, n. vibration f.
vacation, n. vacances f.,pl.	vice, n. vice m.
vaccinate, vb. vacciner	vicinity, n. voisinage m.
vaccine, n. vaccin m.	vicious, adj. méchant
vacuum, n. vide m.; (vacuum cleaner) aspirateur m.	victim, n. victime f.
	victor, n. vainqueur m.
vagrant, adj. vagabond	victory, n. victoire f.
vague, adj. vague	view, n. vue f.
vain, adj. vain	vigil, n. veille f.
valiant, adj. vaillant	village, n. village m.
valid, adj. valide	villain, n. scélérat m.
valley, n. vallée f.	vine, n. vigne f.
valuable, adj. de valeur	vinegar, n. vinaigre m.
value, n. valeur f.; vb. évaluer	vintage, n. vendange, (year of wine) année f.
valve, n. soupape f.	
vanilla, n. vanille f.	violence, n. violence
vanish, vb. s'évanouir	violent, adj. violent
vanity, n. vanité f.	violet, n. violette f.; adj. violet
vanquish, vb. vaincre	violin, n. violon m.
vapor, n. vapeur f.	virgin, n. vierge f.
varied, adj. varié	virtual, adj. virtuel, defait
variety, n. variété f.	virtue, n. vertu f.
various, adj. divers	virus, n. virus m.
varnish, n. vernis m.; vb. lernir	visible, adj. visible
vary, vb. varier	vision, n. vision f.
vasectomy, n. vasectomie f.	visit, n. visite f.; vb. visiter
vast, adj. vaste	visitor, n. visiteur m.
vault, n. voûite f.	visual, adj. visuel
vegetable, n. légume m.	vital, adj. vital
vehicle, n. véhicule m.	vitamin, n. vitamine f.
veil, n. voile m.	vivid, adj. vif m.; vive f.
vein, n. veine f.	vocabulary, n. vocabulaire m.
velvet, n. velours m.	vocal, adj. vocal
vengeance, n. vengeance f.	voice, n. voix f.
vent, n. ouverture f.	void, adj. (law) nul
venture, n. aventure f.; vb. hasarder	volcano, n. volcan m.
verb, n. verbe m.	volume, n. volume m.
verdict, n. verdict m.	volunteer, n. volontaire m.; vb. s'engager
verify, vb. vérifier	
verse, n. vers m., pl.	vomit, vb. vomir
version, n. version f.	vote, n. vote m.; vb. voter
vertical, adj. vertical	vow, n. voeu m.
very, adv. très	vowel, n. voyelle f.
vessel, n. vaisseau m.	voyage, n. voyage m.
vest, n. gilet m.	vulgar, adj. vulgaire
veteran, n. vétéran m.	vulnerable, adj. vulnérable

wade, vb. traverser à gué

waffle, n. gaufre (américaine) f.

wag, vb. agiter

wage, vb. (war) faire la guerre

wages, n. salaire m.

wagon, n. chariot m.

wail, vb. gémir

waist, n. taille f.

wait (for), vb. attendre

waiter, n. garçon m.

wake, vb. éveiller, réveiller

walk, n. promenade f.; vb. marcher; (take a walk) se promener

wall, n. mur m.

walkcovering, n. tenture f.

wallet, n. portefeuille m.

wallpaper, n. papier peint m.; papier à tapisser m.

walnut, n. noix f.

walrus, n. morse m.

waltz, n. valse f.

wander, vb. errer

want, n. besoin m.; vb. vouloir

war, n. guerre f.

ward, n. (hospital) salle f.; (charge) pupille m.f.

ware, n. marchandises f., pl.

warlike, adj. guerrier

warm, adj. chaud, avoir chaud; vb. chauffer

warmth, n. chaleur f.

warn, vb. avertir

warning, n. avertissement m.

warp, vb. détourner

warrant, n. mandat m.; vb. garantir

warrior, n. guerrier m.

wash, vb. laver

washing machine, n. machine à laver f.

washroom, n. salle de bain f.

wasp, n. guêpe f.

waste, n. perte f. gaspillage m., prodigalité f.

watchful, adj. vigilant

watchmaker, n. horloger m.

watchman, n. gardien m.

water, n. eau f.

waterbed, n. aqualit m.

water color, n. aquarelle f.

waterfall, n. chute d'eau f.

waterproof, adj. imperméable

wave, n. vague f.; (sound) onde f.; permanente; vb. agiter; (hair) onduler

waver, vb. vaciller

wavy, adj. ondoyant, onduleux

wax, n. cire f.

way, n. (road) chemin m.; (distance) distance, manière f.; côté m.

we, pron. nous

weak, adj. faible

weaken, vb. affaiblir

weakness, n. faiblesse f.

wealth, n. richesse f.

wealthy, adj. riche

weapon, n. arme f.

wear, vb. porter

weary, adj. las fatigué

weasel, n. belette f.

weather, n. temps m.

weave, vb. tisser

weaver, n. tisserand m.

web, n. (fabric) tissu m.; (spider) toile f.

wedding, n. noces f., pl.; adj. de noces, de mariage

wedge, n. coin m.

Wednesday, n. mercredi m.

weed, n. mauvaise herbe f.

week, n. semaine f.

weekday, n. jour de semaine m.

week-end, n. week-end m., fin de semaine f.

weekly, adj. hebdomadaire

weep, vb. pleurer

weigh, vb. peser

weight, n. poids m.

weird, adj. mystérieux

welcome, adj. bienvenu

welfare, n. bien-être m.

well, n. (water) puits m.; adv. bien

well-known, adj. bien connu

west, n. ouest m.

western, adj. de l'ouest

wet, adj. mouillé; (weather) pluvieux; vb. mouiller

whale, n. baleine f.

what, adj. quel m.; pron. ce qui (subject), ce que (object), qu'est-ce qui, quoi, qu'est-ceque

whatever, adj. quel quesoit...qui, quelque...que ce soit; adv. quoi que ce soit; pron. tout ce qui, tout ceque, quoi que ce soit

wheat, n. blé m.

wheel, n. roue f.

when, conj quand

whenever, conj. toutes les fois que

where, con. où

wherever, conj. partout où

whether, conj. soit que; (if) si

which, adj. quel; pron. (relative) qui; lequel; (interrogative) lequel

whichever, pron. n'importe lequel

while, conj. pendant que; (whereas) tandis que

whim, n. caprice m.; lubie f.

whip, n. fouet m.; vb. fouetter, battre

whirl, vb. faire tourner, tourner

whirlpool, n. tourbillon d'eau m.

whirlwind, n. tourbillon de vent m.

whisker, n. (man) favori m.; (animals) moustache f.

whiskey, n. whiskey m.

whisper, vb. chuchoter

whistle, n. siflet m.; vb. siffler

white, adj. blanc m., blanche f.

who, pron. qui, qu'est-cequi

whoever, pron. qui que cr soit, quiconque

whole, adj. entier

wholesale, adj. and adv. en gros

wholesome, adj. sain

wholly, adv. entièrement

whom, pron. que; lequel; qui est-ce que

whose, pron. dont; de qui; duquel m., de laquelle f., desquels m., pl.

why, adv. pourquoi

wicked, adj. méchant f.

wickedness, n. mechanceté f.

wide, adj. large

widen, vb. élargir

widespread, adj. répandu

widow, n. veuve f.

widower, n. veuf m.

width, n. largeur f.

wield, vb. manier

wife, n. femme f.

wig, n. perruque f.

wild, adj. sauvage

wilderness, n. désert m.

wildlife, n. faune f.

will, n. volonté f.; testament m.; vb. vouloir; (bequeath) léguer

willful, adj. obstiné

willing, adj. bien disposé

wilt, vb. flétrir

win, vb. gagner

wind, n. vent m.

window, n. fenêtre, (shop) devanture f.

windy, adj. venteux

wine, n. vin m.

wing, n. aile f.

wink, n. clin d'oeil m.; vb. clignoter

winner, n. gagnant m.

winter, n. hiver m.

wipe vb. essuyer

wire, n. fil de fer m.

wireless, adj. sans fil

wisdom, n. sagesse f.

wise, adj. sage

wish, n. désir m.; vb. désirer

wit, n. esprit m.

witch, n. sorcière f.

with, prep. avec

withdraw, vb. retirer

wither, vb. flétrir

withhold, vb. refuser

within, adv. dedans

without, prep. sans

witness, n. toin m.

witty, adj. spirituel

wizard, n. sorcier m.

woe, n. malheur m.

wolf, n. loup m.

woman, n. femme f.

womb, n. matrice f.

wonder, vb. se demander; (be

surprised) être étonné
wonderful, adj. merveilleux
woo, vb. faire la cour à
wood, n. bois m.
wooden, adj. de bois
wool, n. laine f.
woolen, adj. de laine
word, n. mot m.
work, n. travail m.; vb. travailler
worker, n. travailleur m.
workman, n. ouvrier m.
world, n. monde m.
wordly, adj. mondial
worm, n. ver m.
worn, adj. usé
worry, n. souci m.; vb. tracasser,
préoccuper
worse, adj. pire; adv. pis
worship, n. culte m.; vb. adorer
worst, adj. le pire; adv. le pis
worth, n. valeur f.; vb. valoir; adj.
valant, qui mérite
worthless, adj. indigne; (without value) sans valeur
worthy, adj. digne
would, vb. vouloir
wound, n. blessure f.; vb. besser
wrap, vb. envelopper
wrapping, n. couverture f.
wrath, n. courroux m.
wreath, n. couronne f.
wreck, n. (ship) naufrage m.;
(remains) débris m., pl.
wrench, vb. tordre
wrestle, vb. lutter
wretched, adj. misérable
wring, vb. tordre
wringer, n. essoreuse (à linge) f.
wrinkle, n. ride f.; vb. rider, plisser
wrist, n. poignet m.
wrist watch, n. montre-bracelet f.
write, vb. écrire
write-off, n. annulation, non-valeur f.
writer, n. écrivain m.
writhe, vb. se tordre
written, adj. écrit, par écrit
wrong, adj. faux m., fausse f.;
wrongdoer, n. injuste, méchant m.

x-rays, n. rayons X m., pl.
xylophone, n. xylophone m.

Y

yacht, n. yacht m.
yam, n. igname f.
yard, n. (house) cour f.; (lumber)
chantier, (measusre) yard m.
yarn, n. fil m.
yawn, n. bâille(ment) m.; vb. bâiler
year, n. and m.; (duration) année f.
yearly, adj. annuel
yearn (for), vb. soupirer (après)
yell, vb. hurler
yellow, adj. and n. jaune m.
yes, adv. oui
yesterday, adv. hier
yet, adv. encore; conj. néanmoins
yield, vb. (resign) céder; produire
yoke, n. joug m.
yolk, n. jaune m.
you, pron. vous
young, adj. jeune
your, adj. votre, vos pl.;
ton m., ta f., tes pl.
yours, pron. le vôtre; le tien m.,
la tienne f.
yourself, pron. vous-même; toi-même;
(reflexive) vous, te
youth, n. jeunesse f.
youthful, adj. (young) jeune;
(of youth) de jeunesse

Z

zap, vb. frapper d'une façon
soudaine et inattendue
zeal, n. zèle m.
zealous, adj. zélé
zebra, n. zère m.
zero, n. zéro m.
zest, n. entrain m.; (taste)
saveur f.
zip code, n. code postal m.
zone, n. zone f.
zoo, n. jardin zoologique